Unless indicated below photo credits are annotated in the individual captions.
Delaware Legislative Council Research Library: Front and Back Covers and Endleaves
University of Delaware Photo by Robert Cohen: Portrait of Ms. Hoffecker

Democracy in Delaware

The Story of the First State's General Assembly

Carol E. Hoffecker

Cedar Tree Books
Wilmington, Delaware

Carol E. Hoffecker

The Right in the People to Participate in the Legislature is the Foundation of Liberty and of all Free Government

*Declaration of Rights and
Fundamental Rules of the
Delaware State
    September 11, 1776*

First Edition

Published by: **Cedar Tree Books**
9 Germay Drive, Wilmington, Delaware 19804

ISBN: 1-892142-23-6

Title: Democracy in Delaware
Copyeditor: Barbara Benson
Cover design: Sandy Hughes
Layout and book design: Phil Maggitti

©2004 by Carol E. Hoffecker

Library of Congress Catalog in Publication Data

Hoffecker, Carol E.
 Democracy in Delaware : the story of the First State's General Assembly / Carol E. Hoffecker.
     p. cm.
 Includes bibliographical references and index.
 ISBN 1-892142-23-6
 1. Delaware. General Assembly—History. 2. Delaware—Politics and government. I. Title.

 JK3766.H64 2004
 328.751′09—dc22
                                    2004004298

Printed in the United States of America

Made from recyclable materials.

Table of Contents

Dedication	vii
Acknowledgments	ix
List of Illustrations	xi
Foreword	xiii
Introduction	1
Chapter 1: The Three Lower Counties on Delaware, 1682-1763	7
Chapter 2: Creating the Delaware State, 1764-1781	29
Chapter 3: The First State, 1782-1815	51
Chapter 4: The Border State, 1816-1860	73
Chapter 5: Delaware's Inner Civil War, 1861-1875	99
Chapter 6: Setting a New Course, 1876-1905	117
Chapter 7: The Du Ponts and Delaware, 1906-1921	141
Chapter 8: The Legislature Faces Good Times and Bad, 1922-1951	169
Chapter 9: Federalism in Action, 1952-1972	195
Chapter 10: The Citizen Legislators, 1973-2004	229
Notes	275
Index	287

Carol E. Hoffecker

Dedication

This book is dedicated to past, present, and future legislators of the Delaware General Assembly, and especially to the memory of my great-uncle Frank R. Zebley, member of the House of Representatives, 1935-1940, Speaker in 1939-1940, a man who loved Delaware and its history.

ACKNOWLEDGEMENTS

The task of reconstructing the Delaware General Assembly's long history has involved the assistance of many people. Librarians and archivists are the historian's guides into the materials of the past. At the Historical Society of Delaware Dr. Constance J. Cooper, Ellen Rendle, and Edward Chichirichi were unfailingly helpful, as were Joanne Mattern, Bruce Haase, Dawn Mitchell, and other staff members of the Delaware Public Archives. Those who assisted in the search for appropriate illustrations included Randy Goss of the Delaware Public Archives, Ellen Rendle of the Historical Society of Delaware, Barbara Hall and Lisa Gensel of the Hagley Museum and Library, Charlotte Walker of the News-Journal Papers, Chief Clerk of the House of Representatives JoAnn M. Hedrick, Supervisor of Legislative Printing Debby Messina, and Madeline E. Dunn, Jenna Hickman, Beverly Laing, Cindy Snyder, and Ann B. Horsey of the Delaware State Museums.

In writing the story of the modern legislature I was most grateful for the insights of a variety of people who have lived that history first hand as legislators, governors, lobbyists, legislative staff, and observers. The names of those who provided those interviews include, in alphabetical order: Thurman Adams, Jr., Steven H. Amick, Myrna L. Bair, Patricia M. Blevins, John Brook, Michael N. Castle, Nancy W. Cook, Richard S. Cordrey, Joseph G. DiPinto, Pierre S. du Pont IV, Orlando J. George, Jr., Robert F. Gilligan, Bethany Hall-Long, Margaret Rose Henry, George C. Hering III, Andrew G. Knox, Jerome R. Lewis, Margaret R. Manning, Jane Maroney, Robert L. Maxwell, Ruth Ann Minner, William S. Montgomery, Lisa M. Moreland, James P. Neal, Russell W. Peterson, Roger P. Roy, Thomas B. Sharp, Wayne A. Smith, Alan V. Sokolow, Liane M. Sorenson, Terry R. Spence, Stephanie A. Ulbrich, and Mary Margaret Williams.

The book would not have been written but for the leadership of House Majority Leader Wayne A. Smith; and it is much richer for the aid of others as well. Mary Margaret Williams, Richard B. Carter, and William S. Montgomery offered valuable suggestions and helped me make contact with several key political figures. Former House Speaker George C. Hering III loaned his collection of the *Legislative Roster*, an annual publication of the Delaware Chamber of Commerce, which was an invaluable resource. The present House Speaker, Terry R. Spence, and Majority Leader Wayne A. Smith invited me to observe a meeting of the

House majority caucus. Ryan Thompson undertook several tasks including an analysis of the increasing length of service of twentieth-century legislators. Walter G. Feindt, the director of the Delaware Legislative Council, and his co-worker Debby Porter managed the finances for the project. Marie Perrone, an expert in word processing, put my raggedy typed version of the manuscript into final publishable form.

Lastly, the author and readers owe a huge debt of gratitude to Dr. Barbara E. Benson, the book's editor. Her deep knowledge of Delaware history, high editorial standards, and painstaking work are an unseen but invaluable presence on every page. The responsibility for any remaining errors lies entirely with the author.

Carol E. Hoffecker
Hockessin, Delaware
October 2003

Illustrations

1. William Penn	6
2. Map	13
3. New Castle plan	23
4. Laws of Delaware title page	26
5. Thomas McKean	34
6. Caesar Rodney	37
7. Mason-Dixon boundary marker	39
8. George Read	41
9. Resolution	43
10. A communication dated February 3, 1787	54
11. The Delaware State House.	61
12. The first floor of the Delaware State House	63
13. The restored Senate Chamber	66
14. Senate chamber with George Washington portrait	72
15. John M. Clayton	74
16. Willard Hall	77
17. School Law of 1829 pamphlet	78
18. Broadside announcement	85
19. A recruitment poster for the 3'd Delaware Regiment	104
20. Draft lottery wheel	108
21. The interior and exterior of the State House	112
22. Capitol Hotel	118
23. Bayard House	119
24. The Dover Railroad Station	120
25. John Edward O'Sullivan Addicks	121
26. This map from 1885 illustrates the importance of railroads	122
27. Members of the House of Representatives elected in 1888	124
28. Hotel Richardson	127
29. The first known photograph of the House of Representatives in session	137
30. This visualization of T. Coleman du Pont's proposal for a multi-use highway	144
31. Old muddy road	146
32. T. Coleman's highway	147
33. At the climax of a public ceremony held in Dover on July 2, 1924	148
34. Pierre S. duPont	152
35. John G. Townsend, Jr.	153
36. Suffrage rally on Dover Green, May 1920	163
37. Wooden school	166

38. New school	166
39. A last hurrah for the old State House	175
40. The preliminary plan for the first floor of Legislative Hall	176
41. Legislative Hall under construction in 1932	178
42. One view of Legislative Hall	180
43. One more view of Legislative hall	181
44. Vera G. Davis	190
45. An election ballot of 1952	197
46. Speakers of the House of Representatives of the 1960s through 1980s	205
47. Governor Elbert N. Carvel	211
48. State police evicted welfare demonstrators from Legislative Hall	216
49. Governor Russell W. Peterson	224
50. A reunion of the "Class of '74"	234
51. Two Republican governors	237
52. New members of the House of Representatives being sworn in	240
53. The Senate of 1987-88.	247
54. Legislative Hall is a beehive of activity	264
55. President William J. Clinton	268
56. Governor Ruth Ann Minner	270
57. Photograph by Kevin Fleming	273

Foreword

WAYNE A. SMITH
Majority Leader
STATE REPRESENTATIVE
Seventh District

HOUSE OF REPRESENTATIVES
STATE OF DELAWARE
LEGISLATIVE HALL
DOVER, DELAWARE 19901

COMMITTEES
House Administration, Chair
Ethics, Chair
House Rules
Legislative Council

It is with great pleasure that I accepted the invitation to write these brief words in front of Carol Hoffecker's wonderful history of the Delaware General Assembly's first 300 years, *Democracy in Delaware, the Story of the First State's General Assembly.*

We are fortunate to have one of our state's great historians to describe this story. We have also been fortunate to have the support of the General Assembly's Legislative Council, under the leadership of Senate President Pro Tempore Thurman G. Adams, Jr., and Speaker of the House Terry R. Spence, in marking the tercentenary of the *First State's* Legislature. This book is a major part of that effort.

Our small state rightly boasts a close relationship between the legislature and those they serve. While this has been an important constant in the years between 1704 and today, that intimate relationship has not always produced working, effective or good government. It took many years to develop fair rules, broad suffrage, equal representation and yes, even the right mind set, to come to where we stand in 2004 – a vibrant and functioning democratic institution.

Dr. Hoffecker shows that the journey to this time has been in fits and starts. The history of the Delaware General Assembly has produced great moments where a body has risen high to meet the sweep of progress and carry our ideals forward -- as well as occasions where the unblinking lens of hindsight revealed another to be lacking in the foresight or even basic functionality needed to join that progress which today seems inevitable, preordained and just plain right.

Like other legislative bodies, the Delaware General Assembly has seen high moments and low. This story serves as both a lesson in how a people can govern themselves in our great democracy as well as how bodies of politicians at different times have often failed to fulfill their intended constitutional purposes or even their basic democratic obligation to provide a forum through which the public can conduct its business. Dr. Hoffecker concludes her book with the admonition that *"maintaining democracy will require constant vigilance to keep a General Assembly that is truly representative of the people and effective in resolving their problems..."* She is correct and has assembled the history to prove it. It is also worth noting that she views today's General Assembly as the positive product of much of this history, and one which stands proudly at the height of its stature as such a body.

Besides the intimate relationship of the citizenry to the General Assembly, the other constant Dr. Hoffecker reveals is how well our General Assembly has reflected Delaware's body politic over three centuries. Prides, prejudices, interests and party faction have all clashed around our state and throughout our history. Those clashes have always echoed loudly in Legislative Hall and serve to remind all that while often unsightly, our basic reason for having a Legislature is to provide the forum where those clashes can occur and find some resolution without resort to bloodshed, violence or lawlessness.

The history buff and the Delaware patriot, as well as the citizen desiring to be informed, will appreciate this fine effort to describe how the Delaware General Assembly has progressed through – while often making – three hundred years of time.

Rep. Wayne A. Smith
House Majority Leader
Chair, Delaware General Assembly
 Tercentenary Committee

December 7th, 2003

INTRODUCTION

The General Assembly is the root of representative democracy in Delaware. The Assembly was the first elected body in Delaware, and it remains the most powerful. It is no exaggeration to say that the Assembly's actions have affected and continue to affect every aspect of life in the state. The Assembly is the citizens' voice in their government. In the course of the Assembly's long history, the definition of citizenship has grown to embrace all adult Delawareans. In that process the General Assembly has sometimes supported the extension of democracy, while at other times it has stubbornly refused to do so. This book explores the evolution of the General Assembly as a democratic institution that continues to shape the State of Delaware and the lives of Delawareans.

On May 22, 2004, the Delaware General Assembly will celebrate its tercentenary. That date marks the three-hundredth year in which representatives of the three counties of New Castle, Kent, and Sussex have met together to make the laws that govern Delaware. One must go back further, however, to seek the beginnings of representative government in the little colony that then had the long descriptive name "Three Lower Counties on Delaware."

William Penn is the father of representative government in Delaware. In 1681 this idealistic English Quaker became proprietor of two colonies in America: Pennsylvania and the Three Lower Counties on Delaware. He tried to unite the two into one. In 1682 Penn called on the freedmen of both colonies to elect their neighbors most noted for "Sobriety, Wisdom, and Integrity" to attend a joint General Assembly. That Assembly's inaugural meeting took place at Upland, now Chester, Pennsylvania, in December 1682. To Penn's intense regret, the representatives of his colonies refused to unite into one. Like a bad marriage, time only made their relationship worse.

In 1701 the proprietor reluctantly agreed to disconnect his colonies' unified assembly. The Assembly of the Lower Counties met for the first time as a separate legislative body in the town of New Castle on May 22, 1704. For the remainder of the colonial period Pennsylvania and Delaware shared a governor, but their representative assemblies met separately. It is difficult to imagine how Delaware could have emerged from the colonial period as an independent state had not that separation already taken place.

The pre-Revolutionary years were the most significant period in the long history of the Delaware General Assembly. The Assembly was the fulcrum for major issues that led to the American Revolution as the assemblymen worked to redefine their colonial status, to examine the source of sovereign power, and to proclaim their understanding of liberty. In that era the Assembly was the only elected body to which Delaware's politically gifted men might aspire. In the crucial period that preceded the Revolution, the Assembly included the most stellar group of leaders ever to serve in that body. Three of the men who led the Assembly—Caesar Rodney, George Read, and Thomas McKean—were chosen by their fellow assemblymen to represent Delaware in the Continental Congress.

The Lower Counties' Assembly voted to separate from Great Britain on June 15, 1776, and in so doing renounced the proprietary rights of the Penn family over them. Less than a month later, Congress declared the independence of the American colonies and created the new nation of the United States of America. In Delaware the Assembly was now the only legitimate source of power to make laws and to bind the three counties together. In the summer of 1776 the Assembly called for a convention to draft Delaware's first constitution. The convention emphatically embraced the doctrine of legislative primacy, declaring: "The Right in the People to participate in the Legislature is the Foundation of Liberty, and of all free Government." Legislative supremacy would remain the hallmark of Delaware's government for more than a century.

The Constitution of 1776 created a two-house legislature whose members elected the state's chief executive. The state's subsequent Constitution of 1831 mandated that the voters would choose the governor, but the governor's office remained largely ceremonial throughout the nineteenth century. Power resided in the legislative branch. It was not until a new constitution was written in 1897 that the relationship of the two branches began to approach equality.

Delaware's proudest historical achievement is its position as the first state to ratify the Constitution of the United States. Although it was a specially elected convention that carried out the ratification on December 7, 1787, it was the General Assembly's rapid action in calling for the election of delegates to that convention that gave Delaware its head start on its sister states. Certainly no state has taken greater pride and satisfaction in being a part of the United States than Delaware. That loyalty received its most severe test on the eve of the Civil War when the General Assembly rebuffed the entreaties of the slave states to the South to abandon the United States for the Confederate States.

Throughout the nineteenth century the greatest prize for Delaware's political leaders was election to the United States Senate. That election took place within the General Assembly. The conceptual basis for that practice was the notion that state legislators were more politically enlightened than the electorate at large and could, therefore, better discern who should represent the state in national affairs. The reality was that the legislature became a pawn in the political leaders' quests for national power.

In the course of the century many states enacted the popular election of their United States senators, but Delaware clung to its old ways. During the 1890s a wealthy political aspirant named John Edward O'Sullivan Addicks tried to buy his way into the United States Senate through the Delaware General Assembly. His efforts had a corrosive effect on the integrity of the ballot in Delaware and helped pave the way for the Seventeenth Amendment to the Constitution of the United States, enacted in 1913 to provide for election of United States senators by the people.

The General Assembly proved unwilling to abandon other undemocratic ways as well. Such important extensions of democracy as the abolition of slavery, the enfranchisement of blacks and women, and the equalization of representation in the General Assembly on the basis of "one man, one vote" originated at the federal, not the state, level. The modern General Assembly is the product of those changes, not their creator.

The role of the General Assembly has changed in response to the growth of the economy and the development of a more complex society. In its early history the Assembly spent much of its time responding to petitions from individual citizens. The legislators granted divorces, determined the placement of roads, altered the boundaries of Delaware's several hundred public school districts, and gave landowners permission to dig drainage ditches. As state government matured, the Assembly transferred those responsibilities to the executive branch or the courts. In place of dealing with ditches, divorces, and boundaries, the Assembly was increasingly called upon to decide the fate of institutional applicants such as banks, turnpike companies, and railroads. Those organizations hired lawyers and lobbyists to secure favorable legislation. Incrementally the Assembly also took on responsibilities for providing public education and certain social services such as the care of the mentally ill.

In 1897 a convention of leading citizens drafted a new state constitution that made possible a more responsive government, establishing an executive branch that could provide leadership and administration for the state. Delaware's government got a major boost in the early twentieth century from several extraordinary private citizens. T. Coleman du Pont and his cousin Pierre S. du Pont provided the money and vision to bring sorely needed improvements to transportation and public education throughout the state. Thanks to the General Assembly's acceptance of the du Pont cousins' plans, Delaware made great strides toward modernization. During the 1920s and '30s the state built many new schools, but it maintained the strict segregation of the races that had characterized life in the First State since the end of the Civil War.

The constitution of 1897 did little to repair the increasingly unbalanced representation among the three counties. For the first two thirds of the twentieth century intense partisan politics and up-state versus down-state rivalries were played out in the General Assembly. Just as there was no political will to integrate black Delawareans into majority society, there was no likelihood that the people of Kent and Sussex counties would acquiesce in renouncing their power over far more heavily populated New Castle County. Then in the 1950s and 1960s the United States Supreme Court intervened with a series of landmark decisions that changed life in Delaware, especially in the General Assembly. Legal segregation died; and reapportionment remade the General Assembly into a body composed of members selected under the banner "one man, one vote."

In the spring of 1920, the General Assembly also lost its opportunity to be the final state needed to adopt the Woman's Suffrage Amendment to the United States Constitution. After the Nineteenth Amendment had passed without help from Delaware, the state's women began to engage in politics. By the 1960s women legislators had become a force for change in the General Assembly and throughout state government.

As the responsibilities and accompanying budget of state government expanded, the actions of the General Assembly took on increased significance. Traditionally, the Assembly had attracted men who viewed brief service in the legislature as a step in building careers in other fields, but by the 1960s members became more committed to serving multiple terms. The trend toward legislative longevity paralleled the growth in the complexities of state government.

In the 1950s and 1960s politically inspired stubbornness often frustrated needed developments in government. Fortunately, during the 1970s a remarkable transformation took place in Legislative Hall. The overall quality of the legislators improved, and committed members chose to remain for multiple terms. Leaders emerged from the two parties in both the executive and legislative branches who respected one another and took responsibility for bringing Delaware's government through the financial difficulties of that decade. Simultaneously, each party gained control of one house of the legislature and used its power over the redistricting process to maintain its majority. As a result, the Democrats have held the majority in the Senate and the Republicans in the House for several decades. The earlier politics of confrontation has been replaced by the politics of compromise.

Three hundred years after its founding, the Delaware General Assembly is composed of citizen legislators who reflect the nature of their state. There are men and women, blacks and whites, people with backgrounds in education, labor unions, the chemical industry, and agribusiness. Legislators keep in close contact with the people in their districts. Legislators know that their constituents will re-elect them or cast them aside, not only on the basis of their political affiliation, but more likely on the basis of how well they serve their districts. There is a greater sense of pride and of responsibility in Legislative Hall now than existed fifty years ago. Representative Wayne Smith of Brandywine Hundred expressed his colleagues' spirit when he exclaimed: "When I look up and see the cupola on Legislative Hall I think what a lucky guy I am!"

A note on the numbering of legislative sessions
The custom of numbering the sessions of the General Assembly did not begin until 1913 when it was determined that the session beginning that January was the 94th since Delaware had gained its independence.

In 1944 State Archivist Leon deValinger discovered a mistake in the previous calculation. At its 110th session in 1945 the legislature accepted deValinger's view and ordered that the next session, due to begin in January 1947, would be numbered the 114th. Subsequent sessions have been numbered accordingly.

William Penn (1647-1718), engraving by John Sartain from a painting by Henry Inman, ca. 1850. As proprietor of Pennsylvania and the Three Lower Counties on Delaware, Penn introduced representative government to his colonies. (Courtesy of the Delaware Public Archives)

1
THE THREE LOWER COUNTIES ON DELAWARE, 1682-1763

No representative government existed in Delaware under the colony's first three governments. The Swedes and Dutch who colonized Delaware in the mid-seventeenth century appointed autocratic military governors to rule the frontier settlement. Neither Sweden nor the Netherlands established elected assemblies to give settlers a role in their government. Neither did the brother of King Charles II, James, Duke of York, who commanded the English navy that conquered the Netherlands' American settlements in 1664. The Duke of York introduced the English common law into his colony on the Delaware, but the colony retained its military-style administration. The most lasting contribution those early colonial administrations made to Delaware's future government was the division of the land into three counties: New Castle in the north; St. Jones in the middle; and Whorekill in the south.

In 1681 Charles II made William Penn the proprietor of a large unsettled domain called Pennsylvania to be located on the west bank of the Delaware River north of the Duke of York's counties on the Delaware and of Lord Baltimore's proprietary colony of Maryland. At Penn's request, the Duke of York agreed to lease his three counties on the Delaware River to Penn so that Pennsylvanians could have an uncontested path to the sea. Only then under Penn's rule did the inhabitants of the three counties on the Delaware take their first steps toward political unity and representative government.

The three counties that Penn acquired from the duke in 1681 had a total population of fewer than 2,000 people. Most of the land was either marshy or heavily forested. The territory boasted only two towns, New Castle and Lewes. The northernmost county was centered on the commercial town of New Castle. This county had a polyglot population of Swedes, Finns, Dutch, along with some English and Africans. Except for the townsmen, most settlers farmed on clearings near the Delaware River.

Englishmen, Africans, and some remaining native people made up the population of the two counties to the south. Many of the landowners there had migrated from neighboring Maryland, where they had received their first land grants from Lord Baltimore, Maryland's proprietor. Together with their African slaves, those Maryland migrants established farms on clearings hacked from forests of hardwood, pine, and holly, and from diked and drained marshland. Like other Eastern Shore Marylanders, they raised tobacco as their primary export crop.

Settlers felt a closer affinity to their particular county than they did to the colony as a whole. The colony was strung out along a major river and had the more settled colony of Maryland to its west. Delaware's settlements had not sprung from a single starting point, nor had they been settled by a single people. In addition, before Penn no overall governing authority had lasted for more than a few years.

William Penn introduced Delawareans to a colonial government wholly different from what they had known. Penn was an idealist. As a young man he had renounced the Church of England to embrace the radical new faith of the Society of Friends, popularly known as Quakers. While enduring occasional imprisonment and other hardships, Penn became a major figure in his new faith. Unlike most Quakers of his time, Penn was a well-educated aristocrat. He used his skills to write Quaker tracts and to investigate philosophical approaches whereby governments might realize the Quakers' belief that the "Inner Light" of God could guide mankind toward peace and happiness.

The Quaker proprietor was a man of contradictions. On the one hand, Penn was a convert to a religious sect that stressed human equality and simplicity of living; on the other hand, he was an aristocratic Englishman determined to live in style by collecting quitrents from his colonists. He expected his colonial venture to set a new standard of human harmony, but he also expected it to yield him a profit. He is famously pictured purchasing land from the Native American inhabitants rather than driving them westward at the point of a sword or gun, as was the practice among other colonizers in America. Yet Penn was to spend most of his later years embroiled in a bitterly contested legal battle with Lord Baltimore and his heirs over their conflicting claims to southern Delaware. Finally, William Penn, the serious student and dedicated practitioner of representative government, found much to abhor when confronted by the results of his democratizing enthusiasm.

The Delaware General Assembly originated in the mind of that idealistic proprietor, who was enmeshed in the complexities of English colonial politics. Before he ever came to America, Penn constructed a plan, which he called the Frame of Government, on which to base his colonial enterprise. He intended to bring his province, Pennsylvania, and his territories, the Three Lower Counties on the Delaware, into one unified, harmonious whole. To ensure equality between the two, he established three counties in Pennsylvania—Philadelphia, Chester, and Bucks—to match the three in the territories. Penn was required by his charter from the king, as well as by his own inclination, to establish a representative body in his colonies to assist in the government.

Americans like to romanticize their colonial history into a series of tableaux. Among the images that form many Delawareans' vision of their state's colonial past is that of William Penn arriving in New Castle on October 24, 1682.

In our mind's eye we can see the portly, plain-clad Quaker proprietor being rowed to shore from his ship, the *Welcome*, to be met by a gathering of joyful townspeople. Penn then makes a brief speech about the purpose of his coming and assures the colonists of his intention to uphold their rights. A quaint ceremony follows in which the Duke of York's representative presents the new landlord with the symbols of his ownership and authority: the key to the fort; a twig protruding from a mound of turf; and a porringer of river water. Everyone present rejoices that the Three Lower Counties on Delaware are to be under a benevolent governor who promises civil liberties and the right of the citizens to participate in making the laws under which they will live.

This pleasant image is only partly true. About 100 Quakers, mostly from the southern English county of Sussex, sailed with Penn. In the course of the journey thirty of them died of smallpox, so the inhabitants of New Castle had reason to keep their distance from the newcomers. It is also likely that the inhabitants were apprehensive about how those strangely dressed Quakers intended to develop and rule their frontier colony. The fort to which Penn received the key was the only public building in the Three Lower Counties. It was not much to behold, being merely a roughly built wooden structure of two floors that contained a jail and a courtroom. Penn cannot have been unaware that this primitive building represented what had been up to then an equally primitive government.

Penn's Frame of Government of 1682 was Pennsylvania and Delaware's first constitution. It began with the optimistic observation: "Let men be good, and the Government cannot be bad . . . ." The Frame guaranteed the people the right to practice the religion of their choice, a freedom that was almost unknown anywhere in the world at that time. It also promised ordinary colonists a role in law making, but it was to be a minor role. The Frame created a General Assembly to be composed of two houses: a council and an assembly. Penn's original design called for the General Assembly to consist of forty-two members: three councilors and four assemblymen to be chosen by the freemen of each of the six counties from those most noted for "their Sobriety, Wisdom, and Integrity."[1]

Under Penn's Frame of Government only the governor and the council could propose legislation. The role of the assembly was limited to reacting to what was presented to them. In this respect Penn's initial Frame departed significantly from the English Parliament, where bills could originate in either the House of Lords or the House of Commons. The Frame required that elections be held annually in First Month, known by non-Quakers as January. Shortly thereafter the council was to meet with the governor to draft legislation. In Third Month (March) the lower house would assemble for a period of nine days, either to give its assent to the bills presented to it or to reject them.[2]

Shortly after his arrival, Penn put his Frame of Government into practice. He directed the sheriffs of each county to hold elections for assemblymen and council members on November 20. There was no set list of candidates for voters to choose among. Voters could choose any qualified residents of their county, and those who received the most votes were declared elected. The only surviving election return is for Whorekill County, later renamed Sussex, which includes the seven names that John Vines, the county sheriff, submitted to the proprietor.

The voters' choices reflect the fact that they lived in a deferential society. It was assumed that the wealthiest, best educated, and best connected should rule. Of the seven names on Sheriff Vines's list, four were local judges. Of the remaining three, one was a Quaker who was a large landholder in southern Delaware, and the others were also prominent farmers who had served in the county court.[3] In contrast to the population at large, those men were literate and knew something about administering laws.

The first General Assembly met at Upland, soon to be renamed Chester, in Pennsylvania, on December 6, 1682. Penn called this first assembly together for the purpose of endorsing two major documents: the Frame of Government and an Act of Union that would bind his two holdings, the Province of Pennsylvania and the Three Lower Counties on Delaware, into a single government. The act promised the same freedoms and privileges to inhabitants of both colonies. Representatives from the province and territories assented to this act on December 7.

Penn had been most anxious to have the Lower Counties agree to The Act of Union in order to stifle Lord Baltimore's claim to their land. Toward that end, he took pains to affirm the landholdings of settlers whose titles came from Lord Baltimore and to offer them rights equal to those of Pennsylvanians. Even with those steps he must have been aware that many in the Lower Counties felt a closer affinity to Maryland than to Pennsylvania.

At that first meeting of the General Assembly, the lower house, called the House of Assembly, established rules by which it would govern itself. Drawn from Parliamentary precedents, the rules permitted the members to choose their speaker and to form the house into a "Grand Committee" to discuss business. Its members also agreed to establish an orderly procedure for the reading and enrolling of bills. The clerk of the assembly was to stand and read the title of each bill. He would then deliver it to the speaker who would read the bill's title and declare that to be the first reading of the bill. Each bill was to have at least two, sometimes three, readings. No member was to speak to the bill until after the second reading, unless to call for its removal.[4]

Penn took the occasion of the assembly's first meeting to naturalize the Swedes and Dutch as citizens of his commonwealth. They, in turn, promised to "serve and obey him with all they had."[5] Despite a disagreement over the election returns submitted by the sheriff of New Castle County, Penn was pleased with the harmony that characterized the proceedings. The "great variety of dispositions, rawness and inexperience" of the assembly's participants had not prohibited them from taking the steps that the proprietor had desired.[6] Penn's new government appeared to be getting off to a good start.

The second General Assembly met in the newly established town of Philadelphia in January 1683, notably out of sequence with the timing prescribed in the Frame. The proprietor opened the meeting by reading several statements, including a lesson in decorum and proper procedure entitled "The orderly Method of Parliaments, and the Demeanor of the Members thereof observed in England . . . ."[7]

The proprietor and council then presented to the assembly a series of laws that dealt with pressing concerns in the frontier settlements. The assembly agreed to new laws that addressed matters such as encouraging the killing of wolves, controlling servants, marking cattle, and burning of woods and marshes. The assembly also adopted statutes concerning the disposition of estates, the recording of deeds, the licensing of ferryboats, and other contracts between citizen and government. Then the assembly went on to consider and adopt laws respecting murder, manslaughter, fornication, breech of the Sabbath, and other crimes.

Penn took the occasion of his second General Assembly to announce a revision of the Frame of Government, raising the number of county representatives to the assembly from four to six. This change was unpopular in the Lower Counties, where petitioners complained that there were as yet too few educated people to send such large delegations to the assembly. Their point was made in a telling fashion, for most of the petitioners signed with a mark, not a signature.[8]

On March 10, 1684, the third General Assembly met in New Castle. This was the first time that a representative body had ever assembled in what was to become the state of Delaware. Thereafter, until the legislatures of the two proprietary colonies began meeting separately in 1704, the assembly met annually in Philadelphia, except in 1690 and 1700, when the assembly returned to New Castle.

William Penn had two reasons to convene the assembly in the Lower Counties. The obvious purpose was to bind the Lower Counties as equal partners in Penn's government. Another reason, however, may have been more salient in the proprietor's mind: that of defending his right to the Lower Counties from the legal claims of Lord Baltimore and his family, the Calverts. It is noteworthy that the meetings in New Castle always coincided with major phases in the proprietors' lawsuit in England.

In the same month in 1684 that the assembly was meeting in New Castle, Lord Baltimore was authorizing his agent in Maryland to lay claim to the Three Lower Counties. The Marylanders were ordered to build a fort on the Christina River in central New Castle County. The incursion was stopped, but some New Castle County residents, including two members of the council, were implicated. Their "treachery and rebellion" disturbed Penn mightily.[9]

The meeting in New Castle in 1684 most likely took place in the fort's upper courtroom, where William Penn had received his twig and river water less than two years before. There were only two other buildings in town capable of containing such a large group. Both were homes of former governors under the Duke of York.

Shortly after the session of 1684 ended, Penn reluctantly sailed back to

England to defend his land title in court. It was to be a long struggle that kept him away for fifteen years. In his absence, he appointed a succession of deputy governors. None proved capable of establishing harmonious relations with the colonists. Factions formed around different religious, geographic, and economic interests. Settlers in both the province and the territories resented paying quitrents, a fixed rent that they were required to pay to the absent proprietor. A time of troubles had begun that would end only with the separation of the two colonies.

Despite the Act of Union, differences between the upper and lower counties became magnified, not diminished, with time. While the dispute over proprietary titles discouraged settlement in Delaware, settlers flocked into Pennsylvania. In just its first two years, ships brought several thousand Quakers to Pennsylvania from England, Ireland, and Wales. Thousands more arrived in subsequent years, drawn by the promise of the religious freedom that they did not enjoy at home.

Philadelphia grew rapidly into a city that left the river town of New Castle in its wake. In the region around Philadelphia, Quaker farmers grew wheat for an international market. Exporting their produce and importing the goods that it bought made Philadelphia a major Atlantic port, and made some of the city's merchants wealthy. Meanwhile, in Kent County, Penn's name for the county formerly called St. Jones, tobacco continued to be the principal export crop, while in Sussex County farmers raised tobacco and chopped trees for lumber. In both Kent and Sussex the Church of England remained the major religion, and slavery was more prevalent than in the wheat-growing region to the north.

Instead of the harmony that William Penn had intended, and for which he had so carefully planned, his government was racked with conflicts. Wealthy Pennsylvanians objected to the proprietor's restrictive land policies. The House of Assembly resented the greater power of the council, which was dominated by Philadelphia's richest Quaker merchants. Inhabitants of the Lower Counties believed that their lesser wealth and fewer numbers rendered them ever weaker with respect to Pennsylvania, while the Pennsylvanians complained about sharing power with the less populous Lower Counties.

Penn was dismayed by the reports of discontent that he received from America. He developed "grave misgivings" concerning the colonists' capacity to participate in government. In 1688 the proprietor appointed Captain John Blackwell to be deputy governor. Blackwell was an experienced administrator, but as a former military officer and a Puritan he was bound to clash with the Quakers of Pennsylvania. Under the direction of this autocratic man, matters sank to a new low point. Blackwell found the colonists so frustrating that he wrote to Penn that the wild animals in the American forests would be better able to govern themselves than could the "witless zealots who make a monkey of his assembly."[10]

Deputy Governor Blackwell's acts of tactless provocation demonstrated his disdain for the assembly. He took a particular dislike to John White of New Castle County, who was elected speaker of the assembly every year from 1685 through 1689. In that latter year, Blackwell ordered White arrested for a minor misdemeanor to prevent the speaker from attending the meeting of the General Assembly. The sheriff of New Castle County refused to make the arrest, and White appeared in Philadelphia to take his seat.

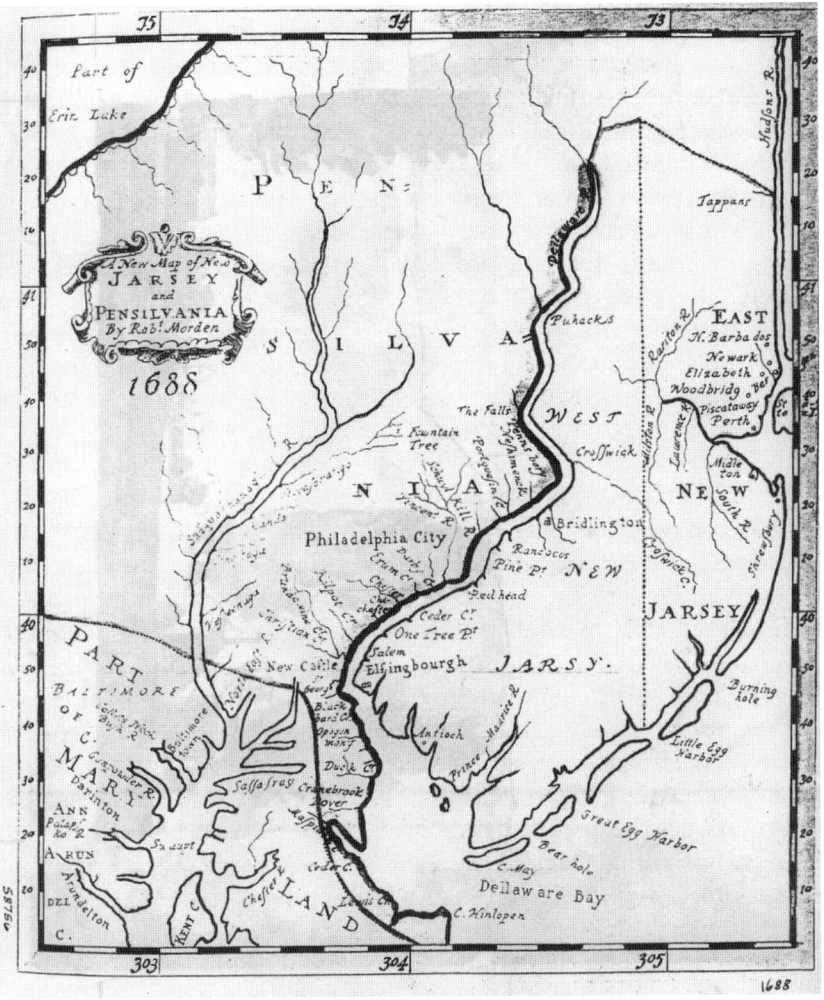

Cartographer Robert Morden of London produced this map in 1688. It is among the earliest maps to show the lands of William Penn in North America. Note particularly Morden's belief that Penn's claim to the Three Lower Counties extended very little westward from the Delaware Bay. Penn's long but ultimately successful court battle to expand his holdings made the State of Delaware possible. (Courtesy of the Delaware Public Archives)

Blackwell then ordered the sheriff of Philadelphia to arrest White while the house was in session. When the sheriff came to the place where the assembly was meeting, Speaker White escaped by climbing out a window. White remained in Philadelphia, where he was twice dragged from his lodgings in spite of his assertion that members of the assembly were immune from arrest during the session except for a serious crime. House members were infuriated by the deputy governor's highhanded action, which was contrary to English law that protected members of Parliament from arrest while Parliament was in session. Fellow assemblymen viewed Blackwell's action as contemptuous "of the dignity of the House" and a clear indication of "the present Arbitrariness in Government."[11]

Penn's Frame of Government had not created two legislative houses of equal weight. The council functioned as both an executive and a legislative body. With the governor it appointed judges and other governmental officers. It shared the governor's responsibility for the treasury, and, as noted before, the councilors worked with the governor or deputy governor to propose legislation to the assembly. The governor and council also had the power to decide when to adjourn the lower house, a power that in England was reserved to the House of Commons to decide for itself.

After a few years under the Frame, the assemblymen demanded more power. If the proprietor wanted them to be governed by the decorum of Parliament, they should also have the rights of Parliament. In 1695, for the first time the assembly defied the most onerous of their limitations by taking up issues for discussion and possible action that had not been forwarded to them from the council.

In the meantime, in England William Penn was adjusting to government under a new king. Following the death of Charles II in 1685, his brother, formerly James, Duke of York, ascended the throne as King James II. James was a convert to Catholicism, and his policies threatened the country's Protestant majority. Only three years after his ascension, most of the nation's Protestant gentry, aristocrats, and merchants coalesced to overthrow him in a bloodless revolt known as the Glorious Revolution. The displaced king's daughter Mary and her husband, William of Orange, a Dutch prince, became England's joint rulers.

The Glorious Revolution could not have come at a worse time for William Penn. James II had lost his crown and fled his kingdom just as he had been on the verge of signing a document that would have given William Penn clear title to the Lower Counties. Thus, legally, in 1688 the Delaware colony reverted to the crown. In the eighty-eight years from England's Glorious Revolution to the American Revolution, the Penn family held Delaware by sufferance, not by legal right. To retain control of the little colony, Penn and his heirs would have no choice but to defer to the wishes of the government in London.

William and Mary introduced new policies into England. They accepted a Bill of Rights that guaranteed Englishmen and Parliament greater rights and powers. But those concessions did not mask the fact that King William was strong willed. He pulled England into the Netherlands' struggle against France, thus initiating a series of wars between England and France that were to persist intermittently until the fall of Napoleon in 1815.

The new sovereigns also demanded a more purposeful approach to the administration of England's growing empire. William and Mary's government favored royal colonies that were directly subject to control from the crown and Parliament in London. Royal administrators were hostile to proprietary colonies and determined to bring them into line with the evolving imperial program, most especially with regard to trade. Those changes powerfully affected Penn's governance of his colonies.

In 1696 the embattled Penn, still fighting Baltimore's claims to the Lower Counties in the courts, issued a new Frame of Government. The new Frame was designed to mollify the colonists and to bring his charter into line with common English practice. Reacting to complaints, especially from the Lower Counties, he reduced the size of the council from three to two members per county and the House of Assembly from six to four. He also acknowledged the right of the lower house to initiate legislation, to elect its speaker, to judge the qualifications of its members, and to decide the time of its adjournment.

The Frame of 1696 provided more detailed rules on running the assembly. It defined eligibility for voting and for membership in the assembly and said that voters who accepted payment for their vote would forfeit their right to vote for that year. Electors and assemblymen had to be at least twenty-one years old and own fifty acres of land, of which ten acres must be cleared, or have other assets worth fifty English pounds. The Frame also set the pay for assembly members at four shillings per day and for the speaker and the council members at five shillings per day.[12]

The English government accused Penn of failing to enforce Parliament's Navigation Laws, which were designed to control colonial commerce in the interest of the empire. To maintain his charter, the proprietor had to demonstrate his ability to enforce those laws. The Lower Counties presented a challenge to that enforcement. Tobacco was being smuggled across the peninsula from Maryland to the Delaware River in the Lower Counties to elude Maryland's taxes. This trade was economically important to some Delawareans and they resisted Penn's efforts to stamp it out.

Piracy represented another form of disobedience to the imperial system. That lurid illicit trade posed a threat to the British Empire in the 1680s and 1690s. The high point of England's response to piracy came in 1701 with the execution of Captain William Kidd in London. While Delawareans stood accused of evading the tobacco tax, it was Pennsylvanians who winked at piracy. The Quaker merchants of Philadelphia and their representatives in the General Assembly were suspected of conspiring with pirates. At the least, they demonstrated an unusual complacency toward the menace posed by these sea-borne thieves.

Colonists in the Lower Counties feared pirates. Those who lived near the Delaware Bay or River, as most Delawareans did at that time, were among the pirates' victims. Pirates never attacked so far up the river as to endanger Pennsylvanians. The geographical difference in vulnerability to attack from the sea drove a significant wedge between Penn's two colonies.

In September 1698 fifty armed men sacked Lewes, the principal town of Sussex County. The pirates carried off valuables from peoples' homes and captured farm animals. Local men were forced at gunpoint to carry the loot to the pirates' ship, leaving the residents of Lewes with little more than the clothes on their backs. The following year another pirate ship sailed up the Delaware River as far as New Castle, where the thieves captured a merchant ship. The leading citizens of the Lower Counties appealed to the deputy governor and the council to take action to protect them from such brazen attacks, but their appeals were ignored.

The pirates' attacks provoked irreconcilably different responses in Pennsylvania and the Lower Counties. Residents of the Lower Counties urged the construction of fortifications at Lewes and on the river to be fitted with cannons to fire at the marauders from the sea. Pennsylvania's Quaker majority opposed military defense on religious grounds. A cynic might also note that they were not directly threatened. The situation appeared very different from the perspective of residents of the embattled Lower Counties. There the chief religious denominations were the Church of England (Anglican), Presbyterian, and Lutheran, none of which placed a moral impediment on defensive war.

The piracy issue caught William Penn in a serious bind. As a Quaker he was conscience-bound to oppose bloodshed, but as a proprietor he was required to demonstrate his government's zeal to combat illegal trade and the robbery of his colonists. If he failed to do so, he risked losing the Lower Counties, and possibly Pennsylvania as well.

The Quaker proprietor's awkward position regarding warfare became more precarious yet when England went to war with France in 1689. The war was fought not only in Europe, but also along the frontiers and coastlines of North America, where it was known as King William's War. The French commissioned privately owned merchant vessels that were armed for war. They were called privateers and behaved much like pirates. French privateers prowled the Atlantic Ocean in search of cargo ships engaged in England's imperial trade. The privateers were drawn to the unprotected Delaware Bay where they could prey on ships bound to and from Delaware River ports.

King William's government required the colonies to erect defenses. The government in London agreed to renew William Penn's charter only on the condition that he comply with that order. Residents of the Lower Counties rejoiced that Penn would have to fortify the bay and river or risk losing his colonies. Pennsylvania's Quaker assemblymen, however, responded with a tepid promise to comply only "so far as our religious Persuasions shall permit."[13]

Serious troubles erupted in the Lower Counties in the wake of the Quakers' refusal to defend the Lower Counties. A broadside appeared in New Castle County in 1690 declaring that the time had come "for us to assert our Right before it be quite lost."[14] Later that year councilmen from New Castle attempted, unsuccessfully, to withdraw the Lower Counties from the union.[15]

In their petition, the Lower Counties' councilmen complained that Penn's government had failed to provide the equality that had been promised. As proof they noted that there were so few judges appointed in the Lower Counties that persons engaged in lawsuits there often had to travel to Philadelphia to have their cases heard. The petitioners cited the particularly egregious instance of a widow accused of murdering her bastard child. Her trial was postponed so long for want of a judge that she had the opportunity to murder her two other children.[16] Writing from England, Penn replied poignantly to the petitioners' request for separate colonies. "Your Division has torne me to pieces . . . . I am a man of sorrows and you Augment my Griefs, not because you don't love me, but because you don't love one another."[17]

Despite Penn's efforts at reconciliation from afar, the wound that divided his commonwealth did not heal. In 1698 several assemblymen from the Lower Counties refused to attend the General Assembly in Philadelphia. In 1699 none of the members elected from New Castle County appeared, nor did several from Kent and Sussex. In response, the rump assembly adopted a law that would fine not only the absentees but also those qualified to vote for assemblymen and councilors who abstained from doing so.[18]

William Penn returned to America in 1699 a chastened man. He was deeply in debt and had become far more pragmatic than in his younger days. Penn was desperate to find a compromise to save his proprietorship over both his province and his territories. He continued to believe that the Three Lower Counties were an essential part of his commonwealth. But he recognized that holding on to them would be difficult. The Lower Counties' assemblymen had made their dissatisfactions clear. They regretted their predecessors' action in agreeing to the Act of Union. They believed that Penn's failure to get clear title to the Lower Counties from James II, coupled with a temporary suspension of Penn's charter in 1693, had invalidated the proprietor's claim to the Lower Counties and erased their union with Pennsylvania.

The proprietor's return signaled that a showdown was imminent. In October 1700 Penn called the assembly to meet in New Castle. The meeting most likely took place in the new courthouse that had been completed in 1687. That building was set afire and destroyed in 1730. Within a year the New Castle County Levy Court rebuilt the courthouse. It stands today as the center section of the historic courthouse.[19]

When the legislators had assembled, the members from the Lower Counties raised the issue of equality. They offered a proposal "That the Union shall be confirmed on Condition that at no Time hereafter the Number of Representatives of the People . . . in the Province (Pennsylvania) shall exceed them of the annexed counties; but if hereafter more Counties be made in the Province, and thereby more Representatives added, that the Union shall cease."[20]

Penn immediately recognized the danger, but he could offer only a feeble promise to mollify representatives of the Lower Counties. If Pennsylvania were to gain additional legislators, as the Province's far greater population clearly warranted, Penn pledged that no legislation that dealt with the Lower Counties would be adopted without a two-thirds vote. Since the representatives of the Lower Counties believed that they were already being short-changed by their larger neighbor, this offer seemed to them but a hollow promise.

Neither colony was willing to back down on what each saw as its rights. With a rapidly growing population and a large frontier territory yet to be settled, why should Pennsylvanians accept equality of representation in the assembly with three poorly populated counties that were locked between the Delaware Bay and River to the east and Maryland to the south and west?

The one issue on which representatives of the province and the territories could agree was the need for a new Frame of Government. The proprietor strove to find a formula that might satisfy his quarreling colonies, the government in London, and his own interests.

In 1701 Penn convened the General Assembly in Philadelphia to consider a new Charter of Privileges. But before he could put his proposed charter before the assembly, the Pennsylvania members introduced a bill to re-confirm the laws adopted at the previous session in New Castle. That action was necessary, they insisted, because laws passed in the Lower Counties were not binding in Pennsylvania. The Act of Union was dead.

On hearing that insult, the representatives of the Lower Counties walked out of the assembly room. They gathered separately to write a remonstrance, which they presented to Penn. The representatives called the action of their sister Province "highly injurious and destructive to the Privileges of the Lower Counties . . . ." When he received the document, Penn called the representatives of the Lower Counties to meet with him. At the meeting the Lower Counties' representatives told the proprietor that the refusal of the Pennsylvanians to accept laws passed in New Castle made a mockery of equality between the colonies.[21]

William Penn was now at his wits' end. He told the assemblymen from the Lower Counties that their behavior was "very unkind" to him personally but that "they were free to break off and might act distinctly by themselves," if they insisted on doing so, "at which they seemed pleased."[22] Shortly afterward, Penn set down his thoughts on the impending rupture in a letter addressed to the assembly. "Your Union is what I desire," he wrote, "but your Peace and Accommodating of one another is what I must expect from you." He begged both sides to "Yield in Circumstantials to preserve Essentials."[23]

It was Penn, however, who had to yield. In his Charter of Privileges, dated October 28, 1701, the proprietor acquiesced to the demands of many politically active men in Pennsylvania to increase the assembly's powers. Thus, the new Charter was more about Pennsylvania than it was about the Union. But it did contain some important changes that affected both the province and the territories.

The Charter reduced the influence of the once powerful council. The council lost its legislative function and became merely advisory to the governor. The Charter directed that the assembly would meet annually in Philadelphia, "unless the Governour and Councell . . . shall . . . appoint another place within the said Province or Territories."[24] Everyone knew that Penn was most anxious to leave for England immediately to defend his land grant to the Lower Counties from both Lord Baltimore and King William, but arguments over the proposed Charter kept the legislators in session for over a month, making the General Assembly of October 1701 the longest to that time.

Finally, on October 28, 1701, as his ship lay in harbor at New Castle about to depart, Penn most reluctantly agreed to accept a proviso to the Charter of Privileges. The proviso read: "I am content and doe hereby Declare That if the representatives of the Province and Territories shall not hereafter Agree to Joyne together in Legislation . . . anytime within three yeares . . . That in such case [he would accept their] separation . . . in Respect of Legislation." To which he added that "Inhabitants of both Province and Territories shall separately Injoy all other Liberties, Priviledges and Benefitts granted Joyntly to them in this Charter."[25]

Penn would never again see America. The union that he had worked to achieve between his adjacent colonies was now very close to rupture. Throughout 1702 Penn's deputy governor, Andrew Hamilton, worked with the council to avert a separation that would both deprive Pennsylvania of the Lower Counties' lucrative tobacco trade and provide ammunition to those in England who sought to strip the little colony from Penn's control.

There remained a fragile chance to affect reconciliation. In October 1702, pursuant to the terms of the new charter, the authorities in Philadelphia called on the six counties of the combined colonies to elect representatives to the annual assembly just as in the past.

The assembly that met in November 1702 not only failed to restore harmony, it proved highly frustrating to all who participated. Representatives of the Lower Counties came to Philadelphia, but they refused to sit with their Pennsylvania brethren as an assembly on the grounds that the Lower Counties were not subject to the Charter.

The deputy governor was at a loss for what to do. England was once again at war with France. Deputy Governor Hamilton had received orders from England's new monarch, Queen Anne, to build defenses on Pennsylvania's western frontier against attacks of Indians allied with the French. The Lower Counties professed their willingness to comply with the Queen's command. They refused, however, to do so as part of an assembly whose powers derived from the new Charter. As a result, nothing was accomplished. Division offered the only way to save Penn's proprietary rights.

The much-anticipated split between the colonies finally occurred in 1704, the third year noted in Penn's proviso. Even then, Penn's newly appointed deputy governor, John Evans, tried valiantly to reunite the quarrelsome colonies. To that end, he called the council and assembly members from both colonies to meet at the home of Joseph Shippen in Philadelphia on the afternoon of April 11, 1704.

When the assemblymen had gathered, the speaker, a Pennsylvanian, told the deputy governor and council that the assembly could not conduct government business while non-members were in the room. He was referring to the assemblymen from the Lower Counties. After the delegates from the Lower Counties had departed, the speaker expressed his surprise that representatives from the Lower Counties had been summoned to the meeting. He then stifled Governor Evans's last-ditch effort to maintain the union with the observation "that they of the Province were a House of themselves, and it might, they feared, infringe their Privileges to admit any other . . . . " This meeting marked the last time that legislators from Pennsylvania and the Lower Counties on the Delaware would assemble together.[26]

The separation was, no doubt, very sad news for William Penn. In the end, the Quaker proprietor would have to content himself with what was perhaps a lesser victory, but given the circumstances, a major one, nonetheless. Against all the odds, he kept his proprietorship over both his province and his territories, and, at his death, was able to pass the two colonies, and his lawsuit with Lord Baltimore, on to his sons.

In the meantime, John Evans was pressing forward with his instructions from Penn to comply with Queen Anne's orders to defend the colonies. With that purpose in mind, he called upon the assemblymen of the Lower Counties to meet with him in New Castle on May 22, 1704. It was the first meeting of the House of Assembly of the Three Lower Counties on Delaware. From that time until the Revolution, Pennsylvania and the Lower Counties were separate in every sense except that they shared the same proprietary governor.

For the remainder of its colonial history, the Lower Counties would be uniquely invisible among Britain's North American colonies. As a colony the counties never captured much attention in London. For one thing, they had no official name, and because the Penn family's title to the Lower Counties was precarious, they were neither quite proprietary, nor quite royal. All of the other American colonies, including Pennsylvania, were required to send laws adopted by their legislatures to England for approval. The Lower Counties were not. The effects of this neglect can still be seen today in the British Government's Record Office, where there are files for all of the thirteen colonies, except Delaware.

Delaware was unique in another way as well—it had a unicameral legislature. The other colonies had councils that, like the council in Pennsylvania, advised the governors. Typically the members of those councils were the richest and most powerful members of the colonial elite. The councils served as nascent upper houses in the legislatures. In the Lower Counties, however, there was no council. There, well-to-do colonists with political aspirations ran for seats in the House of Assembly and the governor dealt directly with the assemblymen. Delawareans accepted the proprietary family's governor of Pennsylvania as their own chief executive, although the British government gave those governors no specific authority over the Lower Counties.[27]

John Evans was the first governor to work with an independent assembly in the Lower Counties. He was a young man with a mission. He had failed to prevent the rupture between Penn's colonies, but he was determined to fulfill his orders to protect the colonies on the Delaware River from the French. To achieve that goal, he developed a strategy to make use of the Lower Counties' eagerness to defend the bay and river. His goal was to force the Pennsylvanians to assist in paying for the necessary fortifications. He found the Lower Counties' assembly willing to comply.

In 1706, at Governor Evans request, the Lower Counties' assembly voted to build a fort to protect New Castle from pirates and French privateers. To pay the cost of constructing and maintaining the fort, the assembly required all passing ships to stop and pay a fee. Pennsylvanians were incensed. It was obvious that their ships would be paying the bill for a fort that many of them found incompatible with their religion. One Philadelphia merchant defied the Lower Counties' law by refusing to stop. Soldiers in the crudely built fort opened fire on the defiant merchant's ship, but their cannon balls did little damage as the ship sailed by.

Although the Pennsylvanians complained about John Evans's high-handed methods, they had even more reason to hate his successor, Charles Gookin, who became governor in 1709. Delawareans didn't much like him either. Gookin was a professional soldier. This may seem an odd choice of governor for a Quaker proprietor to make, even in wartime, but Penn was desperate to placate Queen Anne's government. Based on the governor's odd behavior, historian John Munroe speculates that Gookin may have been mentally ill.[28] He certainly went out of his way to make enemies.

A telling example of Governor Gookin's impolitic and hostile behavior occurred in 1715 when the governor quarreled with the Lower Counties' assembly over landowners' failure to pay quitrents to the proprietor. The governor became so angry at the obstinacy of the colonists that he attempted to dissolve the assembly on the grounds that the members were engaging in "an unlawful riot." Gookin ordered Speaker John French to adjourn the session. When French refused, the governor threatened to arrest him and to remove him from his elected position as sheriff of New Castle County. French retreated to his office in the New Castle jail and refused to leave.

At that point a real riot did occur. Governor Gookin and his men descended on the jailhouse. They attacked the door with axes. Seeing and hearing what was happening, the entire assembly and most of the residents of New Castle rushed to the scene and struggled to stop the governor's henchmen. Gookin and his men retreated amid bitter cursing and violent oaths. The victorious assemblymen and their speaker then reconvened. They drafted a petition to Penn demanding that Gookin be removed as governor. The proprietor, who was by then a sick old man, agreed to replace Gookin with a less contentious governor.

When William Penn died in 1718 the proprietorship passed to his sons—John, Thomas, and Richard. In the years that followed, the sons sometimes appointed deputy governors and sometimes served as governors themselves. Penn's sons carried on their father's legal battle with Lord Baltimore's descendants for the ownership of the three counties on Delaware. The people who lived in the Lower Counties were content that their land be part of the Penn family's domain so long as they were left free to manage their own affairs without interference from their neighbors in Pennsylvania.

By the mid-eighteenth century the small colony had developed an "Independency" for which the members of the assembly gratefully said "we esteem no small part of our Happiness."[29] The Lower Counties' more settled condition helped to swell the population and support development. Where once there had been only narrow trails, now roads, bridges, and ferries were constructed to carry wagons. Villages were built, often in conjunction with millponds and mills, where farmers brought their grain to be processed and brought produce to sell at weekly markets. In Kent, a county seat was established in the village of Dover on the banks of the St. Jones River. In New Castle County, Quaker merchants established the town of Wilmington on the Christina River, while at nearby Brandywine Village millers built large commercial gristmills.

The evolution of the little colony is evident from surviving minutes of the Lower Counties' Assembly. Unfortunately, the records covering the years from 1704 until the end of the colonial period are sparse. Only those from 1739, 1740, 1741, and 1762 have survived. Those surviving minutes provide a window into the assembly's activities in the mid-eighteenth century.

The House of Assembly of the Three Lower Counties on Delaware consisted of eighteen members, six from each county, who were elected at the county seats of Lewes, Dover, and New Castle on October 1 of each year. Voters were defined as freemen who were subjects of the English monarch and who could meet at least one of two qualifications: be at least twenty-one years old and own fifty acres of land, of which at least twelve acres were cleared; or have valuables, such as buildings or tools, worth at least forty pounds. All of those eligible to vote were required to do so on penalty of fine. Servants, slaves, and women, a group that collectively made up a majority of the population, could not vote.

Each county conducted its own at-large election for its representatives to the assembly. Voting took place at the county seat under the supervision of the county sheriff. A resident of each hundred in the county was present to prevent fraudulent voters from casting ballots. Soliciting votes or accepting bribes were crimes punishable by fine. Voters had the choice of placing a paper ballot into a box or, in the case of illiterate voters, telling the sheriff their choice. The sheriff wrote down the name of each voter's choice in "distinct columns on fair paper" to give to clerks who "shall then pronounce publickly to the People, him whose name is oftenest mentioned . . . to be first elected" and so on until the sixth choice was named.[30]

America's first professional architect, the English-born Benjamin Henry Latrobe, prepared a water-colored plan of the town of New Castle in 1804. The section shown here is the earliest known illustration of the New Castle County Courthouse, also the home of the Delaware General Assembly from the 1730s through 1776. (Courtesy of the Delaware Public Archives)

The assembly met annually on October 20 in New Castle. In the early years, the members probably gathered in the courthouse, although since it was unheated, they may have met in private homes or taverns in cold weather. As late as 1739 records show that the assembly met in a private home even though the courthouse that still stands was constructed by that time.

The first act of business each year was the election of the speaker, a position that rotated only infrequently. The assembly's rules required members to appear each day for roll call or pay a hefty fine equivalent to the annual income of most workers. The body had the power to judge the qualifications of its members, to set its adjournments, to appoint committees, and to prepare bills. It could also impeach criminals and redress grievances. The assembly had "all other Powers and Privileges of an Assembly according to the Rights of free-born subjects of England."[31]

At the first meeting of a session each assemblyman stood before the speaker's chair and swore to be "faithful and bear true Allegiance" to the king, to "profess Faith" in the Trinity and the Old and New Testaments and to renounce Roman Catholicism as a "heretical," "superstitious" and "damnable Doctrine."[32]

Since most of Delaware's colonists were protestant Christians, this was not an onerous oath. It was more liberal than the regulations of some colonies that restricted participation in government to members of particular Protestant sects.

The assembly had the power to decide how much money to provide to the governor for his salary and for the management of the colony. The assembly's funds came from two major sources: an excise tax on liquor, and the interest earned from the paper money issued by the colony's land bank. The bank was created in 1723 to supply a much-needed medium of exchange. Paper money was printed at the order of the assembly for distribution to loan offices in each county. Farmers could apply for loans using their land as security. The 5 percent interest that the bank charged its borrowers constituted the colonial government's largest source of income.

To judge from the records, the strict decorum adopted from parliamentary procedure ruled the meetings. Once a session began, no one could leave the room without the speaker's permission, nor could a member interrupt the speaker or whisper to his neighbor. Members could speak no more than three times to an issue unless the house dissolved into a committee of the whole.

After the House of Assembly was organized and the governor arrived in New Castle, the speaker met with him to receive his instructions. The governor typically began the meeting by conveying new requirements from the British government, then went on to give instructions from the proprietor, and ended with his own requests and suggestions. Since bills were not valid unless the governor affixed the Penn seal, it was essential that the governor and the assembly cooperate or nothing could be accomplished.

During the years for which we have records there were occasions when the assembly and the governor sparred, each trying to assert its dominance over Delaware's nascent government. In 1740, in response to a petition from inhabitants, the assembly passed a bill to establish ferry service across the Christina River at Newport. Governor George Thomas declined to sign the bill on the grounds that the power to grant a ferry was his alone. The assemblymen pointed to precedents in support of their right to establish ferries. The records fail to show who won the argument.

The previous year, in 1739, a clash had arisen over the disposition of money accruing from a fine against a convicted counterfeiter of Delaware bills of credit. Part of the fine was designated for the colony's government. Did that mean that the money should go to the governor for his personal disposal or to the assembly to pay for public needs? The attorneys general of Pennsylvania and Delaware agreed that the money should go to the governor, but the assembly disagreed, saying that it "belongs to the people of this Government."[33]

In most important areas of governance the assembly and Governor Thomas worked together with little friction. One such area of harmony was the construction of Delaware's first code of laws. No one could argue that codification of the laws was not desperately needed. Many laws had been lost or were disputed. As a result, judges had to make rulings that were more than usually arbitrary and inconsistent.

Creating a code of laws fell to the colony's assembly. It consumed much of the members' attention during the 1730s. The codification was an exasperating job. Governor Thomas complained that the assemblymen were reinventing the proverbial wheel, passing new laws that contradicted old ones when they could more easily have borrowed a law code from some other more established colony. The assemblymen refused to follow his advice.

The Lower Counties' assemblymen wanted to write the code themselves. Perhaps the members were embarrassed by the confusion left by earlier assemblies, for they replied to Governor Thomas, ". . . we beg leave to say that many of our laws being lost and others lying in the offices of this Government in great disorder made it absolutely necessary to us to endeavor to get the whole revised which were to be found and to supply the place of those which were lost to the Addition of new ones . . . for the press."[34] The early laws that had disappeared by the 1730s have yet to be found.

The assembly's efforts resulted in a book entitled *Laws of the Government of New Castle, Kent, and Sussex Upon Delaware*.[35] Benjamin Franklin, the official printer for Pennsylvania, published the book in 1742, and it provides our best guide into the society and customs of eighteenth-century Delaware. The laws were organized in the chronological order in which they had been adopted, dated by the year since the accession of the reigning monarch. They cover a multitude of subjects that can be grouped into several categories.

One set of laws dealt with the establishment and procedures of governmental offices. Those included laws regarding the establishment of courts and county offices such as the recorder of deeds, overseers of the poor, and assessors. The costs of running those offices were borne by each county under laws adopted by the assembly. County officials met yearly as a levy court to decide their budget for the following year and then to calculate how much each landowner must be charged, or levied, based on his assessment, to raise that amount.

Laws that dealt with crime and punishment were generally in keeping with English statutes as adapted to the special needs of a New World colony. Punishments escalated from fines to lashing and standing in the pillory, the latter two penalties being most often meted out to slaves and the poor. Death was the prescribed penalty for a number of offenses, including stealing horses or slaves and housebreaking.

Laws respecting the regulation of slaves, free blacks, and servants give insights into a harsh world of racially based prejudice in an economy where personal service was the common lot for all blacks and many whites. The manumission of slaves was discouraged, and a white woman who bore a mulatto child was subjected to a severe public whipping. The child was to be sold into service until he or she reached adulthood. If a slave was found guilty of a capital offense and executed, the master could claim two thirds of the slave's value from government funds.

Title page from the first compilation of Delaware laws. Initially published by Benjamin Franklin in 1742, this page is from the reprinting of 1752 by Benjamin Franklin and David Hall, who had taken over the operation of the press when Fanklin retired in 1748. (Courtesy of the Delaware Public Archives.)

Laws that dealt with the land and the environment included subjects such as transportation, farming, and the control of wild and domestic animals. The assembly legislated on the draining of marshes, improvements to navigation, laying out of highways, and building of bridges. A law was passed against setting fire to woodlands since that method of clearing ground had proved destructive to valuable timber. Farmers were required to erect post-and-rail fences to protect their fields from stray animals. Owners of pigs were ordered to put rings in the noses of those beasts so that swine could be led away from town centers, where their presence was obnoxious. A reward awaited anyone who killed a wolf and brought the beast's severed head to the authorities. Colonists were restricted to hunting deer in fall and winter, but, in a rare concession to Delaware's first inhabitants, Native Americans were permitted to hunt deer throughout the year.

The publication of the *Laws of the Government of New Castle, Kent, and Sussex Upon Delaware* must have brought a degree of consistency to court proceedings that had been previously impossible to achieve. Another edition of the laws was printed a decade later. Those volumes, now lying unused and forgotten in libraries throughout the state, are not just quaint historical relics. They represent the basis upon which Delaware's later laws have been built. Given the difficulties that members of the assembly faced in bringing order from the chaos of past legislation, the codification and publication of the laws was a considerable achievement.

Defense continued to occupy much of the assembly's attention. It was an area where the legislators and the governor were likely to agree. In the 1740s England was again at war with France in what the American colonists called King George's War. The Delaware Bay and River were once more "naked and defenseless" against assault.[36] In 1745 an enemy privateer brazenly sailed up the Delaware as far as Reedy Point, only a few miles below New Castle. Two years later a shipload of pirates landed a few miles above Bombay Hook and plundered two houses, carrying off several black people. Fears of slave insurrections heightened white Delawareans' sense of vulnerability.

Now free of Pennsylvania's check on military expenditures, Delaware's freemen were eager to cooperate with the mother country's call for troops. Assemblymen were not pleased, however, when indentured servants began signing on with the militia. Masters complained about losing their servants' labor and the assembly promptly disallowed that practice.

In 1740 the Duke of New Castle, Britain's principal secretary of state, commended the Lower Counties' Assembly for its members "dutiful behaviour" in "chearfully complying with his Majesty's Instructions" to assist in provisioning troops raised here for the expedition against Louisburg in Canada.[37] At last the little colony had come to the attention of a major figure in the British government, and in a positive way.

The climax of Anglo-French fighting in America came in the French and Indian War of 1754-1763. Once again Delawareans responded to the call for action.

The assembly provided several thousand pounds in money and supplied provisions for General Edward Braddock's ill-fated march through Pennsylvania to Fort Duquesne. Delawareans revived their militia and the assembly authorized a lottery to support the colony's troops and to purchase cannon for the fort protecting New Castle. For those patriotic exertions the colony received compensation from a grateful British Parliament.

The assembly's meeting in 1762, the only one during the war years for which we have a record, was a veritable love feast among the assemblymen, their governor, and the British government. "With hearts full of gratitude we received the Information of the generous Gift of the Parliament of Great Britain to this Government" began the assembly's letter of thanks for the compensation the colony had received. The letter went on to proffer "the most unfeigned Thanks of every freeman" of Delaware for this recompense.[38] Who could have foretold that only a little over a decade later revolution would sever this tiny, loyal colony's ties to Britain.

2
CREATING THE DELAWARE STATE, 1764-1781

By the 1760s the Lower Counties had evolved from a frontier of forests and marshlands to a settled community that included farms and towns. The work of the assembly reflected those changes. Whereas in the early period of settlement the assembly of the Three Lower Counties on Delaware had legislated a bounty to encourage the killing of wolves, in the later period they enacted a bounty to kill squirrels. Efforts to control nature had progressed from the dangerous to the merely annoying. The assembly was now devoting considerable time to the issues of road and bridge building, marsh draining, and regulating the construction of mills on tidal streams. The Delaware colony was an integral part of a trade network centered in Philadelphia, which interacted with the entire British Empire. The growing network made transportation and economic improvements ever more important.

While there is no way to know for certain the population of late colonial Delaware, an estimate made by the U.S. Census Bureau suggests that by the 1770s about 37,000 people lived in the Lower Counties, of whom roughly seven thousand were of African descent. The population had not only grown, it had changed. In the mid-eighteenth century there was a mass movement of Scotch-Irish immigrants of the Presbyterian faith from Northern Ireland to the middle colonies. Many of them landed in New Castle and settled nearby. Those newcomers demonstrated a great regard for education. Villages hired schoolmasters to teach the three "R"s. One Scotch-Irishman, the Reverend Mr. Francis Alison, began an academy to prepare young men for the professions. Illiteracy, although still common, became less pervasive.

To meet the growing market for food, farmers enlarged their fields to plant corn, wheat, and hay and to raise horses, cattle, and hogs. Tobacco ceased to be a major crop in the colony. On Delaware's many streams and rivers enterprising men built mills and milldams to grind wheat into flour and corn into meal. The shift in agriculture from tobacco to grains was linked to the development of Wilmington as the colony's chief center for milling and commerce. By 1770 the collection of Quaker-owned flourmills at the Brandywine Bridge in Wilmington comprised one of the greatest concentrations of manufacturing in the British colonies. Wilmington flour was shipped to the West Indies. Mill owners, ship captains, and the more prosperous among the farmers used the proceeds from that commerce to purchase English manufactured goods that would have seemed luxurious only a generation before.

Wood and brick were the major building materials of the era. In Sussex County landowners found a ready market for cedar and pine logs in Philadelphia and beyond. Farmers, merchants, and millers with money to spend attracted skilled artisans to the colony to build substantial residences of brick that boasted interiors decorated with carved wainscoting of pine or poplar and filled with well-crafted furniture, clocks, and silverware.

The growing prosperity and sophistication of colonial life did not, however, bring an end to unfree labor in its various forms. Many immigrants from England and Northern Ireland began their stay in America as indentured servants. Servitude for a period of years was also a common punishment for minor crimes, and household service provided an easy way to find homes for orphaned children.

Slavery represented the most all-encompassing infringement of freedom. In Delaware slavery reached its peak in the mid-eighteenth century. Then the institution slowly began to decline. Manumissions became more common; some slaves bought their freedom; and there was a change in public sentiment regarding the morality of slavery and the slave trade. There were two basic reasons for this change: the shift from raising tobacco to less labor-intensive grains, and a growing religiously based revulsion to slavery, especially among Quakers. Delaware had no large plantations of the sort common in tidewater Virginia, where hundreds of slaves were often employed. In contrast, Delaware's wealthiest farmer and largest slave owner was John Dickinson of Kent County, who owned only thirty-seven people. Dickinson served briefly in the assembly. The second largest slaveholder among assemblymen owned nineteen slaves.[1]

Economic and social developments altered the composition and business of the assembly. Although assemblymen continued to be selected from the colony's largest landowners, and most would have described themselves as farmers, by the 1770s the assembly also included practicing lawyers, physicians, and businessmen. A number of members were veterans of the French and Indian War. A study of the composition of the assembly describes its members as, "practical men . . . who were used to solving problems they encountered on farms or in business."[2] Some assemblymen had studied the English Common Law and were familiar with legal procedures, either in their capacities as practicing attorneys or as judges in the colony's courts.

There were no political parties in Delaware, but there were family and interest-based factions. Colonial historians refer to those groups as the Court Party and the Country Party to distinguish those whom the governor of the moment favored with preferments from those whom he overlooked. One should not set too much store on these designations in Delaware, however, because the colony enjoyed a comfortable relationship with the Penn family, whose members continued to govern Delaware and Pennsylvania until the Revolution.

After William Penn died his sons abandoned their father's Quaker faith and reverted to the Church of England. Their religious apostasy made them unpopular with the Quakers of Pennsylvania, but Quakers had little impact on politics in the Lower Counties. Religion did, however, play a role in politics in Delaware, not between Quakers and non-Quakers, but between adherents of the Church of England, who made up the largest segment of the electorate, and Presbyterians from Northern Ireland, whose rapid ascent to influence attracted the enmity of some established colonists.

To get elected to the assembly in the Lower Counties it helped to have a large family of supporters, a number of freemen who felt some connection, and a background of service in another government post or in the militia. Wealth and status continued to be keys to success. Although the distribution of alcohol for political purposes was illegal, pre-election parties where liquor flowed freely were still expected. At those gatherings ordinary freemen had the chance to interact with their betters on something approaching equal terms.

The rituals of the assembly meetings remained the same as in the past until the Revolution changed them forever. The assembly continued to be elected early each October and to meet at the beginning of the third week of that month in New Castle. The first order of business was the election of the speaker. Once that decision was made, the speaker led a small committee of assemblymen to wait upon the governor at the boarding house kept by Ann Clay, which was the governor's residence throughout the session. Having heard the governor's report and recommendations concerning affairs that affected the colony, the speaker and committeemen returned to the courthouse to tell their colleagues what the governor had presented to them. The assemblymen then read petitions they had received from constituents and drafted legislation to address the various concerns that had been put before them.

Toward the end of the session the assemblymen reviewed the land bank accounts for the previous year. This was an important responsibility because the county land banks were not only the major source of capital for entrepreneurial colonists, they also constituted the government's largest source of income. At the end of the session the assembly presented the bills that had been passed to the governor for his acceptance. The governor had the power to withhold his ascent, but the Penns and their deputies rarely exercised that power. A bill became law when the governor fixed the Penn family seal to it.

During the final years of the colonial era the governorship passed among descendants of William Penn. The warm but formal tone that characterized relations between legislature and executive appears again and again in the assembly minutes. In 1773, for example, John Penn returned to the governorship after a period during which his uncle, Thomas, had held the post. Caesar Rodney, the speaker of the assembly, delivered a letter of congratulations to the returning governor that included the following language: "The Felicity the good People of this Government enjoyed under your former Administration . . . gives us a well-grounded Prospect of future Happiness whilst one of your Honorable Family presides over us . . . ."[3]

The mutual respect and affection that bound the Penns so contentedly to the Lower Counties was shattered in 1765. In that year Parliament adopted the infamous Stamp Act. The purpose of the act was to raise revenue from the American colonists to help defray Britain's enormous debt from the French and Indian War. This ill-starred revenue law unleashed a torrent of protest in America from which imperial relations never recovered.

After 1765 the assembly of the Lower Counties continued to pursue its usual agenda of issues dealing with roads, dams, and sluice gates. The main subject of its attention, however, shifted to protesting the increasingly hostile actions of the mother country. For the next decade the majority of the assemblymen would seek after the elusive brass ring of a mutually acceptable accommodation with the kingdom that many still thought of as home, though few had ever been there.

During this period of protest, three leaders emerged within the assembly: Caesar Rodney; George Read; and Thomas McKean. Those men were destined to lead Delaware to independence and to help create the United States of America. They risked everything for the ideal of maintaining the right of citizens to elect those who had the power to tax them, and they worked selflessly to create a new political entity that would fulfill their ideals. Because of their accomplishments during a time of unprecedented significance and stress, those three leaders were the most important members ever to serve in a Delaware legislature.

Caesar Rodney was born in 1728 on a farm in Kent County, the first of eight children born to a prosperous farmer and the daughter of a minister of the Church of England. The Rodneys were part of the Kent County gentry that included other politically powerful families such as the Dickinsons and the Ridgelys. Caesar Rodney was educated at home and later at a Latin academy in Philadelphia.

Although farming would always be his main source of income, Rodney was early attracted to public life. His grandfather, William Rodeney, had been elected the first speaker of Delaware's assembly when the Lower Counties split from Pennsylvania in 1704, and his father was also active in politics. While still in his twenties Caesar Rodney helped organize militia for the French and Indian War. He went on to be selected justice of the peace and a lower court judge, and was then elected sheriff of Kent County. After building a strong record in government, in 1761 Rodney defeated his neighbor John Dickinson to become an assemblyman at the age of thirty-three.

Rodney's clear judgments and responsible behavior inspired the confidence of voters and colleagues for many years to come. We are fortunate that many of Rodney's letters written to his brother Thomas during the Revolutionary period have survived. Those documents provide insight into this important leader's thoughts and actions. The letters also attest to the seriousness of Rodney's chronic health problems, which included asthma and the facial cancer that finally killed him in 1784.

George Read was born in Cecil County, Maryland, in 1733, the first of six sons of a farmer who had migrated from Ireland. Although Read's family was neither so prosperous nor so prominent as the Rodneys, George's father recognized his eldest son's intellectual talent and had the resources to send him to study at Francis Alison's academy. It is an indication of young Read's integrity that he later renounced all claims to his father's estate in favor of his brothers because they had not received such expensive educations.

At age fifteen George Read began reading law with a prominent Philadelphia attorney. He was admitted to the bar in New Castle County in 1754. While in Philadelphia, Read developed a lifelong friendship with John Dickinson, also a budding lawyer from Delaware. By the time George Read was elected to the assembly in 1765 he had become the most sought after lawyer in Delaware, known for his hard work and deliberate approach to legal problems. Like Rodney, he was a member of the Church of England, which became the Episcopal Church after the Revolution.

Thomas McKean was the son of a Scotch-Irish immigrant tavern keeper. His mother, who was also born in Ireland, was a member of the Finney family, which achieved prominence in New Castle. Thomas was born in 1734 and orphaned at the age of eight. Like George Read he attended Francis Alison's academy. He then read law in the office of his kinsman David Finney in New Castle and was admitted to the bar in 1754.

Bright, vigorous, industrious, and ambitious, McKean set out to rival his wealthy relatives, and by his ceaseless labors he ultimately surpassed them. In 1757, at the age of twenty-three, McKean was appointed clerk of the assembly. He served two terms in that position before being elected to the assembly in 1762. In 1774 he moved his main residence to Philadelphia and became increasingly involved in Pennsylvania politics, but McKean was continually elected to the Delaware assembly until he withdrew from Delaware politics in 1779.

The Stamp Act of 1765 was greeted in America with riots and rejection. Massachusetts' leaders called on their sister colonies to meet together to formulate a united response to Parliament and the king. When word of the proposal to hold a congress of all thirteen colonies reached the Lower Counties it was already late summer. Recognizing that Governor Penn could not call a special session to allow the assembly to elect delegates, the assemblymen of each county met to choose one delegate each from among their number. Jacob Kollock, the assembly speaker, was selected in Sussex County, but was too unwell to attend. Caesar Rodney, the choice of Kent County's assemblymen, and Thomas McKean, the choice in New Castle County, did participate in the Stamp Act Congress when it met in New York City in October 1765.

That same month the assembly of the Lower Counties convened for its annual meeting in New Castle. Amid handling their usual petitions for draining marshland, the members appointed a committee that included George Read to draft a resolution in response to the Stamp Act. The assembly adopted the committee's words, which put forward the "Liberties and Privileges of the

Inhabitants of this Government, and Setting forth the Grievances . . . from some late Acts of Parliament."[4] They forwarded their resolution to the British government through the colony's agent in London.

Thomas McKean (1734-1817), painting by Rembrandt Peale. A New Castle lawyer, McKean became a leading figure in the Revolutionary era politics of both Delaware and Pennsylvania. (Courtesy of the Historical Society of Delaware)

About that time George Read wrote to an acquaintance, an English merchant who had recently departed the Delaware Valley to return to Britain. "The scene in America has greatly changed since you left us," Read said. "Then political disputes were confined to parties formed in the respective colonies. They are now all resolved into one, and that with the Mother-Country. The Stamp-act you made on your side of the water hath raised up such a ferment among us . . . that I know not when it will subside." He went on to comment that if the law were not repealed, the colonists would believe that "they are to become the slaves of Great Britain by the Parliament's making laws to deprive them of their property without their assent by any kind of representation." In that case, Read predicted, the Americans would cease importing British goods and develop their own industries, which would destroy the mother country's economy.[5]

When the assembly met in May 1766 tempers had cooled. Parliament had repealed the Stamp Act. Thomas McKean was sufficiently sanguine about the restoration of good relations with Britain that he proposed that a committee be appointed to draft an address of thanks to King George III. The assembly agreed.

The speaker chose McKean, Rodney, and Read to fill the ad hoc committee. It was the first of many times that those three men would be called upon to fulfill an enterprise on behalf of the Lower Counties' assembly.

The committee's "Address to the King's Most Excellent Majesty" made two basic points. The Address recalled the Lower Counties' "ardent zeal for His Majesty's service" as attested in their alacrity to provide both men and money to assist in past imperial wars; and the Address reminded the king of the colonists' "inherent Rights and Liberties" to tax themselves.[6] The assembly approved the committee's work. In October 1767 the assemblymen were gratified to receive word from their agent in London that George III had been so pleased with their Address "that he read it over twice."[7] Not long after, Parliament repealed the Stamp Act. Most colonists concluded that they had won their battle with Parliament over "taxation without representation."

At that same session, Thomas McKean reported his successful completion of an assignment from the assembly to track down the Lower Counties' land records from the years when the Duke of York had controlled the colony. Those documents had been found in New York, the Duke's other colony. They were important because they provided evidence concerning the ownership of land in the pre-Penn period. *The Duke of York Record* is still consulted today because it offers the best guide to land titles in early colonial Delaware.

The assembly of 1767 is also notable for another action, or rather, for an action that almost happened, respecting the institution of slavery. In that year, Caesar Rodney, a slave owner, led an effort in the assembly to end the slave trade in the Lower Counties. His bill failed to pass by two votes. Opposition came from Sussex and New Castle counties. All of Kent County's members, together with a few from the other counties, voted for the bill. Had it passed, it would have been a first step toward eradicating slavery in Delaware. The institution of slavery was no longer taken for granted in the Lower Counties, but the practice of involuntary service in its various forms still retained a stronghold in society. It is noteworthy that in that same session the assembly adopted an Act for Relief of the Poor that bound out orphaned children into service until they reached adulthood.

In 1767 Parliament adopted a new tax measure called the Townshend Duties, which were taxes to be applied to a list of specified items that the colonists imported from Britain. News of the Townshend Duties hit the American colonies like a thunderbolt. The law demonstrated Parliament's continuing determination to tax the American colonists. In the Lower Counties on Delaware the assembly took up this new challenge to their rights at their annual session in October 1768.

By the time that the assembly gathered in New Castle a great many Delawareans had read John Dickinson's denunciation of the Townshend Duties in his "Letters of a Pennsylvania Farmer," published in a Philadelphia newspaper. His "Letters" were reprinted in papers throughout the colonies and made Dickinson famous for his legal defense of American liberties. Dickinson's farm was, of course, in Kent County, not in Pennsylvania, but "Letters of a Lower Counties on Delaware

Farmer" did not roll from the tongue. Furthermore, Dickinson was living in Philadelphia, where he practiced law and was involved in Pennsylvania politics. Dickinson had close ties to many of the Lower Counties' political leaders, including his neighbor and onetime political opponent, Caesar Rodney. He was also friendly with his fellow lawyers George Read and Thomas McKean, who shared his outrage at Parliament's act.

Most of the assembly's session of 1768 was given over to considering the issues posed by the Townshend Duties. Rodney, Read, and McKean were appointed to be the body's committee of correspondence, which was authorized to keep in touch with the colony's London agent and with sister colonies. The assembly then resolved itself into a committee of the whole to formulate its response to Parliament's latest revenue scheme.

After meeting for several days as a committee of the whole the house reconvened to adopt the resolutions that its members had written. The first resolution denounced the Townshend Duties. "It is the opinion of this Committee," the resolve read, "that some late acts of the British Parliament . . . have a Manifest Tendency to deprive the Colonists in America of the exclusive Right of taxing themselves . . . ." This was followed by a second resolve, which was another petition to "our most gracious sovereign . . . with the utmost Decency and Submission, to assert our inestimable Rights and Liberties: delivered from God and Nature, handed down from our Ancestors, and confirmed to us by the constitution . . . ."[8]

Legislators in the Lower Counties, as in sister American colonies, believed that they were in a contest with Parliament over the question of legislative power. At that stage of the contest the Americans liked to believe that King George was above the fray and could be persuaded to recognize the legitimacy of the colonists' arguments. The assembly's continual assertions of loyalty, which appear obsequious to a later generation, should be read in light of the assemblymen's hopes that the king would see their point and intervene to protect them from a rapacious Parliament. But, amid their protestations of loyalty to the crown, the colonial legislators were not about to surrender even a tiny portion of what they viewed as their rights as Englishmen, lest in sacrificing a little they risked losing all rights.

The final version of the resolves was fashioned by the committee of correspondence and signed by Speaker John Vining on behalf of the assembly. The document included the following words: "with the most humiliating sorrow we behold your Majesty's Ancient Colony of New York deprived of her legislative Authority . . . and with equal Concern we observe that Duties for the sole and express purpose of raising a Revenue in America" that had been adopted by Parliament. ". . . our Assemblies will be no longer the Representatives of a free people . . . ."[9] That was the nub of the issue.

Delawareans were proud to be a part of an empire that guaranteed certain liberties to the king's subjects. "No taxation without representation" stood high among those ancient liberties. The assemblymen could not comprehend why this truth was not as clear in England as it was in America. Perhaps, they thought, if they but reminded the king one more time all would be well. Otherwise their assembly and the assemblies of their sister colonies would become but feeble reeds indeed.

This time Parliament did not act swiftly to repeal the duties. In reaction the committees of correspondence in the various colonies spread the word to resist by boycotting the taxed articles. In the Lower Counties George Read organized the boycott and led its enforcement. Believing as he did that the British could best be persuaded through their pocketbooks, he was a zealous enforcer. The tactic worked, but only partially. Pressed by English merchants and manufacturers, Parliament abandoned all the Townshend Duties but one, the tax on tea, which was retained as a symbolic statement of Parliament's authority to treat the colonies as subordinate to British control.

For the next three years the annual meetings of the assembly resumed their ordinary routine. The legislators dealt with matters of local concern such as crooked streets in Wilmington, election fraud in Sussex County, the efficacy of lotteries, and the establishment of the Trustees of the Common in New Castle. Relations with the Penn family were never more cordial.

In 1773 the assembly received disturbing news from other colonies, especially Massachusetts. There, British troops, stationed in Boston to enforce

Caesar Rodney (1728-1784), a Kent County planter, was Delaware's most important leader during the Revolutionary era. He served sequentially as Speaker of the Assembly, delegate to the Continental Congress, and Delaware's Chief Executive. No contemporary likeness of Rodney exists, probably because his face was disfigured by cancer. This line drawing by James E. Kelly, done in preparation for the casting of the statue in Wilmington's Rodney Square, shows an idealized Rodney riding to Philadelphia to vote in Congress for independence on July 2, 1776. (Courtesy of the Historical Society of Delaware)

Parliament's will, came into conflict with local people who called themselves "Patriots" and "Sons of Liberty." Parliament tested the resolve of the colonists by authorizing the shipment of a large quantity of tea to America's major ports. In Boston, Patriots dressed as Indians tossed the tea overboard.

The British Parliament retaliated against Massachusetts with a series of punishing laws known collectively as the Coercive Acts. Civilian government was suspended and martial law took its place. If the intention of the British ministers was to demonstrate their absolute power and to isolate the Bay Colony from her sisters, the tactic backfired. The war of words had failed; a war of guns, bayonets, and swords was soon to begin.

A call went out through the committees of correspondence to convene a Continental Congress in Philadelphia in 1774. Normally, the assembly would choose the colony's delegates, but the leaders of the Lower Counties' assembly knew that it would be impossible to expect Governor Penn to convene the assembly for such a purpose. It was time for the colonists to take matters into their own hands.

The Lower Counties' three leading committeemen—Read, Rodney, and McKean— arranged to hold public meetings in each county. A resolution, probably drafted by George Read, was presented at these county meetings. The resolution called for the assembly to meet as a special convention for the purpose of electing delegates to Congress. All three meetings attracted large crowds that endorsed the proposals put before them.

The meetings revealed tensions among the counties. Those who attended the meetings in Kent and Sussex expressed their displeasure that the proposed convention of assembly members was to be held in New Castle instead of in more centrally located Dover. Dr. Charles Ridgely, a Kent County assemblyman and recent addition to the committee of correspondence, led the campaign on behalf of his hometown. It was the first salvo in an inter-county fight to relocate the assembly's place of meeting.

The assembly's speaker, Caesar Rodney, took the responsibility to summon his fellow legislators to this unprecedented meeting. The meeting convened in New Castle on August 1, 1774, and elected Rodney, Read, and McKean to represent the colony in Congress. Once in Philadelphia, they were ordered by the assembly "to consult and advise with the deputies from the other Colonies, and to determine upon all such prudent and lawful measures as may be judged most expedient . . . in order to obtain relief for an oppressed people . . . ."[10]

The words "prudent" and "lawful" illustrate the delicacy of the assembly's position. The assemblymen sought to compromise in order to maintain the support of members such as Thomas Robinson, a recent addition to the committee of correspondence and a leader in Sussex County who maintained a strong devotion to the king. When war came Robinson chose the British side. The implacable loyalty to the crown represented by Robinson and a few other members acted as a brake on the assembly's actions. How else to explain the near groveling of their addressing George III as "our most gracious Sovereign and rightful liege Lord," only to follow those anachronistic words with an assertion in the same sentence of the colonists' "Liberties, Privileges, and Immunities of free and natural born Subjects" who had the unquestionable right to rule themselves through their own assembly. Though members with Tory leanings had to be assuaged through equivocal language, they were by no means in control. The assembly continued to choose its three leading defenders of colonial rights to represent Delaware in Congress.

Boundary marker placed at the southwest corner of Delaware in 1765/66 at the completion of the Mason-Dixon survey to determine the border separating the proprietary lands of the Penns from those of the Calverts of Maryland. The photograph was taken in Maryland looking toward Delaware and bears the armorial shield of the coat of arms of the Calvert family. The Penn shield appears on the other two sides. Stones marked each mile of the border with the proprietary coats of arms shown at five-mile intervals. (Courtesy of the Delaware Public Archives)

In October 1774 Governor John Penn summoned the assembly to its annual meeting. The governor tried to behave as if everything was proceeding in its usual way. He stayed at Mrs. Clay's during the assembly's session and had very good news to share with the speaker and the other delegates sent to meet with him there. He reported that the ancient boundary dispute that his family had fought to save the Lower Counties from Maryland had finally been resolved in the Penns' favor in England's Court of Chancery. Under the court's decree, the western boundaries of the three Lower Counties were to be extended westward to meet the permanent border that the Mason-Dixon survey had determined several years before.

Delawareans who prize their state's independence from Maryland can only wonder at the timing of the conclusion to that seemingly endless lawsuit. How fortuitous that this thorny issue was put to rest immediately before the Revolution. The most perplexing issue of Delaware's colonial era was settled just in time for the three Lower Counties to assert their geographic integrity as a state.

The assembly met again without their governor in March 1775 to select delegates to a second Continental Congress. The Congress was scheduled to meet in Philadelphia in May. Rodney, Read, and McKean were again the assembly's choice. They were given "full power" to vote for measures to restore relations with Britain to a "constitutional Foundation" and were urged to avoid being unnecessarily "disrespectful" to the king; but the obsequious tone toward the monarch that had characterized the assembly's earlier instructions was gone.

A bridge had been crossed. Britain and even the Penn family were no longer the places from which power flowed. The united colonies were in the process of discarding their masters. The source of political power that is called sovereignty was already moving from the king to the people. A new nation was being formed from what had been thirteen distinct colonies. As their instructions showed, the most important concerns for the delegates from the Lower Counties were to act in concert with the other colonies and to demand that the little colony, still called the Three Lower Counties on Delaware, be accepted as an equal.

Events moved rapidly now. Less than a month after the assembly adjourned, militiamen exchanged fire with British regulars at Lexington and Concord in Massachusetts. A few weeks later Congress appointed George Washington of Virginia to organize a Continental army and called upon each colony to supply troops. Before the new commander in chief could assume control, a bloody encounter between New England militia and the Redcoats took place on Bunker Hill within sight of Boston. The American Revolution had begun.

What proved to be the final meeting of Governor John Penn with the assembly of the Three Lower Counties opened in New Castle on August 21, 1775. Both sides played their parts as if by script. The rupture was more wistful than angry. In response to the request from Congress, the assembly voted a loan to pay for recruiting and outfitting troops for the Continental army and for local defense. Governor Penn, who was under instructions from the British government to deny such measures, withheld his assent to the loan. The assembly's majority respectfully but unhesitatingly took measures into their own hands. They paid the governor the usual 150 pounds for his support and he, in turn, affixed his seal to all the bills adopted except the loan. It was to be the last time the Penn seal would make legal a bill passed by a Delaware assembly.

In early 1776 Washington's army, reinforced by cannon taken from Fort Ticonderoga, dislodged the British from Boston. The ministry in London was, however, hardly in a mood to surrender. The American colonies were declared to be in rebellion and were placed outside the protection of the king. A large army, made up in part of mercenaries hired from the German principality of Hesse, was readied to cross the Atlantic to crush the rebellion. It was in this context on May 15, 1776, that Congress adopted a motion of Virginia's Richard Henry Lee calling upon the colonies to "adopt such Government as shall in the opinion of the Representatives of the People best conduce to the happiness and safety of their constituents...." Caesar Rodney expressed the situation well just two days later when he wrote that "continuing to swear Allegiance to the power that is cutting our throats... is certainly absurd."[11]

George Read (1733-1798), engraving by Samuel Sartain. Read, a New Castle lawyer, was a leader in the Delaware Assembly's resistance to Great Britain. He represented the state in the Continental Congress and was the leading figure in drafting Delaware's first constitution. (Courtesy of the Historical Society of Delaware)

In a legal, constitutional sense in the spring of 1776 there was no government in the Lower Counties, or anywhere else in the American colonies. Nonetheless, assemblies met; laws were passed; money was raised; and an army supported. In the Lower Counties, as elsewhere, the assembly WAS the government, and of their own free will the assemblies followed the dictates of Congress. Thus, on June 15, 1776, meeting in New Castle, the Assembly of the Three Lower Counties on Delaware voted to separate from the Crown and Parliament of Britain and lifted the restraint that had previously bound its representatives in Congress to seek reconciliation with Britain. Citizens of the Lower Counties were simultaneously freeing themselves from the Penn family's proprietary rights, which depended on England's sovereignty. Delawareans now celebrate June 15 as Separation Day.

A little over two weeks later Speaker Caesar Rodney made his famous ride from Dover to Philadelphia "through thunder and rain" to break the tie within the Lower Counties' three-man delegation in Congress on the question of independence.

Thomas McKean favored the Declaration, but George Read was reluctant to vote for independence before the United States could form a proper government. Once Rodney had put Delaware in the yea column, Read agreed to join his colleagues in signing the Declaration of Independence.

The colony known as the Lower Counties on Delaware was now challenged to write a constitution that would legitimatize the authority of its government and establish a legal basis for the liberties of its freeholders. Acting on their belief that the assembly was not the appropriate body to remake the government, the members voted on July 27, 1776, to call elections for a special convention of ten representatives from each county to frame the state's new constitution. In adopting this act, the Assembly of the Three Lower Counties on Delaware voted itself out of existence.

The election of delegates to Delaware's constitutional convention took place on August 19, 1776, in an atmosphere permeated with apprehensions and partisan wrangling. By then the long-awaited British invasion had occurred. Sir William Howe had disembarked his large, well-prepared force on Staten Island, while General Washington's untried troops prepared to defend New York from Long Island.

Meanwhile, British warships patrolled the Delaware Bay and kept up contacts with the Tories, the disaffected, and the fearful in Sussex County. In Kent County zealous patriots joined the Dover Light Infantry, which was commanded by Caesar Rodney's zealous but imprudent younger brother, Thomas. The Light Infantry whipped up partisan feelings so much that the backlash cost Caesar Rodney election to the state's constitutional convention in favor of more moderate men such as Dr. Charles Ridgely and the recent Methodist convert Richard Bassett. Rodney was one of only four members of the 1776 assembly who failed to be elected to the convention.

The constitutional convention chose George Read as its president and adopted procedural rules similar to those familiar to assemblymen. All thirty members took an oath to support the independence of the state and to create a government that would insure its citizens' civil and religious rights. In partial contradiction of that pledge they also swore their faith in the Trinity and their belief in the divine inspiration of both the Old and New Testaments. The statement of rights in the new constitution provided to Delawareans a "Natural and inalienable Right to worship God according to the dictates of their own Consciences" but only Christians were guaranteed "equal Rights and Privileges in this State."[12]

The convention met from August 27 through September 21, 1776. During that time word of Howe's victory over Washington's army at the Battle of Long Island must have had a sobering effect on the members. The bad news from the battlefield did not deflect them from their responsibility. Most of the work was done in two committees, both chaired by George Read, who was the constitution's principal author.

In the HOUSE OF REPRESENTATIVES for the Counties of *New-castle*, *Kent* and *Sussex*, upon *Delaware*, at *New-castle*.

SATURDAY, *July* 27, 1776, P. M.

THE House taking into Consideration the Resolution of Congress of the 15th of *May* last for suppressing all Authority derived from the Crown of *Great-Britain* and for establishing a Government upon the Authority of the People, and the Resolution of this House of the 15th of *June* last, in consequence of the said Resolution of Congress, directing all Persons holding Offices Civil or Military to execute the same in the Name of this Government until a new One should be formed; and also the Declaration of the UNITED STATES OF AMERICA, absolving from all Allegiance to the *Brittish* Crown, and dissolving all Political Connection between them and *Great-Britain*, lately published and adopted by this Government as one of those States, are of Opinion, that some speedy Measures should be taken to form a regular Mode of Civil Polity, and this House not thinking themselves authorized by their Constituents to execute this important Work,

Do Resolve,
That it be recommended to the good People of the several Counties in this Government to chuse a suitable Number of Deputies to meet in Convention, there to ordain and declare the future Form of Government for this State.

Resolved also,
That it is the Opinion of this House, That the said Convention consist of the Number of Thirty Persons, that is to say, Ten for the County of *New-castle*, Ten for the County of *Kent*, and Ten for the County of *Sussex*; and that the Freemen of said Counties respectively, do meet on *Monday* the 19th Day of *August* next at the usual Places of Election for the County, and then and there proceed to elect the Number of Deputies aforesaid, according to the Directions of the several Laws of this Government for regulating Elections of the Members of Assembly, except as to the Choice of Inspectors, which shall be made on the Morning of the Day of Election by the Electors, Inhabitants of the respective Hundreds, in each County.

Resolved,
That every Elector shall (if required by one or more of the Judges of the Election) take the following Oath or Affirmation, *to wit*;

I *A. B.* will, to the utmost of my Power, support and maintain the Independence of this Government, as declared by the Honorable CONTINENTAL CONGRESS.

Resolved also,
That it is the Opinion of this House, That the Deputies when chosen as aforesaid, shall meet in Convention in the Town of *New-castle* on *Tuesday* the 27th Day of the same Month of *August*, and immediately proceed to form a Government, on the Authority of the People of this State, in such Sort as may be best adapted to their Preservation and Happiness.

Extract from the Minutes,

Published by Order,
JAMES BOOTH, Clk. of Assembly.

By this resolution, dated July 27, 1776, Delaware's colonial assembly voted itself out of existence. The resolution called for the election of delegates to meet in convention in New Castle on August 27, 1776, to draft the state's first constitution. (Courtesy of the Delaware Public Archives)

Scholars of the American Revolution have looked at the original state constitutions to discover the political philosophy that animated the revolutionary generation. The revolutionaries saw themselves as reformers intent upon limiting the exercise of power. Their documents stressed citizens' rights as opposed to government power, and deliberately sought to erect barriers to separate the legislative, executive, and judicial functions from one another. Among those three branches, they tipped the scale of power toward legislatures and away from the executive. Revolutionary constitution writers were particularly fearful of granting too much power to an individual. In Delaware as elsewhere, chief executives were accorded very little independent authority.[13]

Article One of the constitution renamed the Lower Counties on Delaware "The Delaware State," just in case anyone should doubt Delaware's equality with her larger sister states. The second article created a two-house legislature called the General Assembly, which would consist of a House of Assembly made up of seven representatives from each county to be elected annually and a Council of three members from each county to be elected for three-year terms. The purpose of that measure was to divide power between one house that featured breadth of representation and another smaller house that would be filled by men of more mature and measured judgment. The property qualifications for voters remained unchanged from colonial times.

The executive, to be called president, was to be elected by the two houses of the legislature for a single three-year term. The president had no veto power and was further circumscribed by a privy council of four members, who were also to be chosen by the legislature. To prevent dual office holding in two branches of the government and to preserve the separation of powers, any member of either house who was selected to serve as a privy councilor was required to vacate his seat in the General Assembly.

The legislature rather than the executive was empowered to appoint judges. Judges were to be selected through a vote of the two houses of the assembly and the president. Those infrequent judicial elections were the only times when the assembly and president were mandated to meet together.

Delaware's first constitution made it impossible for the president to become a tyrant and unlikely that either house of the assembly could dominate the other. Liberty would be protected. But, as a commentator in a Philadelphia newspaper pointed out, the structure was unwieldy. "All these opposite and incoherent powers . . . must produce endless jars and confusions . . ." out of which, he predicted, there might arise a tyrant.[14] The constitution writers of 1776, both in Delaware and in the other states, were engaging in an experiment in self-government. It would have been asking too much to expect them to get it completely right on the first try.

Among the most significant portions of the constitution of 1776 was its Article 26, which read: "No person hereafter imported into this state from Africa ought to be held in slavery . . . and no Negro, Indian, or Mulatto Slave ought to be brought into this state for sale from any part of the world." That provision appeared in no other state constitution written in response to independence. The Kent County moderates, Dr. Ridgely and Richard Bassett, may have seemed lukewarm revolutionaries to Thomas Rodney, but it was they who championed this forward-looking measure. In the assembly the prohibition on the slave trade had twice failed by a few votes, but at the convention Ridgely and Bassett timed the introduction of the motion to take advantage of the absence of enough of its opponents to ram it through. Since the assembly had made no provision for the voters to ratify this first "peoples" constitution, the prohibition on the slave trade in Delaware, like everything else in the document, was beyond challenge.

On September 11, 1776, the delegates adopted a bill of rights, which they called the *Declaration of Rights and Fundamental Rules of the Delaware State*. Among those rights was "the Right in the people to participate in the Legislature," which the writers called, "the Foundation of Liberty and of all free Government."[15]

On October 28, 1776, the General Assembly of the Delaware State held its inaugural meeting in New Castle. All subsequent General Assemblys are dated from that first session. John McKinly, a Scotch-Irish physician from Wilmington, was elected speaker of the House of Assembly and George Read became speaker of the Council. Both houses adopted rules that would have been familiar to members of the old assembly. In the House a quorum of two thirds was required to do business; there was a prohibition on interrupting a member who was speaking; and no one could speak more than three times on a bill unless the House went into a committee of the whole. Members were to stand and address the speaker when they spoke and were subject to a fine of five shillings if they left the room for more than a short time without securing the speaker's permission. Assemblymen were enjoined not to read newspapers or books while meetings were in progress. The Council adopted similar, but simpler rules in keeping with its smaller size.

Having first established their rules of procedure, both houses then turned to the pressing issue of choosing a new state seal. The joint committee assigned to that task proposed a design symbolic of their philosophy of government. It was to show the figure of Liberty fleeing from Britannia to America. This patriotic theme proved to be beyond the engraver's artistic ability, so the committee was sent back to reconsider.

The committee's second design motif aimed to illustrate the state's economy and proved more workable. As described in the House Minutes, it was to show "a sheaf of wheat, an ear of Indian corn, and an ox, in full stature, in a shield, with a river dividing the wheat sheaf from the ox, which is to be cut in the nether part of the shield below the river; that the supporters be an American soldier under arms on the right, and a husbandman with a hoe in his hand on the left, and that a ship be the crest; and that there shall be an inscription round the same near the edge or extremity thereof in the words following, in capital letters, THE GREAT SEAL OF THE DELAWARE STATE."[16]

To our modern minds it may seem odd that lawmakers faced as they were with the possibility of invasion and civil unrest would give such high priority to creating a decorative seal. We have become used to the idea that a bill becomes law when it passes both houses and is signed by the chief executive. Delaware's constitution of 1776 did not provide for a chief executive of such power. Only the affixing of the state seal could turn a bill into a law.

The House of Assembly then took up issues arising from the war. They dispatched a committee to ascertain the condition of the two Delaware battalions that were attached to Washington's army and adopted a bill to root out and punish treason. They elected delegates to Congress and appointed people to collect blankets and woolen clothing for the soldiers. The two houses communicated frequently. The practice was that a member of the House would be sent to knock on the Council's door with a written message or request concerning pending legislation.

Allegations of treasonous dealings with the enemy consumed much of the legislators' time. It was reported that one of the members of Council, Daniel Dingee of Sussex County, had been seen aboard a British ship off Cape Henlopen. Dingee denied the report and refused to sit in Council until he was cleared of suspicion. After a thorough examination of witnesses he was proclaimed innocent and resumed his seat. Other cases were not so happily resolved. In January 1777 two prominent Sussex County residents, Boaz Manlove and former assemblyman Thomas Robinson, were accused of treason. Both escaped to British ships rather than face those accusations in the House. The legislators appointed a committee to revise the state's laws in accordance with independence from Britain. Most of the old laws were allowed to stand. The state's treason law, for example, continued to be modeled on a statute from the reign of Edward III. But some of the old laws had become anachronisms, most notably a law from the reign of James I entitled "An Act against Conjuration, Witchcraft, and dealing with evil and wicked spirits," which was repealed.[17]

It was not until the new assembly's second session in February 1777 that the legislators got around to electing the president of the state. From several nominees they selected Speaker of the House Dr. John McKinly. Thomas McKean replaced McKinly as speaker. Each house then chose two privy councilors to guide and advise the president. In May 1777 the House and Council voted to move the state capital to Dover, a victory for Dr. Charles Ridgely, who had been championing that cause for several years.

The General Assembly's final meeting in New Castle took place in the first week of June 1777. There were pressing and intractable problems to be addressed. Inflation was rampant and getting worse. With each new call from Congress for money to recruit and equip troops the state printed more bills than it could back with collateral. Disaffection was rife in Sussex County where Tories were becoming ever more brazen. The recruitment of fresh troops was going badly, and the state was unable to supply the basic needs of those already in the service.

The General Assembly had to confront serious issues in an environment where members were still struggling to master their roles. For example, President

McKinly complained that the assembly's practice of issuing military commissions in the name of the Delaware State instead of in the name of the president jeopardized his authority as commander in chief.[18]

In contrast to the unsettled relations between the executive and legislature, the two legislative houses formed a workable partnership. The House was the more active of the two, the Council the more reflective. In response to a House bill to provide an inviting bounty to those who joined the army, the Council warned against creating a situation in which the ability of the wealthy to buy their way out of service would make the "bulk of the people" resentful. "The success of the present struggle chiefly depends on unanimity and confidence being supported among all ranks of people," the Council members wrote.[19]

It was during the months that the new legislature was getting organized that Lord Howe's army drove the Americans out of New York and chased Washington's beleaguered troops across New Jersey into Pennsylvania. On Christmas 1776 Washington executed a daring attack on the Hessians at Trenton and followed up his victory with another at Princeton. Colonel John Haslet, the commander of the Delaware battalion and formerly a member of the assembly from Kent County, was killed in the latter action. In the wake of those surprise attacks, Howe pulled his troops back toward his base in New York and awaited the coming of spring for the opportunity to capture the rebel capital of Philadelphia.

In 1777 the British campaign to defeat the rebellion in the middle colonies reached its apogee. As an army commanded by General John Burgoyne attacked New York State from Canada, General Howe left a small force in New York and sailed to the Chesapeake Bay. The British army landed at Elkton, and in early September the formidable force began its march to Philadelphia. The British troops marched through Glasgow and Newark, Delaware. A small American force attacked the Redcoats at Cooch's Bridge in the only Revolutionary War battle to be fought in Delaware.* The British forces pressed onward toward a rendezvous with Washington's rebel army at the Battle of the Brandywine at Chadds Ford, Pennsylvania, in mid-September. There, Howe's flanking action surprised the Americans, and the invaders were able to continue their march northward to Philadelphia.

The day after the Battle of the Brandywine British soldiers marched unopposed and unexpectedly into Wilmington. No place in New Castle County was safe from enemy troops. All of the state's money and many of its most important documents together with its president, Dr. McKinly, had been placed on a ship in the Delaware River in the hope that they would be safe there. The hope proved false, and the state's chief executive together with its money fell into enemy hands.

---

* Circumstantial evidence suggests that the American Stars and Stripes first flew in battle at Cooch's Bridge.

In October, Howe's victorious army occupied Philadelphia. George Read, who had been in Philadelphia representing Delaware in Congress when the British arrived, escaped across the river to New Jersey to collect his family who had been staying there. The Reads proceeded to Salem, where they embarked for New Castle. A British patrol stopped their boat, but Read so convincingly portrayed himself as a private gentleman that the king's sailors not only let them go, but even helped the family to bring their baggage to shore.[20]

During the interval that separated President McKinly's capture from Council Speaker Read's return, Thomas McKean, as Speaker of the House, briefly assumed executive power in the state. With the enemy occupying Wilmington and threatening New Castle from the river, he determined that the usual fall election in New Castle County should take place at the academy in Newark. McKean wrote to Caesar Rodney, who was then serving in the army, that Delaware was in dire straits "without a head, without a shilling, public records and papers in possession of the enemy, together with their capital and principal trading town; the militia dispirited and dispersed . . . ."[21]

For a time frustration and confusion reigned. Speaker Read attempted to call the legislature into emergency session in late October, but his effort failed for want of a quorum in the House because the Tories had disrupted the election in Sussex. With its slower turnover rate, the Council was able to put together a quorum. At that session, the Council's first in Dover, the upper house took steps to raise 600 militiamen to protect the state.[22]

Both houses of the General Assembly met for the first time in their new capital of Dover on December 1, 1777. House of Assembly Speaker McKean opened the meeting of the House with a recital of recent events and concluded on an optimistic note. "The gloomy cloud which hung over this State is dispersing fast," he said, "and a little fortitude and vigour in securing and punishing a few of the principal traitors" together with a more successful militia law would set things right. There were, after all, signs of success. Burgoyne had been defeated at Saratoga, New York, and Washington's troops had given "severe blows . . . to the barbarous and wicked invaders of our country."[23]

Unfortunately, the assembly failed to fulfill McKean's hopes. Only two months later he was complaining to George Read that the legislators had not addressed the problem of inflation, which could only be remedied by imposing a tax; neither had they taken the vigorous steps needed to suppress treason and to fill the state's quota in the army.[24]

McKean was not alone in registering disappointment with Delaware's government. On February 22, 1778, George Washington's forty-sixth birthday, the commander-in-chief wrote to George Read, the state's acting president, from Valley Forge. In his exasperation Washington did not mince words. "It gives me great concern that the Legislature of your State has not taken timely and effectual means for completing the battalion belonging to it." Delaware's effort to recruit volunteers wasn't working, the general said, and should be scrapped in favor of a draft as other states were doing, both as a duty to the state and to the "continent at large." Commenting on the political infighting that was hampering action in Dover, Washington admonished, "it is much to be lamented that, at a season when our affairs demand the most harmony and greatest vigor . . . there should be any languor occasioned by divisions" and counseled Read that "your efforts cannot be better employed than in conciliating the discordant parties, and restoring union."[25]

Even such stern words from George Washington failed to move the assembly to action. The two houses of the legislature wasted much of the session in the spring of 1778 squabbling with one another over the wording of a militia bill and a treason bill. In spite of the virtual collapse of the state militia, they refused to enact a draft. George Read was exasperated. He told Thomas McKean that "Not the warmest whig . . . has taken one step" to aid in recruiting troops. "A great mistake among us," Read complained, "has been to set at naught such acts of legislation as do not exactly tally with our own sentiment; this has been a fatal tendency at all times," he noted, "but particularly at the present, making each individual a judge of what he ought and what he ought not to submit to."[26]

The assembly's one accomplishment in 1778 was to elect Caesar Rodney president of the state in place of the captured Dr. McKinly. At first Rodney was inclined toward a charitable opinion of the assembly, but soon he, too, was disgusted by their lack of accomplishment in the face of great challenges.[27]

In the summer of 1778 General Howe's army abandoned Philadelphia and returned to its primary base in New York. Although the enemy's principal army no longer posed so direct a threat to Delawareans, coastal Delaware remained subject to constant plundering from marauders, called "refugees," who were Tories displaced from throughout the country. Their presence in the bay prevented farmers in lower Delaware from bringing their crops to market. With so little commerce, the legislators were loath to impose the taxes needed to provide for defense and to stem the ruinous inflation that resulted from the state's unsupported bills of credit. Moreover, despite America's new alliance with France and other signs that the revolution would succeed, Tory insurrections persisted in Kent and Sussex.

Increasingly ill from cancer, Caesar Rodney soldiered on in his efforts to push the complacent members of the General Assembly to action. In October 1778 he laid the Articles of Confederation of the United States before them, but the assembly postponed taking action on the nation's first constitution for nearly a year, making Delaware the next-to-the-last state to ratify. The assembly also demonstrated little responsibility for maintaining the state's representation in the Continental Congress. Delaware went without representation for months at a time, in part because the assembly balked at paying their delegates' expenses. It was rare for a Delawarean to be in Congress. The assembly's most successful appointments went to men like Thomas McKean and John Dickinson, both of whom were residents of Philadelphia who agreed to serve under Delaware's banner while still putting their major energies into Pennsylvania's affairs.

A frustrated President Rodney unburdened himself to Dickinson in June 1779. He told Dickinson that he had rejoiced that the General Assembly had come near to completing its work that year when two members went home early, "and thereby dissolved the House." Controlling his anger, the chief executive concluded, "I don't like to make use of harsh expressions relative to these gentlemen's conduct—but wish most heartily they had a deeper sense of their Duty."[28]

The effects of war and the constitution of 1776 had wrought subtle changes in the composition of the General Assembly. The best-qualified men who had once been the leaders of the assembly were now holding positions in the executive branch, the Congress, or the army. After 1776 there was swifter turnover among legislators than had been common in colonial times. Many assemblymen of the late war period were newcomers who served for only a short time, which made it difficult to develop capable leaders.

State politics also played a part in engendering lethargy. Neither the Whigs, who supported the war for independence irrespective of the cost, nor moderates, who would have accepted peace based on a return of the pre-1763 empire, had sufficient power to claim control. As the war dragged on, Delaware's assemblymen became increasingly unable to summon the will to overcome their political divisions to address the many problems of their state and country.

The generation of leaders who had fearlessly opposed British power—those who had helped to create a nation from thirteen disconnected colonies, and those who had brought The Delaware State into being—was passing from the scene. Caesar Rodney died in 1784; Thomas McKean became Chief Justice of Pennsylvania; John Dickinson, who was Rodney's successor to the presidency, abandoned Delaware after only one year to accept that same office in Pennsylvania. Only George Read remained as a continuing presence. Although he was still a powerful figure, his efforts to moderate differences among factions had made him an object of hatred, especially among extreme Whigs.[29]

Delaware was far from alone in having discontents. Her sister states were also bruised by the lengthy war, but Delaware was unusually unfortunate because of its ill-protected shoreline and its die-hard Tories, who disrupted political life especially in Sussex County. How to deal with the Tories became for a time the most divisive political issue in the state. Moderates, such as Read, insisted on extending civil rights to those who were accused of treason. Their position earned the scorn of the most passionate among those Patriots fighting for "Liberty."

The Battle of Yorktown in 1781 brought an end to offensive warfare. Two years later the British government signed a treaty of peace that acknowledged the independence of Britain's former colonies. The Delaware State and the young nation had survived to face a new day that would require every bit as much vision and vigor as had the period of hostilities they were leaving behind.

3
THE FIRST STATE, 1782-1815

The postwar years presented serious challenges as well as unprecedented opportunities for Delaware and for her sister states. State economies that had once rested on the British Empire had to be remade. Wartime debts had to be paid. New and unprecedented government structures had to be created that would be strong and yet protect citizens' liberties. There were many responses to the concept of freedom. Some involved economic development, while others aimed at extending rights to the poor and emancipating the slaves. Delaware's General Assembly confronted all of those difficult issues at the end of the Revolutionary War and had resolved most of them by the end of the War of 1812.

The Articles of Confederation created a very limited national government. Congress, a legislative body in which each state had one vote, was the sole governing authority of the United States. The Articles provided for no national executive, nor for a national judiciary. Consequently, most power and responsibility rested with the states. Like the Articles, the frame of government that Delaware's constitutional convention had created in 1776 was also heavily weighted toward the legislative branch. Because it alone had authority, the assembly met frequently throughout the war and into the immediate postwar period. Typically, the assembly convened for three lengthy sittings a year held in January, May, and October.

Because the national government had so little power, the issues that confronted state governments covered an unusually wide spectrum. In Delaware the assembly dealt with matters that spanned the distance from patents to pigs. There was no national prerogative on patents in the 1780s, so inventors were forced to seek patents from each state. Delaware's legislature granted patents to two of the greatest American inventors of the age: Pennsylvanian John Fitch for his newly invented steamboat and Delawarean Oliver Evans for his pathbreaking continuous-action milling machinery.

The General Assembly was the only governmental authority in the state. It was responsible for a myriad of activities, including the development of Delaware's transportation and economy. Toward those ends, the assembly adopted laws to enable bridges to be built and milldams to be erected along the state's waterways. In response to petitions from residents, the legislators also passed laws to deal with such mundane community needs as preventing pigs from wandering the streets of newly created towns.

In the aftermath of a long and disruptive war, the legislators worried about signs of social decay that seemed to be arising in their new, more dynamic and freer world. In the 1780s a religious revival arose among America's protestant denominations that stressed the importance of morally based self-restraint as the key to salvation. The movement found its most powerful expression in Delaware in the rapid rise of the Methodists, but its effects were also felt among the Presbyterians, Quakers, and former members of the Church of England, now called Episcopalians. Influenced by the revival, legislators took responsibility to ensure that liberty would not degenerate into license. They especially targeted gambling and alcohol.

In 1785 the assembly abolished fairs. The legislators reasoned that stores had replaced the fairs as places where craftsmen and notions salesmen could sell their wares to country folk. Having lost their original purpose, fairs had degenerated into venues for liquor dealers to debauch servants and young people. Fairgoers were being tempted to "lay out large sums of money for many articles that are of no real use or benefit."[1] A few years later the assembly permitted fairs to be reintroduced, but only in rural areas to facilitate the sale of animals and other country produce.

Eliminating fairs was not enough to reinvigorate public morality. In 1786 the assembly took further steps by passing a law entitled an "Act to Suppress Idleness." The law attacked "the practice . . . for people to assemble themselves together under the various pretences of horse racing, foot racing, cock fighting, shooting matches, etc., which are frequently made with intent to vend and sell strong liquors; thereby promoting idleness, vice, and immorality, to the great prejudice of religion, virtue and industry."[2]

Issues involving slavery and race relations also came under increased scrutiny. The Revolution had sparked demands for greater social equality and personal liberty, and the religious revival brought the practice of human slavery into disrepute. In Delaware, Quakers and Methodists particularly condemned slavery and petitioned the assembly to end a practice that they believed was immoral.

Although not everyone agreed with their views, public sentiment was moving toward abolition in the 1780s. Delawareans' growing hostility toward slavery is revealed in two pieces of legislation enacted just eight years apart. In 1779 the assembly looked backward toward the colonial past when it adopted a law that treated the theft of Negroes and of horses as equal crimes.[3] By 1787, however, under the pressure of Quaker petitioners, the assembly acted to prevent black people, both slave and free, from being sold out of state. Such sales, said the assembly, were "contrary to the principles of humanity and justice and derogatory to the honour of this state."[4] The punishment for violating the law was a stiff fine of one hundred pounds. In that same session, the legislators took the further step of forbidding the fitting out of slave ships in Delaware.

The collision of emerging principle and established prejudice among the voters and their representatives is evident from another law of that period that freed any slave brought into the state, but denied freedmen and their descendants the right to vote and the right to serve in the government.[5] A majority of legislators conceded the immorality of unrestrained slavery and made clear their hostility toward the growth of the institution, but an equally strong majority was determined to confine people of African descent to a legal status below that of whites.

The social and moral issues of the 1780s paled, however, before the state's overriding financial problems. Paper money had lost its value and had disappeared from circulation. Citizens and the state government were equally unable to meet their obligations. Bankruptcy was common. Questions of how to pay the state's bills and how to restore a stable circulating currency preoccupied the assembly. Petitions poured into the legislature from citizens in all three counties who complained of the unavailability of a reliable medium of exchange to assist their commercial transactions. Those were serious problems, especially in light of the unusual demands on the state's treasury in the postwar decade. Soldiers and soldiers' widows were owed pensions, and people whose goods had been seized by the British and those who had supplied United States armies were demanding compensation. Creditors looked to Congress and the state governments to pay those war debts.

Every year the legislators passed lengthy bills intended to stem the tide of financial disaster. Nothing seemed to work. In 1785 the assembly took a Draconian step toward solvency when it voted to call in all of the state's outstanding bills of credit and to pay those who held the bills at the rate of one pound on the face value of seventy-five pounds. George Read and Richard Bassett were appalled at the measure, which seemed to them to be a cheap trick to rid the state of debt at the expense of its creditors. Council Speaker Read urged state President Nicholas Vandyke to take action to correct the state's financial problems. Read's pleas met with a response that he, as principal author of the 1776 constitution, must have anticipated. President Vandyke replied that he was helpless. He could neither appoint nor remove state officers. "The executive branch in this state has naught to do with money matters," Vandyke reminded Read, "unless expressly empowered by the . . . General Assembly."[6]

The assemblymen, like the people at large, were divided between creditors and debtors. The House of Assembly, being the more popular of the legislative bodies, paid close attention to the complaints of debtors, while the Council was more sympathetic to creditors. The two houses argued and then produced compromises that satisfied no one. The assembly paid off the state's creditors cheaply, but it also pledged to resist emitting additional unsecured paper bills.

The legislature's actions neither provided a stable medium of exchange nor increased the flow of revenue into the state's treasury. As George Read saw it, the assembly's financial moves were futile since "few mind or obey them . . . ."[7] Delaware had an ineffectual method of tax collection that depended on the counties' levy courts. Whole sections of the state failed to pay taxes for years at a time. The powerless chief executive had no bureaucracy to maintain accounts, no one to do a proper audit, and no means to bring tax delinquents to justice.

> A Verbal Message from the House of Assembly to the Council.
>
> Gentlemen,
>
> The House of Assembly propose to the Honorable the Council, that both Houses meet in the Council Chamber forthwith for the Purpose of nominating and ballotting for Deputies to attend the proposed Convention for revising the Federal Constitution; for an Auditor for this State; and for a Delegate to Congress to supply the Place of Gunning Bedford the elder Esq'r who hath declined to accept of that appointment.
>
> Saturday P.M. Feb. 3. 1787.

A communication dated February 3, 1787, from the House of Assembly to the Council (the upper house of the legislature under the state's constitution of 1776), requesting a joint meeting to vote for Delaware's delegates to the national convention that drafted the Constitution of the United States. (Courtesy of the Delaware Public Archives)

In the midst of that financial crisis the assembly was asked to choose delegates to participate in a convention at Annapolis in 1786. The convention's purpose was to consider the commercial relations of the United States as a whole. The assembly selected five delegates to represent Delaware, all men of proven probity and experience. Jacob Broom, a member of the House, was a manufacturing entrepreneur in Wilmington; George Read, the New Castle lawyer, was a fixture on the Council; John Dickinson, formerly president of the state and once a leader in Pennsylvania's government, was again living in Delaware; Richard Bassett, was a wealthy farmer and Council member from Kent County; and Gunning Bedford, Jr., a New Castle lawyer, was related to George Read by marriage.

When delegations from some states failed to show at Annapolis, those who had come, a group that included the five Delawareans, decided to hold a larger meeting in Philadelphia the following year to consider revising the Articles of Confederation.

The meeting that convened in Philadelphia during the summer of 1787 was the Constitutional Convention. Its members included the same five delegates that the Delaware assembly had sent to Annapolis the previous year. In Philadelphia the Delawareans supported the creation of a strong federal government that would help to secure the nation's finances and provide protection from foreign enemies.

The Delawareans took a leading role in demanding that the small states be accorded equality of representation in the national government. The large states refused. After much discussion, the two sides agreed to a compromise. Each state, regardless of its size, would elect two senators to the upper house of the proposed Congress of the United States. The composition of the House of Representatives, however, would be determined on the basis of the population of each state. Delaware's delegates knew that they had won the best apportionment that was politically possible, and they strongly supported the finished document.

The Delaware General Assembly eagerly awaited the Convention's outcome. In August the assembly was called into a brief special session in hopes that the delegates would have completed their work and that ratification could go forward.[8] It was not until October 24, however, that President Thomas Collins laid the completed document before the General Assembly. Petitions poured in from around the state urging the assembly to take prompt action. Keen though the assemblymen were to move forward on ratification, a familiar obstacle blocked the assembly from immediate action—there had been a contested election in Sussex County that had to be sorted out before the assembly could do anything else.

Contested elections had become commonplace in Sussex County during the Revolutionary period when armed Tories had harassed voters. The conclusion of the war did not end this disruptive behavior. In 1787 witnesses alleged that groups of armed men calling themselves "associators" prevented all but 100 people from voting. The sheriff, who bore responsibility for keeping order, claimed that he had been too sick to challenge the armed mob. The assemblymen had heard similar stories from Sussex before. This time they were particularly eager to get on with business, so they reluctantly accepted those who had been so narrowly and illegally elected into their body.[9] Out of the assembly's investigation came its decision to move the Seat of Justice of Sussex County from Lewes, the place where elections were held, to a more central location on an undeveloped tract that was to be named Georgetown.[10]

On November 7, 1787, the House took a short break from its hearings on the Sussex election. On that day the House adopted a resolution to hold an election later that month for delegates to attend a state-wide convention in Dover to consider Delaware's ratification of the federal constitution.[11] One month to the day later, on December 7, 1787, the Delaware convention unanimously ratified the United States Constitution "fully, freely and completely." Despite the botched assembly election in Sussex, Delaware was the first state to ratify, a fact that Delawareans have never forgotten. The date, December 7, 1787, is emblazoned on the state flag; and December 7 is celebrated in the state annually as "Delaware Day."

The state's ratification convention took place in a room supplied by Mrs. Elizabeth Battell, whose inn faced the Dover Green. Since the General Assembly had moved from New Castle to Dover a decade before, this had been the room in which the Council regularly convened. The House of Assembly met in a room furnished by a rival innkeeper, John Freeman.

In 1790 Freeman and the assemblymen had a falling out over Freeman's refusal to surrender some public papers that he had been charged to keep. If the innkeeper thought that his tactic would cow the assemblymen into paying a storage fee, he was disappointed. The speaker ordered the sergeant at arms to bring Freeman before the House of Assembly. After a brief hearing Freeman was pronounced in "high contempt towards this House" and sent to jail. The realization that there was nowhere to appeal his case soon persuaded him to apologize. Freeman was released from jail, but had to pay the costs of his confinement. Needless to say the House paid no storage fee to get their papers back.[12]

By 1787 plans were afoot for the Kent County Levy Court to build a new courthouse that could also serve as a permanent home for the General Assembly. At first the assembly declined to provide money for the project on the grounds that they were unable to meet the state's debts, let alone provide for additional expenditures.[13] In 1791, when the project was well advanced, the assembly belatedly approved a lottery to raise money to complete the new building. But cramped though they continued to be in their old quarters, in 1787 the House, and in 1788 the Council, agreed for the first time in the assembly's history, to open their doors to "orderly persons" who might wish to attend their debates.

The need for public buildings was endemic throughout every level of government in Delaware. It was especially a problem for the courts. In 1788 State President Thomas Collins urged the assembly to enact legislation to prevent judges from holding court in taverns. The president complained that judicial proceedings meant to be dignified were often interrupted by drunken outcries and brawls. No wonder the assembly sought to restrict its own audience to "orderly persons."

The Constitution of the United States required each state to adopt procedures to fill posts in the federal government and to adapt their practices to conform to a revised distribution of powers and responsibilities. The most crucial role assigned to the state legislatures appeared in **Article 1, Section 3**: "The Senate of the United States shall be composed of two Senators from each state, chosen by the Legislature thereof, for six years."

In the fall of 1788 the General Assembly met in joint session to elect Delaware's two United States senators. They chose George Read of New Castle County and Richard Bassett of Kent County. Both had been longtime assemblymen and had represented Delaware at the Constitutional Convention in Philadelphia. Under the United States Constitution the assembly was also charged to determine how presidential electors were to be chosen and to put in motion the popular election of Delaware's lone member of the United States House of Representative.

In January 1790 the assembly ratified what became the first ten amendments to the Constitution, known collectively as the Bill of Rights. Delaware was the only state to return the original document to federal officials with the legislature's actions on each amendment written at the bottom of the document. Other states kept their copies of the Bill of Rights and replied by letter.

Delaware returned the original document because the legislature had no permanent home. The ratification took place the same month that the House of Assembly had its altercation with innkeeper John Freeman over his refusal to return the assembly's public papers. When the Bill of Rights arrived, the House had just moved from Freeman's inn to another residence that offered no place to store documents. The Delaware legislature probably returned the document to Congress because the state as yet had no space for storage. Hence, the National Archives came to own Delaware's copy of the Bill of Rights. In 2002 an agreement was reached between Delaware and the federal government that will permit the document to be shared. After 212 years, Delaware's copy of the Bill of Rights will return to Dover to be put on display for one half of each year.

In 1789, as the new federal government was being organized in New York under the leadership of President George Washington, the Delaware assembly was contending with the financial disaster that still threatened the state. In January of that year an ad hoc Joint Committee on Finance presented a report that members could not ignore. The most likely author of the committee's report was Jacob Broom. Broom was a member of the House and he had been one of Delaware's five delegates to the Constitutional Convention in Philadelphia. Broom was an unusual figure among the assembly's farmers and lawyers. He was a businessman who possessed an acute aptitude for mathematics and had the ability to comprehend the state's muddled accounts. The financial crisis provided his moment to shine in the assembly.[14]

The Joint Committee on Finance's report was an unsparing indictment of the state's financial policies. The committee blamed the assembly for tolerating faulty tax-collection procedures and poor accounting practices. The county land banks that had been making loans to farmers since colonial times were still operating as loan offices. Those bank offices were so poorly managed that many thousands of pounds were overdue, yet no one was minding the store. The Kent loan office had experienced especially massive delinquencies and embezzlements.

The assembly employed an auditor, but he could not overcome the enormous difficulties. "There may be large sums of money due from individuals to the state, and we presume there are," the committee wrote. "The collectors of Taxes also have been suffered to trifle with the public in a manner that is shameful to tolerate. Many of them have been sued and judgments obtained," but no money was ever recovered to the state treasury.[15]

The financial report woke the assembly members to the necessity for greater accountability and indirectly pointed to the need to reform the organization of state government. More than any other factor, the recognition of the financial morass into which the state had settled goaded the legislators to rethink their constitution. The United States Constitution that Delaware's leaders had embraced so fervently only a short while before offered an obvious model on which to build.

In January 1791 the members of the House of Assembly received a carefully prepared statement that began "Whereas, Governments are instituted for securing the unalienable rights of man, and for the protection of individuals in the enjoyment of life, liberty, and property . . . ." The statement went on to say that the people could alter their government when these objectives were not being met. "The great and important ends of government are not effected by our present form of government," in which "general departments are so blended together, and improperly arranged" that "the burdens and expenses of government are with difficulty borne." No one familiar with the operation of government in Delaware could deny it was the truth.[16]

The constitution of 1776 had given the General Assembly power to amend the document, but the leaders of that body demurred from doing so. They argued that under the doctrine of the sovereignty of the people there should be an elected convention to correct the flaws in the present government.

The legislators' definition of who could participate in the election of delegates to the constitutional convention represented a major step toward expanding democracy in Delaware. The election was to be open to "any free white citizen" of at least twenty-one years of age. With this action the General Assembly for the first time extended the electorate beyond owners of land and wealth to include all adult white males. The lawmakers' action recognized that landless white men had a stake in government. But, non-white men and all women remained outside the world of democratic politics and their disenfranchisement was made more obvious by their exclusion from a political system that now included all white males.

A convention of thirty delegates, ten chosen by the voters of each county, met in Dover in November 1791. The most easily recognizable change to emerge from the convention was the renaming of *The Delaware State* to *The State of*

Delaware. The most important changes, however, were in the organization of the state government.

John Dickinson, Delaware's most experienced citizen in the philosophy and practice of government, led the convention. Others, such as the conservative-minded Nicholas Ridgely, provided a counterweight to Dickinson's morally centered approach. The basic questions that confronted the convention were how to make the state government stronger without making it oppressive and how to build into the structure a balance between the competing interests of wealthy and ordinary folk. The answer that the United States Constitution provided was to create checks and balances among the branches of government.[17]

The delegates agreed that the state constitution of 1776 had made the legislature too strong and the executive too weak. They proposed to strengthen the executive in several ways. Firstly, they adopted the more commonly used name *governor* in place of *president*. They made the governor a popularly elected figure instead of a creature of the legislature, and they eliminated the chief executive's advisory privy council. Under the new constitution the governor had the power to appoint some state officers and he took responsibility for the execution of the laws.

In some ways, however, the office of governor remained weak. There was no restitution of the powers enjoyed by the Penns in colonial times. The governor continued to have no power to shape the state's policies. He could not veto legislation passed by the assembly. Lacking the veto he had no means to bargain with the lawmakers. He could not appoint the state treasurer. That key figure in the administration of the state's affairs would be chosen by, and accountable to, the General Assembly.

The issue of how to design a legislature to provide a balance between the interests of property holders and those of less affluent citizens absorbed much of the convention's time. The General Assembly would continue to be a two-house legislature, but the names of the houses were changed to the House of Representatives and the Senate in conformity with the federal Constitution. The change in the name of the upper house from Council to Senate was not only congruent with the nomenclature of the United States Constitution, it also emphasized the role of the upper house as a legislative body rather than as advisory body to the governor.

The new constitution did not alter the size of the two houses. The House of Representatives would continue to consist of twenty-one members: seven to be elected at large from each county. The Senate would consist of nine members, three elected at large from each county. In keeping with the practice that the legislature had employed in selecting the peoples' representatives to the constitutional convention, the delegates agreed that all adult white males would be eligible to elect both the governor and the members of the House of Representatives. They struggled, however, with the issue of how to define the Senate so that it could represent a perspective different from that of the House.

John Dickinson believed that the Senate should be composed of men who could see beyond narrow, parochial interests toward the more general public good. His idealistic hope was, however, trumped by those, like Nicholas Ridgely, who sought a Senate defined by wealth. For them the only question was whether to achieve that end by restricting the electorate for the Senate or by limiting the Senate to persons of means. In the end, the convention decided that it would be both unpopular and unwieldy to differentiate among voters on the basis of wealth. If there was to be a distinction between the two houses, it was easier and less divisive to make property holding a qualification for membership in the Senate.

The convention failed to address the issue of slavery, although not for lack of pressure to do so. Warner Mifflin, a spirited Quaker abolitionist from Kent County, and a group of Quakers from the Wilmington area made eloquent pleas to the convention to include abolition in the document. Their efforts were ignored. Like white Delawareans generally, the delegates were deeply divided on the issue of slavery. They excused themselves from grappling with the great moral challenge of slavery on the grounds that legislating about that issue lay more properly within the sphere of the General Assembly, rather than that of a constitutional convention.[18]

The General Assembly had given convention delegates the power to ratify their own constitution. The delegates circulated copies of the proposed document for public comment midway into their proceedings, but the voters did not ratify the completed document.

The adoption of the new constitution coincided with the completion of Kent County's new courthouse. At last, the General Assembly would have a permanent home with chambers worthy of the dignity of a legislative body, but not before one final indignity was visited upon them. In May 1792, just as the General Assembly was poised to move into its new quarters, a finishing crew appeared and drove the legislators from the building. The indignant assemblymen accepted an offer to meet in a private home at Duck Creek Crossroads, later called Smyrna.

From their temporary quarters in Smyrna they fired off a complaint against the man responsible for bringing in the work crew at such an inconvenient time. That functionary, they wrote, had "insulted the Legislature of the state," which "ought not to be subject to the caprice of any individual." The assembly resolved not to return to Dover until the "Levy Court of Kent County . . . shall by an explicit act, appropriate to their use the chambers in the said courthouse."[19]

Today we think of the historic brick structure facing on the Dover Green as the Old State House. When it was constructed the building was more commonly called the Kent County Courthouse. It was built largely with Kent County funds, supplemented by the state's appropriation of money from a lottery. Originally the state had use of only three rooms: chambers for the two houses of the assembly and a room for the state auditor. The room assigned to the Senate also served as the headquarters for the Kent County Levy Court and as a jury room. The building's primary role as a courthouse was clear from the erection of a pillory and whipping post on its east side.

The legislators did their best to turn their rooms into a truly permanent home. The House of Representatives purchased bookcases for its growing accumulation of the yearly journals of other state legislatures and the national Congress. The lawmakers also collected books of law and copies of Thomas Jefferson's *Manual of Parliamentary Practice*. In 1800 the assembly commissioned a portrait of George Washington from Denis A. Volozan, a French-born artist then living in Philadelphia. The large, full-body finished portrait of Washington in military uniform was hung in a gilt frame in the Senate Chamber. In 1812 the Senate added a carpet to further dignify their meeting room.

The Delaware State House. This building served as the home of the General Assembly for 140 years, from 1793 until 1933. Built to be the Kent County Courthouse as well as the home of state government, the building underwent many changes and additions before the restoration of 1976 that aimed to return the building to its original appearance both inside and out. The State House is now part of the Delaware State Museums. (Courtesy of the Delaware Public Museums)

As befit its role as the more popular house of assembly, the House of Representatives was less elegantly furnished. Its members were not, however, without amenities. Records show that in 1804 the House members paid their doorkeeper $100 to perform such duties as ringing the bell, providing wood, and making fires. The doorkeeper was also entrusted to purchase a shovel and tongs, inkstands, candlesticks, snuffers, a pitcher, and tumblers for the House Chamber. Both houses had bolts and locks installed on the legislators' desks to secure their property when the assembly was not in session.

The Constitution of 1792 changed the General Assembly's meeting schedule from its marathon three-times-a-year sessions to a less demanding and more predictable one. Under the new constitution the assembly met annually from early January through early February. In presidential and senatorial election years the members convened briefly in the fall to choose Delaware's presidential electors and its United States senators.

On January 11, 1793, the state began its business under its new constitution. The members of the House proceeded across the hallway from their second-floor chamber to be seated with the senators in the Senate Chamber to witness Governor Joshua Clayton, Delaware's first popularly elected chief executive, take the oath of office. The governor, the chief justice, and the speakers of the two houses of assembly sat at the clerk's table facing the assemblymen. Governor Clayton took an oath "on the Holy Evangelists" to support the constitutions of the state and the nation. In the tradition of earlier governors going back to the Penn period, Clayton did not read an address, but instead forwarded his remarks to the General Assembly in writing via his secretary of state.

As neither the size nor the method of selection of the assembly had been altered by the new constitution, business in the two houses followed its usual forms. The speakers of each house appointed committees, usually of three members, to report back to the members on proposals put forward by the governor or by petitioners. Most legislation came from those reports and petitions. When a bill passed in one house it went to the other for concurrence. If the two houses could not agree, the bill often was sent to a joint conference committee for resolution. It was unusual for a major bill to be adopted the first year that it was proposed. The necessary compromises sometimes took years, and it was common for the assembly to add supplementary legislation years after a bill had become law.

In 1797, for the first time in Delaware history, the state judiciary declared a state law unconstitutional. The judges had a vested interest in turning back the law at issue. In 1796 the legislature had created a fund to be used to establish public schools. The constitutional problem was that the school fund was to be raised from marriage and tavern license fees, which by an earlier law had been, in part, committed to paying judges. Challenged by the judges, the legislators passed a supplementary act that provided that the first call on expenditure of the fees would go toward the judges' salaries. Any residue was to be reserved for the school fund.[20]

The first floor of the Delaware State House showing the elegant federal staircase that leads to the assembly rooms upstairs. The restored Kent County Courtroom occupies the main first-floor space in the museum restoration, as it did when the building was first used in the 1790s. (Courtesy of the Delaware State Museums)

In 1806 the House of Representatives voted an impeachment. The action was against Robert Hamilton, a justice of the peace for New Castle County. Hamilton was accused of dispensing unfair, self-serving law. On January 25 of that year a member of the House appeared before the Senate and announced, "Mr. Speaker, I am commanded in the name of the House of Representatives and all the people of the State of Delaware to impeach Robert Hamilton . . . of high crimes and misdemeanors."[21] The legal and political maneuvering that followed took two years to resolve. Finally, in 1808 the Senate quashed the case on constitutional grounds. The senators reasoned that although two-thirds of the members present in the House had voted the articles of impeachment not every member of the House had been present, so two-thirds of the total membership of the House had not voted the impeachment.

While the House majority was digesting its failure to remove Hamilton from office, they were confronted with an equally awkward issue that concerned one of their own members. William Torbert had been elected from Kent County in 1808. Records showed that at the time of his election, Torbert owned a large amount of land in New Castle County and that he had purchased real estate in Kent only after the election, making him an ineligible candidate. Torbert was removed from the House, but in a special election Kent County voters returned him to office.

Politics was a key ingredient in such disputes. The legislative journals from the period did not identify members of the assembly by political party, but we can infer that a majority was Federalist because the legislators chose men loyal to that party to be Delaware's United States senators and presidential electors. Delaware remained loyal to the Federalist Party years after the Democrats became dominant nationally with the election of their candidate, Thomas Jefferson, as president in 1800.

In his book *Federalist Delaware*, John A. Munroe explains why Delawareans clung so long to the old party. He argues that rural Delawareans, particularly those of English heritage who predominated in Sussex County, and to a lesser degree in Kent County, were slow to abandon the party of George Washington. The typical Sussex farmer was a political conservative who associated Jefferson's Democrat Party with the excesses of the French Revolution. Federalists feared that Jefferson's "states' rights" doctrine would undermine the strong union on which a small state like Delaware depended.

By contrast, New Castle County residents were quicker to embrace all that was new and to associate Jeffersonian republicanism with personal rights rather than with the dissolution of the federal government. The Democrats believed that the United States had more to fear from Great Britain than from her enemy, France. "In Delaware," Munroe says, "the Democratic Party represented the liberal, bourgeois, element of the population, whereas the Federalist was the party of the landed gentry."[22]

The political rivalry was reflected in the way the assembly dealt with elections. In 1800 Caesar A. Rodney, a nephew of the Revolutionary patriot, led a Democrat effort in the House of Representatives to shift the choice of presidential electors from the assembly directly to the voters. His resolution was defeated 13 to 7. Rodney and others of his party perceived that because the population of New Castle County was increasing at a much faster rate than that of her sister counties, the Democrats had a reasonable chance to win a statewide popular election. By contrast, Rodney's party had no chance to gain a majority in the assembly, where each county had equal representation.

The Federalists were not unwilling to modify election laws so long as doing so would not undermine their power. In 1811 they agreed to a bipartisan effort to expand the number of polling places throughout the state in order to accommodate elderly voters and others who found traveling to the county courthouse to be an onerous burden. This so-called "district election law" was in fact a major break from the habits of over a century that reflected the increased safety of the election process. It did not, however, alter the practice of countywide at-large elections of members of the assembly.

Party politics was not, however, always the driving force in the assembly. On many issues factors such as religious beliefs, family relations, or attitudes concerning economic possibilities governed members' votes. It is noteworthy, for example, that the most eloquent supporter of humanitarian reforms during those years was Governor Richard Bassett, a Kent County Federalist who was a dedicated Methodist. Delaware's Federalists hung on to an outmoded party label after the party had all but disappeared elsewhere, but their leaders encouraged economic novelties such as turnpikes and banks. Governor Bassett, for one, supported a plan to construct a canal to connect the Delaware River to the Chesapeake Bay, but he despaired that the legislature was composed of a "narrow, selfish, contracted set of beings," both Democrat and Federalist, who were incapable of recognizing the advantages that such a striking improvement in transportation would mean for the state. He believed that the assembly's hostility to the construction of the canal would make them appear as "a laughing stock of the whole world."[23]

Delaware's Federalist voters and legislators were more likely to be farmers than to be aggressive entrepreneurs on the Hamiltonian model. They expressed their party sentiment in their commitment to Washingtonian nationalism. When their hero, George Washington, stepped down from the presidency after his politically contentious second term, the Federalists overcame the objections of the assembly's Democrat minority to send him a message of congratulations.

In the two decades from 1792 until the declaration of war against Great Britain in 1812 the General Assembly took major steps toward Delaware's economic development. Banking entered a new age in the state when the assembly replaced the faulty county land-bank loan offices with chartered banks. The most important new financial institutions were the Bank of Delaware, a private corporation devised and funded by Wilmington manufacturers and chartered in 1796, and the Farmers' Bank of the State of Delaware, chartered in 1807.

The Farmers' Bank was a hybrid of private and public ownership. Its major office was in Dover, but the bank also had branch offices in Sussex and New Castle counties. It was the major repository for the state's money and a source of investment for the state. Delaware purchased 2,000 of the bank's initial 10,000 shares and the legislature directed that the remaining shares be sold in equal amounts in all three counties. The state's investment permitted the General Assembly to select nine (three from each county) of the Farmers' Bank's twenty-seven directors.

In 1792 the Delaware assembly dismissed the Penn family's claim to recover the family's unsold land in the state. The Penn heirs then took their case to federal court. The Penns hired Thomas McKean, the former revolutionary leader, now Chief Justice of Pennsylvania, to represent their interest. Delaware responded with the equally impressive legal team of James A. Bayard and Caesar A. Rodney.

The Penns lost their case. The legislators must have been confident of that victory, for even before the verdict was announced the state had already established a land office to sell the vacant land claimed by the Penns for the benefit of the state treasury. Ironically, Pennsylvania, which in the pre-Revolutionary days had been far more hostile to the proprietors than had the Delawareans, elected to pay the Penns rather than go to court. Delaware had stuck by the Penns until 1776, but felt no need to do so after independence.

The restored Senate Chamber as it would have appeared in the 1790s with plain desks, Windsor chairs, quill pens, and candles. (Courtesy of the Delaware State Museums)

Next to banks, improvements in transportation loomed large in the early days of the Republic. Delaware's legislature was responsive to requests from Wilmington area merchants and manufacturers for improved transportation so long as the petitioners were prepared to pay the bill. The assembly voted to create private corporations to construct bridges over the Brandywine and Christina rivers. It also chartered companies to build toll roads, called turnpikes. Those improved roadways radiated from Wilmington toward the wheat-growing regions in Pennsylvania that supplied the town's flourmills.

The first two highways to be constructed were the Newport and Gap and the Wilmington and Gap turnpikes, both incorporated in 1808. The roads to Gap led into the rich farmlands of Lancaster County, Pennsylvania. They began at rival ports on the Christina River and then joined to become one roadway near Hockessin.

That first turnpike legislation served as a model for the many turnpikes that followed. The incorporators, or more likely their lawyers, drew up the bills for those "artificial roads," as the turnpikes were called. The legislators sometimes introduced modifications into the legislation to mollify dissatisfied petitioners. The final outcomes of that legislative process were lengthy and complicated charters that defined the powers and procedures of the turnpike companies and set the toll rates for hauling common commodities. It was in those laws that Delaware's General Assembly first required traffic to stay to the right hand side of the road.

Authorizing requests for economic developments to be funded by the private sector was easy compared to embracing humanitarian reforms that would draw on the public purse. In 1801 Governor Richard Bassett broke with tradition to deliver his gubernatorial address in person before the General Assembly. In common with the admonitions of all governors of that period he began his speech with an urgent request that the assembly put muscle into the state's ineffectual militia law. He then turned to a hitherto ignored topic: Delaware's care for its insane citizens. At the beginning of the nineteenth century those unfortunates who could not be kept at home were confined in Delaware's county jails.

Governor Bassett told the legislature that mentally ill people might have a chance to recover if they could be transferred to special rooms in the county poorhouses and given appropriate care. He deplored the treatment of mentally ill inhabitants in the Kent County jail. That facility was, he said, a particularly deplorable place even for criminals, where "few persons, if any, however abandoned, wretched and depraved" should be confined. He implored the assembly to expend the small amount of money needed to improve the horrendous conditions there. The assembly committee assigned to report on requests in the governor's address disagreed. They found nothing amiss in the Kent County jail and concluded that the state's insane were "already amply provided for by laws of this government."[24]

Penal reform was another subject of humanitarian interest in some states, notably nearby Pennsylvania. Instead of branding criminals, confining them in stocks, or subjecting them to painful and humiliating public whippings, reformers urged lawmakers to build penitentiaries, or workhouses, where criminals could reflect penitently on their former wrongdoing while learning the habits of work.

Several governors of both parties proposed that Delaware build a penitentiary to replace its "sanguinary inflictions." In 1797 a committee of the House approved the concept of building a small penitentiary, but a majority of the legislators thought otherwise. The assembly again came close to adopting a penitentiary bill in 1810, but then backed off to avoid a possible increase in taxes because "the Practical benefits . . . in so small a state...are yet doubtful and imaginary."[25] The legislators relied, instead, on a law adopted in 1805 that authorized the Delaware Supreme Court to appoint "judicious, sober, and discreet persons in each county" to check periodically on the condition of the jails and the conduct of the jailors.[26]

The assembly's parsimony was hard to justify on financial grounds. Delaware's finances had rebounded since the early 1790s. The upturn was due to several factors: better management of the state's tax collection and accounting; the federal government's assumption of the states' wartime debts; the sale of the Penn lands; and income gained from the state's bank deposits and its investment in the Farmers Bank. In 1807 Governor Nathaniel Mitchell told the legislators that Delaware's financial position was so sound that the state might soon be able to dispense with direct taxes on citizens' property.

The legislature showed the same reluctance to embrace reform in education that it demonstrated with regard to prisoners and the insane. In spite of pleas from successive governors, the assembly's majority refused to draw money from the school fund that had been accumulating since 1796 to actually finance schools. Perhaps legislators feared that the money in the fund could not be spread widely enough to reach many rural neighborhoods.

The legislators were not against education. They were just not willing to pay for it. They did not hesitate to permit towns and villages throughout the state to establish academies and schools at local expense. Those schools provided the opportunity for education to children who lived in towns and whose parents could pay tuition. The academies did nothing for those who were poor, or for those who lived in the countryside far from a town.

The assembly's unwillingness to commit Delaware to embarking on humanitarian reforms was most tragically evident in the state's racial policies. Delaware's location abreast the Mason-Dixon Line made the state both a national bellwether on race and a place where contradictory attitudes toward race and slavery lived side by side. In the swirl of conflicting citizen petitions, gubernatorial recommendations, resolutions, and debates concerning slavery and race relations, Delaware's legislature came closest to embracing abolition in the 1790s and the first decade of the nineteenth century.

In 1796 a gradual emancipation bill passed both houses. The Senate insisted on adding a proviso that the law be submitted to the public for comment before it would go into effect. Apparently stung by negative comment, the bill failed to become law. In 1803 a bill to enact gradual abolition failed by one vote. In 1805 a slender majority of two turned back a bill that had begun with the inspiring democratic preamble: "Whereas we conceive it to be our duty . . . to extend to others a portion of that freedom which hath been extended to us . . . ."[27] The Delaware assembly had come tantalizingly close to moving the state forward toward greater human freedom only to retreat like a tide that could not quite reach the shore.

The legislators recognized that slavery was an evil institution. They passed a number of laws to protect free blacks from being kidnapped and enslaved. The penalty that the legislators set for kidnappers was highly punitive, in fact it was the same as for black males accused of attempting rape on white women: thirty-nine lashes, followed by being nailed by the ears to the pillory, and finally having the soft part of the ears cut off. The assembly also protected free blacks from outright exploitation by permitting them to testify in court in defense of their property. Aside from these narrowly circumscribed safeguards, however, free blacks were essentially outside the protection of the law.

By the end of the first decade of the nineteenth century the mood of the assembly changed to one less sympathetic to free blacks. Several factors may explain that change of heart. Perhaps most important was the successful uprising of the slaves in Haiti, which engendered fear in whites. Another factor was white Delawareans' growing concern that the little state would be flooded with manumitted slaves forced to leave states further south. The legislature took steps to deprive such outcasts of a haven in the First State.

The assembly increased the legal restrictions on all black people, both slave and free. In 1810, for example, the assembly adopted a law that a child born to a slave woman who had been promised her freedom at some future time would be a slave. Another law deprived any black person from testifying against a white man accused of fornication with a black woman. That law made it highly unlikely that a white man could be convicted of raping a black woman.[28]

Following the outbreak of the French Revolution in 1789 war resumed between France and Great Britain. The United States found itself almost constantly on the verge of war with one or another of the combatants. The tension fueled America's nascent political parties as the Federalists leaned toward Britain, while the Democrats sympathized with France. Each of the first three presidents of the United States tried to keep the country out of war, but America's major role in trans-Atlantic shipping drew the young nation ever closer to the European struggle. In 1807 war fever swept the United States when a British warship fired on an American ship of war in the Chesapeake Bay. In an effort to prevent war while preparing for it at the same time, President Thomas Jefferson's administration persuaded Congress to declare an embargo on American trade with the belligerents and to require the states to prepare for war.

The Delaware General Assembly repeatedly failed to heed the pleas of successive governors to revive the state's long-dormant militia. Congress forced Delaware to take action. The assembly called all physically able male citizens between the ages of eighteen and forty-five to duty in the militia. The men were placed under the leadership of officers appointed by the governor as the state's commander in chief. The militiamen were to attend regular musters or be punished by fines. The assembly also empowered the governor to purchase military supplies such as muskets, bayonets and cannon, but he was to do so only if an enemy attack appeared to be imminent.

War did not come in 1807, nor did it come in the years that immediately followed. As the years went by the militiamen became ever more resentful of the calls to muster without weapons. In 1811 sympathetic legislators withdrew the threat of fines for non-attendance for all ranks. Despite the urgings of successive governors to give force to the law, the First State's militia once more became virtually nonexistent. The Federalists, who still dominated politics in southern Delaware, were convinced that war with Britain would be such folly that it was unlikely to happen.

In the spring of 1812 war with Great Britain again threatened. In May, Governor Joseph Haslet, a Democrat and the son of a Revolutionary War hero, called the General Assembly into special session in response to President James Madison's call on the states to hold troops in readiness. "Without your aid," the governor told the predominantly Federalist legislators, "compliance is impossible." The Delaware militia was in shambles, he said, without arms or organization. But he was certain that Delaware would rise to the challenge. "In this state it is not a question of whether the authority of the United States is to be respected. The State of Delaware will never hesitate to co-operate with her sister states in defending the common rights of the nation."[29]

Spurred by Governor Haslet's words, the assembly voted to comply with the national government's request to create a militia force of 1,000 men that could be detached for federal duty in the event of war. The assembly also gave the governor authority to draw up to $25,000 in state funds to equip the militia. One month later, Congress declared war on Great Britain. Delaware's two United States senators, both Federalists, and the state's Federalist Congressman voted against the declaration, not because they excused Britain's many insults, but because they doubted that the national interest would be served by war with so mighty a foe.

The War of 1812 arrived in Delaware in March 1813. A British flotilla, led by the HMS *Poitiers*, a seventy-four gun battleship, took stations at the entrance to the Delaware Bay to blockade American shipping. Several days later the British sent a message to Colonel Samuel Boyer Davis, the military commander of Lewes, demanding that the town supply their ships with provisions or see the town destroyed. Davis refused.

Delaware's defenders sprang into action. In the days that followed, while the British were distracted by opportunities to seize merchant ships, Governor Haslet and companies of soldiers from all over the state descended on Lewes. On April 6 the British renewed their threat to crush the town if provisions were not forthcoming. Again, the proud commander, backed by the equally determined citizens of Lewes and the state's militiamen, turned them down. This time the British were not distracted.

The British ships commenced bombarding Lewes with cannon balls and incendiary Congreve rockets. Boatloads of royal marines attempted to land on the beach south of Cape Henlopen. The fierce bombardment lasted for twenty-two hours. During that time the people of Lewes fired back with their four cannons, and the militia frightened the marines, who retreated back to their ships.

Miraculously, no one was killed and hardly any damage was done. The enemy's cannon fire fell short of the town while the rockets overshot it. Perhaps embarrassed by their failure, the British broke off the engagement. As one town wit put it, "The commodore and all his men, shot a dog and killed a hen."

Delaware was not completely out of danger. Just as in colonial times, occasionally parties of enemy foragers landed along the bay and even sailed to remote places on the river to seize cattle and other provisions. But none of those forays presented significant danger. The enemy flotilla quit their blockade during the winter months but returned in reduced strength in the spring of 1814. By the end of that year the British warships disappeared for good. At this writing, Delaware has not since been directly attacked by a foreign foe.

Throughout the period of Delaware's greatest vulnerability, its General Assembly did not panic; neither did it overspend. The predominant feeling among the assemblymen was that if the Democrats who controlled the federal government wanted a war, than they could pay for it. For several years before the conflict, the legislators had offered to cede riverside land to the national government if the federals would build a fortification to protect the Delaware River. After the bombardment of Lewes both the state and the federal governments got serious about the proposed project. In May 1813 the assembly ceded Pea Patch Island to the United States for the purpose of erecting a fort.

The following year the assembly adopted a resolution requesting the United States government to reimburse Delaware for the cost of defending Lewes. In the view of the legislators a state militia was inadequate to the task of putting up "serious resistance" against a professional army. For proof one had only to look at the success of the British assault on Washington, D.C. in that same year. Fortunately, a peace treaty was signed before the proposition had to be put to further test.

The end of the war did not, however, bring closure to the issue of federal compensation to the state. Under the leadership of its General Assembly, Delaware pressed its case for compensation for the defense of the state. In 1819 the state's persistence began to pay off when the federal government reimbursed Delaware $25,000. Three years later the state was awarded an additional $9,545.

At that point the federal government considered the debt to have been paid in full. The assemblymen disagreed. What about the interest that the state might have earned had its funds remained in bank stock instead of paying for defense, they asked. Based on that reasoning, the General Assembly sent a commissioner to press their case for more money from the United States Treasury. The issue dragged on for years. The bureaucrats in Washington demanded that Delaware deduct the value of the arms that the state had purchased for its militia from their claim. The state's commissioner was embarrassed to report that the state had kept no records of the distribution of weapons to the Delaware militia and that many of the officers had walked off with them at the war's end. The state finally had to admit defeat in 1833 when President Andrew Jackson vetoed a bill that would have paid the $9,480.74 that the state claimed to have lost in dividends some twenty years before.[30] In the end, Delaware's legislators had spent more time and energy fighting the federal government than they had expended on fighting the British.

In 1800 the Assembly contracted with French-born Philadelphia artist Denis A. Volozon to paint a full-length portrait of the recently deceased George Washington. When installed in 1803, it dominated the Senate chamber. (Courtesy of the Delaware State Museums)

4
THE BORDER STATE, 1816-1860

Delaware changed profoundly in the years from the end of the War of 1812 to the beginning of the American Civil War. Public education was introduced, the Chesapeake and Delaware Canal opened, and the state's first railroads were constructed. In the realm of politics, the Federalist Party collapsed; the Whig Party rose and fell; and the Democrat Party became dominant in the First State. During this era Delawareans held two conventions to alter their state's constitution. Nationally, these were years of growing strife over slavery, an issue that resonated deeply in Delaware because of the state's position on the border between slave and free states. The General Assembly stood at the center of Delaware's response to all of those developments and concerns.

During the first half of the nineteenth century the population of the United States grew prodigiously, but that of Delaware did not. In the seven decades from 1790 to 1860 as the nation's population was gaining more than 30 percent every decade, Delaware's population failed to double as it grew from 59,096 to 112,216. A troubling demographic fact hidden in that statistic was that the population of New Castle County was growing much faster than that of either Kent or Sussex. In 1790 each of the three counties had been roughly equal in numbers, but by 1860 nearly 49 percent of Delawareans lived in the most northern county. Furthermore, over 38 percent of New Castle County's residents lived in Wilmington, the state's only city. To put it another way, by 1860 nearly 20 percent of Delawareans lived in an industrial, urban community.

The assembly recognized Wilmington's growing size and importance in 1832 with a new charter that gave Wilmingtonians increased powers to manage their own affairs under a mayor and city council. Yet despite the dramatic changes in the relative population of the three counties, the state constitution continued to mandate equality of representation among them.

The General Assembly was the organ through which the state addressed some challenges of the era positively while ignoring others. To understand why the assemblymen behaved as they did, it is important to bear in mind how state governance worked during that era. Nineteenth-century Delaware's chief executive had little power and its legislators typically served for no more than one or two terms.

John M. Clayton (1796-1856), statue by Bryant Baker in Statuary Hall, United States Capitol. Clayton was Delaware's leading Whig politician. The General Assembly chose him to represent the state in the United States Senate three times. He served as Secretary of State during the brief administration of President Zachary Taylor. His home, Buena Vista, now belongs to the state. (Courtesy of the Historical Society of Delaware)

High turnover in the membership of the assembly prevented the development of the legislators' sense of corporate identity and shared experience that had contributed to the assembly's resistance to British policy in the 1760s and 1770s. During the nineteenth century the names of particular assemblymen did not reappear session after session. Party leadership was most often exercised by men who were not members of the assembly, but looked to the assemblymen to elect them to the higher office of United States senator.

With such a high turnover and little internal leadership, each legislative session seemed a new beginning. In the session of 1857, for example, the newly elected Speaker of the House of Representatives noted in his acceptance speech that he had never served in the legislature before and knew nothing about Parliamentary rules of procedure.[1] The need for such an admission would have been much less likely in the eighteenth century or, for that matter, in the twentieth.

Those factors contributed to the assembly's inability to address many issues successfully. If the majority party were willing, petitioners for banks, railroads, and other private enterprises had little trouble getting the legislators to adopt complex legislation written by company lawyers. In circumstances where the object of a proposal required that the state raise money or that the assemblymen draw up a law on their own, there was much less chance that a thoroughly developed, workable piece of legislation would emerge, or, if it did, that it would pass.

The counties were quite independent of the state. Election to the General Assembly remained at large and countywide, not by election district. The counties' levy courts raised the money that paid for the poor houses, jails, and roads. The state seldom taxed, nor did it administer the counties' roads, poor relief, jails, or care for the insane.

The state's modest revenue came from license fees, dividends from its Farmers' Bank stock, pay-outs to the state from the federal government's sale of western lands, and income earned from its bank deposits. From those sources Delaware paid the state judiciary and supported the cost of maintaining the legislative and executive branches. On the rare occasions when the state supported a large-scale capital project, it did so by permitting the petitioners to hold a lottery, not by issuing state bonds as modern governments do.

When the state did require a tax, it did so based on a tax system inherited from colonial days in which the burden fell almost entirely on farm owners. Tax assessments were done by each county's Levy Court and were based on land, slaves, and luxury goods such as silver and carriages. Mill machinery was not taxed, nor was income from commercial transactions or stock dividends. Why a legislature dominated by farm owners permitted this system to go unchallenged is a good question. The answer may have been that the tax rate was generally so low that well-established farm owners were hardly inconvenienced. Those most affected were young farmers who were paying off mortgages. Such men were always cash-poor and constituted the chief opponents to any proposal, no matter how worthy its goals, that was likely to increase their taxes.

Insistence on localism and resistance to taxation long impeded the introduction of public education in Delaware. The special education fund that the legislature had established in 1796 from marriage and tavern licenses grew so slowly during the succeeding years that no one could envision a time when it alone could suffice to establish free public schools throughout the state.

Governor after governor implored the General Assembly to augment the school fund so that state-supported public schools could be introduced throughout Delaware. In his inaugural address in 1817 Governor John Clark of Smyrna argued that Delaware had a special need to educate its people because the state lacked vacant land for an expanding population. Therefore, he said, "much reliance must be placed on the mental talents of our citizens for the support of our power and importance in the Union."[2] Governors John Collins and Charles Thomas repeated that theme in their addresses to the legislature during the 1820s. "In these portentous times," remarked Governor Thomas in 1824, "it seems rather a hazardous experiment to permit one generation to sleep in ignorance." He advocated a special school tax, which he promised "would be a blessing to the people . . . for it would . . . relieve them of the most intolerable of all burdens, the burden of immorality and ignorance." "In vain," he said, "do we boast of our elective franchise, and our civil rights, if a large portion of our citizens are unable to read the tickets which they annually present at the polls. Such men may think themselves free, but in fact they are slaves . . . . If education is confined to the rich," he warned, "the few will govern."[3] Despite those powerful arguments the legislature failed to act. Its members were held back by their constituents' fears of being taxed and of losing local control over the proposed public schools.

The man who finally broke through the fear of taxation and parochialism that stymied the legislature's adoption of public education was Willard Hall, now known as "the Father of Public Education in Delaware." Willard Hall was a native of Massachusetts and a Harvard College graduate. He had come to Delaware in 1803 to practice law. From his arrival, Hall impressed the members of the Delaware bar as a clear thinker and a very hard worker. He served two Democrat governors as secretary of state and was elected to several terms in both the state Senate and the United States House of Representatives. In 1823 President James Monroe appointed him to the highest judicial position in the state, Judge of the United States District Court for Delaware.

During those same years, the General Assembly frequently called on Judge Willard Hall to draft legislation because the members respected his superior knowledge of the elements that comprised good statutory law. The assembly also commissioned Willard Hall to digest the laws of the state. The task of codification was quite difficult because in the years since the codification of 1742 the legislature had adopted laws that contradicted those that already existed. Willard Hall was the most capable person in the state to undertake this Herculean legal effort, and he succeeded in bringing clarity to the shambles of Delaware's laws.

Willard Hall (1780-1875) from a painting by Laussat Rogers. Hall is known as the Father of Public Education in Delaware for his role in drafting the School Law of 1829. Hall drafted many laws for the General Assembly, even after his appointment as judge of the Federal District Court for Delaware in 1823. (Courtesy of the Delaware Public Archives)

Willard Hall's experience in New England had convinced him of the value of public schools. As a Democrat he was also committed to respecting the views of the common man and to opposing unnecessary government costs and bureaucracy. He was perfectly placed to thread the needle of the school conundrum. It seemed quite natural for him to be entrusted with drawing up a school law in 1829. He knew the arguments of the opposition, and he knew just how far he could push the legislators and the voters to accept responsibility for free public schools.

The bill that Judge Hall presented to the legislature came as close to meeting the poor farmers' concerns as it was possible to go. Hall's plan respected the farmers' demand for local control and it promised to be cheap. At long last the legislators had a school bill they could endorse.

The School Law of 1829 created school districts throughout the state so small that no child would have to walk more than two miles to attend. Each of those tiny districts was to have its own popularly elected school committee. The committee would acquire a school building and employ a teacher. There was to be no state superintendent, no outside person or body to interfere, and no imposed standard of quality to be met. By 1829 the state's school fund had increased to $168,000 and was earning about $9,000 annually. That annual income was to be divided equally among the three counties, and then re-divided among each county's school districts. It was left up to each local school committee to decide whether to tax the residents of the district to make up the difference between what the district received from the school fund and what the committee thought was needed to run their local school. The schools were to be open to all *white* children of both sexes. Students could be expelled for "obstinate behavior."[4]

The Delaware General Assembly acknowledged the unusual significance of the School Law of 1829 by publishing a pamphlet to inform the public of the act's provisions. (Courtesy of the Delaware Public Archives)

The law produced mixed results. Some districts moved expeditiously to build or acquire schools and to hire teachers; others did not. Some squeaked by with very short annual school sessions, and some hired uneducated persons of questionable morals to teach. The district meetings and school committee elections were often scenes of anger and hostility. As a result, the educational benefits for Delaware's children were spread very unevenly.

    Several governors called for the creation of an office of state superintendent to bring standards of order and equality to the system. Those governors were of the

Whig Party, which was usually less hostile to government and its costs than were the Democrats. Their recommendations went unheeded in the assembly. In 1839 a committee of the House of Representatives reported their dissatisfaction with the law. The committee's investigation showed that the schools were "inefficient," "inadequate," and "wretchedly administered."[5]

Willard Hall was not moved by those criticisms. In 1841 he prepared a report for the General Assembly on the progress of the schools. Expressing Democratic Party doctrine, he characterized the public schools as belonging to the people, not to the state. "There is an error, he admonished, "in looking to the *system* to do what the *people* must do."[6] For better or worse the assemblymen heeded his advice.

In 1821 the trustees of the Newark Academy and other friends of education petitioned the assembly to establish a state-supported college. In response, the assembly created a special fund, similar to the school fund, to be collected from license fees charged to stagecoach companies. The income was to endow a college to be located in Newark in conjunction with the long-established academy. Unfortunately, few applied to operate stagecoach companies within Delaware, although many out-of-state transportation lines ran through the state. Friends of the college then turned to the popular remedy of a state-sponsored lottery as a more feasible way to acquire the money needed to construct a college building and hire a faculty.

In 1833 the friends of the college were ready to act. Willard Hall represented his fellow trustees of the Newark Academy in a petition to the legislature to incorporate the college. The petition asked for permission to hold a lottery to pay the cost of constructing an appropriate building. A committee of the Senate reported the bill favorably, and it was adopted by both houses and passed into law. The college was to instruct students in "languages, arts and sciences with power to confer degrees."[7] Like other collegiate institutions of that time, it was open to male students only. The college was the subject of several subsequent laws, most notably "An Act to Prevent the Sale of Spiritous Liquors" to its students, adopted in 1843, a reform as yet to be fully realized.[8]

In 1824 Governor Thomas complained that illiterate voters were casting preprinted ballots. His complaint gives us a window into the way politics operated during that period. By the 1820s political parties had grown from loose associations of like-minded candidates into well-greased organizations. Parties regularly distributed preprinted party voting tickets before elections, and newspaper editorials were strongly influenced by party loyalties. Party rallies and nominating conventions were among the most exciting public events of the time.

Delaware had been one of the last states to abandon the Federalist Party. As the Federalists faltered in the second decade of the nineteenth century, the Democrat Party gained strength. The Democrats were the party of low taxes and unobtrusive government. The party flourished under the leadership of men such as Caesar A. Rodney, Willard Hall, and the descendants of Federalist leader James

A. Bayard, whose two sons, grandson, and great grandson were all to be elected to the United States Senate as Democrats. In Wilmington, as in other American cities, the Democrats captured the votes of workingmen, especially immigrants. In rural areas they defended the rights of farmers to be taxed as little as possible and of slave owners to continue employing that form of labor.

During the presidency of Democrat Andrew Jackson (1829-1837) a new party called the Whigs arose. The Whigs opposed Jackson's vetoes of the national bank and his denial of federal support for interstate transportation. Like the Federalists before them, the Whigs supported a strong federal government held together by a national bank, tariffs to protect America's rising manufactories from cheaper European imports, and federal support for the construction of an internal transportation system. Theirs was the party of manufacturers, most entrepreneurs, and many large-scale farmers. The Whigs also appealed to those, mostly in the Protestant elite, who believed that government had a role to play in improving morals. In Delaware, the party included people sympathetic to temperance reform, the abolition of slavery, and more humane treatment of convicts.

Delaware's Whig leader was John Middleton Clayton, a politician whose formidable skills won him praise and respect, even among his opponents. A native of Dagsboro, Clayton was already clerk of the state Senate at the age of twenty. He went on to be elected to the United States Senate and to serve as secretary of state in President Zachary Taylor's administration.

Party politics played a role in most aspects of legislative life, but never more so than in the election of United States senators. In 1839, when different parties controlled the two houses, the assembly not only failed to agree on the choice of a United States senator, but its members also failed to agree on the method by which the selection should be made. Delaware had but one federal senator for the next two years.

The first half of the nineteenth century was notable for the rise of a wide variety of movements to reform society. Those phenomena were manifest in the issues that came before the Delaware General Assembly, especially with respect to the treatment of prisoners, paupers, and the insane. In several other states legislatures took steps to improve the treatment of those who were wards of the state, but Delaware did not. At the beginning of the century Delaware's practice of relying on county almshouses had not been unusual, but by mid-century the First State had fallen behind many other states in its treatment of its most needy citizens. The state's small size was a factor in explaining such tardiness to embrace reform. Delaware had relatively few insane and handicapped citizens. But the most significant factor to explain Delaware's reluctance to develop specialized care for those unfortunates was the state's antiquated tax system that depended on the counties to collect most revenue and to manage welfare functions.

The state's politicians often seemed paralyzed by their baneful perception that the state was falling behind its more dynamic neighbors in every important category of reform. Because the state's penal code attracted the most attention from reform-minded governors and assembly members, the recital of lost opportunities to bring the code into conformity with nineteenth-century sensibilities makes for particularly melancholy reading. Some members of the General Assembly continued to urge their colleagues to replace the pillory, branding, and the whipping post with a workhouse or prison. In 1818 a legislative committee called the state's penal system "disgraceful." Noting that "the great ends of punishment are the prevention of crime and the reformation of the offender," they declared that the state's "cleaving to that bloody code of laws that stamp their victims for life" was hardly the way to make honest citizens out of criminals. Instead, they continued to promote the construction of a state penitentiary, an idea introduced into the General Assembly as early as 1797. A bill to that effect was introduced in the House in 1818 but failed by one vote.[9] Five years later a Senate committee reported favorably on the construction of a penitentiary, and noted that there was "a great reluctance manifested in our state to inflict sanguinary punishments."[10] But the "great reluctance" to use the whipping post failed to be translated into a law to discard this ancient device.

In 1824 Governor Charles Thomas included a plea for prison reform in his annual message. He noted without pride that "the penal laws of this State are much severer than those of any State in the Union." Governor Thomas also urged the legislature to abolish imprisonment for debt and to revise the poor laws. "An opinion seems to pervade the community," he said, "that our poor houses ... are rather nurseries for vice than asylums for the helpless."[11] His words went unheeded. Again, in 1835 Governor Caleb Bennett admonished the assembly to abolish imprisonment for debt and the pillory, which, he said, "yet remains a stigma to our county towns, and a disgrace to the statutes of the state" in an age otherwise characterized by intelligence, progress and philanthropy.[12] Again, no law was changed.

In 1839 Governor Cornelius P. Comegys, a man otherwise noted for his reluctance to tamper with the legal code, told the assembly, "I cannot believe that the whipping post and pillory are consistent with the genius of the age." The governor failed to persuade a majority of the legislature to alter the law, but he used his power of pardon to delete the whipping portion from the sentences of several men convicted of petty thefts. His leniency aroused the ire, not the admiration, of the assembly, some of whose members introduced a resolution to restrict the governor's power to pardon on the grounds that "the frequent exercise of the pardon power is ... a great public evil, which threatens seriously to interfere with the due and regular administration of justice."[13]

In the 1841 session Governor Comegys adopted a different strategy to reform the legal code's punishments. He appealed to "public opinion," a mantra then much in vogue as the justification of any action in a democracy. "The criminal enactments on your statute books," he told the assembly, "are, in the estimation of the people, a mere bug-bear." He challenged the assembly to remove "the taint of cruelty and barbarism" from the state's criminal code.[14] Despite a report from a

House committee that upheld the governor's position, the legislature once more failed to act. That pattern continued, not only in 1841, but in every session for the next 131 years. Although Delaware last used the whipping post in 1952, this bloody punishment was not eliminated from the state's legal code until 1972.

During the first half of the nineteenth century reformers sought not only to improve the condition of criminals, but also to teach the blind, deaf and dumb, to ease the suffering of the dependent poor, and to heal the mentally ill. A succession of governors urged the assembly to address those problems, but there was never a majority to support action. As a result, by mid-century Delaware lagged behind other states, especially its neighbor Pennsylvania, in caring for its disabled citizens.

In 1849 the legislators took a modest first step on behalf of the insane when they provided a charter to a private corporation that hoped to raise enough money to build an asylum. According to the charter, the state would supply the funds necessary to complete the project once the philanthropists had raised $20,000.[15] Unfortunately, the fund-raising effort was unsuccessful. In a similar effort to address the needs of the mentally ill without spending state money, the legislature agreed to permit the county levy courts to send patients to a Pennsylvania asylum rather than keep them in the almshouses. But the moves were to be conditional on the levy courts paying the cost. Similarly, the assembly agreed to permit the governor to send the state's blind, deaf, and dumb children to specialized institutions in the Quaker state using money from the already overburdened school fund.[16]

Women as well as men introduced petitions on behalf of reforms. Women's names appeared prominently in requests to the legislature for the incorporation of Sunday Schools and for similar philanthropic organizations, most often associated with particular religious denominations. Moral reformers of both sexes also petitioned the assembly to prohibit lotteries and to abolish, or at least moderate, the sale of intoxicating liquors.

The reformers' efforts received modest support from legislators determined to reflect public opinion rather than to lead it. Many people resented the reformers' efforts to interfere with their freedom. In 1847 the assembly passed a law to allow county option on the sale of liquor and to prevent its sale on Sundays. Beyond those changes the legislature would not go.[17] As a House committee charged to examine temperance petitions reported in 1843: "The Legislature of this state ought not to regulate arbitrarily the appetites, passions, and private habits of men . . . . The people of this state never designed that their legislature should assume a rigid supervision of their personal habits, or thrust its hand into their private and social relations."[18]

In 1855 the short-lived American Party, better known as the "Know Nothings" because of their fraternity-like pledge to secrecy, won control of the assembly. The party's appeal was based on its hostility to foreign immigrants and their supposedly immoral ways. The Know Nothings pushed through a bill to further restrict the sale of liquor by making it illegal to give or sell intoxicating beverages to a drunken person and to fine drunks who appeared in public. John Munroe, the most knowledgeable historian of pre-Civil War politics in Delaware, attributed the Know Nothings' rapid demise to their identification with the "unpopular prohibition law."[19]

The assembly also reflected the public's mixed views on the controversial question of lotteries. In 1841, a House committee considered abolishing lotteries on the grounds that they ensnared the unwary into gambling and squandering their money. Nevertheless, the committee concluded that the assembly should take no action to outlaw lotteries until the citizens demanded their demise.[20] Members were not about to destroy a fund-raising mechanism that saved the state the burden of paying for its needed capital improvements.

In the 1830s the General Assembly took its initial steps toward protecting Delaware's fragile coastline environment. In 1830 the legislature adopted a law designed to maintain the oyster beds in the Mispillion River from the "wanton destruction" caused by throwing oyster shells off the wharf, "thereby injuring the channel thereof and destroying the young oysters."[21] This law was the first in the state's history designed to protect a natural resource. An additional act in 1835 prevented dredging for oysters or gathering them in the summer months.[22] In 1839 the assembly went even further to limit the depletion of its aquatic resources by prohibiting nonresident hunting and fishing in or near the Delaware River or Bay.[23] A few years later, in 1847, the assembly voted to limit the season for hunting game to the fall, and in 1851 it required non-Delawareans to obtain a license to catch terrapins, clams, and oysters. That same law also encouraged the planting of oyster beds and prohibited the destruction of terrapin eggs.[24]

The rapid development of transportation technology in the years following the War of 1812 and the new enterprises that those advances spawned commanded much attention in the assembly. By 1816 the age of turnpike building was drawing to a close, soon to be replaced by faster methods of travel. As early as 1801 the Delaware Assembly adopted a bill to permit a canal to be dug through the state to link the Delaware River to the Chesapeake Bay. Although nearly all of the proposed C & D Canal would pass through the First State, the project belonged much more to Pennsylvania and Maryland than to Delaware because its principal purpose was to move heavy commodities between the harbors of Philadelphia and Baltimore. The Chesapeake and Delaware Canal required legislation in all three states. After many delays, the canal was constructed in the 1820s and opened for use in 1829.

In the 1820s and 1830s canals were all the rage. Some residents of southern Delaware dreamed of building a canal across the peninsula to connect their part of the state to the lower Chesapeake towns of Maryland and Virginia. A number of bills were introduced in the legislature to permit the construction of canals to link the Mispillion River or Broad Creek to the Nanticoke River. The assembly granted permission for those ventures and wished them well, but without state financing or adequate support from private businessmen, the projects died.

A construction project that did benefit southern Delaware was the Lewes

Breakwater. The project had its beginnings in 1826 when the Philadelphia Chamber of Commerce urged Congress to build a breakwater inside the entrance to the Delaware Bay to provide a safe harbor for ships caught in rough waters. They argued that a breakwater would also be a defense should the United States again go to war with a maritime foe. Delaware's assembly readily granted the federal government permission to build the breakwater in the bay, just as it had provided state land on Pea Patch Island for the construction of Fort Delaware.

In 1829 the General Assembly chartered Delaware's first railroad. The act authorized the New Castle and Frenchtown Turnpike Company to construct a railroad along their existing right of way. The railroad would provide an overland link to transport passengers along the Baltimore-Philadelphia corridor between the Delaware River and the Chesapeake Bay. The venture potentially posed competition for the newly opened Chesapeake & Delaware Canal. But since the railroad was intended to serve passengers while the canal carried freight, the canal interests did not oppose the railroad bill.

Several years later, in 1832, a competing set of powerful businessmen, including a number of Wilmingtonians, petitioned the legislature to charter yet another trans-peninsular railroad, to be called the Wilmington and Susquehanna Railroad Company. The new road was to be Delaware's part of a nearly all-land rail link to connect Philadelphia to Baltimore. The only break in the all-land route would be a ferry to cross the Susquehanna River. Unlike the earlier trans-peninsular projects, the W & S Railroad stood to provide considerable direct benefits to Delawareans, principally to Wilmington's manufacturers.

As was typical in business charters, the W & S Railroad bill provided that subscription books for the company's stock were to be opened at a certain time and place. Once the shares were taken up, the shareholders were to meet to elect a board of directors who would run the company. To no one's surprise, once Maryland, Pennsylvania, and Delaware had all agreed to incorporate the portions of the new railroad that were to run through their respective states, the three companies merged to form the Philadelphia, Wilmington, and Baltimore Railroad Company. Later in the century the Pennsylvania Railroad acquired the PW & B Railroad. At the Pennsylvania Railroad's demise in the late 1960s, the line originally known as the PW & B became part of Amtrak. From the first, the PW & B Railroad's route was far superior to that of the New Castle & Frenchtown, but just to make sure of their monopoly the PW & B bought a controlling share in the New Castle and Frenchtown Railroad in the 1840s.

The final major link to the emerging railroad network in Delaware was the Delaware Railroad. The legislature chartered the Delaware Road, as it was known, in 1836. With John M. Clayton as one of the commissioners charged to determine the direction of the company, the new railroad, like the Wilmington and Susquehanna before it, had strong support from the Whig Party. As the first railroad to serve southern Delaware, the project was bound to capture the support of legislators from all parts of the state. The rails were to be laid southward from

This broadside announces the schedule for the Delaware, Junction & Breakwater Railroad, which was completed in 1869 to connect the towns of eastern Sussex County with the Delaware Railroad. The illustration shows a typical engine, fuel car carrying wood not coal, freight car, and passenger car of the period. (Courtesy of the Delaware Public Archives)

either the New Castle and Frenchtown or the Wilmington and Susquehanna to the southern border of the state, where it would join a possible line down the peninsula to Cape Charles, Virginia. In contrast to the legislature's earlier charters for transportation companies, in the case of the Delaware Road the state not only chartered the railroad, it also legally bound itself to support the railroad financially.

Written into the Delaware Railroad's charter were provisions to exempt the company from taxes for fifty years and a requirement that the state subscribe $25,000 toward the company's shares.[25]

In 1852 the General Assembly passed a pork-barrel law that distributed money raised through a state-sponsored lottery among several privately owned transportation companies, most especially the Delaware Railroad.[26] Not to be left out of the state's largess, the PW & B applied to Delaware for funds to help the company over the hump of hard times in the late 1830s. Delaware's assembly agreed to loan $80,000 to the rail company from the state's share from federal lands sold in the West.

All did not run smoothly in the execution of those large, capital-intensive projects. For legislators the problems that arose must have provided a painful learning process. First of all, there was the legal battle that pitted the C & D Canal Company's chief engineer, John Randall, Jr., against the company. In 1825 the canal company abruptly dismissed Randall. He sued, and in 1834 a Delaware court awarded him huge damages. When the company balked at paying, Randall's lawyers forced the Delaware legislature to hold a special session in 1836 for the purpose of changing the canal company's charter so that creditors, such as Randall, could have a voice on the company's board.[27]

The outcome of Randall's suit led to yet another battle over the canal's carrying policies. To pay its debt to Randall the canal company decided to permit passengers to use its waterway. This decision riled the New Castle and Frenchtown Railroad and the PW & B Railroad. The railroads charged that the canal had no right to earn income from passengers. The Maryland legislature disagreed and added passenger tolls to the canal company's charter in 1844.

The canal's future rested upon whether Delaware's General Assembly would agree to alter the C & D's charter to permit passenger service. The C & D Canal was a major link in America's rapidly evolving transportation network. The eyes of the nation were on Delaware. It was well known that most members of the Delaware legislature were closely tied to the railroads. The Whigs commanded the legislature and their political sponsor was John M. Clayton, the railroads' legal counsel. Delaware's wealthiest residents owned stock in both the canal and the railroads.

Torn by powerful political and financial rivalries in the state, the General Assembly decided to hold a public hearing on the canal question in the House of Representatives. The hearing was scheduled for January 1845.

In an age that treated political speeches as the highest form of entertainment, the conflict among the rival transportation companies stirred great public interest. On the day set for the hearing, the Representatives' Hall was packed with legislators and citizens, including women, whose attendance was specifically welcomed on that occasion. Even many who had little or no financial interest in the outcome came to the hall for the rare opportunity to hear the state's two most respected lawyers and statesmen, John M. Clayton, the Whig leader and railroad champion, and James A. Bayard, the state's leading Democrat and the attorney for the canal. As Ralph Gray, the historian of the canal has written, "two giant corporations were met in deadly battle . . . ."[28]

The question of the canal's right to charge its passengers agitated Delawareans for weeks. It provided fodder for newspapers and presented the assemblymen with a difficult choice. After hearing the rival lawyers' arguments the legislators debated the issue among themselves. Then, predictably, they passed a law to deny the canal the right to charge passengers. The title of the law gave the game away: "A Law for the Protection of the Investment of This State in The Loan of the PW & B RR. Company."[29]

In the 1850s the General Assembly became even more mired in railroad politics. By that time the PW & B had merged with the New Castle and Frenchtown Railroad. The New Castle railroad owed the state money from a past loan, which its successor railroad was discharging by paying a special state tax. In 1852 legislators from southern Delaware pushed for a bill to use the income from the tax levied on the New Castle and Frenchtown Railroad to buy stock and bonds in the Delaware Railroad. This action would accomplish two goals dear to the railroads. It would provide funds for the needy Delaware Railroad and it would guarantee the junction of the Delaware Road with the existing upstate railroads.

New Castle County's Democrat representatives were indignant. They called the proposed transfer of funds a "bribe" and a "highly obnoxious" violation of their oaths as assemblymen. Despite those objections, the Whigs of southern Delaware prevailed. The assembly adopted several bills to benefit the Delaware Railroad. One extended the transfer of funds from the New Castle and Frenchtown to the Delaware Railroad; another assigned the lion's share of earnings from the state lottery to the Delaware Railroad; and a third made the two upstate railroads the guarantors of the Delaware Railroad's bonds.[30]

A few years later, a legislative committee charged to report on a host of petitions from existing and would-be railroad companies felt compelled to justify the state's blessing of the recent merger of the Delaware Railroad with the PW & B. They argued that the merger had assisted the Delaware Railroad and had tied the PW & B more firmly to the state. What wasn't said was that had the merger not occurred, the Delaware Railroad might have looked southward to connect with a proposed railroad down the peninsula to Virginia rather than toward the north.

The legislative committee tried to make it appear that the legislature could remain aloof from transportation politics. Relative to the recent merger, the committee reported, the only act in which the state had participated was one that had given the respective corporations power to contract with one another.[31] Henceforth, they said, the state should remain unattached to any particular company and should abstain from becoming a party to disputes among transportation carriers. This was an exceedingly disingenuous statement of hope rather than reality. It seemed an easy position to take after the basic transportation decisions had been made. The fact was that the big transportation companies already exercised great influence in the General Assembly and the assembly had taken on long-term involvement in the financial affairs of the state's railroads. It was ostrich-like to expect legislatures of the future to be free of pressure from transportation companies. For the next century the railroads were to be the best financed, most persistent, and ever-present lobbyists in the State House.

As the General Assembly was taking an increased role in the state's economic development it took steps to shed other responsibilities that had previously consumed a great deal of the legislators' time and attention. The assembly shifted some of the private petitions that flooded its docket to the state courts. A new law gave people petitioning for divorces the option to go to court rather than to the assembly. Similarly, the legislature received numerous petitions from slave-owning farmers seeking permission to move individual slaves between the owners' farms in Maryland and Delaware. The *Laws of Delaware* of the antebellum years are filled with names of slaves who were being moved about on the Delmarva Peninsula. It was illegal to bring slaves into Delaware, but the legislature could override the law. The lawmakers re-directed those petitions to the courts. The assembly also reassigned its responsibility over draining marshes to state courts.[32]

In 1829 the General Assembly relinquished the right to choose Delaware's presidential electors for president and vice president of the United States to the state's voters. But the assembly was not about to surrender too much of its power. In 1825 the legislators turned down a proposed general incorporation law at a time when a number of other states had enacted such statutes. In Delaware the legislature continued to exercise the power to decide the specific rights and restrictions to be extended to each organization that sought a state charter.

By 1830 there were numerous voices in Delaware calling for a stronger state judiciary. Newspapers agitated for changes in the state constitution to bring greater order and professionalism to the state's courts. In 1831 a convention was called to rewrite Delaware's constitution. Aside from overhauling the judiciary, the constitution of 1831 made few significant changes in state governance. The spirit of democratic reform was evident in the convention's decision to eliminate property qualifications for nearly all state officials, with the striking exception of state senators, who were exempted from this democratic change. The convention debated a measure to eliminate the requirement that citizens must pay the county tax to be eligible to vote. The delegates decided to retain the "poll tax" even though some recognized its potential for manipulation by unscrupulous politicians.[33]

From the perspective of the General Assembly, the most important changes in the new constitution were the institution of biennial elections and biennial legislative sessions. Elections were to be held in even-numbered years on the second Tuesday in November, in place of October, which had been the custom since colonial times. Under the new constitution the legislature was to convene in early January as before, but in future it would meet only in odd-numbered years, unless the governor called the legislature into special session.

Although the General Assembly would meet only half as often as before, it was found that legislative sessions were not much longer than those of previous years. It would appear that the lawmakers were relying ever-more heavily on petitioners, or their lawyers, to draft bills, and on party discipline to replace each individual's assessments of proposed legislation.

There is an insightful comment concerning the consequences of Delaware's short legislative sessions to be found in Willard Hall's report to the assembly in 1829. Speaking from his experience as a former state senator and as the codifier of Delaware's laws, Judge Hall noted that a major cause of the tangles in the state's laws was hasty lawmaking. Legislators spent so little time in Dover that they failed to search out and expunge inadequate legislation from the past and instead cobbled together new bits and pieces to make already badly confused statutes even worse. After 1831 the shortened legislative calendar made it even less likely that legislative committees could create well-researched and thoughtfully composed bills.[34]

Paradoxically, once the assemblymen began spending only half the time in the State House than had once been the case, the members of the House complained that their chamber was too small.[35] The legislators decided to build a two-story extension onto the rear of the State House to provide more "suitable rooms for the Legislature of this State."[36] They undertook the addition in conjunction with Kent County's Levy Court, which remained the building's principal tenant. The first floor of the new rear space was intended for the use of the state's growing archives, while the second floor became the Hall of the House of Representatives. The Senate moved into the former House Chamber.

Within two decades the assembly had outgrown those arrangements. In 1855 the cramped General Assembly adopted a resolution that called for the construction of an entirely new statehouse to replace the structure that they continued to share with Kent County. In their resolution the legislators described the 1792 building as "wholly insufficient . . . and . . . not such a building as the capitol of a state should be."[37]

In 1852 yet another constitutional convention was called to consider further democratization. At that time Delawareans were nearly equally divided in their political loyalties. The Whigs, who had dominated the state's politics since the 1830s, were about to unravel and the Democrats were fast gaining ground. It was the Democrats who wanted the convention, primarily for the purposes of eliminating the poll tax and reapportioning the legislature to reflect the increased population of New Castle County, most particularly in the rapidly growing city of Wilmington. To achieve those ends, some delegates from New Castle County sought to create legislative districts in place of countywide at-large elections. But in one last flourish of power, the Whigs gained control of the convention and blocked the proposed changes.

There were other agendas at work at the convention, including an effort by United States Senator James A. Bayard to write slavery into the state's constitution so that no future legislature could abolish it. When Bayard's amendment lost he quit the convention in a huff. Battles over reapportionment were equally bitter. It was no surprise that when the proposed constitution was put before the voters it lost in all three counties.[38]

Of all the issues that came before the General Assembly during the first six decades of the nineteenth century none were more important and none evaded compromise more completely than did those that dealt with race and slavery. As Patience Essah concluded in her aptly titled book, *A House Divided, Slavery and Emancipation in Delaware*: "For well over a century the Delaware legislature struggled in vain to break ... the stubborn and persistent stalemate over slavery."[39] Like the nation of which they were a part, white Delawareans were deeply divided over the question of the status that should be accorded to blacks.

Throughout the decades that preceded the Civil War the number of slaves in Delaware continued to decrease while the number of free blacks increased. By the 1850s Delaware had a higher proportion of free blacks in its population than any other state in the Union. It would be incorrect to conclude, however, that the movement toward greater democracy that characterized some aspects of Delaware's political evolution in that era was extended to include the state's free persons of African origin. Indeed, calls for the abolition of slavery in the first half of the nineteenth century actually decreased from the level of the last decade of the eighteenth. Similarly, free blacks remained at best "residents," never citizens, and had few rights. Regardless of how many generations they may have lived within the borders of the United States or in Delaware, their status was, at best, analogous to that of the foreign "guest workers" in some European countries today.

Textbooks in United States history label Delaware a "border state" because it was a slave state that remained loyal to the Union when states further to the south seceded in 1860-1861. The decision of this little slave state to reject the Confederacy was, however, but one of many contradictions that can be found in the General Assembly's actions concerning race relations during the pre-Civil War years. An examination of Delaware's legislative journals and laws make clear that during the years 1816-1859, when the legislature was increasing the rights of white men, it was also constricting the rights of blacks, both slave and free.

A good place to start this examination might be with the entwined issues of runaways and kidnapping. In 1818 a committee of the House of Representatives examined a complaint from the governor of Maryland that Delawareans were harboring runaway slaves from his state. The committee declined to take any action and reported to the House that because their predecessors had adopted a bill in 1740 against harboring runaways, no further action was necessary. They then added a counter thrust, demanding that Maryland must reciprocate by stopping its citizens from stealing Delaware's free blacks "forcibly and by stealth" to place them in "perpetual and cruel bondage."[40]

The following year the legislature helped to rescue a free black man named Benjamin Benson who had been kidnapped from Delaware and sold into slavery in

North Carolina.[41] Benson protested his capture in court and the Delaware legislature paid the cost of sending witnesses to North Carolina to testify on his behalf. This thoughtful action on behalf of freedom was, however, but a glimmer of light. More often the legislators agreed with the position of private petitioners who asked the assembly to set aside its earlier prohibition on bringing slaves into the state to permit owners to move their slaves from other states, primarily Maryland, into Delaware. Perhaps some legislators justified their acquiescence on the grounds that the likely alternative was for the owners to sell those unfortunate people into even worse conditions farther south. How else can one explain the seemingly contradictory actions of a legislative body that called slavery "cruel bondage."

Although the high noon of abolitionist sentiment passed in Delaware after the advances of the 1790s, Delaware's Quakers, together with like-minded people from other religious denominations, continued their campaign of abolitionist petitions to the legislature. After many years of fruitless effort, finally in 1829 the abolitionists appeared to be close to victory. In that year a committee of the House reported favorably on a bill to enact gradual abolition. The committee's views adhered closely to Whig Party doctrine. They acknowledged the "degrading influence of slavery upon the morals of a free people" and called slavery a "stain" on Delaware that was retarding the state's development. "But," they admitted, "it is a question full of difficulties." The committee might wish that slavery had never been introduced into America, but they could not reverse history. In the best equivocating style of people stuck on the horns of a political dilemma, the committee recommended against the House legislating gradual abolition, but instead suggested that slave owners voluntarily free their bondsmen.

That same House committee also addressed the issue of race. Taking a position that was common in the Whig Party, the committeemen argued that although slavery might be wrong, it was equally true that the two races could not function side by side within the same country. Proof of this position appeared to be all around them. Free blacks were "ragged, dejected and forlorn . . . shut out from respectable society . . . deprived by the laws and constitution from participation in the government . . . freedom to them, in this country, is but a mockery and a profanation of that sacred name."[42] The answer to this condition, the House committee suggested, lay not in removing those legally inflicted impediments but rather in sending free blacks to Africa to colonize the newly created nation of Liberia. Colonization appeared to be a compromise solution to a seemingly intractable problem. It was both liberating and racist. There were, however, two implacable impediments to its realization: most free blacks were determined to remain in the United States, the land of their birth, and, even had that not been the case, no one was prepared to pay the cost of their migration.

The response of Delaware's lawmakers to slavery and race issues was conditioned both by local and national conditions. Slavery had been declining in importance in much of the nation during the 1790s, but it was then rejuvenated throughout the southern states by the invention of the cotton gin and the rapid expansion of cotton production. Delaware was too far north to grow cotton. The First State's crops did not require year round attention as cotton did. The *Journals of the General Assembly* in the nineteenth century reveal no economic arguments in favor of maintaining slavery in Delaware. Those in Delaware who supported the "peculiar institution" did so not on the grounds of economic need but on the right of slave owners to maintain their historic right to their property. Advocates of that position were deeply influenced by those Southern politicians in the national political arena who argued that the United States Constitution guaranteed the right of each state to determine whether or not it would permit slavery.

Delaware behaved as the slave state it was in a number of ways. In 1832, for example, following Nat Turner's bloody slave rebellion in Virginia, fearful white Delawareans reacted in a manner similar to their southern brethren. Governor David Hazzard urged the legislature to adopt stronger laws to control blacks. It was free blacks, not slaves, who most occupied the minds of fearful white Delawareans. The General Assembly adopted An Act to Prevent the Use of Firearms by Free Negroes and Free Mulattoes.[43] Notably, this law was not aimed at the state's remaining 3,000 slaves but at its much larger and less controllable group of 16,000 free blacks.

The law put a number of restrictions on free blacks. They could no longer possess guns "or any warlike instrument" without a written certificate from a justice of the peace signed by five or more "respectable and judicious citizens of the neighborhood" who could testify to the applicant's good conduct. The statute also outlawed late-night meetings of free blacks for religious or any other purpose unless three respectable white men were present. Black preachers who did not reside in Delaware were required to obtain a preaching license from a judge or justice of the peace for fear that they might be spreading sedition.[44]

Delaware's white majority did not know how to handle the challenge posed by the free black minority. In his message to the assembly in 1837, Governor Charles Polk lamented the decline in the state's agriculture, which he blamed, in part, on the difficulty of finding sufficient workers. The problem, he said, lay with "the wretched condition of the colored population which infests the state," whom he characterized as "irresponsible, lawless, and miserable . . . a migratory tribe without fixed abode, alternately roving from city to country."[45] His solution was not to provide education or assistance for those unfortunates, but to urge the enforcement of existing restrictions to prevent more free blacks from coming into Delaware.

In the year of Governor Polk's address, the American Anti-Slavery Society sent William Yates, a free black man, to Delaware to examine conditions for free blacks there. Yates reported that his fellow blacks in the First State were "only nominally free" under a "wretched system of laws . . . designed to degrade, to crush and to render them ignorant and powerless."[46] In subsequent years the legislature did nothing to modify Yates's assessment. In 1849 and again in 1851 the assembly adopted laws to discourage the migration of blacks into the state, to deny re-entry to blacks who had left the state in search of seasonal work elsewhere, and to put idle, vagabond blacks to work under a master.[47] In 1843, the assembly entertained a bill that would have prevented free blacks from owning land in Delaware, but it fell short of a majority.[48]

During the thirty years from the Nat Turner rebellion of 1831 until the Civil War began in 1861, Delaware's lawmakers became progressively less inclined to abolish slavery. The old system of unfree labor was dying out on its own, many argued, without the intervention of intrusive busybodies or the passage of laws. The reaction of a House of Representatives committee to a petition from Wilmington's female Quaker abolitionists is revealing. It was one of the few times that the legislators took the state's abolitionists seriously enough even to comment on their petitions. The committee ignored the subject of the petition to concentrate on the gender of the petitioners. In the legislators' view, "the petitioning of women to our National and State Legislatures, which they regret to see is becoming so general a practice, is derogating from that refinement and delicacy which should . . . accompany the female character." The petitioners, the committeemen said, should "confine their attention to matters of a domestic nature, and be more solicitous to mend the garments of their husbands and children then to patch the breaches of the Laws and Constitution."[49]

In the 1820s the notorious Patty Cannon of Johnson's Crossroads in western Sussex County was brought to justice as a kidnapper of blacks and murderer of whites. In response to that sensational case, the legislature briefly focused attention on protecting free blacks from kidnapping. By the 1840s, however, the lawmakers' attention was instead directed toward preventing abolitionists, such as Wilmington Quaker Thomas Garrett and Maryland escapee Harriet Tubman, from spiriting slaves northward from Delaware. Yet, although the lawmakers strove to protect the right of Delaware's declining number of slave owners to keep their property, their support for the pro-slavery agenda of the southern states was lukewarm at best.

The communication among the states that had started with the committees of correspondence in the pre-Revolutionary era continued after the adoption of the United States Constitution. State governments regularly exchanged information with one another, and delivering that correspondence to the assembly was one of the governor's major duties. Through that route Delaware's lawmakers knew what amendments were being proposed to the Constitution and what other national initiatives sister states were promoting. When the Delaware General Assembly adopted a resolution in support or condemnation of some proposal, such as the Virginia and Kentucky Resolutions, South Carolina's nullification claim, or the abolition amendments proposed by northern states, the legislature's resolution was usually in response to receipt of one of those communications. Delaware's resolutions, in turn, were sent to all of the other states for their information.

Delaware's resolutions made it clear to her sister states that the First

State would never support any action that might jeopardize the integrity of the federal union as established by the Constitution. As far back as 1799 the assembly went on record against the states' rights position put forward in the Virginia and Kentucky Resolutions. Again, in 1833 the legislators listened approvingly as Governor Caleb P. Bennett, a Revolutionary War veteran, denounced South Carolina's attempt to nullify a federal tariff. Bennett called the nullification doctrine a "rebellion" based on "heresy." "It was in *union,*" he reminded his audience, "that we wrested our liberties from the grasp of oppression. The *union* is *our whole* strength, our sole support."[50]

No matter how much Delawareans disagreed with one another on the morality of slavery, very few wavered from their state's bedrock support for the union of states under the United States Constitution. In 1833 a committee of the state Senate voiced its strong opposition to South Carolina's attempted nullification of a federal law. The Constitution was not a mere treaty among sovereign states, the committeemen wrote, but an unbreakable compact. Governor David Hazzard agreed, declaring, "As the people of this state were the first to adopt the present government, they will be the last to abandon it."[51]

One had only to read the newspapers, however, to know that by the late 1840s disunion was becoming ever more likely. At the end of the Mexican War southern states insisted upon their right to extend slavery into the Western frontier while northern states disputed that right. Both sides knew that the outcome of their struggle for the West would eventually cause the death of slavery in the United States or give the institution new life. What was a tiny state like Delaware, located between two great antagonistic forces and totally dependent on the protection and freedom provided by the United States Constitution, to do in that situation?

One response was to practice patriotism. It was no coincidence that it was in 1849 that the assembly first ordered that a flagpole be erected in front of the State House and that the American flag be flown every day while the legislature was in session.[52] Another way to be patriotic was to turn to the sage advice of America's greatest hero and unionist, George Washington. Toward that end, the General Assembly adopted the practice of joining together during each biannual session to hear the reading of Washington's Farewell Address.

Flying the flag and hearing the words of Washington were strongly symbolic of Delaware's union-centered position amid the bitter disharmony that suffused the increasingly un-United States. Those nationalistic actions bespoke Delawareans' strong attachment to the union, but they were hardly likely to protect the little state from a future inter-state conflict or from the disintegration of the United States. Following the divisive Mexican War, the nation's most powerful political leaders rallied in Congress to prevent disunion. They crafted the Compromise of 1850, a bundle of bills that gave some victories to both North and South. Most importantly, California, newly acquired from Mexico, was admitted as a free state, while on the other side, Congress passed the Fugitive Slave Act, which gave federal support to apprehending runaway slaves no matter where in the United States they might be hiding.

In 1850, the year of the compromise legislation in Washington, D.C., Delawareans elected William H. Ross, a slaveholder from Seaford, to be their new governor. In his inaugural address to the General Assembly in January 1851, Governor Ross proclaimed his support for the compromise and blamed northern agitators for causing the national crisis. Slavery might be dying in Delaware, he said, but he was convinced that a majority of citizens in the First State supported the rights of the slave states. Perhaps he was right.

On at least one occasion the assembly proved to be even more pro-slavery than Governor Ross. In 1855 the governor told the legislators about a case in which a murderer had been acquitted because the only witness to his crime was a slave. In light of this miscarriage of justice, he suggested that the law should be modified to permit slaves to testify in court under certain conditions. The committee of the House appointed to consider the governor's recommendation vehemently opposed the idea on the grounds that "there could not be a jury of twelve men . . . of our state that would, upon the testimony of a Negro slave, convict a man . . . ."[53]

Throughout the 1850s race consciousness remained very high and may have grown in Delaware. In 1859 the assembly decreed that the P W & B Railroad must prevent black passengers from sitting in cars designated for whites while traveling through the state. Exceptions were permitted only in the case of servants or slaves who were traveling with their employers or masters.[54]

The 1850s marked a major shift in political power in Delaware. In the course of the decade the Whig Party disintegrated as a force in the nation and in the state. The party's demise in Delaware was heightened by the death of John M. Clayton, long Delaware's most powerful politician, in 1856. The Whigs disappeared nationally and in Delaware because they had tried to ameliorate the slavery issue but had found that it could not be done. After a few years of political upheaval in mid-decade the two-party system reemerged. The Republican Party came forward to link the capitalistic nationalism that had characterized the Whigs with opposition to the further spread of slavery. Meanwhile, the Democrats continued to be a loose alliance of pro-slavery, states-rights southerners, urban immigrants and workers, and people who adhered to the Jeffersonian doctrine of minimalist government.

The political churning that characterized the decade resonated strongly in the General Assembly. As late as 1853 the Whigs controlled the House of Representatives. On the final day of the session that year Eli Saulsbury, the leading Democrat in the House and one of a triumvirate of brothers who were emerging as major political leaders in the state, paid tribute to the fairness with which John R. McFee, the Whig Speaker, had conducted the proceedings. Saulsbury remarked that the "vehemence of manner" that had characterized the debates did not mean that proponents of the two parties did not respect one another. "We have shared together the labors and responsibilities of a protracted session . . . . We met at the commencement of our session comparatively as strangers; today at its close, we part as friends," he said.[55] Inter-party friendships would be sorely tested in the years that followed.

In 1859 the term of Governor William Burton, a Democrat, began as that of Peter F. Causey, a Whig, came to an end. Both men resided in Milford and they must have known one another well. Causey owned a large flour mill in town, and Burton was a physician and farm owner. Their speeches before the General Assembly reveal a great deal about political life and government in Delaware on the eve of the Civil War.

The outgoing governor, like so many of Delaware's Whig Party chief executives before him, concentrated his remarks on the state's responsibilities for the well-being of its citizens. He admonished the legislators to come to the aid of Delaware's children. The existing public schools, he said, were dilapidated and the teachers untrained. "It [public education] has been the theme of much debate in our legislative halls for many years," he remarked, "and yet each succeeding session has ended in little or no alteration for the better." The tiny school districts run by committees elected by the residents most hostile to taxation simply were not working. Governor Causey anticipated the assemblymen's excuse that they could not take on so large a topic as school reform during their short legislative session. But if they had the will to improve the schools, he said, "there will be time enough during the present session for much to be done."[56]

Governor Causey also challenged the assembly to address the needs of the insane, who, he said, "more than any other portion of our community [were] . . . dependent upon our care and protection." He noted that despite rising incidences of crime, especially in Kent and Sussex counties, the legislature had failed to build a penitentiary.[57] In short, Delaware had made little progress to improve education, care for the mentally ill, or rehabilitate criminals during the six decades since governors had first begun urging legislative action to address those issues. Suffice to say, the assembly of 1859 did no better.

It was not the time to make improvements in the state. The attention of the General Assembly, as indeed that of the whole country, was focused on events beyond the borders of Delaware. Both the outgoing and incoming governors could hardly fail to discuss the question of slavery in the United States territories. The issue preoccupied all Americans and was on the verge of destroying the United States. In taking up that great issue Delaware's governors demonstrated the paradox of the little state's southern leanings coupled with its unbreakable support for the Union. Both the Whig Causey and the Democrat Burton pleaded for a compromise that might reunite the country. Both supported the concept of "popular sovereignty" in the territories, even though that remedy had been found unworkable in Bloody Kansas. Both blamed Northern abolitionists, not Southern secessionists, for threatening the stability of the Union.

In his inaugural address Governor William Burton captured the essence of Delaware's political position within the nation. He urged Delawareans, "whose fond boast it has been that she was the first state to ratify . . . the federal Constitution, to use all their moral influence in allying the fierce storms that now threaten us with destruction. The perpetuity of the Federal Union, to all a matter of deep interest, is to us of Delaware an absolute necessity. It is our salvation—the ark of our safety, within which we have naught to fear; out of which we have nothing to look to for protection."[58] This principle would guide Delawareans through the fiery trials that were about to descend upon them.

5
DELAWARE'S INNER CIVIL WAR, 1861-1875

The Civil War was *the* central American experience. This titanic struggle, which cost over 600,000 lives, ended slavery and forged semi-independent states into an indivisible national union. It is incorrect, however, to view the war in simple terms of Yankee blue versus Confederate gray. Like all civil wars, the struggle was highly political, and combatants on the Union side were not all agreed on the war's causes or on its desired consequences. Nowhere were the confusions that marked the war years more vividly displayed than in Delaware, Maryland, Kentucky, and Missouri, the states collectively known as the "border states." Border states were geographically situated between North and South. They were slave states that did not join the Confederacy.

Delaware ha perhaps the most peculiarly ambiguous reaction to the war of any state. Although secession was never seriously considered in Delaware, the First State's legislature remained defiantly hostile to many federal government policies throughout the war and during the period of reconstruction that followed. The actions of the General Assembly during those years reveal the deep political divide inside a state that engaged in a protracted political war within itself. For Delaware the period of the Civil War and the Reconstruction that followed were times of bitter internal differences that were played out in the General Assembly.

Important demographic and economic factors help to explain the General Assembly's actions in the war years. By 1860 more Delawareans lived and voted in New Castle County thn in Kent and Sussex combined. New Castle County, led by its major city of Wilmington, had been transformed by the industrial revolution and the transportation revolution. By contrast, the two southern counties remained rural and had a relatively undeveloped transportation system and little access to financial resources. Slavery was legal in Delaware, but the institution was moribund everywhere in the state except in western Sussex County. The 1860 census reported only 1,798 slaves in the state, together with 19,829 free blacks and 90,589 whites.

Despite the population tilt toward the norhernmost county, each county retained its equality ofrepresentation in the General Assembly. The political issues that confronted the assembly in that period might have been resolved differently had the guiding principle of representation been one man, one vote rather than county equality. By 1860 the Democrats had become the major party in Delaware primarily by assuming an anti-plutocratic stance that captured the support of Wilmington's immigrant, mostly Irish, workers and by playing on fears among citizens throughout the state that the Republicans would institute racial equality.

The Democratic Party had competing centers of power in two families: the Bayards of New Castle Couty, led by United States Senator James A. Bayard and his son and later United States Senator Thomas F. Bayard; and the Saulsburys of Kent County, who were known collectively as the "party of the three brothers." The brothers were United States Senator Willard Saulsbury and his equally politically active siblings, Eli Saulsbury and Gove Saulsbury. The Bayards and the Saulsburys each possessed a newspaper to trumpet their competing views. Despite their differences, both Democratic factions staunchly opposed the policies of the Republican Party, which they viewed as anti-slavery and oppressive to white citizens. Simply put, the Democrats wanted to keep the state and nation as they once had been, with slavery and states rights upheld under the umbrella of a non-intrusive federal government.

The Republican Party, in Delaware as elsewhere, inherited the allegiance of many former Whigs. It was the party of middle- and upper-class industrialists, of opponents to slavery, of nationalists, and of Protestant social reformers. While the party's strength n the First State was primarily in New Castle County, it also claimed a surprising number of adherents in Sussex County. Republicans believed that slavery was immoral and economically backward. They supported the preservation of the Union as the paramount necessity for an economically progressive, democratic nation. In the 1860 election those in Delaware who supported the Republican position voted for candidates of the Peoples Party, a short-lived fusion party of Republicans, nativists, and former Whigs that marked a stage in thestate's transition to a new two-party system.

The parties disagreed on a variety of issues that included parochial interests as well as transcendent national principles. An example of a local issue that divided the political parties and the sections of the state was the use of lotteries. During the early decades of the nineteenth century lotteries had been the legislature's favorite means of assisting all manner of public and private projects. The legislators passed many bills that allowed lottery agents to come into the state to raise money to build highways, railroads, churches, mills and schools. The lotteries cost the state nothing, and sometimes even earned it a portion of the profits.

By the late 1830s lottery agents had gained a reputation as tricksters who swindled their victims with misleading promotions. Social reformers turned against them and urged the state legislature to outlaw lotteries as mere gambling. Most of the protests came from New Castle County and primarily from Whigs-later turned Republicans who accused the protectors of lotteries in the legislature of accepting bribes to keep the shell game going. Those protests struck some southern Delawareans as unfair. The major transportation needs of the northern part of the state had already been met, but those of southern Delaware had not. The people of eastern Sussex County were especially eager to promote the Junction & Breakwater

Railroad that was planned to link the Delaware Railroad at Harrington to Milford, Georgetown, and Lewes. In the early 1860s the railroad was unfinished and to complete it would require the infusion of capital that a lottery could provide. The value of the railroad's stock, not to mention the improvement's potential for economic development, was at stake.[1]

After years of debate on the lottery issue, some Democrats joined the Republicans in the legislature to abolish lotteries in 1862. This action marked an important moment in the history of public finance in Delaware. Having taken away the lottery, the state turned to bonds as the best means to assist projects just at the time when the federal government was raising money for the war through this same device. The Junction & Breakwater Railroad became the first private project in Delaware to receive support from state bonds. Bonds have been the mainstay of public financial support for capital projects in Delaware ever since.

Although state matters, such as lotteries and railroad construction, continued to be important issues before the General Assembly in the 1860s, it was the assembly's reactions to the national issues of secession, war, and emancipation that were most historically significant during those years.

On the issue of federal authority over slavery, Delaware stood with the South. In November 1860 the Republican candidate for President, Abraham Lincoln of Illinois, defeated the divided Democratic Party's two candidates, Stephen A. Douglas of Illinois and John Breckinridge of Kentucky, plus a third-party candidate, John Bell of Tennessee. Lincoln won because he gained solid majorities in the Northern states. In Delaware, however, the clear winner was Breckinridge, the candidate most sympathetic to the South, who captured about one half of the vote. By contrast, Lincoln won less than a quarter of Delaware's vote.

The General Assembly met for its regular biennial session in January 1861, two months before Abraham Lincoln was to take office. Southern states in the nation's lower tier, led by South Carolina, had already seceded in anticipation of the Republicans' rule and were in the process of organizing the Confederacy. Governor William Burton, a Democrat from Sussex County, told the legislators that he feared "a terrible calamity." He blamed abolitionist fanatics who, he said, were driving the country apart by their refusal to enforce the Fugitive Slave Act. Many of Delaware's lawmakers agreed.

A majority of First State legislators believed that reconciliation could still be achieved. They looked hopefully to a proposal to placate the slave states put forward by Kentucky Senator John C. Crittenden. Supporters of Crittenden's plan proposed to hold a national convention to save the union. But the compromise bubble burst when incoming President Abraham Lincoln refused to commit his administration to the plan. President-elect Lincoln opposed the Crittenden Plan because it would have permitted the spread of slavery into United States territories in the West. Lincoln's candidacy had been based on rejection of the further spread of slavery. In Delaware, only one member of the General Assembly, Edward Betts, of Wilmington, had the temerity to oppose the Crittenden Plan. Betts was denounced throughout the state and was even hanged in effigy in Middletown.²

Delaware's support for the Crittenden Plan suggested to some that the First State was primed to join the Confederacy. It was in that expectation that the Honorable H. Dickinson, Chancellor of Mississippi, arrived in Dover early in 1861. Dickinson requested the opportunity to address a joint session of the General Assembly. The legislators lstened to his arguments with courtesy but then expressed their disapproval of secession. The Delaware legislators later rejected another opportunity to join the Confederacy proffered by a commissioner from Georgia. Their disapproval was, however, qualified in the Senate, where the Democrats held a slight majority that counterbalanced the Peoples Party's one vote majority in the House. The House summoned the votes to oppose secession on principle. In the Senate, however, a substitute motion was adopted. It proclaimed that Delaware would retain its attachment to the union "so long as a lingering hope of its preservation remains."³

A similar division between the houses marked the vote on the symbolic issue of displaying the national flag. The House resolved to purchase a thirty-four-star national flag representing all the states then in the union, including those that had seceded, to fly from the State House cupola. The resolution was lost in the Senate in a tie vote.⁴ A narrow majority in the Senate also blocked a resolution to commend United States Army Major Robert Anderson for his decision to maintain the federal presence at Fort Sumter in the harbor of Charleston, South Carolina. In reaction to Anderson's refusal to surrender the federal fort the Confederates fired on Fort Sumter. This was the spark that started the war. The General Assembly's ambiguous reactions to those proposals reflected the division in the state between those who blamed the approaching calamity on abolitionists and those who blamed secessionists. The events of the war would further deepen that division.

Perhaps the most important actions of the First State's government during the war were not what it did but what it chose not to do. The state refused to secede and it refused the opportunity to be a guinea pig in President Lincoln'sproposal for the compensated emancipation of the state's few slaves. The President conceived of the plan in the fall of 1861 when it occurred to him that the least costly way to end the war and save lives and money would be to offer slave owners in the loyal border states the opportunity to obtain cash from the federal government in exchange for freeing their slaves. If the plan worked, the seceded states might be inclined to accept a similar offer and renounce secession. What better place to try out the idea than in little, loyal Delaware. Under the proposed plan Congress would pay the bill. The federal government would then use the First State's action as an example that might be enacted in other border states, and ths entice the states of the Confederacy to reenter the Union on similar terms.

The President met with Delaware's United States Representative George P. Fisher, who agreed to sound out the proposal in his home state. Fisher assisted in drawing up a bill to put before the General Assembly that called for gradual emancipation to be completed in ten years. The contents of the bill appeared in the press and were widely discussed and debated throughout the state. In January 1862 the legislature met in special session to decide the fate of the compensated emancipation plan. Representative Fisher met with legislators behind the scenes to urge them to adopt the measure. His proposal created great excitement in the legislature. But the "Abolition Bill" did not attract a majority, and the sponsors withdrew it before it was formally presented for a vote.

Why did compensated emancipation fail? Some opponents objected to using the money of non-slaveholding citizens to pay off slave owners. Most, however, refused to accept the idea that the federal government should play a role in determining a state's right to decide for itself whether slavery would be legal or illegal in that state. The Democrats stood by the principle that Delaware must decide on its own when and if to free its few remaining slaves. They feared the dissolution of states' rights on the slavery issue. The Democrats, like the President, believed that the whole nation, including the Confederacy, was watching to see what Delaware would do. With that spotlight in mind they managed to pass a states' rights resolution by the smallest of majorities. "When the people of Delaware desire to abolish slavery within her borders, they will do so in their own way," the resolution proclaimed.[5]

As a result of Delaware's refusal to adopt his plan, President Lincoln abandoned his quixotic compensated emancipation scheme and turned instead to freeing the slaves in the rebellious states by Presidential decree, using his powers as commander-in-chief. Five days after the Union Army had won a significant victory over the Confederates at Antietam in western Maryland in September 1862, Lincoln issued a preliminary Emancipation Proclamation. The announcement came just two months before the election of a new Congress and, in Delaware, of a new governor and legislature.

The election of 1862 was unlike any that Delaware has ever known. Democrats were enraged at the audacity of the President's Emancipation Proclamation. They had long predicted that the Republicans would destroy slavery and now warned that racial equality would shortly follow. The Democrats' campaign tactic in Delaware was built around constant use of derogatory terms in reference to blacks and of racial scare tactics. State Republican leaders claimed to fear that there would be riots and intimidation at the polls, especially in the southern counties. To counteract this perceived threat, they requested troops from the War Department. Soldiers stood guard near polling places on election day.

The election produced a deeply divided government in the First State. The Republican candidate for governor, William Cannon of Bridgeville, polled virtually even with his Democratic rival in Sussex County, won New Castle County, and lost Kent. At the final count Cannon won by a statewide majority of only 111 votes, but that was a large margin of victory compared to the Democrats' candidate for Congress, who won by just thirty-seven votes. The Republicans rolled up

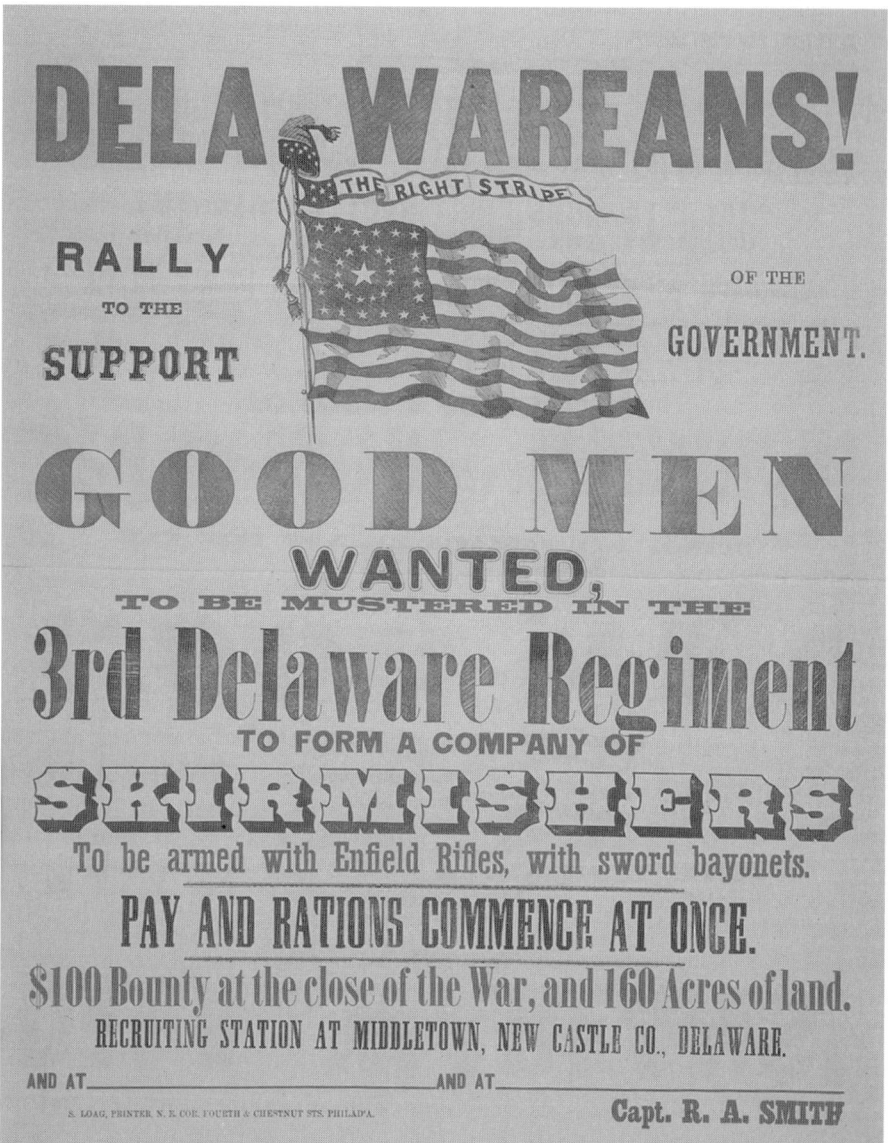

A recruitment poster for the 3rd Delaware Regiment. The regiment was recruited from volunteers in the fall of 1861, but a year of hard fighting left it short of men. In the fall of 1862 the federal government authorized the promise of bounties of $100 in addition to free land in the West as a one-time offer to attract new recruits to Union Army regiments. (Courtesy of the Historical Society of Delaware)

majorities in nearly every part of New Castle County, but could not prevent the Democrats from gaining control of both houses of the General Assembly. Despite their victories, the Democrats were enraged by the presence of troops at the polls and determined to make the most of the perceived assault on civil liberies.

In his final speech before the assembly on January 6, 1863, the outgoing governor, Democrat William Burton, proclaimed both his loyalty to the United States and his hatred of the Lincoln administration's policies. He said that Delaware had loyally provided the troops required by te federal government but that the state had refused to supply any state funds in support of the war. He also described his intense indignation at what he regarded as the shameful way in which the national government was treading on the civil liberties of Delawareans. Burton particularly condemned the federal government for disarming militia units raised by Democrats in Delaware, for arresting and imprisoning the state's citizens on suspicion of treason without benefit of trial, and for sending troops into the state at election time.[6]

A few days later a large crowd gathered to witness the inauguration of the new governor, Republican William Cannon. A local brass band played as carriages bearing the new governor and other dignitaries arrived on the green. Governor Cannon entered the State House to take the oath and address members of both houses in the courtroom on the first floor.[7]

Facing an audience of assembly members in which the Democrats had a slight, but all-powerful edge, Cannon did not shy away from proclaiming his version of the issues. The war, he said, was a "gigantic rebellion" that "threatens to destroy the nation." He denied the doctrine that the United States Constitution was a "mere compact between states." "The claim of the United States is paramount," he said, ". . . its jurisdiction supreme." In contrast to the grudging support that his predecessor had given to the war effort, Governor Cannon called on the assembly to demonstrate its gratitude for Delaware's suffering soldiers by voting money to support their families.

With regard to the two questions that most troubled the Democrats, slavery and the use of troops at the recent election, the governor was clear. The General Assembly, he said, should acknowledge the fact that slavery in Delaware "was doomed" by abolishing it on their own. He noted that the war was bringing change and "the longer the contest is protracted, the more radical will be the change wrought." Cannon was one of the Republicans that the Democrats blamed for bringing the federal troops to guard the polls. Cannon, in turn, justified that action by noting that the soldiers had been a force to ensure voters' rights against the intimidation of mobs and that the soldiers had not trampled upon the rights of anyone.[8] It was the first and the last time that Republican views would prevail in the General Assembly of 1863. To make their opposition perfectly clear, the legislature adopted a joint resolution condemning Governor Cannon's inaugural address.[9]

A number of serious issues confronted the General Assembly in the winter of 1863, but all were submerged in the effort to tar the Republicans with the charge of intimidation at the election. The leader of that effort in the Delaware Senate was Senator Gove Saulsbury, whose brother Willard Saulsbury joined in the denunciation in a speech before the United States Senate. In Dover, Gove Saulsbury called for the creation of a joint committee to investigate the election incident. He chaired the committee, which was composed exclusively of Democrats.

The joint committee conducted extensive hearings that took place before the entire assembly. Over a hundred witnesses were called to testify. When the hearings ended, the committee published a lengthy report that, to no one's surprise, found the Republicans and their intimidating soldiers guilty as charged. The assembly then adopted an "Act to secure the freedom of elections in this state," which made it a felony to invite soldiers into Delaware at election time or for federal troops to be stationed closer than five miles from a polling place.[10]

While the assemblymen were castigating the Republicans for sending troops to the polls, they indefinitely postponed consideration of the governor's request to aid soldiers' families. They did, however, find time to adopt a series of measures designed to keep newly freed slaves from the rebellious states out of Delaware and to further reduce the few freedoms that native-born "free Negroes and mulattoes" enjoyed in the First State. It became illegal for free blacks to "attend or be present at any political meeting," to vote, to hold office, or to possess a gun or a sword. A mere five-day hiatus from Delaware would cost a black person the right to maintain residency status, and further limits were adopted to govern blacks' religious meetings and preachers.[11]

In a similar spirit, the assembly placed pro-slavery restrictions on the federal government's plan to build defenses at Cape Henlopen. At the outset of war, Pennsylvania and New Jersey had requested that fortifications be built to protect shipping at the entrance to the Delaware Bay. Delaware's legislators were slow to agree to cede the land for a fort. When they finally did agree, the assembly attached the provisos that no escaped slaves could find sanctuary there and tha no nonresident black workers could be employed in the construction or maintenance of the fort. The federal government refused to accede to Delaware's conditions and did not build the fortification because the government no longer felt the urgent need to do so.[12] By 1863 it had become accepted practice for escaped slaves to gain their freedom by entering federal lines, and the threat of a Confederate attack on the Delaware coast had diminished.

The legislature met in January 1863, the month when the Emancipation Proclamation went into effect. It was also one month after the Union Army's debacle at Fredericksburg, Virginia. The Democrats were encouraged to push their opinions to the fullest. They adopted a joint resolution that called on the Lincoln administration to restore the old union and to provide civil liberty for whites only. Hardly masking their intense anger, the authors of the resolution noted the shift that had taken place in the purpose of the war from one of the restoration of the union to one of emancipation. "In the opinion of this General Assembly and a majority of the people of the State, this war ought never to have been made; that it is the result of wickedness on both sides."[13]

The Democrats' resolution in the General Assembly called for a national convention of reconciliation "to end this dreadful war." Their hope for such a peaceful restoration was rather fanciful since the Confederacy had proclaimed that it would never return to the United States no matter what conditions were offered. Finally, the assembly declared "we do most emphatically condemn, and in the name of the people of Delaware, protest against the proclamation of emancipation . . . ."[14] It is not surprising that the Republican press labeled the General Assembly of 1863 "the copperhead legislature," using the Republicans' term of derision to describe pro-Confederates in the North.[15]

By 1864 the war had turned around. With the fall of Vicksburg on July 4, 1863, the Confederates lost control of the Mississippi. The day before, General Lee's army had been turned back at Gettysburg. From then on the Confederates were fighting a defensive war against a determined nation with superior forces. The shift in the momentum of war influenced the General Assembly. When Governor Cannon called the assembly into special sessions in January, July, and October 1864 there were no more calls for conventions of reconciliation with the seceded states. Instead, the Democrat majority seemed resigned to the prospect of Union victory and concentrated on rearguard actions to limit the social and political changes that the victory would bring.

Delaware Democrats in the General Assembly continued to display no enthusiasm for the Union cause. In January 1864 Governor Cannon asked the legislature to provide $425 toward the national cemetery at Gettysburg where the bodies of Delaware's sons who had fallen on that field of battle lay buried. The Senate declined to provide state funds for that purpose. Fortunately, private donations of more than double the amount requested saved the state from embarrassment. The assembly also refused to provide support for the families of the state's soldiers. The Democrat majority studiously ignored Governor Cannon's proposal to emancipate Delaware's few remaining slaves, in spite of the fact that neighboring Maryland had recently eliminated slavery. Delaware was now completely, but defiantly, surrounded by free states.

The state could no longer refuse to assist recruitment for the army. Other states were paying bounties of several hundred dollars to encourage volunteers. Delaware had not done so, yet up until 1864 the state had managed to produce several regiments of fighting men. In July 1864 Governor Cannon called the legislature into special session to announce that Preident Lincoln had just called for a new draft to ensure that each state would fill its assigned quota. Delaware's leaders much prefered to recruit volunteers rather than resort to a draft. Therefore, the state had to accept the necessity of offering bounties to keep Delawareans from joining units from other states that did offer bounties. The title of the law that the assembly adopted proclaims the majority's attitude: "An Act to relieve the people of this state from the draft."¹⁶ The bounties were to be financed by the sale of state bonds. The act succeeded in attracting volunteers to the army, but not enough to fill the state's quota. Delaware still had to resort to the draft.

This draft lottery wheel now in the collections of the Historical Society of Delaware was used at Wilmington's Old Town Hall to select draftees to fill Delaware's quota in the Union army in May 1864 and again in February 1865. (Courtesy of the Historical Society of Delaware)

The Democrats battled the Republican governor on other issues as well. They passed a law designed to prevent military interference at the upcoming general election. They denounced the national Republican administration's suspension of Habeas Corpus. They deplored the governor's request that bounties be paid to recruits irrespective of race. They especially demanded that Governor Cannon provide them with information concerning the recruitment of colored troops from the First State into the regiments of other states.

Governor Cannon was not to be intimidated. He noted that the legislature had refused to recruit or pay bounties to blacks. The assembly's resistance was shortsighted, he said, because the state would be forced to resort to the draft to make up its quota. The Democrats declared the governor's words to be an "insult," and they charged "no one has contributed so much as he has done to the unjust and cruel oppression of the people of this state."¹⁷

The battle lines of the state's political future were clearly marked. In a further exchange, the governor referred to the "unfriendly legislation" that characterized the assembly's treatment of blacks. The legislative Democrats responded defiantly, "the African race has ever been considered by us an inferior and subject race. While our laws have extended to them all the privileges to which the most prudent and humane could possibly consider them entitled...."[18]

The November election of 1864 brought no surprises in Delaware. The state was one of only three to choose Democrat George McClellan over Republican Abraham Lincoln. The Republicans won all the legislative seats being contested in New Castle County, but lost by a large margin in Kent and by a narrow margin in Sussex.

In January 1865, the newly elected legislators confronted for the last time the opportunity for Delaware to abolish slavery on its own. Once more Governor Cannon urged the assembly to "make Delaware a free state."[19] He and all the legislators were well aware that Congress was about to pass the Thirteenth Amendment to the federal Constitution, which, once it was ratified, would make slavery illegal throughout the United States. This was Delaware's final chance to take responsibility for the emancipation of its few remaining slaves. The General Assembly stubbornly declined the opportunity. Later in that same session the legislature received the Thirteenth Amendment and predictably refused to ratify it on the grounds that slavery was a state issue.

The legislature's back-to-back endorsements of slavery attracted national attention. Horace Greeley of the New York *Tribune* wrote derisively: "Well here is Delaware with a Legislature that might abolish slavery if it would, or might ratify the Constitutional Amendment; but it will do neither, because its Democratic majority knows that it owes its ascendancy to Slavery and to nothing else—that, but for Slavery, this old Federal and Whig State would not pretend to be Democratic."[20] A newspaper in Albany, New York, agreed. "Delaware," its editor said, "is progressing backward."[21]

On March 1, 1865, Governor William Cannon died of typhoid fever at his home in Bridgeville. The members of the General Assembly recessed their deliberations to attend the funeral of the man that a majority of them had battled for two years, often resorting to vicious invective. Under Delaware's constitution, the Speaker of the Senate, who was Gove Saulsbury, became the state's chief executive. The Democrats were thus firmly in control of both the legislative and executive branches of the state's government when the war ended the following month.

Historians have labeled the decade that followed the Civil War the Era of Reconstruction. During much of that period former Confederate states were disqualified from participating in the national government as the Republicans who ruled in Washington tried to remake the South. The federal government sent troops to occupy the South and attempted by various means to force Southern whites to accept the political and social equality of blacks. The Freedman's Bureau dispatched teachers to set up schools to educate former slaves. Only when rebel states had conformed to the Republicans' political agenda were they permitted to rejoin the Union as reconstructed states. The key elements in the Republican program were expressed in the Thirteenth, Fourteenth, and Fifteenth amendments to the United States Constitution and in laws designed to guarantee the freedmen's civil rights.

Because Delaware had remained loyal to the Union, most Reconstruction programs only indirectly affected the state. No federal troops were stationed in Delaware, nor could the Republican-dominated Congress force Delaware to ratify the Reconstruction Amendments. Delawareans were deeply split over the goals of Reconstruction. A determined minority of blacks an committed white reformers established a privately funded charity to educate black residents. Called the Association for the Education and Moral Improvement of the Colored People, the organization worked with black communities throughout the state to build schools and to hire and pay teachers.

In the General Assembly, however, a narrow majority opposed the Republicans' Reconstruction measures. As a border state, Delaware was one of only four former slave states that had the freedom to choose to reject the Reconstruction Amendments to the United States Constitution. The First State's Democrats were determined to make their "unqualified disapproval" of all three amendments loud and clear. A special committee of the House of Representatives was appointed to advise their colleagues on the Fourteenth Amendment, which would prevent states from denying equal rights to blacks. The committee reported that the proposed amendment represented "a breach of faith" with the rights of the states guaranteed in the original Constitution of 1787; and the legislature refused to ratify it. But it is worth noting that the vote was very close. In the House supporters of the amendment lost by only one vote.[22]

The opponents of civil rights for blacks had won a razor-thin victory in the state House of Representatives. That vote demonstrated just how closely matched the two major parties were in Delaware during Reconstruction. During that most politically charged era in the state's history the Democrats maintained their ascendancy, but often only by a few votes at the polls and in the legislature. In several elections they would have lost their hold on the state legislature had it not been for the peculiarities of the state constitution that mandated equality of representation by county in countywide, at-large elections.

Delaware's Democrats were particularly hostile to the Fifteenth Amendment. The amendment's purpose was to prevent racial discrimination in voting. Once given the vote, Democrats knew that black males would flock to the Republican Party and tip the balance in state politics.

The story of how the state's savvy Democrats thwarted the Republicans who governed in Washington, D.C., is a parable of how political infighting worked in Reconstruction-era Delaware. Each state's right to determine its own rules for voters was a cardinal principle of the Democratic Party. Coupled with this principle was the belief held by most adherents of Delaware's Democratic Party that people of African descent were inherently inferior to those of European ancestry.

In 1866 Delaware's Democratic majority in the General Assembly denounced a proposed act of Congress to extend the suffrage to the black residents of Washington, D.C. According to the legislature's resolution, the federal act was unconstitutional because it violated the wishes of the majority of the capital city's white inhabitants. The measure, the legislators wrote, "would be a lasting stigma upon the nation, tending to degrade and disgrace the free white men of this country." Black suffrage was not only disgraceful, but morally reprehensible they said, as it flew in the face of "the immutable laws of the Creator" who had made white people the superior race.[23]

Black Delawareans rallied in support of the Fifteenth Amendment and rejoiced when it was ratified, without Delaware's support, in 1870. That same year Congress adopted three Enforcement Acts to ensure that the new amendment would be respected. With the force of a Constitutional amendment and federal statutes behind them, it appeared that Delaware's black males would face no obstacles to voting in the election of 1870 and all the statewide elections that would follow. But the wily Democrats had some tricks up their sleeves.

It was not for nothing that United States Senator Thomas F. Bayard stood at the head of the Delaware bar and that the Saulsbury brothers were the state's cleverest politicians. The battle against the Fifteenth Amendment drew those rivals within the Democratic Party together into a common cause. They would prevent as many blacks from voting as possible. More than a decade before the former rebel states became free from the constraints of Reconstruction to hatch similar schemes, Delaware's Demorats seized upon the poll tax as the most legally defensible means to exclude black voters from casting ballots.

A long-standing Delaware law required voters to demonstrate that they had paid their county tax. Landowners sowed a receipt from the county tax collector to qualify to vote; those without land or other taxable property paid a modest poll tax to the collector in exchange for a similar receipt. According to the Democrats, most blacks were too poor and too unsettled to pay either tax. They charged the Republicans wit paying the poll tax for those blacks who did qualify. To keep blacks from qualifying, in 1870 Democrat tax collectors slipped away when they saw black men approaching to pay. Once the potential black voters departed in frustration, the tax collectors marked those persons as "delinquent" or "left the state." The trick worked. In 1870 Democrats won every contested seat for the General Assembly.

The furious Republicans fought back. Republican Anthony Higgins, United States District Attorney for Delaware, prosecuted several New Castle County collectors under the federal Enforcement Act. The case of the first defendant was heard in the United States District Court for Delaware in October 1872. On the testimony of thwarted black voters, the collector was found guilty and fined. Using the power of federal law, a federally appointed prosecutor, and a federal court, the Republicans appeared to have won a major victory. They had even more reason to rejoice in November 1872 when the Republicans gained a statewide majority at the polls that elected a Republican to Congress.But the Republicans were concentrated in New Castle County, and they failed to capture the General Assembly because Kent and Sussex counties returned Democratic majorities.

The interior and exterior of the State House underwent a major transformation in 1874. In keeping with Victorian tastes, the building acquired a third floor covered by a mansard roof. A new cupola and entryway were constructed, and the building was sheathed in plaster. This photograph was taken ca. 1909 during the first stage of another restoration project. Note the scaffolding from which workmen were removing the plaster to reveal the brick underneath. (Courtesy of the Delaware Public Archives)

By the time the assembly gathered in Dover in January 1873 the Democrats had already worked out a plan to disfranchise blacks. The newly elected governor was James Ponder, a businessman from Milton in Sussex County. Ponder was well connected politically. He was a former state senator and was the son-in-law of Willard Saulsbury. The governor laid out the major provisions of the Democrats' plan in his inaugural message. Governor Ponder suggested that the legislators adopt a new election law to re-define the responsibilities of tax assessors and collectors. Under the new law, those officials could not be held accountable should taxpayers complain that they had tried in vain to pay their taxes but could never find the collector available to receive their money. The assembly promptly complied by adopting the Assessment Act of 1873, which closely followed the governor's proposal.[24]

The Assessment Act of 1873 won the state notoriety as well as admirers in the 1870s. It has since attracted the attention of Delaware historians.[25] It is difficult to gauge the law's effectiveness. No doubt many property-less blacks were discouraged from attempting to qualify to vote, but some persisted, especially in New Castle County, where the Republicans were often in control of the assessments. Seen in its historic perspective, the law damaged the state's political integrity. But it was the poll tax itself that opened the way for vote buying on a massive scale, although that result did not become evident until the 1880s.

Despite the extreme racism that characterized majority sentiment in the General Assembly of the 1870s, the legislators occasionally paid heed to the wishes of their black constituents. During the Reconstruction era black Delawareans and their white supporters were as interested in promoting educational opportunities for black Delawareans as they were in gaining political power. Black leaders and white Republicans urged the state legislature to assist private endeavors in funding schools for black youngsters. Interestingly, no one suggested that black students should share in the state's School Fund. That modest fund, which dated back to 1796, had been established for the benefit of the state's whites-only public schools, and so, for a time at least, the money continued to be used exclusively for that purpose. Integrated public education was not considered. Instead, supporters of state-assisted education for blacks practiced the politics of the possible. They urged the assembly to adopt a bill to permit blacks to be taxed to pay for their own schools.

In 1875 the General Assembly adopted a law to establish schools for the state's black children to be supported by black taxpayers. Under the law the counties were to tax black property owners to create "a separate and distinct fund" for the support of segregated schools. The schools were to be administered by the Delaware Association for the Educational Advancement and Mral Improvement of the Colored People, which was the private agency that had begun most of Delaware's schools for black children.[26] In its first year of operation the fund for black schools collected $3,200 to support twenty-eight rural schools. The Association for the Education of the Colored People provided an additional monthly sum of $6 to each school. Those schools enrolled over 1,100 pupils throughout the state.[27]

During its 1875 session the General Assembly also turned its attention toward improving the quality of the state's public schools for whites. The legislature created the post of state superintendent and made the superintendent responsible for oversight of hiring teachers, organizing summer institutes for teacher training, and annually inspecting the condition of each school. The superintendent was to report to a state board of education to be composed of the president of Delaware College, the secretary of state, and the state auditor.[28] The superintendent and the board could make reports but lacked the power to force the taxpayers in a deficient district to improve their schools. None of those provisions applied to the schools for blacks. The state's sole responsibility for them lay in the legislature's mandate to the counties to collect the tax from black property-owners.

While Delaware's General Assembly was in session in February 1875 the United States Congress adopted its final Reconstruction law. The Civil Rights Act of 1875 was intended to protect black Americans from discriminatory practices in public accommodations such as railways and hotels. Even when the bill was before Congress, some of its supporters expressed doubts about its constitutionality, and the federal government did little to enforce its provisions. Delaware's Democrats seized the opportunity to nullify the potential effect of this strong sounding, but weakly administered national act.

Only one month after Congress passed its public-accommodations bill, the General Assembly adopted its own version of public accommodations. The state's act permitted an owner of an inn, restaurant, theater, steamboat, railroad, or other public accommodation to refuse service to persons "offensive to the major part of his customers."[29] No word about race appeared in the law. The supporters of the measure were correct in their assumption that the federal government would not challenge its constitutionality. The Delaware Public Accommodation Act of 1875 was to remain in effect in the First State for eighty-eight years until the federal Civil Rights Act of 1963 superseded it.

In addition to the racial tensions that divided Delawareans, the state also faced the problem of paying off its war-related debt. During the war the legislature had reluctantly issued bonds to pay for wartime bounties. The assembly had also committed the state to assist the construction of in-state railroads. After the war, the assembly was eager to pay off the debt without increasing taxes on real estate. Toward that end, in 1869 the legislature voted to impose a series of new taxes on large companies doing business in the state. Those included insurance companies, banks, and railroads. The legislature also adopted laws to tax the earnings of lawyers and physicians, and to tax inheritances that were not assigned to family members. The assembly's goal was to leave the state debt-free by 1890.[30]

The PW & B Railroad challenged the constitutionality of the state's railroad tax in court, but lost. The railroad company then agreed to pay Delaware a set sum of $27,000 annually in lieu of paying a per-capita tax on its passengers. Aside from paying off its bonds, demands on the state's revenue were slight. It cost only $33,000 to pay for all three branches of Delaware's government in 1874.[31]

The state passed another major milestone in 1867 when the legislature accepted Delaware's entitlement from the federal Land-Grant College Act of 1862. Under the terms of the act Delaware received scrip from the United States government representing ownership of 90,000 acres of public land in the West. The state treasurer sold the scrip to a land speculator in Cleveland, Ohio, for

$80,000. The money became an endowment for Delaware College to be used to teach the useful arts of agriculture, engineering, and military science.

Delaware College had closed during the war years for want of funds, and the infusion of the land-grant money gave the institution a new lease on life. When the college reopened in 1870 the professor of chemistry offered his services to the state to become the state chemist, an offer that the state readily accepted, thus inaugurating a new age of active cooperation between the state and its major institution of higher learning.[32] The main job of the state chemist was to test fertilizers for their chemical content.

During the post-war period the legislators also expanded the rights of married women. In legislation that mirrored acts adopted nearly twenty years before in New York and other northern states, Delaware extended to married women the right to maintain their own property, to hold on to their property and earnings if they were separated from their husbands, and to bequeath that property by will without their husbands' consent.[33]

In the Civil War and Reconstruction era Delaware's legislature demonstrated the extreme contradictions that made this little border state unique among the states of the Union. On the one hand, Delaware remained steadfastly loyal to the United States. On the other hand, Delaware's elected leaders constantly proclaimed a states' rights doctrine and refused to support federal efforts to improve the status of black Americans. It is worth remembering that although Delaware prides itself on being the first state to ratify the United States Constitution, it and Kentucky were the last states to outlaw slavery. Only the action of those sister states who ratified the Thirteenth Amendment forced Delaware to take that necessary step forward toward human freedom and equality.

Slowly the bitterness engendered by the war faded. In 1885 the legislature voted to provide $2,000 to erect a monument to the state's soldiers who had fallen while fighting at Gettysburg.[34] In 1901, when the Republicans finally wrested control of the General Assembly from the Democrats, Delaware tardily ratified the Thirteenth, Fourteenth, and Fifteenth amendments to the United States Constitution. Appropriately, the vote took place on February 12, the ninety-second anniversary of the birth of Abraham Lincoln, the President who had called for "a new birth of freedom" throughout the United States.

6
SETTING A NEW COURSE, 1876-1905

The latter decades of the nineteenth century were neither the most productive nor the proudest in the Delaware General Assembly's long history. Yet, the legislative inertia and political corruption that marked those years ultimately produced a reaction that led to reshaping the state's constitution and laying the groundwork for a more effective state government. Simply put, the problems of the 1880s and 1890s galvanized state leaders to recast the state's constitution into a stronger form that proved able to meet the challenges of the twentieth century.

Delaware's history during the last quarter of the nineteenth century must be seen in the context of unprecedented national growth. Post Civil War America experienced the rapid settlement of the western plains, free-wheeling economic boom and bust, the completion of the intercontinental railroad, and the dominance of railroad companies and big city bankers, often at the expense of farmers and other small producers. A massive immigration of people from southern and eastern Europe filled the nation's fast-growing, unruly industrial cities. In government it was an age of often-corrupt party politics and laissez-faire attitudes. The federal government proved reluctant to impose rules on the nation's dynamic, if unstable, economy; nor did the federal courts impose a rigorous interpretation of the recently enacted Fourteenth and Fifteenth amendments to the federal Constitution that had seemingly guaranteed equality to Americans of African descent.

Delaware's population growth and economic development in those years fell below the national standard. The state remained overwhelmingly agricultural, but increased competition from the West made its farmers poorer and their land less valuable. Farm owners who had welcomed the construction of the Delaware Railroad and its branches as links to urban markets had not anticipated the high freight charges that absorbed their meager profits. Rural Delaware's ongoing economic depression fueled resentment of Wilmington, the state's only industrial city.

Wilmington was the most dynamic place in the state. Its population in the post-Civil War era increased from fewer than 30,000 in 1870 to 76,500 by 1900. The city's locally owned and managed foundries, tanneries, carriage-making factories, and, most particularly, its builders of railroad cars, trolley cars, and steamboats, attracted workers from around the region and from Ireland, Germany,

The Capitol Hotel, built in the 1860s, was a favorite among late-nineteenth-century legislators. The building faced the Green next door to the Ridgely House on the ground where once had stood Elizabeth Battell's Golden Fleece Tavern. Fires in 1881 and the 1920s destroyed the old hotel. (Courtesy of the Delaware Public Archives)

Poland, Russia, and Italy. Wilmington's Market Street was the premier retail district in the state, and the city's churches, opera house, hotels, schools, and homes attested to the city's wealth and prominence.

In Wilmington, as throughout the First State, black residents lived and worked at the bottom of the social and economic scale. In the city blacks were most often servants, draymen, or laundresses. In the rural areas blacks lived in small settlements or on farmland where they were occasionally owners but were more usually tenant farmers or day laborers. Instead of creating opportunities for genuine equality, the Reconstruction amendments had seemed merely to fasten on black people a post-slavery world of segregation and poverty.

The legislative branch of the state's government reflected those economic and social realities. It was also the product of the peculiarities of the state constitution of 1831, whereby the three counties were qually represented in both houses of the assembly and the members of the assmbly were elected at large in each county. In practice, that meant that rural voters controlled elections in Kent and Sussex counties while Wilmington's voters had the upper hand in choosing the representatives and senators from New Castle County.

Rural dominance might have suggested legislative sympathy for the plight of the farmers who complained of the railroad's high freight rates. Sympathy there may have been, but no action was forthcoming. It would not have been easy for the mostly small-time men chosen to represent the people to go up against the Pennsylvania Railroad, the largest corporate power in the United States and owner of the Delaware Railroad. The Pennsylvania Railroad kept a lobbyist in the State House every day the General Assembly was in session to prevent any action that might adversely impact its interests. In addition there were the free passes to consider. The time was gone when most legislators traveled by horse and stayed in Dover throughout the session. Now, many traveled to and from Dover daily on the railroad. The railroad's management graciously gave free passes to the legislators. Critics considered those gifts a form of bribery.

Service in the General Assembly failed to attract the state's best talent in the final years of the nineteenth century. Legislative activities were so mundane, the assembly's powers so ineffectually exercised, and its political factionalism so nasty that most men of substance—rising lawyers, well-educated farm owners, and successful businessmen—either refused to run for office or served only a single term. Such men could not have found their service very meaningful or even comfortable.

The General Assembly's physical facilities were deplorable. In 1885 the House and Senate chambers had become so cold that frailer members were forced to leave. Those who wrapped up and stuck it out through the frigid mid-winter weather were sickened by the stench that arose from the cesspool that lay under the building. The "foul air," they complained, "permeates every part of the building." Disgusted by those unhealthy conditions, the assembly finally resolved to install steam heat in the State House and to connect the building to the Dover sewer system.[1]

The biennial sessions were long and tedious. Legislators devoted much of their time to a plethora of minor concerns that centered primarily on granting divorces, perpetually rearranging school-district boundaries, approving the laying out of myriad dirt roads often intended to suit private landowners, and approving the ditching of marshes. Delaware's legislatively granted divorces were an embarrassment to respectable people. Years earlier the legislature had tried to shift divorce decisions to the courts, but the legislation still left an opening for the assembly to continue to grant divorces. In the late nineteenth century, wealthy couples who decided to divorce hired lawyers and went before a court. It was those with little means who petitioned for divorces from the General Assembly, where there would be no hearing and no precedents that legislators would be compelled to follow. Much of the first two weeks of every legislative session was consumed with handling divorce petitions. In 1891, a typical year, the legislature granted fifty-four such petitions.

The Bayard House barroom. The Bayard House stood at the corner of Loockerman Street and Governor's Avenue. During the 1890s the hotel was the unofficial headquarters for John E. Addicks and supporters. (Courtesy of the Delaware Public Archives)

Another major legislative activity was chartering corporations. Most states had enacted general incorporation laws in the pre-war era, but not Delaware. Now the assemblymen were paying the price of their predecessors' decision. Many charter applicants were nonprofit organizations such as churches, women's charity organizations, patriotic societies, and the like. Businesses also applied to the assembly for the privilege of incorporation. Most business petitioners were in-state, but sometimes non-Delawareans sought incorporation in Delaware. Those were called "foreign" corporations.

By the 1890s Delaware was one of only four states that had no general corporation law. The legislature had made several attempts to adopt such a law, but their efforts had been narrowly defined and did not encompass business corporations, which all agreed constituted the most significant category. Legislators seemed to lack the will or the expertise to draft a general incorporation law that a majority could support. They, therefore, soldiered on, still granting petitions written by lawyers who represented businesses asking for individually constructed corporate privileges.

The Dover Railroad Station, where legislators arrived and departed from the capital, stood at the western end of Loockerman Street. (Courtesy of the Delaware Public Archives)

Pressure to enact a general corporation law finally reached the boiling point in the late 1880s. The catalyst for action came in the 1890s when the legislature granted a charter to the Peninsular Investment Company. The head of the company was John Edward O'Sullivan Addicks, a Philadelphia-born resident of Claymont whose financial interests in urban gas companies had earned him the nickname the "Napoleon of Gas." From the proposed company's name the assemblymen presumed that the company intended to invest in some new enterprise on the Delmarva Peninsula. But they were wrong. Addicks had bamboozled them with the name to get their assent to a corporation with broadly defined powers by which he intended to control a Boston gas company. Many legislators and others who followed legislative affairs were furious. They were soon to have greater reasons to be enraged by Mr. Addicks and his unorthodox methods.

John Edward O'Sullivan Addicks (1841-1919). Known as the "Napoleon of Gas," his effort to induce the Delaware legislature to elect him to the United States Senate split the state's Republican Party and preoccupied the General Assembly from 1889 until 1906. (Courtesy of the Historical Society of Delaware)

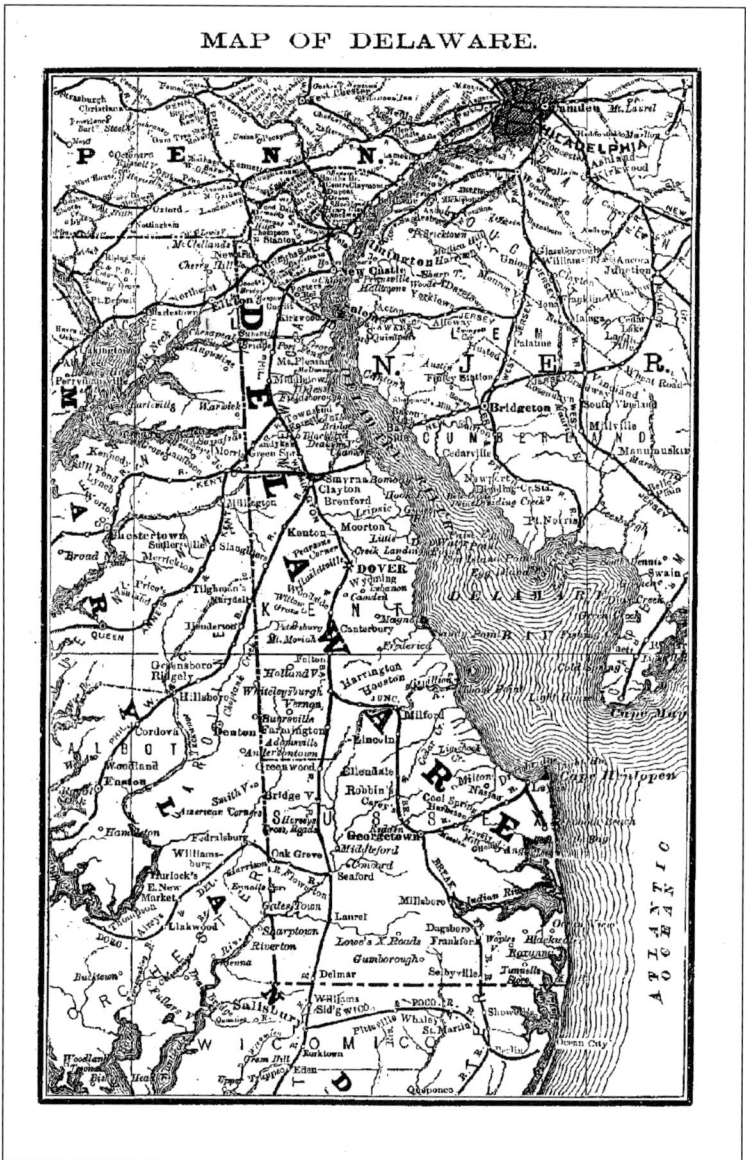

This map from 1885 illustrates the importance of railroads to late-nineteenth-century commerce and travel. Except for those who lived in or near Dover, legislators reached the capital by rail and many returned home most evenings during legislative sessions. (Courtesy of the Delaware Public Archives)

The Addicks phenomenon is surely among the most bizarre in the history of Delaware. By the time of his Peninsular Investment Company deception, Addicks had already acquired a reputation as a financial buccaneer. Having achieved wealth through his gas franchises, he turned his attention to the quest for political power and the prestige of high office. He decided to become a United States senator from Delaware.

The General Assembly elected the state's United States senators by majority vote in joint session. Since the Democrats held the upper hand in the legislature during the post-Civil War years, their candidates inevitably won. The Democrats maintained their control in part because of the poll tax legislation they had enacted in 1873 to prevent blacks, and anyone else the Democratic assessors didn't like, from voting. Fraud was rampant throughout Delaware's voting system. Poor party loyalists received money to pay their poll taxes, and, if that failed to secure the vote, other tactics came into play to prevent the taxes of one's opponents from being paid. Given the existing corruption of the ballot, the small size of the state, and a split within the ranks of the Democratic Party in 1888, the situation was ready made for a political adventurer such as John Edward Addicks.

In 1888 the dispute among the state's Democrats gave the Republicans a majority in the legislative session to commence in January 1889. The triumphant Republicans could not have anticipated the political roller coaster that awaited them. On the day that the assemblymen were gathering in Dover, John E. Addicks entered the lobby of the Hotel Richardson and, standing before a group of astonished Republican legislators, announced his candidacy for Delaware's vacant seat in the United States Senate. More astonishing still, the gas magnate predicted that he would win the upcoming contest. Some of his audience may not have known who he was, but his long golden moustache and immaculate attire, including a high silk hat, sealskin coat, and gold-headed cane, surely made an unforgettable impression.

A few days later the legislators gathered in joint session to hear Governor Benjamin T. Biggs give his address. Governors always laid their suggestions for legislative action before the General Assembly, which typically ignored them. Not since the days of the Penns had governors possessed the power to compel the legislature's attention, much less its action. Regardless of whether his party held the majority or not, the governor was not a powerful figure in Delaware politics. Governor after governor had urged the legislature to improve the schools, provide decent care for the insane, build a penitentiary (also called a workhouse) for criminals' rehabilitation, and undertake other reforms, usually to little effect. On this occasion, Governor Biggs did not disappoint. In his remarks he renewed those time-honored pleas. He also criticized the legislators for lavishing so much time and attention on insignificant matters such as granting divorces, "changing the school districts and laying out, opening, and vacating roads," all of which, he said, amounted to "a waste of time."[2]

Members of the House of Representatives elected in 1888 posed on the front steps of the State House for the first group portrait of Delaware legislators known to exist. These were the first House members to confront John E. Addicks' quest for a seat in the U.S. Senate. (Courtesy of the Delaware Public Archives)

In contrast to those relatively trivial activities, Governor Biggs drew the General Assembly's attention to a truly important concern: the corruption of the election process by "wholesale bribery." He declared that "the use of money at elections everywhere is alarmingly on the increase. That use has, in this State, become so great as to call forth a protest by all who favor the purity of the ballot." In Delaware, he said, "the votes of men are openly bartered for," a practice that called into question "the safety of the state, its welfare and its good name."[3]

The assembly was not wholly unresponsive to the governor's message. The legislature adopted a bill to assist New Castle County in the construction of the building at Farnhurst that in 1889 became the State Hospital for the Insane. The hospital's superintendent boasted that the assembly's timely action made "proud, plucky, little Delaware" the first state in the nation to assume responsibility for the institutional care of all its mental-health patients.[4]

The assembly failed, however, to heed Governor Biggs's plea to reform the election process. Instead, the members spent much of their time balloting for a new United States senator. The Republicans held the majority and would have had an easy time electing their candidate had they not been divided between choosing Anthony Higgins, a longtime party loyalist, and the newcomer, John E. Addicks. To the surprise of many it took forty-three ballots for Higgins to win election.

The Democrats won majorities in the next two biennial elections. In 1891 the legislature took a step toward election reform by adopting the secret ballot, also called the Australian ballot. The new law was seriously flawed, however, by a provision that permitted an "assistant" to accompany a voter into the voting booth. Allegedly that provision was necessary because the ballot was so long and complicated that few could understand it without help. In reality, however, the Voter's Assistant Law was an invitation to corruption.

In 1893 Addicks began to campaign in earnest for a seat in the United States Senate. In Democratic Kent County and in Sussex County he paid the poll taxes of potential Republican voters and provided campaign funds to Republican candidates. His money gave vitality to the GOP in parts of the state that had been solidly Democratic since the nearly forgotten days of John M. Clayton. The Republicans of southern Delaware felt ignored by their state party chiefs in Wilmington. Addicks provided a way for them to succeed in spite of the upstate party leaders' neglect. Addicks's tactics produced a Republican majority in the General Assembly in 1894. The gas king boasted that it had cost him $140,000. But he could not purchase the affection of New Castle County's established Republican leaders. The lawyers and businessmen of Wilmington labeled him a "carpetbagger" and vowed to block his senatorial aspirations.

The General Assembly session of 1895 provided a test of strength for the Republican factions. On January 1, the opening day, Governor Robert Reynolds admonished the legislators to uphold the "honor of the State" against "the taint or suspicion of corruption." The ballot, he said, should be the expression of the voter's intent, not a commodity for sale. He warned that if reforms were not made "the end of free government is not far distant."[5] Two weeks later the houses began voting to choose a United States senator to fill Anthony Higgins's expired term. The first day the vote was split among several candidates from both parties. The second day's vote produced two more inconclusive ballots.

Every day thereafter the houses adjourned at midday to meet in joint session to resume the balloting. Addicks's supporters shouted their slogan "Addicks or Nobody" as they held firm to their six unshakable votes. Higgins held onto nine other Republican votes. The votes of the remaining legislators were spread among several Democrats and other Republican candidates.[6]

Day after day the voting continued. Recognizing that Higgins could not get a majority, the anti-Addicks Republicans substituted other names that they hoped might attract enough additional votes to win. On May 8 they placed Colonel

Henry Algernon du Pont's name in nomination. The seignior of Winterthur, a Medal of Honor winner from the Civil War, did a bit better than the others, but he, too, failed to secure the necessary majority. The assembly voted forty-eight times that day without gaining a winner. On the following day, May 9, the final day of the session, the assemblymen balloted twenty-eight times. At one point it appeared that du Pont had won by one vote, but it proved an illusion. No one could win in that frustrating, crazy time.

The Republican governor had just died, and under the Constitution of 1831 his successor was the president of the Senate, a Democrat. The Senate president/governor chose that moment to insist on his right to vote, and du Pont's majority of one dissolved into a tie. The anti-Addicks Republicans were livid with rage. It was clear that no more could be done for any candidate, so the embittered and exhausted assembly members adjourned *sine die* at three o'clock in the afternoon. There had been 210 fruitless ballots in all. Delaware would be one United States senator short in the next Congress.

The split in Delaware's Republican Party appeared irreconcilable. In 1896 the Addicks faction proclaimed itself the Union Republicans and held a convention separate from that of the Regular Republicans. A Democrat, Ebe W. Tunnell of Sussex County, won the governor's race that year, and the Democrats successfully challenged enough of Addicks's candidates for the legislature to secure Democratic control in the 1897 session. Freed from Republican dominance, the Democrats elected their own candidate, George Gray, to fill the seat in the United States Senate that had lain vacant for two years.

Despite the acrimony that characterized Delaware's politics in the late-nineteenth century, citizens from all factions recognized the need for a new state constitution. During that interval of relative political calm no one in any faction doubted that the basic structure of government in Delaware needed improvement. The only obstacle was the Constitution of 1831, whose authors had defined a laborious process for the replacement of their work. It took the passage of a constitutional amendment in the legislature of 1893 and an overwhelming vote in the general election of 1894 to fulfill the constitutional requirements. Finally in 1896 the voters chose delegates, ten from each county, from slates proposed by the two parties. The disputed outcome in Kent was resolved by compromise, and the final result produced an almost evenly balanced convention composed of sixteen Democrats and fourteen Republicans.[7]

The thirty delegates held the first of their many meetings on December 1, 1896. They met on the second floor of the newly completed library building adjacent to the State House. Among their number were several prominent lawyers, including William C. Spruance and Edward G. Bradford of New Castle County and Charles F. Richards of Sussex County, all Republicans. Leading Democratic members were J. Wilkins Cooch of New Castle County and William Saulsbury of Kent County. Many delegates were businessmen and farmers, and nearly all participated actively in the vigorous debates that were to occupy them for the next six months. We are very fortunate to have a complete stenographic copy of the convention's proceedings, published in five large volumes in 1897. Those volumes give a rare look into life in the First State at the end of the nineteenth century; and they provide the reasoning behind provisions in the constitution that, with some modifications, still governs the state over a century later.

The Hotel Richardson, built in 1881 in the triangle at the intersections of State Street, Loockerman Street, and the King's Highway, was the most elegant of Dover's late-nineteenth-century hotels. It was here that John E. Addicks first announced his candidacy for the U.S. Senate before an astonished group of Republican legislators. The building was demolished in the 1950s to make way for a branch office of the Wilmington Trust Company. (Courtesy of the Delaware Public Archives)

The bitter divisions that wracked Delaware politics, particularly within the Republican Party, were mercifully absent from the convention's discussions. Regardless of political affiliation, a majority of the delegates agreed that Delaware's new constitution should be modeled on the United States Constitution and that it should aim to eliminate vote buying. The delegates were equally determined to force the General Assembly to enact a comprehensive corporation law. The delegates were well prepared for their work, fortified by reading the constitutions of many other states, including the recently rewritten documents of New Jersey and New York. In the course of their deliberations they frequently referred to those state constitutions as guides and examples.

In 1896, 120 years after Delaware adopted its first constitution as a free and independent state, its government still retained the all-powerful legislature and weak executive that had seemed appropriate to a people who were in the process of overthrowing a king and a proprietary governor. Times had changed since 1776, and even since 1831, when a very slightly altered constitution had been put in place. It was clear to the delegates, especially to those among them who had served in the General Assembly or had done business with it, that Delaware's government was in serious need of repair. The delegates recognized that the tradition of localism and the insistence on county sovereignty that had characterized Delaware since colonial days was no longer fair nor effective.

Delaware needed a structure of government that would permit the state to take on additional responsibilities. The effects of modernization in transportation, industry, and communication had increased the demands for state government services and for state intervention beyond what a part-time law-making body and a nearly powerless governor could provide. The delegates were aware of the many complaints about laws that were poorly conceived and poorly written, or were merely the expressions of whichever private interests had gotten to the General Assembly first. In addition, because there was so little legislative memory, contradictory and overlapping laws that defied interpretation cluttered the law books.

The legislature's most conspicuous problem was evident from how the House and Senate spent their time and effort. Delegates to the convention who had served in the legislature and had sat through long legislative sessions reported their disgust at the pace at which the General Assembly worked. Members waited around with little to do during the early weeks of a session only to be rushed at the end to vote on laws that they hardly had time to read. More disturbing still, a plethora of private issues ranging from divorces to ditches occupied too much of the assembly's attention.

Based on the experiences of those who had served in the General Assembly, the convention delegates agreed to remove such minor activities from the assembly's supervision and to distribute them among other branches of government that were better suited to handle them. The delegates expected that a legislature freed from many mundane but time-consuming activities would direct its energies toward more important legislative concerns, such as public welfare, the improvement of public education, and the quality of the state's wretched roadways.

The new constitution provided a tentative step toward the reform of Delaware's segregated approach to public education. The delegates provided equal state funds to support the schools of both races. The new constitution did not, however, require the legislature to alter the practice whereby taxpayers of each race paid separately to provide the bulk of funding to support the schools within each segregated school district. That practice was not eliminated until the enactment of the School Code of 1919.

The convention also altered the structure of public education. The delegates made the office of state superintendent a permanent position in Delaware's government. The legislature had created the post of superintendent in 1875, but had discarded it twelve years later in favor of county superintendents. Some delegates argued that compulsory school attendance should also be a constitutional provision. When rural delegates pointed out that some rural children lived as far as seven miles from the nearest school, the convention equivocated. They wrote into the constitution: "The General Assembly . . . may require by law that every child . . . shall attend public school. . . ."[8] It would be up to a future General Assembly to get beyond the word "may."

The convention delegates included a constitutional provision to require the assembly to adopt a general incorporation statute. Recollection of the Peninsular Investment Company charter still rankled, but it was only one case among a number of instances where petitioners had badgered the legislators into making unwise concessions to private companies. Delegates were especially uneasy about the power that the railroads, especially the Pennsylvania, had over the legislature. Merely by giving the legislators free passes, the railroad company appeared to have the Delaware General Assembly in the palms of their mighty hands. The delegates expected that a general corporation law would resolve those problems by removing the General Assembly's power to grant or withhold special favors to specific corporations. Judging from the effect of New Jersey's recently enacted incorporation statute, a liberally written general corporation law might also generate income since firms would pay a fee to the state for the privilege of incorporating in Delaware.

The delegates eagerly set about constructing a framework in which legislative sessions could be shorter and yet more productive. Complaints had been heard around the state that the assemblymen deliberately dragged out their sessions in order to increase their per-diem pay. The convention considered, but ultimately rejected, a plan to limit regular biennial sessions to sixty days and special sessions to twenty days. They did, however, agree to limit per-diems to that number of days. It was generally believed that the legislators could get more work done in fewer days if they spent their nights as well as their days in Dover during the sessions. The evening committee meetings that had speeded along legislative action in the horse-and-buggy days had all but disappeared in the railroad era because too few assemblymen remained in Dover overnight to conduct business. The convention's members hoped to change that pattern.

The most forward-looking among the convention delegates recognized that the model of a weak governor that had seemed suitable in the wake of colonialism was no longer tenable. By the 1890s the legislature was taking on responsibilities that required executive oversight. In 1879 the legislature had created the post of insurance commissioner. Later legislatures added a Board of Agriculture and the hospital at Farnhurst, which like all similar state boards, commissions, and institutions reported to the legislature, not to the governor.

It seemed likely that the state would also soon take responsibility for the prisoners in county jails. Already there were plans afoot in New Castle County to build Delaware's first workhouse. In 1899, two years after the new constitution went into effect, the General Assembly gave the county permission to bond itself to construct the workhouse. Designed to incarcerate convicts from all three counties, the building had the potential to become a state facility. In 1907 the assembly gave the courts of Kent and Sussex counties permission to send their long-term convicts to the New Castle County Workhouse.⁹

In response to those developments, the delegates increased the power of the courts and the governor at the expense of the assembly. Today we would use the term "checks and balances" to describe their idea of the best way to distribute power among the three branches of government. Although that expression was never used in the convention, the concept was at the heart of the convention delegates' decision to make the courts the sole authorities over divorces and interpretation of the incorporation law, and to give the governor the power to veto legislation passed by the assembly and to administer the state's growing bureaucracy.

The veto power was the key to strengthening the governor's power in dealing with the legislature. Colonial governors had exercised the veto absolutely. When the Penn family maintained the Lower Counties as part of their proprietorship, governors and the leaders of the assembly had met to work out their differences in order that laws might be adopted. Give and take between the executive and the legislature had disappeared with the Revolution and had never been replaced. For over a century governors had pleaded in vain with legislatures to enact one piece of legislation or another, but the governor had no bargaining chips to play against the all-powerful, but often leaderless, General Assembly.

Not all delegates believed that the governor should have the veto power. Some believed that a simple legislative majority should be sufficient to override the governor's negative, but this would have been no veto at all. A majority of the delegates accepted the proposition that the legislature would take greater care in drafting bills knowing that the governor would scrutinize them before he signed. With that concept in mind, debate then centered on whether the number of legislative votes needed to override should be two thirds or three fifths. It was typical of the spirit of the convention that they adopted the compromise figure of three fifths.

The delegates also voted to give the governor the item veto in money bills, a power denied to the president of the United States but available to the governors of many states. Their decision to permit governors to run for a second four-year term was also intended to strengthen the office and to make service as governor more attractive to able candidates. On the other side of the equation, the new constitution adopted the federal model of requiring the Senate's consent to confirm the growing number of gubernatorial appointments to administrative positions and to the judiciary.

The creation of the office of lieutenant governor marked another important change in the relationship of the executive to the legislative branch. Under Delaware's earlier constitutions, the Senate, like the House, selected its own presiding officer, called the speaker, from among its members. In that plan, the speaker of the Senate had replaced the governor if the chief executive died or became incapacitated. That provision had occasionally produced painfully awkward situations, as when the Republican governor Joshua H. Marvil died in 1895 and the Democratic presiding officer of the Senate who took his place insisted on maintaining his right to vote in the Senate and had thereby denied Henry Algernon du Pont a seat in the United States Senate.

The office of lieutenant governor was in some ways similar to that of vice-president of the United States. The lieutenant governor would be the state's second-ranking officer and was to be elected statewide. Unlike federal practice, however, the governor and lieutenant governor were not to run for office as a team. In the future the lieutenant governor, like the vice-president of the United States, would preside over the Senate and be empowered to vote in order to break a tie. The Senate would elect its own president pro tempore who would be its chief internal officer and would preside over the Senate in the lieutenant governor's absence.

The change that became the greatest hallmark of the Constitution of 1897 was the redistribution of seats in the legislature. Ever since William Penn had convened the first meeting of the General Assembly in 1682 legislators had been chosen in countywide at-large elections to represent the people of their counties, and each county had had an equal number of assemblymen. Initially, when the population of the three counties was roughly equal, this system made sense, but by the 1890s it was grossly unfair. According to the federal census of 1890, 97,182 of Delaware's 168,493 people lived in New Castle County. What's more, nearly two thirds of New Castle County residents lived within the boundaries of Wilmington. The city's population was only a bit less than those of Kent and Sussex counties combined, and the city's population was growing far faster than that of any other part of the state. In light of demographic developments, Edward G. Bradford, a delegate from the Wilmington area, maintained that the county sovereignty so dear to inhabitants of Kent and Sussex had become "trivial if not grotesque."[10]

The convention delegates addressed the issue of representation in several ways. First, they decided that henceforth members of both houses of the General Assembly would be elected from districts, not at large. Second, after a long debate, they agreed to award New Castle County a small number of additional seats to be filled from the city of Wilmington. Third, they enlarged both houses of the legislature.

The constitutions of 1776, 1792, and 1831 had mandated a Senate of nine members, three from each county, and a House of Representatives of twenty-one members, seven from each county. By contrast, the constitution of 1897 created a Senate of seventeen members to include five each from districts in Kent and Sussex counties and seven from districts in New Castle County, of whom two were be elected from Wilmington. The new constitution required that senators be at least twenty-seven years of age, as opposed to twenty-four in the lower house, and it retained the old constitution's provision that senatorial terms be four years. Notably, no one among the delegates disagreed with the convention's decision to remove the wealth requirement for membership in the Senate.

The Constitution of 1897 aimed to make the Senate a more effective legislative body. The Senate had evolved from the colonial governor's council and had never functioned well in its legislative capacity. Delegate William C. Spruance of New Castle County posited that "there isn't much standing of manly discussion and debate in the senate of Delaware, and never has been . . . . You cannot very well get up a lively debate when one man stands up and addresses his whole audience, his eight others, and it doesn't amount to much." As a result, he said, lobbyists had gained great power over the body. Another delegate described an ideal Senate as one where members would be so broad-minded as to think and act with regard to the best interests of the state as a whole, rather than to focus on the interests of their own districts, as he expected members of the lower house to do.[11] In theory at least, longer terms and larger districts would accomplish this hoped-for broad senatorial vision.

There were to be thirty-five members in the new House of Representatives in contrast to twenty-one under the former constitution. Sussex and Kent counties were to have ten districts apiece, and New Castle County was to have fifteen districts to include ten from the rural portion of the county and five from the city of Wilmington. Members of the lower house would continue to be elected every two years to insure that they kept in close touch with popular opinion.

It doesn't take a mathematical genius to recognize that the concession made to the premier city of the state was scant indeed. In fact, Wilmington actually lost power in the legislature because its voters could no longer control the election of New Castle County's entire delegation to the General Assembly as had become the case in at-large elections. In a convention that was otherwise remarkably free from angry cant, the issue of Wilmington's representation brought out the worst. The delegates wrangled all winter over the issue of the city's representation. Some delegates from the southern counties were determined to maintain the concept of county sovereignty that had reigned from the days of the Three Lower Counties on Delaware. By their thinking, the counties, not districts or people, were represented in the General Assembly. The concept of county equality had governed the composition of the constitutional convention itself. To expect a group so constituted to give Wilmingtonians the democratic representation inherent in their numbers was beyond the most sanguine hopes of the city's supporters.

Wilmington's delegates confronted a hostile and suspicious audience. A delegate from Seaford in Sussex County characterized Wilmington as "an immense octopus that had its tentacles throughout the state."[12] Farmers had been hit hard by the agricultural depression of the late nineteenth century, and everywhere throughout the land, including Delaware, they focused blame on the prosperous and populous cities where bankers and railroad executives ruled, immigrant workers toiled, and nobody felt the ties to the land as did a farm owner trying to earn a living from a diminishing resource.

Much of the convention's work was done in committees. The delegates from each county met together to decide on the boundaries of their county's legislative districts. When they had reached agreement, they then presented their recommendations to the full body. After much discussion and some disagreements, the boundaries that emerged from the process generally followed the lines of the existing hundreds in each county. Because the districts were embedded into the constitution, they could not be altered except through a deliberately difficult amendment process. As a result, those provisions remained in place until the United States Supreme Court overturned them in 1964.

Convention members often expressed the hope that the enlarged General Assembly would behave more responsibly than its predecessors had sometimes done. The convention delegates foresaw a legislature where the serious consideration and thoughtful debate of issues would replace the power of lobbyists. That concept lay at the heart of the constitutional provision mandating that the assembly enact a general corporation statute. Not all delegates agreed. William Saulsbury, a Democratic lawyer from Dover, argued that general incorporation laws were perhaps necessary in large states, but not in Delaware where legislators knew everybody. His argument might have held merit in the distant past, but by the 1890s the Delaware legislators were receiving petitions for incorporation from out-of-state companies. The argument that a general law would eliminate the bribery that, it was claimed, was too often part of the process no doubt influenced many delegates to reject Saulsbury's view.

When it became clear that Delaware was to have a general incorporation statute, William Saulsbury abruptly changed his position. He told his fellow delegates to look to the provisions of New Jersey's recently enacted incorporation act as an appropriate model for Delaware.[13] An unconvinced delegate asked Saulsbury how, aside from collecting fees, New Jersey benefited from incorporating firms whose principal businesses were in New York. Saulsbury replied, "that is where it does good, the money it puts into the Treasury. That amount would be enough to run our State Government, schools and everything else." He characterized New Jersey's policy as "liberal" as opposed to the "narrow, restrictive and hampering policy in some other states." Then rising to his full eloquence, the delegate from Dover said, "I want our State to reach the highest possible point of development. I do not want to give unjust powers to corporations. I want the Legislature . . . to use reasonable and proper care. But if corporations can be induced to come to our State to take out their charters and pay their money into our State Treasury and relieve our people from taxation, instead of going to New Jersey to get their charters—I would like to have them come here . . . ."[14] In that statement lay Delaware's strategy for enacting a corporation law whose effects have surely eclipsed William Saulsbury's fondest dreams. Moreover, with a general corporation law the state's courts, rather than its legislature, would decide disputes that involved companies incorporated in Delaware.

The delegates recognized that their efforts to improve Delaware's government would amount to nothing if vote buying were to continue to corrupt state politics. They were experienced men and were under pressure from many citizens to do something effective to put an end to blatant corruption of the ballot. The convention's Committee on Elections searched mightily to find a formula to curb the blight that affected their beloved state's reputation for governmental integrity. It was not an easy task because all manner of election frauds abounded. Party workers and candidates paid poll taxes for poor citizens. Fake names were added to the election rolls while those of legitimate voters mysteriously disappeared. Bribery was commonplace. The Voters' Assistants were really political enforcers.

Delegates admitted that both parties engaged in those deceits. To counteract them, the convention members considered various tactics to reclaim what they called "the purity of the ballot." William Spruance, an anti-Addicks Wilmington Republican, urged the convention to eliminate the poll tax and to make it illegal to disqualify a voter for non-payment of taxes. The convention agreed to those reforms, but then imposed an undemocratic literacy test, supposedly to keep those most susceptible to bribery from voting.[15] Some delegates argued unsuccessfully for a clause to deny jury trials to those accused of voter fraud. Disagreement over the imposition of a voter-registration fee proved to be so divisive that the convention ultimately decided to leave the matter for the General Assembly to resolve.[16]

Woman's suffrage was another election-related issue to come before the convention. The National American Woman Suffrage Association and the Delaware Equal Suffrage Association made a strong effort to win the convention's support for votes for women in the First State. Major national leaders, including the redoubtable NAWSA president Carrie Chapman Catt, were invited to appear before the convention to present arguments for woman's suffrage. Margaret Houston representing the Equal Suffrage Club of Sussex County made the most memorably persuasive case. She urged the delegates: "As the little Diamond State was the first to adopt the [U.S.] Constitution, so let her be first of her Eastern sisters to enfranchise the woman."[17]

The men paid attention. Delegate David S. Clark took the floor to argue in favor of woman's suffrage on the grounds that women would "raise the moral standard" of public life.[18] But in the end Edward G. Bradford's observation that women, although the equals of men in intelligence, were best confined to their own "sphere" won the delegates' vote by 17 to 7.[19] The suffragists were disappointed that Delaware had turned down its opportunity to be the first East Coast state to extend democracy to its women. But they were not discouraged and looked forward to carrying on their fight.

The convention had to decide how the new constitution was to be implemented and amended. Early in their sessions, J. Wilkins Cooch proposed that the constitution be submitted to the voters for ratification. His democratic view was shared by the General Assembly, but it was not in the tradition of earlier constitutional convention documents in Delaware, except for the document of 1852, which the voters had rejected. Cooch's proposal was defeated. There would be no ratification process. The convention decreed that the new constitution would go into effect on June 10, 1897, just six days after the delegates completed their work.

An equally undemocratic view prevailed respecting the amendment process. To prevent easy or hasty changes to the document, the convention decreed that amendments could only be made following a two-thirds vote of two successive general assemblies. The standard was above that needed to overturn a gubernatorial veto. Given the nature of two-party politics and inter-county rivalries, it was a standard that would prove nearly impossible to meet. The majority's primary fear was that at some future time New Castle County, and especially the city of Wilmington, would find a means to increase their constitutionally established representation in the General Assembly. The hurdles built into the amendment process virtually guaranteed that rural power would continue to predominate in the legislature and prevent that change, no matter how great the population of Wilmington might become.

During the early months of 1897, while the convention met in the new library annex, the General Assembly held its regular biennial meeting next door in the State House. The assembly faced several ugly disputes over contested elections, but overall the session proved less contentious than its predecessor. The Democrats had the votes to elect their candidate to the United States Senate seat that had lain vacant for two years.

In 1898 the members returned to Dover for a special session to enact legislation required to carry out the mandates of the new constitution. It would be the final meeting of the General Assembly elected under the constitution of 1831. Governor Ebe Tunnell opened the special session by reminding the assemblymen that the new constitution "has placed around you many restrictions and has deprived you of many . . . powers." No longer would the assemblymen "be annoyed by divorce legislation so disgraceful to our state," nor would they be "called to sit in judgment on conflicting claims and disputes of corporations involving questions which a legislative body finds so difficult to understand and intelligently deal with." No more would local fences, stray animals, ditches, and similar minor matters consume their time.

To make that transition, the assembly was required to enact a plethora of new laws. The legislators were asked to adopt a new divorce law, to replace the poll tax with a capitation tax, to create permanent boards of agriculture and health, to increase the state's control over the public schools, and to bring into being the mechanisms necessary to fulfill other constitutional mandates, including, most importantly, the enactment of a general corporation law. By hiring three lawyers, one from each county, to do the most complex work, the legislators accomplished all the tasks required of them, except that of the corporation law. That job was left to the next legislature, which would be elected in the fall of 1898 according to the terms laid out in the new constitution.

Not least among the special session's accomplishments was the assignment of space in the newly refitted and enlarged State House. Offices for the governor, state treasurer, secretary of state, auditor of accounts, judiciary, and state librarian were located on the first floor. To mark the governor's new powers, the assembly voted to provide him with a stenographer and a new technological device called a typewriter.

The expanded legislature was given rooms on the second and third floors for their exclusive use. The legislators took pains to repair and re-hang their portrait of George Washington. The massive painting had been acquired so long ago that the assemblymen needed the services of a historian to research its background. News of the improvements to the state government's home encouraged private citizens to contribute portraits of past governors. The assembly gratefully accepted those gifts and hung the portraits in the State House.[20]

The first session of the fifty-two member General Assembly convened in its newly expanded quarters in the State House on January 3, 1899. The first piece of legislation to come before them was "An Act providing a general corporation law." The bill drew liberally from New Jersey's corporation law of 1896. It permitted companies incorporated in Delaware to do business anywhere in the United States or beyond its borders. It laid down rules to cover stockholders' meetings, the sale of stock, and the dissolution and merger of corporations. The bill prescribed rules to govern several types of business enterprises that were especially significant at the time, including railroads, gas and water providers, and telegraph and telephone companies. The bill also described the role of the state chancellor as arbiter of legal disputes involving Delaware corporations. Another related bill fixed the incorporation fees and annual fees that companies would pay to Delaware's secretary of state for the privilege of being incorporated in Delaware. The fee structure was strategically positioned to be just under that of New Jersey. The bills passed both houses of the legislature unanimously and were signed into law on March 10, 1899.[21]

The unanimity that speeded the corporation bills through the General Assembly was in complete contrast to the political warfare that otherwise governed the session. In the House of Representatives it took ninety-two ballots to elect a speaker. That exhausting contest was merely a prelude to what followed. The assembly had to select a United States senator to replace Democrat George Gray, whose term was at an end. The Democrats held a one-vote majority in the Senate. The Republicans held the majority in the House. Since there were more Republicans than Democrats in the combined houses, the GOP would have had a majority except for the fact that the Republicans remained hopelessly split between the "Addicks or nobody" faction and the "anybody but Addicks" faction. Day in and day out the tedious balloting continued with no end in sight. Suspicions rose and tempers flared when a few turncoat Democrats agreed to support the Republican "carpetbagger" Addicks in early March. The stratagem failed. When the assembly finally adjourned after 113 fruitless ballots Delaware was once more one United States senator short.

The General Assembly convened its first meeting of the twentieth century on January 1, 1901. Outgoing Governor Ebe Tunnell happily reported that in 1899, the corporation law's first year of operation, the secretary of state had collected

$69,000, and that money from corporation fees was continuing to pour into the state. He cautioned, however, that the public impression "that the state treasury is suddenly overflowing" was exaggerated, especially in light of the needs of Delaware's schools to increase teachers' salaries to cover the recently lengthened school year.[22]

The first known photograph of the House of Representatives in session, taken in 1897. This was the legislature's last meeting under the Constitution of 1831. Note the gas lamps, shuttered windows, wall clock, and carpeting that decorated the House chamber of the 1890s. The House then met on the second floor of an extension, since removed from the rear of the State House. (Courtesy of the Delaware Public Archives)

On a less optimistic note, Governor Tunnell reported that the election reforms contained in the Constitution of 1897 had failed to fulfill their goal. In the general election of 1900, he said, "bribery, corruption, and intimidation walked brazenly through our state . . . ."[23] Legislators chosen through recourse to such methods may have blushed at the accusation as they prepared to do battle on behalf of the party or faction to which they owed their seats. Once more the chief activity of the assembly was fixed on seemingly endless balloting for the United States Senate seat that ever-eluded John E. Addicks and his competitors.

The most exciting event to emerge from the balloting tedium of 1901 was a Sussex Democrat's claim that he had been offered a bribe to assist Addicks's election. An ad hoc legislative committee held a public hearing designed to publicize the allegation. The story was that the young representative from Nanticoke Hundred had been riding the train en route to a dance in Wilmington when a well-known Addicks lieutenant offered him a sum of money rumored to be $1,500 or $2,000 to be absent from the legislature's next meeting. It was an old legislative trick for one or more members to absent themselves from an important vote to reduce the size of the whole and thus make it easier to secure a majority. Instead of playing along, the legislator squealed and the stratagem failed. Although the committee reported that the evidence was inconclusive, the Addicks faction sustained a public black eye.[24] The voting went on. After forty-five ballots Delaware still had no one elected to hold either of its two seats in the United States Senate.

In between their fruitless balloting, the legislators managed to enact some important measures. The state legislature was gradually asserting its responsibility over activities that had once been the province of local and county government. The assembly provided funding for the State Hospital for the Insane. It assisted the completion of the New Castle County Workhouse that a previous legislature had authorized. A majority voted funds to provide teacher training and textbooks for the public schools. The legislators also took their first tentative steps toward applying a statewide standard for roadways and they approved the use of oyster shells to strengthen the surfaces of dirt road beds in Kent and Sussex counties.

Those important advances seemed to be drowned in the ongoing story of Addicks's quest for a seat in the United States Senate. By now the Addicks saga had made Delaware notorious throughout the United States. The popular weekly political magazine *Outlook* featured the little state's embarrassing political imbroglio in numerous articles. The state's inability to elect a United States senator allowed observers from populous states to raise the question of why little Delaware should have the right to hold its two Senate seats, especially if the state left them both unfilled. In 1902 *Outlook* sent a reporter to cover the general election in the First State. The reporter described what he saw to be "from all evidence...a carnival of vote buying," and claimed that Addicks had spent $130,000 in Kent and Sussex counties to elect General Assembly candidates pledged to him.[25]

When the assembly met in January 1903 the Republican factions agreed to compromise on the organization of the houses. But, on the day appointed for the all-important vote on United States senatorial appointments the factions deadlocked as usual. The Democrats had managed to drive an additional wedge between the Union and Regular Republicans with a proposal to eliminate the Voters' Assistant

Law. Fearing that the Regulars would strike a deal with the Democrats to outlaw the mechanism that greatly assisted Addicks's candidates' successes at the polls, the Union Republicans set aside their "Addicks or Nobody" position. Various deals were floated. The final result was a compromise by which Addicks agreed to take himself out of the running in exchange for allowing one of his supporters and one anti-Addicks Republican to be chosen to fill Delaware's two empty seats in the United States Senate. Meanwhile, the Voters' Assistance repeal moved forward. The bill gained majorities in both houses by combining the votes of the minority Democrats with those of a few Regular Republicans.[26]

In 1905 Addicks experienced business reversals. He knew his hope to claim a seat in the United States Senate had to be fulfilled now or never. Addicks refused to make further deals and pulled out all the stops to win. For the final time his ambition was thwarted. But as the former gas king's star faded that of Colonel Henry A. du Pont rose. The colonel's money was not running out, and he had in his cousin T. Coleman du Pont a crafty and determined political manager who was prepared to play the political game to win. Thus, in 1906 Colonel du Pont finally realized his ambition to be a United States senator as the bankrupt John E. Addicks drifted into obscurity. The Addicks phenomenon that had blighted Delaware's politics for over a decade was at an end, but the corrupt practices that it had generated would not be swept away for many years to come.

In retrospect the remarkable legacy of the Addicks period was one of both progress and corruption. Perhaps it took the desire to thwart corruption to induce a steadfastly complacent and conservative state to break with the past and to embrace a new constitution. Despite the bitterness engendered by the contest for the United States Senate in those years, the state legislature was setting a new course. It was beginning to grapple with issues that really affected the state's citizens, particularly public education and highways. Those issues would dominate state government in the next century.

7
THE DU PONTS AND DELAWARE, 1906-1921

Historians call the early years of the twentieth century the Progressive Period. It was a time when Americans confronted the problems and opportunities of the industrialized society that their nation had become. Progressives worked through private agencies and within government to increase opportunities to pursue "the American dream" and to bring greater fairness to economic competition. At the national level Presidents Theodore Roosevelt and Woodrow Wilson backed measures that ensured the purity of the foods Americans ate, broke up business monopolies, and recreated the nation's central banking system. At the state and local level Progressive governors and mayors instituted and expanded government services and introduced regulations on the private sector.

At first glance it might appear that tradition-bound Delaware would be slow to embrace Progressive forces. The state was just emerging from the embarrassing political trauma of the Addicks period. Its General Assembly was reactive and had generally been unwilling to commit the state to new endeavors, especially ones that cost money. The state legislature was content to permit the counties to raise most of the taxes and to provide most public services. Meanwhile, the du Pont family had become dominant in the state's politics and business. The du Ponts must have seemed anything but "Progressive." The Du Pont Company was, after all, prominent among the "trusts" that the United States Justice Department "busted."

But for all those seeming negatives, Progressive forces were about to revolutionize Delaware. The state had a new constitution that provided the opportunity for a more dynamic government, and there were people in the state who envisioned how that government might be used to improve the lives of Delawareans and to bring the First State into the new twentieth century. The General Assembly was to be the instrument through which those developments were realized.

The Progressive Movement took many forms. Its leaders were often well-educated professional people who embraced modernity and expertise as integral to social progress. While some battled big business, others embraced the efficiencies, technical sophistication, and synergy that large systems could bring not only to business enterprises but also to government bureaucracies. Within that broad framework, Thomas Coleman du Pont and Pierre Samuel du Pont were Delaware's leading Progressive reformers.

The du Pont cousins' vision, civic-mindedness, and money transformed Delaware and brought the state into the twentieth century. T. Coleman du Pont gave Delaware its first modern highway, and Pierre S. du Pont provided modern public schools to communities throughout the state. The du Pont cousins also created the professionally staffed governmental organizations that carried on and expanded their innovations.

The du Ponts could not have made those remarkable contributions without the cooperation of the General Assembly, but that cooperation was not easily achieved. The du Pont family's direct involvement in state politics came in the wake of the political storms of the Addicks era. Many Delawareans, especially rural folk, were inclined to look gift horses in the mouth. The story of the du Pont cousins' dealings with the General Assembly demonstrates the negotiation necessary for members of a wealthy elite to introduce new concepts into a conservative, democratically governed society. It is also the story of how Delaware became part of the new age.

In 1902 the Du Pont Company, America's largest manufacturer of gunpowder and explosives, celebrated its centennial year at the company's original site on the Brandywine River just northwest of Wilmington. The company was family owned and administered. About the time of the centennial the company elders had been on the verge of selling the company to its largest competitor when three cousins of the younger generation of du Ponts— Alfred I., T. Coleman, and Pierre S.—came forward to purchase the company and thus keep it in the family. T. Coleman du Pont became the company president, Pierre S. its treasurer, and Alfred I. its chief of production. For T. Coleman and Pierre, the goal of the purchase was not to continue the ways of the past, but to remake Du Pont and the entire American explosives industry into an efficiently managed monopoly under their leadership. Alfred I. remained apart from his cousins' determination to exchange the familiar ways of the past for consolidation and the imposition of new business methods.

T. Coleman du Pont was a tall, vigorous man, a native of Kentucky, a graduate of the Massachusetts Institute of Technology, and an experienced businessman. His was a dynamic, robust temperament that craved power and was alive to the opportunities made possible by new technologies. His ambitions included politics as well as business. As president of Du Pont, he moved quickly to dominate rival powder and explosive makers and then absorb them into his company. Meanwhile, he continued his dominance of Delaware's anti-Addicks Republicans, a position that he had gained when he had led Henry Algernon du Pont's campaign for the United States Senate. When Addicks ceased funding his Union Republicans after 1906, T. Coleman du Pont became the acknowledged head of the state GOP.

Among T. Coleman's passions was his love of automobiles. In the first decade of the twentieth century automobiles were expensive luxuries available only to the rich. But T. Coleman could foresee the day when autos and trucks would alter the way everyone lived and worked. His political activities gave him insight into all parts of the First State. He was acutely aware of the plight of Delaware's farmers, especially those whose farms were remote from railroads and those whose farms were too small to be able to afford the rates the railroads charged to carry their crops to market. Du Pont was a trained civil engineer and he could foresee the transformation that good roads and the internal combustion engine might mean, especially in the poorest and most remote parts of rural Delaware. Unlike most visionaries, however, T. Coleman du Pont had the money to make his vision come true. The only question was did he have sufficient persuasion, backed by the political clout, to realize his concept? If so, he could help Delaware and attract favorable state and national press upon which to build a political career that might take him to the United States Senate and even to the White House.

Du Pont's vision for a statewide system of improved roads contrasted sharply with long-established practice in Delaware. Road construction and repair had been a county responsibility since colonial times. The state legislature had the sole power to authorize the creation of roads, but the counties did the work from money that each county's levy court raised from real-estate assessments. There was no state supervision, no state standards. Most roads were unpaved, poorly drained, and rutted by wagon wheels. The motorcar posed a challenge to this low-cost, low-quality approach to transportation.

Legislators were unsure how to react to the dawning of the automobile age. In 1903 they passed an act to provide state funds for "the Permanent Improvement of the Public Highways." The law directed the governor to appoint a state highway commission charged with developing a statewide highway plan to be implemented by the counties with state assistance.[1] The next legislature repealed the act. The opposition was not so much to the use of state aid for roads, which was allowed to continue on a small scale, but to the imposition of state commissioners into county business. New Castle County, home to most of Delaware's few hundred automobiles, was authorized to appoint commissioners to rationalize its roadways, but neither of the other counties was required to do so because so few of their residents owned automobiles. The General Assembly of 1905 did recognize the growing importance of automobiles by enacting the state's first motor-vehicle registration law. The law outlawed speeding, and required cars to use lights at night and to give the right-of-way to horse-drawn vehicles.[2]

Other states were undertaking statewide programs to construct highways to accommodate the new mode of transportation, but Delaware seemed to be trapped in its tradition of county responsibility for roads. Could the perception of upstate-downstate differences in the need for modernization be resolved?

In 1908 T. Coleman du Pont announced a plan to construct the most advanced highway in the United States and to build it the length of Delaware. As was typical for that colossus of business, du Pont's plan seemed larger than life. He proposed a technically advanced concept that envisioned a broad swath of

This visualization of T. Coleman du Pont's proposal for a multi-use highway was much scaled back through political compromise by the time the General Assembly authorized construction of the du Pont Highway. (Courtesy of the Hagley Museum and Library)

highway running the length of the state to accommodate not only automobiles, but also trolleys, horse-drawn vehicles, and various communication lines. Most astonishing was du Pont's offer to pay for it all from his own pocket.

While many Delawareans greeted du Pont's proposed gift enthusiastically, others were suspicious of the millionaire's motives. Predictably, the proposal was most popular among upstate Republicans and least acceptable to downstate Democrats. Opponents suspected that the wealthy financier was planning to use the state's power of eminent domain to build a multi-channel highway from which he would profit.

Du Pont had to do a great deal of explaining to overcome perceived "gift horse" problems. Ultimately he was forced to pare back his original multi-use concept. But not all downstate residents opposed his road plan. While some farmers clung to their traditional ways, others were quick to see the benefits that a modern roadway might provide.

In its session of 1909 the General Assembly provided a forum to thrash out the issues involved in T. Coleman's unprecedented scheme, but the assembly took no action on it that year. At the next legislative session in 1911 du Pont's lawyers, former Attorney General Robert H. Richards, and Daniel O. Hastings, who was the chief counsel for the General Assembly, presented a draft bill designed to meet the legal obstacles to building the road. The chief impediment was the Corporation Act of 1899, which had established a policy that the legislature would no longer enact one-client-only charters such as du Pont had in mind.

As the road bill awaited action in the General Assembly, du Pont launched a media campaign. In February 1911 the Wilmington *Sunday Star* informed its readers that du Pont had offered $1,000,000 toward the project. A week later the paper reported that he had doubled his offer. "This plan . . . is massive," a reporter wrote. "It may, in fact, be too great a departure for Delaware." In March the paper informed its readers that du Pont had no ulterior motives and the writer observed ironically that no such suspicions had prevented scores of "greedy men" in the past from getting the assembly to enact special legislation on their behalf.[3]

Debate over the highway proposal continued until the final midnight hours of the 1911 session. Frantic to conclude their work, the legislature finally adopted the bill they had received from T. Coleman du Pont's lawyers. The bill cleverly sidestepped the general corporation statute by authorizing any corporation that wanted to give Delaware a well-designed highway the length of the state to do so. The law merely laid out the ground rules that such a corporation must follow. A qualified "Boulevard Corporation" could accept gifts of land or purchase its right-of-way. The highway could reach a maximum of 200 feet and could include lanes for several types of transport as well as communication lines. A commission composed of major state officers was to supervise the construction work, but that group could not interfere with a boulevard corporation unless the builders failed to observe the terms of the law.[4]

It would appear that du Pont had gotten all that he wanted from the

This photograph and the one opposite show the dramatic changes wrought by T. Coleman du Pont's highway. A typical mud-rutted road photographed in 1920 (above) contrasts with the intersection of the du Pont Highway (U.S. 13) with U.S. Route 40 as it appeared in 1931. (Courtesy of the Delaware Public Archives)

legislature, but there was one thing missing. His Coleman du Pont Road Corporation lacked the power to condemn land. Without the power of eminent domain, construction could proceed only as fast and as far as landowners could be persuaded to sell or give their property. If a strategically located landowner balked, the corporation could initiate condemnation proceedings, but the road builders could not take the property until a court had settled on the price.[5] In 1913 du Pont asked the legislature to give his corporation the power to proceed with construction ahead of a court's determination of a land's price. Du Pont even offered to pay farmers up to five times the current value of their properties if he could lay claim to the right-of-way immediately.

The assembly met in joint session before a large audience to hear lawyers

argue both sides of the condemnation issue. Although condemnation laws such as du Pont requested were a common practice in some states, the legislature refused to enact such a law in Delaware. Du Pont took his case to court. In 1914 the Delaware Supreme Court resolved the issue in du Pont's favor. But in the meantime, the limitation had slowed construction and was in part responsible for T. Coleman's decision to forego the wide right-of-way and multiple uses that he had originally planned to include in the project.

    The official groundbreaking for the new road took place at the border of Delaware and Maryland just below Selbyville on September 18, 1911. Among the most enthusiastic supporters of the new road was Selbyville businessman and former Union Republican legislator John G. Townsend, Jr. He was what people at the time would have called a "go getter." Townsend manifested insatiable energy and had the ability to perceive opportunities for development in what others thought was a backwater environment. Townsend was an ideal champion of the highway project. As a familiar figure at land auctions, he could purchase property for the roadway with greater ease than could T. Coleman.

    For the next several years T. Coleman du Pont supervised the construction of his road. He was usually addressed as "General du Pont" in recognition of his

At the climax of a public ceremony held in Dover on July 2, 1924, Governor William D. Denney (left) presented T. Coleman du Pont with a map of Delaware fashioned by Tiffany and Company of New York City. The map was made of silver with a gold thread representing the du Pont Highway. The map is now in the collections of the Delaware State Museums. Former U.S. Senator George Gray stands at the right. (Courtesy of the Hagley Museum and Library)

rank in the National Guard. The general traveled in a large motorcar that included an expandable tent. As his road progressed from south to north, it "ended the profound isolation that had characterized life in Southern Delaware for generations."[6]

In 1916 the cause of improved roads got a big boost nationally when Congress adopted the Federal Aid Highway Act. The act provided federal matching funds in support of state highway improvements. To qualify for assistance, states were required to create professionally managed highway departments. That fall Delaware's voters chose John G. Townsend, Jr., to be their governor. Townsend, a friend to many Progressive causes, came to Dover with a strong determination to enact numerous reforms. Among them was a proposal to create a state highway department so that Delaware could qualify to receive federal matching funds.

The Republicans controlled the Senate and the Democrats controlled the House in the General Assembly that greeted the new governor in January 1917. Overcoming their state's deep-seated traditionalism, the assembly passed the necessary legislation to create a state highway department in an unusual show of bipartisan harmony. Henceforth, the state, not its counties, would be responsible for public roads. But the counties could not be forgotten. The composition of the new department was to include members from each county. The department was to employ a chief engineer to oversee its work using money collected from motor-vehicle registrations and drivers' license fees.

The friendship and mutual respect that existed between Coleman du Pont and Governor Townsend ensured a smooth transition from the Coleman du Pont Highway Corporation to the State Highway Department. The chief engineer and staff of the Corporation simply became the employees of the new Department. Coleman du Pont continued to pay for the road, as he had promised to do. The team that he had assembled proceeded with the construction of the highway northward through its completion in 1924. In the final reckoning, T. Coleman du Pont supplied nearly $4,000,000 toward the construction of the highway that bears his name.

In the years that followed, the Du Pont Highway more than lived up to its creator's expectations. Southern Delawareans discovered that they could truck farm produce to major urban markets in Philadelphia and New York in less than a day and that they could do it on their own schedule without paying railroad rates. The independence, convenience, speed, and relatively low cost of this new source of transportation encouraged farmers to produce truck crops, raised farm income, and increased the value of farmland. Most significantly for the future, in the 1920s the highway made possible the inauguration of the broiler-chicken industry in eastern Sussex County. By the 1940s that industry had become the central pillar of Delaware agriculture.

The legislative session of 1913 was significant in the history of Delaware's General Assembly for a host of actions in addition to the highway legislation. It was the last meeting of the assembly to choose the state's United States senators.

On a more parochial note, the session marked the end of a practice going back to colonial times whereby each bill that passed the two houses was enrolled by hand before it went forward to the governor for his signature. Beginning in 1913 the official copy of each piece of legislation was to be typewritten. The new practice got off to a rocky start. It showed up the deficiencies of the assembly's typists. Governor Charles R. Miller complained that he had to return many bills to correct numerous typographical errors.[7]

By a small margin the Delaware General Assembly of 1913 failed to pass the Seventeenth Amendment to the United States Constitution to mandate popular election of United States senators. The House approved the amendment by a unanimous vote, but it lost in the Senate by a vote of six yeas to ten nays. Delaware's failure to pass the Seventeenth Amendment was ironic. For years the First State had been the object of unflattering national news stories concerning John E. Addicks's flamboyant efforts to win a seat in the Senate. Those stories had helped to convince a majority of Americans of the need for this reform. On May 31, 1913, the Seventeenth Amendment went into effect without Delaware's endorsement.

The Seventeenth Amendment had a profound effect on politics in Delaware, especially with respect to the General Assembly. From 1789 when the United States Constitution had gone into effect, the greatest political plum in Delaware had been election to the United States Senate. Every political figure in the state aspired to a seat in the United States Senate, and the only way to get there was through election by the General Assembly. John E. Addicks was hardly unique in his effort to elect men to the General Assembly who would support his senate candidacy. Political leaders from the days of George Read through those of John M. Clayton and Thomas F. Bayard had done the same, only with a bit more grace and a lot less money. In future there would be no reason for aspirants to the United States Senate to interfere in the selection and cultivation of those elected to sit in the legislature in Dover.

Women played a major advocacy role in the national Progressive Movement. In Delaware, women's groups championed several important measures in the legislative session of 1913. It was in large part thanks to the efforts of women's organizations that the assembly passed laws in 1913 to establish a Child Labor Commission, to regulate the hours and working conditions for female factory workers, and to appoint a cannery inspector. Women's organizations proved to be innovative publicity-conscious lobbyists. To convince the legislators of the need for a maximum ten-hour-workweek for women, they presented a "monster petition" signed by 5,000 supporters.

The Delaware Federation of Women's Clubs and the Delaware Grange adopted equally effective, if less flamboyant, measures to convince the legislature to create the Women's College of Delaware. The new college was to be located in Newark and to operate in conjunction with all-male, state-supported Delaware College. The state committed $125,000 to acquire a campus for the Women's College and to construct two buildings, a residence hall and a classroom/laboratory.

In 1914, for the first time, Delaware offered its white young women the opportunity to attend a state-supported college. In the years to come the state could look to its graduates to find well-prepared schoolteachers.

In that same session the legislature voted to give Delaware College a perpetual charter, thus relieving the college's trustees from seeking renewal of their charter every twenty years. With a perpetual charter the college could more easily attract endowment support from alumni and friends. That year the assembly also provided funds to permit Delaware College to offer tuition-free summer institute training to Delaware's public schoolteachers.

Corrections reform was another important item on the agendas of early-twentieth- century General Assemblies. In 1905 the assembly voted to discontinue the use of the pillory, but multiple efforts to remove the whipping post proved unsuccessful. The whipping post had been a frequent target of reforming governors in the first half of the nineteenth century. Calls for its elimination disappeared in the Civil War years. By the first decade of the twentieth century abolition of the whipping post was once more in the news. Progressive writers for national magazines and newspapers criticized Delaware for retaining bloody corporal punishment. In 1907 a group of Wilmington Quakers petitioned the assembly to rid Delaware of that "brutal and degrading" practice, but to no avail.[8] Many Delawareans and their legislators rejected the critics' view. One such was Governor Simeon S. Pennewill. In his final address to the General Assembly in January 1913, the outgoing governor declared his support for the whipping post as a deterrent to crime and rejected the accusation that whippings were being inflicted "in a barbarous manner."[9]

The Voters Assistance Law and Local Option in the sale of liquor were two other perennial issues of the era. Those who hoped that Delaware had seen the last of Voters Assistance in 1903, when a Democratic majority repealed the law, were disappointed when the Republicans brought the practice back. The GOP justified Voters Assistance on the grounds that without help many voters couldn't understand Delaware's complicated ballot. For proof they pointed to the large number of invalid ballots cast in statewide elections. The Republicans showed no interest in creating a more comprehensible ballot and thus removing this alleged obstacle to reform. They much preferred to have their workers "assist" voters.

Local option proved to be an equally tricky issue. At first glance it seemed to make sense to allow the voters of each county to decide whether alcoholic beverages should be manufactured and sold in that county. But the local-option law passed in 1907 failed to stem the flow of liquor, even into Kent and Sussex counties where liquor sales were declared to be illegal. Despite victories by dry proponents, men's "clubs" sprang up in every southern Delaware town to serve alcohol imported from outside the state.

In New Castle County, local option intensified hostilities between Wilmington and the rural parts of the county. City residents urged the legislature to treat Wilmington as a separate entity so that Wilmingtonians could vote on local option for themselves. Their efforts failed. The battle of "dries" versus "wets" was but one element in Wilmingtonians' often-disregarded efforts to obtain a greater degree of home rule from the General Assembly.

Pierre S. du Pont (1870-1954). Although shy by nature, he was a crusader for public education and prohibition reforms in Delaware. Du Pont is seen here in 1932 in front of the city-county building in Wilmington's Rodney Square urging the end to Prohibition. (Courtesy of the Hagley Museum and Library)

In January 1917 John G. Townsend, Jr., took the oath as governor. The ceremony took place at the Dover Opera House, the only building in the capital capable of holding the crowds that attended gubernatorial inaugurations. In his address Townsend promised to apply business methods to the administration of the state. Looking at Delaware's government from the point of view of a businessman and a Progressive, Townsend called for the creation of a state "budget system" that would significantly alter how the state raised revenue.[10] In particular, the new governor sought to replace Delaware's traditional reliance on county real-estate taxes with a state income tax.

    Tax reform was overdue in Delaware. With each legislative session the state took on more responsibilities, and the cost of state government rose accordingly. In 1914 the state's total expenditures were $780,458. This was a substantial increase from the $612,666 that Delaware had spent only two years previously. Revenues were rising too, but were barely keeping pace with expenditures. By far the largest source of revenue came from licenses and fees, which earned Delaware $158,000 in 1914. Next in significance was the tax on railroads, which accounted for another $112,000, closely followed by the corporate

John G. Townsend, Jr. (1871-1964). As governor from 1917 to 1921, Townsend championed reform causes that included highway construction, woman suffrage, and public education. (Courtesy of the Historical Society of Delaware)

franchise tax, which earned the state an additional $95,000. The state's ability to raise revenue through a variety of devices demonstrated that, in future, citizens would look to the state rather than to the counties' land assessments for increases in government funding.[11]

In 1913 the General Assembly ratified the Sixteenth Amendment to the United States Constitution to permit a federal income tax. Delawareans did not oppose the notion of an income tax to spread the federal tax burden more fairly to embrace salaries, investments, and other sources of income beyond landholding, but they would have to be shown an important benefit to justify enacting that reform at the state level. In the next few years the enactment of a state income tax in Delaware would take a circuitous route that was intertwined with the ambitions and goals of leading members of the du Pont family.

The First World War had a major impact on the du Ponts and on Delaware. In the spring of 1917 the United States declared war on Germany. By 1917 the armies of Europe had fought one another for more than three years in the most destructive war in world history. In the first years of the European conflict the United States sought to remain neutral, but the Great War had a powerful impact even on the non-combatant United States. The war fired the flames of patriotism and gave urgency to the perceived need for "preparedness."

The war had a profound effect on the United States economy, especially in the manufacture of weapons that were purchased by Britain and France. Among the American industries that benefited from this increased trade, none was more important than powder making, and the Du Pont Company of Wilmington, Delaware, was America's greatest producer of military explosives.

The Du Pont Company had developed rapidly since the three cousins had taken control in 1902. Du Pont gobbled up its main competitors, and in 1906 the company opened a large corporate headquarters building in the center of Wilmington. A few years later the company added a hotel and theater to the Du Pont Building. In 1912, the company lost an antitrust suit that challenged its domination of American powder manufacture. The result was the creation of two spin-off companies, Hercules and Atlas, both of which also chose Wilmington to be their corporate headquarters. Du Pont remained the largest powder maker in the country and kept its exclusive contracts to supply military explosives to the United States government.

By 1912 T. Coleman was eager to reach beyond the confines of Wilmington and the explosives industry. Leaving the management of Du Pont to cousin Pierre, he moved to New York where he became involved in developing hotels and building an insurance company near Wall Street. By 1914 he decided to sell his Du Pont stock to finance those enterprises.

The disposition of T. Coleman's shares in Du Pont, which accounted for more than one third of the company's total capitalization, produced a bitter family feud. The feud had a major impact, not only on the management of the company but also on politics in Delaware. In reaction to the privately negotiated sale of

Coleman's shares to a syndicate composed of Pierre and his immediate family, Alfred I. du Pont sought redress in the federal courts. The case was ultimately settled in Pierre's favor in 1917. By then the company was in the midst of massive wartime expansion that vastly increased the company's profits and its stock's value. Through their syndicate, called Christiana Securities, Pierre and his siblings controlled the Du Pont Company and were the major beneficiaries of the company's phenomenal wartime growth.

In the second decade of the twentieth century all three of Delaware's daily newspapers were published in Wilmington. The Bancroft family owned the *Every Evening,* a Democratic paper. Senator Henry Algernon du Pont owned the *Evening Journal,* which trumpeted his Republican perspective. In 1911 Alfred I. du Pont had purchased the state's only daily morning paper, *The Wilmington Morning News,* which was also Republican in its politics. With the Addicks phenomenon now behind them, by 1916 the state's Republicans were once again a united party. Their unity did not last long, for in that year Alfred I. du Pont entered state politics and picked up the remnants of the old Union Republicans. The du Pont maverick continued to be a factor in state politics until 1920, when he moved to Florida.

In 1916 Alfred I. du Pont sought to deny Henry A. du Pont re-nomination to his seat in the United States Senate on the grounds that the old colonel was merely a stalking horse for T. Coleman. Alfred depicted his newly created faction as the Republican Party's progressive reformers in opposition to the "Old Guard" as represented by T. Coleman and Henry Algernon. Alfred's accomplice in this endeavor was J. Frank Allee of Dover, formerly an Addicks lieutenant and an influential member of the state Senate. Alfred's tactics were in part successful. As a result of the split in the state GOP, in 1916 Democrat Josiah O. Wolcott captured Henry Algernon's former seat in the United States Senate.[12]

The legislative session of 1917 found Alfred squarely behind John G. Townsend's call for tax reform in Delaware. Dr. Caleb Layton, another former Addicks politician now in Alfred's camp, attracted statewide attention when he addressed a mass meeting in Wilmington on the subject. "We Delawareans are living in the past," he said. "Every man . . . should pay a tax in proportion to what he is worth."[13] With even T. Coleman's old-guard Republicans coming out in favor of a more fairly based tax system, the taxation issue before the legislature was going to be not if, but how much.

First, however, the two Republican factions butted heads over the organization of the Senate, where the GOP held a majority of ten to seven. The battle over who would serve as Senate president pro tempore went on for three weeks before a few Democrats decided the issue by swinging their votes to Alfred's candidate on the forty-first ballot. With that victory behind them, the Senate leaders brought up their inheritance-tax bill. The bill provided a graduated tax rate and taxed widows' inheritances at a lower rate than money left to more distant relatives. The bill passed both houses by unanimous votes. The income-tax bill came up next. It required more negotiation and compromise, but ultimately it passed. Like the newly enacted federal income-tax law, the state income-tax law provided for graduated rates and included a number of deductions.

The General Assembly also adopted in 1917 its first law to provide non-institutional welfare. The law created the Mother's Pension Commission to assist needy widows and abandoned mothers of children under the age of fourteen. Qualified applicants were entitled to receive up to $8.00 monthly for one child plus an additional $4.00 for each additional child. The program was to be administered by a commission made up of women, one member from each county. The commissioners were to supervise the payments and hire the welfare workers charged with conducting periodic checkups on the recipients.[14]

The introduction of new, potentially major sources of state income set the stage for the next big reform: the development of a well-financed, state-supported, professionally managed system of public schools throughout Delaware. Delaware's legislature had been moving haltingly toward that goal for many years, but with mixed results at best. In 1907, for example, the assembly passed a mandatory school attendance law. The law required children between the ages of seven and fourteen to attend school for five months a year, but then made an exception by reducing the requirement down to three months for children whose labor was needed on farms.

The farm-labor exemption was not the only weakness in the school attendance law of 1907. There was no provision for state funds to enforce the act. Each of the state's 521 school districts was free to employ a truant officer at its own expense.[15] Given the sorry state of most of the districts, there was little likelihood that many would take advantage of the opportunity. Similarly, the legislature created a State Commission of Education, but it failed to give the Commission the money or the power to provide the graded schools, adequate salaries for teachers, and teacher training that the commissioners endorsed.

Large landowners had come to dominate the elections in the tiny rural school districts. Their votes ensured that school taxes would be kept to a minimum. The new state income tax opened the door a bit to show at least the possibility that public education might be funded through a tax on incomes rather than on land. That welcome possibility may have gained the votes of some rural legislators for reform. In 1919 they agreed to a bill appointing a gubernatorial commission to reorganize Delaware's anarchistic school system.

Only a few weeks after the assembly adjourned in March 1917, the United States Congress declared war on Germany and its allies. The declaration of war demanded a rapid mobilization of the nation's resources on a scale not seen since the Civil War. The federal government moved swiftly to create agencies and boards charged with bringing the maximum number of men and material into the fight in the least amount of time. In President Woodrow Wilson's war cabinet the task of coordinating those activities fell to a subset of department secretaries known as the Council of National Defense. The Council called for the individual states to play their part by organizing their populations, farm production, and industries to the highest level possible.

In response to that national mandate, Governor Townsend summoned the General Assembly into special session in March 1918. "In a crisis," he reminded them, "Delaware has never failed."[16] The legislature responded positively to the governor's major request to create a state Council of Defense. The Delaware State Council of Defense proved to be a more important element in Delaware's development than its war-related charge might have suggested. Its chair was Everett Johnson, Governor Townsend's secretary of state and a strong supporter of education and other reform causes. Another influential member was John J. Raskob, a close advisor to Pierre S. du Pont. The council brought a broad perspective to its responsibilities for coordinating the state's contribution to the war effort. It instituted an educational program of Americanization for Delaware's immigrant population, and also undertook surveys of public health and literacy throughout the state.

The surveys uncovered shocking information that called into question the ability of Delawareans to fight a war or to participate in the modern economy. Parts of the state were much like what we presently envision third-world countries to be like. There were large numbers of sickly people, even among draft-age men. The dismal effect of Delaware's ill-funded, localized approach to public education was also painfully evident. In 1915 a report of the National Commissioner of Education put Delaware at the bottom of the nation in school attendance and close to the bottom in every other school-related category. The council's findings confirmed that view and demonstrated the high price that Delaware was paying for its inadequate schools.

Meanwhile, the Commission on Education that the General Assembly had created in 1917 struggled along without professional support. Lacking state funds to undertake its work on educational reform, Governor Townsend turned to Pierre S. du Pont, who supplied the money to hire two nationally known experts, Doctors Abraham Flexner and Frank P. Bachman. Flexner and Bachman had made a similar study in Maryland that had led to significant reform in public education there. The education experts now undertook to study Delaware's educational needs and to provide an educational plan for the First State that the Commission on Education might take to the General Assembly.

Pierre S. du Pont was so aroused by the need for educational reform that he took time from his burdensome schedule as wartime president of the Du Pont Company to host a meeting of eighty civic-minded Delawareans in July 1918 to address the problem.[17] An organization called Service Citizens of Delaware grew out of that meeting. The majority of Service Citizens' members were business and professional men who took as their major mandate the reform of Delaware's public schools. It was through this organization that P. S. du Pont led the cause for the most significant, and most difficult, reform in Delaware's history. He not only provided leadership, he also generously provided a trust fund of $1,500,000 to Service Citizens for a period of four years to hire staff and to set educational reform in motion.[18]

Pierre S. du Pont was a scientist by training and inclination. He had concentrated on chemistry at the Massachusetts Institute of Technology before entering the business world. He brought a cool-headed, scientific approach to every issue that he encountered in business and public affairs. He was impressed by systematically acquired data, not by arguments based on emotion. That is why he found the State Council of Defense surveys so compelling. He was also by nature reticent. He did not like to speak before crowds; he disliked publicity; and he was no backslapper. In short, unlike his cousin T. Coleman, he had no interest in entering politics. But he did own a newspaper, the *Wilmington Evening Journal*, which he acquired from his cousin Henry A. du Pont.

The General Assembly met in January 1919, less than two months after the armistice that ended World War I. In his address, Governor Townsend praised Delawareans' response to the war crisis. The governor then challenged the legislators to fill the urgent needs that had been made public from the work of the Council of Defense in the fields of health, education, and child welfare. He also drew the legislators' attention to Abraham Flexner and Frank P. Bachman's recently completed report to the Commission on Education. He challenged the assembly to realize the goals of those reports for a better Delaware.

The governor's message fell on the ears of men who were in no mood to advance reforms of any kind. For most purposes, the Progressive Era had died in the trenches of France. In Delaware, as elsewhere in the United States, politics was becoming mean spirited and parochial.

Thanks to a "unity" agreement between the competing party blocs that owed allegiance to T. Coleman and Alfred I., the Republicans had won control of both houses of the assembly in the 1918 election. Unfortunately, the "unity" stopped when the last vote was counted. As a result, the session proved to be among the most acrimonious in Delaware's legislative history. Bickering among the Republicans got things off to a slow start, and there were plenty of controversial bills to increase hostilities and prevent actin. As late as March 21, when the legislature was assumed to be on the verge of adjournment, the editor of the Wilmington *Every Evening* lamented the lawmakers' lack of accomplishment. "It is doubtful if ever there was . . . a less profitable or more unsatisfactory session of the General Assembly," he wrote.[19]

In 1918 the General Assembly had endorsed the Eighteenth Amendment to the United States Constitution, which made the manufacture and sale of liquor illegal. In 1919 the legislators spent much of their time debating and amending a state prohibition bill that was unlikely to have much significance in light of the recently adopted federal amendment. The state Senate also went on record as opposed to President Woodrow Wilson's proposed League of Nations. Since state legislatures had no responsibility for the ratification of treaties, that, too, was a gratuitous waste of time.

The legislature considered, but ultimately rejected, a bill to increase Wilmington's representation in the assembly. It also opposed a bill to replace

Wilmington's city council with the commission-style government then much in vogue. Another loser was a bill to permit horse races in the First State; and yet another was a bill, strongly supported by the Consumer League, to enact a minimum wage for female employees. In the Senate the minimum wage bill received only two votes, both from the Wilmington senators, a Republican and a Democrat. Elsewhere in the state, senators accepted the canning lobby's contention that if the bill were enacted rural Delaware would lose its canning industry.

The two most entertaining struggles of the session emerged from the political factions and party struggles that were never far below the surface. Led by J. Frank Allee, Jr., the Republicans attempted to reduce the size of the Kent County Levy Court from ten to three. Allee's bill was called a "ripper" because it was a politically motivated piece of legislation flying under the banner of government reorganization. The purpose of this "ripper" legislation was to replace the Democrat-controlled levy court with one in which Republicans would have the upper hand and therefore be in charge of collecting county taxes. Following a bitter debate the measure passed the Senate by a strict party vote. This action so enraged the Senate Democrats that they vowed that if the House also passed the "ripper' bill they would vote "no" on every piece of legislation for the remainder of the session. The unseemly battle consumed about a week of the legislators' time in mid- March. The stalemate finally ended when enough Republicans in the House voted with the Democrats to kill the Kent County reorganization plan.

Another memorable struggle pitted Alfred I. du Pont and Republicans loyal to him against the T. Coleman wing of the party, now supported by P. S. du Pont. At stake was a bill to amend Delaware's corporate law. On March 7, 1919, P. S. du Pont's *Wilmington Evening Journal* proclaimed in a banner headline "P. S. du Pont and Associates Win Powder Suit, Decision Geat Vindication For Men Who Bought Disputed Stock." The federal circuit court had spoken, and Alfred I. had lost his suit disputing Cousin Pierre's purchase of T. Coleman's shares.[20] Two weeks later, Alfred's political associate, J. Frank Allee, Jr., introduced a bill in the state Senate to permit a stockholder to vote all of his or her shares for one candidate to a corporate board of directors instead of spreading those votes among a full slate of candidates.

The editor of Pierre's *Evening Journal* concluded that Alfred I.'s goal was to elect himself to the board of the Du Pont Company. In reply, Alfred I. told a reporter at his *Wilmington Morning News* that he had no intention of sitting on the Du Pont Company Board so long as Pierre was in power there. His interest, Alfred said, was solely one of fairness to minority stockholders.[21] Alfred I.'s bill won a majority in the Senate, but it failed to receive the two-thirds vote necessary to move a proposed amendment to the state constitution to the House of Representatives. And so the matter died, but not before it gave Delaware newspaper readers and assembly-watchers an entertaining spectacle of the du Pont family quarrel.

All of those legislative bills and debates paled, however, before the really big battle that hovered in the wings of the General Assembly of 1919: House Bill 144, the school code bill. The bill came to the legislature from the Education Commission that Governor Townsend had appointed in response to action of the previous legislature. The authors of the commission's report were Abraham Flexner and Frank Bachman, the experts that the commissioners had hired with funds supplied by P. S. du Pont. Bill 144 was unusually long and complex. Its text ran about one hundred pages in length. Its provisions grew directly from Flexner and Bachman's overwhelmingly negative observations of public education in Delaware. Their recommendations mirrored the reforms that Maryland had recently enacted.

The Flexner-Bachman report, entitled *Public Education in Delaware*, blamed the state's educational failures on the existence of the tiny, locally controlled school districts that were the relic of the School Law of 1829. The keys to improvement, the experts said, lay in creating statewide standards of education that would mandate better-trained and better-paid teachers, and in consolidating districts to provide a graded education and access to high school for every Delaware child. Pierre S. du Pont was so impressed with the report that he had Service Citizens print 7,500 copies for distribution to people throughout the state. Service Citizens also set up a group to lobby the legislature for reform.

It took no crystal ball to anticipate that many would oppose reform. Many rural Delawareans were satisfied with education on the cheap in districts that could be controlled easily by a few voters. It would also be necessary to do a lot of convincing to win over townspeople and especially Wilmingtonians, who would be reluctant to surrender control over their communities' incorporated school districts.

The essence of the proposed reforms lay in the seeming contradiction between two concepts of democracy: voters' sovereignty versus equal opportunity. By empowering educational professionals at the expense of local voters the state could realize the goal of giving every child an opportunity to succeed in a society and economy that increasingly rewarded educated workers at the expense of the illiterate and semi-literate.

Information about the school code proposal was in the hands of legislators and the public when the General Assembly met in January 1919. To spread the word of what the reform might mean, Governor Townsend proclaimed the week of February 16 to be Education Week throughout the state, and he encouraged religious leaders, women's clubs, and men's service clubs to discuss the proposed bill during that time. In early March the legislators held a public hearing on Bill 144. Every commissioner spoke enthusiastically in favor of the bill, as did a number of educational leaders such as Abraham Flexner and Frank Bachman, Samuel Chiles Mitchell, the president of Delaware College, Winifred Robinson, the dean of the Women's College, and several school principals.

Supporters of the legislation demonstrated their willingness to meet the critics of the plan part way. They agreed to an amendment to reduce the power of the proposed state superintendent (called commissioner in the bill) and thus removed a major criticism that was being voiced around the state. Proponents did not, however, retreat from their insistence on a 180-day school year, which was being attacked by some because it would remove child laborers during critical times in the planting and harvesting of crops. All of the state's daily newspapers favored the school bill. Even Alfred I. du Pont, who owned a number of downstate weeklies in addition to the *Wilmington Morning News*, supported his estranged cousin's crusade for better schools.

When the bill moved onto the docket of the Senate's Education Committee, it appeared that it might have smooth sailing to enactment. But by March 21, two weeks after the public hearing, the legislature was threatening to adjourn without taking action on the school code or on many other bills. The *Every Evening* castigated the assembly for its profitless "time-wasting" when an important piece of legislation remained unaddressed.[22] Fortunately for the friends of school reform, the assemblymen voted to extend their session by a few more days. Three days into the extension the Senate spent the entire afternoon angrily debating the bill and then voted nine to eight in its favor. The measure needed a two-thirds vote to pass, so it was defeated.

On the final day of the legislative session lawyers for the cause of school reform slapped together a series of amendments designed to eliminate the requirement for a two-thirds vote. The amended version was presented to the assembly on the night of March 26, quite literally at the eleventh hour. Opponents were furious at this last-minute effort to force a vote on such hastily conceived legislation concerning a topic that, they believed, did not have the support of the majority of Delawareans. The last speaker before the vote, Senator James W. Robertson of Wilmington, replied to the bill's opponents: "It is not so much what the people want, but it is what the children need."[23] It was a photo finish. The bill passed the Senate by a margin of two votes. It would have failed in the House had not Representative John E. McNabb, a Wilmington Democrat who had previously opposed the school code, bowed to Governor Townsend's personal plea and changed his vote.

Despite being dead tired, in the early hours of March 27, 1919, the lawmakers pressed forward, hurriedly adopting a host of measures. Lobbyists anxiously waited to see if their particular bills would be taken up or be left unaddressed. It was 5:15 in the morning when the legislative frenzy finally stopped. Fatigued beyond sleepiness, the assemblymen burst into song. They entertained one another and the surprised reporters and lobbyists who had endured the night with a number of popular songs ending with "Home Sweet Home," which was where they all sought to be.[24]

The new school code gave authority to the state and responsibility to the counties. It empowered the State Board of Education to set minimum standards for each grade level and for high-school diplomas. The state board was to establish the length of the school year and to create certification requirements for teachers. But the implementation of those standards would be assigned to county school boards elected by the voters of each county. In the first statewide extension of the franchise to include women, female Delawareans who could prove their status as taxpayers were permitted to vote in county school-board elections. The law abolished the old rural school districts and transferred their powers to the county school boards. The county boards were to be responsible for consolidating schools that would guarantee every child access to a graded primary school, a grammar school, and a high school. The state board set the standards. The county boards had the responsibility to increase teachers' and administrators' salaries and to build the many new schools needed to meet those standards. The money necessary to achieve those mandates was to come primarily from the traditional county taxes on real and personal property in the amounts determined by the each county board.[25]

The service of the members elected to the General Assembly in 1918 was not at an end. In March 1920 Governor Townsend called them back into special session to consider the proposed amendment to the United States Constitution that would extend the suffrage to women. For one of the few times in its history the entire nation was watching the Delaware General Assembly. Since Congress had passed the suffrage amendment two years earlier, thirty-five states had ratified. Delaware's positive vote would put the Nineteenth Amendment into the United States Constitution. In his address to the lawmakers the governor called the issue of woman's suffrage a question of "right and wrong," and he urged the assemblymen to do their duty to their state and their nation by joining a large majority of the states that had already ratified the amendment.[26]

Woman's suffrage had come before lawmakers in Delaware several times before, always with negative results. In 1897 the state constitutional convention had rejected pleas from a delegation of national and local suffragist proponents. Again in 1913 supporters of votes for women had high hopes that the legislature might vote their way but once again were disappointed. In those cases the issue had been limited to Delaware's women. Now, however, a positive vote in Dover would insure the suffrage for all the women of the United States.

No issue had ever brought so much attention or so many people, letters, and telegrams to the General Assembly. Dover's hotels were crammed with visitors. The major national figures in the American Woman's Suffrage Association, led by their president, Carrie Chapman Catt, came to Dover to testify before a joint hearing on March 25. Delaware's own nationally prominent suffrage leaders, Florence Bayard Hilles and Mabel Vernon, organized a parade and held rallies. The "suffs" handed out yellow jonquils to any man, especially a member of the legislature, who would wear one as a sign of his approval of votes for women. The opponents, known as the "antis," led by the indomitable Mary Wilson Thompson, a Wilmington socialite, gave out red roses, the symbol of chivalry, as boutonnieres for their male supporters. The colorful floral duel came to be known as the "war of the roses."

By 1920 the arguments raised by both sides in the suffrage debate were well worn. The suffragists pointed to the undemocratic nature of restricting the vote to one sex. Mrs. Hilles, of Delaware's politically active Bayard family, argued that as taxpayers women should have the right to vote under the old Revolutionary War slogan of "No taxation without representation." The most prominent political figures in the state and nation, including President Woodrow Wilson, T. Coleman, Alfred I., and Pierre S. du Pont all urged the legislature to adopt the amendment, as did the leadership of the national Republican and Democratic parties.

Suffrage rally on Dover Green, May 1920. In a final effort to win over a majority of the Delaware legislature, suffragists set up a speaker's platform on the Green and decorated the trees with banners showing their colors of purple, gold, and white. (Courtesy of the Historical Society of Delaware)

By contrast, Mrs. Thompson took the view that women could be more effective advocates for causes if they were seen to be apolitical. Her supporters in and out of the legislature included those who sought to repeal the recently enacted Prohibition Amendment, opponents of the school code, and those who embraced the "states' rights" doctrine, which held that the federal government had no business interfering with a state's decisions regarding who among its residents should have the right to participate in government. Representative John E. McNabb of Wilmington, known as "Bull," the man whose change of vote had saved the School Code bill in 1919, was the antis' most effective and colorful advocate in the House of Representatives. When he used the strongest language to denounce the suffs on the House floor, Mrs. Thompson abandoned all pretense to lady-like behavior and cheered him on from the sidelines.

In late March the Senate voted in favor of the amendment, but the victory was of little consolation to the suffragists as they rightly foresaw that their resolution would face a much more difficult time in the House. Both sides resorted to unconventional tactics to advance their positions. At one point, to prevent a vote that they knew they would lose, the suffs kidnapped Representative Walter E. Hart of Townsend, the chair of the House committee that was to report on the bill, and spirited him off in Mrs. Hilles's automobile. After he returned, Mrs. Thompson made Hart sign a proxy so that she, who would deny herself the right to vote in general elections, could act on his behalf in the House of Representatives should he again mysteriously disappear.[27]

After more than six weeks of frenzied effort the moment of truth came on June 2, 1920. A motion for the House of Representatives to resolve itself into a committee of the whole to consider the suffrage amendment lost by a vote of ten yeas to twenty-four nays. Shortly after, the General Assembly adjourned *sine die*. Delaware had failed the suffragists and the First State had lost its opportunity to be the state that gave all American women the vote. Little more than two months later the Tennessee legislature won that honor when, by a one-vote majority, it adopted the Nineteenth Amendment on August 18, 1920. At its next regular session in 1921, the Delaware legislature amended the state constitution to remove sex as a disqualification for holding state office.[28]

In the meantime, the battle over the school code had gathered steam since the assembly's last minute endorsement in 1919. Many people wanted to repeal the code. The biggest problems were its cost and where that cost was placed. County property taxes could not be raised enough to pay for all that the law required. At that critical point Pierre S. du Pont took a major step that averted repeal. Du Pont created and personally funded the Delaware School Auxiliary Association (DSAA), through which he offered to pay for the construction of schools to meet modern standards throughout the state. His offer conspicuously included schools for African American children as well as white children. The financier's dedication to school reform went even further. Much against his nature, in the fall of 1919 he decided to take two months off from business to tour he state and speak about the need for the code before audiences in any community that would have him.[29]

Daniel and Landreth Layton, former Addicks Republicans in Sussex County, and now political friends of Alfred I. du Pont, led the opposition to the code. They asserted that the code represented an un-American and undemocratic "decline into autocracy."[30] The autocrat that they had in mind was, of course, P. S. du Pont. They could not, however, get far by accusing P. S. du Pont of harboring selfish motives. The philanthropist's pledge of several million dollars to build new schools, a gift that was to grow even larger in the decade to come, was already the largest contribution ever made by anyone in the United States toward public education.

The "Great School War" was still in full swing when Governor Townsend called the legislature into special session on March 22, 1920. Several days before the session began, ten Sussex County assemblymen held a strategy session to plan how to defeat the code. In his opening address to the General Assembly, the governor acknowledged the necessity of making adjustments in the school law. In light of the fact that teachers' pay was less than that of "the poorest unskilled labor," he could see no way to cut costs. Townsend proposed, therefore, to shift the tax burden from the counties to the state.[31]

Among the many letters and telegrams both for and against the code that poured in upon the legislature was one that Senator J. Frank Allee, Jr., singled out as sufficiently important to be read into the Senate's minutes. It was a letter from Allee's constituent W. C. Jason, president of Delaware State College, a small coeducational institution created and funded by a federal supplement to the Land Grant College Act since 1891. Writing in his capacity as the presiding officer of the Delaware Negro Civic League, President Jason began with the observation that although Negroes "have no voice in legislation" they had a great stake in seeing the school reform succeed. "It would be a calamity," President Jason wrote, "if after the hopes raised by the events of the past year we should be thrown back upon the school system we had hoped was gone forever. For the first time in the history of the State the Negro is offered a fair chance to prepare for intelligent participation in the responsibilities of citizenship. Do not repeal it, we beseech you."[32]

President Jason's appeal was seconded by another no doubt more persuasive voice, that of Pierre S. du Pont, who was given the privilege of the floor to argue the case for retaining the code. As he had done in his recent appearances around the state, P.S. du Pont patiently laid out the facts about Delaware's deplorable educational resources and how the code would provide for great improvements.[33] On April 7 a motion to repeal the code lost in a close vote. The battle was, in effect, postponed until the next regular legislative session set for January 1921.

As had been predicted, the school-code issue dominated the General Assembly of 1921. In the first week of the session, while committees were being organized in both houses, the legislators were entertained at a dinner at the Hotel Du Pont honoring outgoing Governor John G. Townsend, Jr., and the newly elected governor, William D. Denney, a Republican who was in the P. S. du Pont camp. With Alfred I. du Pont's withdrawal from politics, the Republicans stood united for the first time in many years, but riding on the back of the school-code issue, the Democrats had won control of the House in the election of 1920. It was difficult to predict the outcome of the school-code battles that were sure to come.

Opponents of the code were most hostile to two features of the 1919 law: the tax burden that it placed on the county property tax, and the 180-day school year, which interfered with farmers' use of child labor. To meet these criticisms a Citizens' Committee had drafted a revised version of the law that would move the tax burden to the state by imposing an annual 3 percent tax on Delaware corporations. When the Citizens Committee's bill came before the Democrat-controlled House of Representatives in early March no one was surprised by the big majority that voted against it. Some feared that a 3 percent tax would drive corporations from the state. A majority in the Senate was also committed to

Before and after photographs taken in 1922 illustrate the effects of Pierre S. du Pont's contribution to public education in Delaware. Similar scenes could be shown from throughout the state. These photographs show the old one-room, clapboard "colored" school in Georgetown (above) and its replacement, a modern, two-room brick building. (Courtesy of the Delaware Public Archives)

opposing the Citizens Committee's substitute law, but the opposition in the Senate lacked the votes to overcome a predicted veto by the governor. If that were to happen, the law of 1919 would remain in place for another two years.[34] To thwart such an outcome the Senate voted to repeal the school code altogether and to substitute a much weakened version.

Among proponents of retaining school reform were the chairman of the State Board of Education, Charles I. Miller, and P. S. du Pont. Miller threatened to quit the board if the reform was abandoned. Yet both men continued to work toward a compromise that might save the major features of the 1919 law. Du Pont told the press that he would continue to support the cause of better public education in Delaware no matter what the legislature did. He also let it be known that he was opposed to the idea of changing the State School Board from a group appointed by the governor to an elected body, as some wished to do, because the board would then become mired in politics. He also opposed a plan being advocated by some in the legislature to eviscerate the law by dropping the provisions for truant officers and for teachers' academic qualifications. Du Pont advocated an increase in the state income tax rather than a 3 percent corporation tax to pay for the educational program. He said that the income tax could give Delaware a school program that would be well attended and well taught.[35]

Meanwhile behind the scenes, attorneys were working on two bills designed to overcome the major obstacles that had torpedoed the Citizens' Committee's bill in the assembly. One bill dealt with the schools, the other with taxes. The school-code bill was weaker than the proponents of reform might have wished. It reduced the qualifications for teachers and principals from what the experts, Flexner and Bachman, had recommended, and it reduced the number of mandatory school days from 180 to 160, but it contained a provision for a State Board of ducation to be appointed by the governor, and, most important, it maintained the goal of giving every Delaware child an education in graded schools that culminated in high school.

The tax bill was equally significant. "An Act to Provide Revenue for School Purposes" eliminated the need for the county boards of education that had been written into the 1919 law as mechanisms to raise revenue. For the first time in Delaware's history the responsibility for funding public schools was to be placed squarely on the state. The bill raised the graduated income tax rate from 1 percent to 3 percent and created the post of State School Tax Commissioner to make sure that the money was collected.[36] The state's schools remained segregated, but the differential in funding between black and white schools was eliminated. The result of the legislation would be a school system that looked to the state for centralized leadership.

In typical General Assembly spirit, the two bills were rushed through both houses with little discussion late in the final day of a session that did not actually adjourn until 6:30 a.m. the following morning. This time there was no outburst of song from the weary legislators. Perhaps the chorus of Delaware State College had satisfied the legislators' need for music when it had serenaded them the night before. Despite the compromise victory, the editor of P. S. du Pont's *Evening Journal* had little good to say about a legislative session that, in his view, had been "marred by undignified and unstatesmanlike bickering" and by "attitudes of some . . . on matters of finance and education" that were "simply outrageous."[37]

Whatever Pierre du Pont may have thought of the General Assembly of 1921, he was sufficiently pleased with the new school laws to accept Governor William Denney's request that he serve as a member of the State Board of Education. From that position he oversaw the transformation of Delaware's schools, which his money, coupled with his unstinting commitment, had made possible. In two decades P. S. du Pont gave $5,000,000 through the Delaware School Auxiliary Association to build over 120 modern schools for the consolidated districts that emerged from the school law. He championed the schools in other ways as well, fighting against those, including his cousin Alfred I., who tried to reduce state taxes. In 1927 Pierre even took on the responsibility for overseeing the collection of Delaware taxes by accepting the position of State Tax Commissioner. Largely as a result of his unyielding support, by 1930 state funds were supplying 88 percent of the cost of maintaining Delaware's public schools. Delaware had moved from its position near the bottom of the United States in state support for education to become the national leader.[38]

In the decade from 1911 through 1921 Delaware underwent profound changes in transportation and public education that catapulted the state from the nineteenth to the twentieth century. Credit for those developments must go primarily to T. Coleman du Pont and Pierre S. du Pont. Their contributions to Delaware's development were not merely financial, for both men could well afford to be generous with their gifts to the state. What was remarkable was both men's vision of how state government could serve the people more effectively. The state legislature was their reluctant partner in driving those advances forward. At the beginning of the century the assemblymen were devoting a great deal of their time to approving very minor requests for laying out new unpaved roads or altering the boundaries of the state's hundreds of school districts, each with its one-room school and its ill-trained, poorly paid teacher. By 1921 those conditions had been replaced by two strong, professionally managed state agencies: the State Highway Department and the State Board of Education, each capable of delivering first-rate services to the people of Delaware.

In January 1921 John G. Townsend delivered his farewell address to a joint secession of the General Assembly. His closing words bear witness to the spirit in which the transformations that marked that era were realized—and they remain a challenge to every subsequent General Assembly. "Standing here four years ago in the shadow of the history of Dover Green, there came to me a realization of the great work of those who made this State possible. Today, I am dreaming of the Delaware of tomorrow. Facing the future, I present its responsibilities to you."[39]

8

THE LEGISLATURE FACES GOOD TIMES AND BAD: 1922-1951

Few periods in American history have presented such striking contrasts as did the period from the 1920s through the 1940s. It was an era that defies efforts to impose thematic unity. During those thirty years the nation moved from the heights of prosperity to the depths of depression and from an uneasy peace through a second world war into a tension-filled Cold War. The monumental political figure of the time was President Franklin D. Roosevelt, who moved the Democratic Party from its traditional Jeffersonian small-government moorings to become the party of the interventionist state.

The challenges that marked the era had profound influences on Delaware's government. During those years the role of the executive branch increased in shaping state policy as the state added more offices and employees for the governor to appoint and manage. The state increasingly assumed financial responsibilities for areas previously handled by local governments, and federal mandates imposed a new relationship between the national government and the states. There was little continuity in the issues that faced the General Assembly because each decade presented novel problems. As the era progressed the once dominant Republicans began to lose their grip on state affairs to the rising power of a rejuvenated Democratic Party. The clarity of goals set by P. S. du Pont and his cousin T. Coleman in the previous era became lost amid ceaseless squabbling between evenly matched political parties, neither of which could command more than a fragile hold on power.

In our national memory, the 1920s was the prosperous "Jazz Age" decade sandwiched between the more somber eras of the First World War and the Great Depression. In Delaware, the decade's most important developments were the construction of modern schools and roads. Those developments affected everyone in the state. By the decade's end most of Delaware's children were attending bright, new fireproof schools; farmers delivered their produce to market in trucks; and legislators drove their automobiles to Dover rather than taking the train.

Nationally, the Republican Party dominated the era. In Delaware the GOP controlled the governor's office throughout the 1920s, but the Democrats continued to be a powerful force in the General Assembly. Democrats controlled both houses of the assembly in 1923. In 1925 and 1927, though they lost the House of Representatives, the Democrats maintained a slight majority in the Senate. Only in 1929 did the Republicans gain control of both houses.

With the parties so evenly divided, political infighting and crafty maneuvering were prominent features of legislative life. In 1923 the Democrats used their legislative power to enact "ripper bills" to replace Republican office holders and to limit the governor's power of appointment by requiring bi-party representation on state commissions. In certain circumstances the mere threat of a Democrat ripper bill encouraged Republicans to compromise on unrelated pieces of legislation.

In the Senate, where the Democrats maintained a tiny majority, a member could sometimes control the outcome of a vote by announcing during roll call that he was present but "not voting." This tactic could doom a bill without forcing a member to declare his opposition since the constitution required a majority of the House, not merely a majority of those present and voting. Another practice was the use of "skeleton bills." A skeleton bill contained only a title and an enacting clause, but nothing else. The flesh was to be filled in by a legislative committee after the bill was passed. Because it was incomplete, the skeleton bill received no first or second reading, so only committee members knew what they were voting for on the floor. Skeleton bills could be introduced at any time during a session, but they were most commonly used during the frantic rush of business as the legislature approached adjournment.

Life in the legislature followed a reasonably predictable pattern. The General Assembly met immediately after the first of the year n odd-numbered years and adjourned in early April on its sixtieth day, or as soon afterward as possible. Members did not receive their per diem pay beyond the sixty-day maximum. During the first week in January the majority party in each house chose its leaders, who then assigned members to the standing committees. It was not uncommon for that process to drag on while rival candidates fought over which member of the majority party would become leader and which members would take other important positions. In the 1920s it was the Democrats, rather than the Republicans, who were inclined toward such time-consuming battles. The major party in each house also named the clerks, stenographers, sergeant-at-arms, and other appointed assistants called attaches.

The next step was the presentation of the governor's message, which typically concentrated on laying out his budget recommendations for the next biennium. Once legislative committees were established, the members took inspection tours of state facilities. They visited state-run facilities such as the State Hospital at Farnhurst. Sometimes the legislators dropped by to inspect agencies that received state appropriations, such as the St. Michaels' Day Nursery and the Layton Home, a facility for aged black people, both in Wilmington. The University of Delaware entertained the legislators at dinner in the Old College dining room.

Back at the State House, the assembly received bills up to an agreed upon day in mid-March. Then they began the rush to take action on several hundred pieces of legislation before their sixty-day session came to an end in April.

Members received $600 per session plus a travel allowance. In 1929 legislators' travel claims became the object of controversy because some who made claims were riding to Dover in cars owned and driven by fellow members. After much debate and a veto by Governor C. Douglass Buck, the assembly adopted a compromise measure whereby members who drove could claim ten cents per mile while passenger members could claim three and one half cents per mile.[1] One supposes that the latter payment was to cover wear and tear on passengers' clothing.

By the 1920s a state bureaucracy was beginning to emerge. The state as yet had no civil-service system. That explains why the political parties were so intent on controlling the commissions that hired state employees, especially those in the labor-intensive State Highway Department. When one party wrested control from the other it was common practice for the new majority of commissioners to replace all the employees with members of the prevailing party. Those employees had neither job security nor benefits. During the 1920s the assembly turned down bills to provide pension benefits to retired state employees and schoolteachers.

The most difficult ongoing problem that faced the General Assembly in the 1920s was how to pay for the massive improvements to education mandated by the School Codes of 1919 and 1921. P. S. du Pont had always intended that his school-building program should be a partnership between the professionally managed agencies that he had helped to create and the people of Delaware acting through their General Assembly. He would prime the pump, but the state would then take over the pumping. With the adoption of the School Codes, he believed that his Delaware School Auxiliary Association could begin to shift the cost of building new schools to the school districts and the state. By 1923 du Pont's organization had built eighty-eight schools and was on the verge of completing the philanthropist's commitment to construct new schools for black children throughout Delaware. The time had come for the people of Delaware to rise to the challenge to fund the remaining school construction with modest additional assistance from the DSAA.

P. S. du Pont's expectations were sorely tested by the General Assembly of 1923 and that of 1925. In 1923 State Superintendent Harry V. Holloway, a former school administrator from Sussex County, asked the legislature for two distinct sums of money: one to pay the teachers and run the schools; the other to build new schools. The state superintendent told the assembly's education committees that Delaware could not attract the best-trained teachers because the state's teachers' salaries were not competitive with those of Maryland or other nearby states. But the legislators considered the superintendent's request for a $2.5 million annual school budget excessive and cut it to $2 million. The assembly also refused to provide any money for school construction. The story in 1925 was not much different. The legislators were loath to enact new taxes and were intent upon living within the state's pre-School Code budget.

P. S. du Pont urged the legislators to raise additional funds. He suggested that Delaware establish a funding formula whereby the state would provide 80 percent of the financing for additional schools and the local districts would supply the remaining 20 percent. He estimated the total cost of constructing new schools to be $9.7 million.[2] When it became clear that the legislature would not pass a tax increase, du Pont revised his plan to stay within the state's current income. The assembly increased the budget for school administration, but at the very end of the session the votes of six determined Republican senators killed the school-construction bond bill because it would lead to higher taxes. Du Pont suspected that a few wealthy men, including his cousins Alfred I. du Pont and former U.S. Senator Henry Algernon du Pont, were behind the obstructionists.[3]

For P.S. du Pont and for other school reformers the outlook would have been bleak indeed, except for one significant factor: by the mid-twenties the state school fund was accumulating money from its two largest sources, the state income tax and the corporate franchise tax. Those sources produced enough money to undertake school improvements without increasing the tax rate or adding new sources of revenue. To those knowledgeable about such things it was clear that the fund could be considerably richer yet if all those who owed income tax actually paid. What Delaware needed was a well-managed tax collection bureau directed by a determined person with executive experience. In 1925 Governor Robert P. Robinson found the perfect recruit: P.S. du Pont, himself.

Under du Pont's leadership the tax office was transformed into a model of efficiency and effectiveness. Du Pont hired several people to undertake the day-to-day management of the office and paid them from his own pocket. The tax officials created a list of taxpayers, and those who owed back taxes were politely but firmly pressed to pay. The money earmarked for schools fell only lightly if at all on working class, or even middle-class, families. The state income tax fell mainly on the wealthy, as did the property tax, with its rate of .25 cent per $100 valuation. Only one tax touched everyone, the filing fee, or capitation tax, which all voters were required to pay. By 1926 those revenue streams had produced $3.8 million to be used exclusively for the state's public schools.

Finally convinced that school construction bonds would not lead to a tax increase, in 1927, at the height of the twenties prosperity, the General Assembly agreed to provide $1 million a year to fund the construction of schools in districts not as yet covered by the DSAA program. As P.S. du Pont kept reiterating in speeches to PTAs, civic groups, legislators, and anyone else who would listen, Delawareans were getting a great bargain: new schools at very little cost to themselves. To make certain that the cost to less affluent citizens would be negligible, the legislature of 1927 also did away with the unpopular voters' filing fee. The bonds could be retired from the state's remaining sources of income.

The legislature's willingness to make strategic alterations in the state's incorporation law during the late twenties should be viewed in the context of the state's commitment to fund the school program. The legislators did not hesitate to make changes in the corporation statute as recommended by the Delaware Bar Association because they were determined to keep Delaware ahead of other states in the quest for the incorporation revenue that fueled the school fund. Wilmington's growing fraternity of corporate lawyers kept the legislators abreast of changes in the field, and the lawyers drew up the necessary legislation. Because the laws of incorporation had become so technical, the changes received little publicity, nor were they subject to much legislative debate. From the perspective of the average legislator or citizen, the important thing was to keep the stream of money flowing from the franchise tax.

The state's other major consumer of revenue was the State Highway Department. In the 1920s the state used the revenue generated from drivers' licenses, car tags, and a tax on gasoline to expand highway construction beyond the T. Coleman du Pont Highway. As income from those new sources grew, some could foresee the day when the state would relieve the counties of responsibility for all major public roadways. The result of such a shift would not only bring greater uniformity to Delaware's roads, but, equally important, it would remove the cost of highway building and maintenance from the counties' land tax, thus saving farmers from an unfair tax burden. For the time being, however, legislators were content to accept the view expressed by several successive governors that the state should adopt a "pay as you go" road-building plan and move gradually to assume the counties' bonded indebtedness for local roads.

In addition to Delaware's increasing responsibilities for schools and roads, the state was also gradually becoming more accountable for public welfare. The day of the county almshouse was nearly at an end. In 1925 those legislators who visited the county almshouse in Sussex County came away convinced that the place was a "disgrace." They became advocates of the view that the time had come for Delaware to build a single modern facility for poor, elderly persons. The almshouse issue arose again in the 1929 session, but a bill to replace the antiquated county facilities with a state welfare home failed to pass. The assembly was shy about taking on the burden of welfare, but its members proved willing to assist in the area of public health. They increased the funding for existing state institutions such as the State Hospital at Farnhurst, and in 1925 agreed to purchase and maintain the Delaware Anti-Tuberculosis Society's hospital at Hope Farm in New Castle County.

The sponsor of the Hope Farm bill was Representative Florence M. Hanby, a Republican from Brandywine Hundred and the first woman tobe elected to the General Assembly. According to newspaper accounts, her fellow assembly members greeted her most cordially. She arrived at the outset of the January 1925 session to find two floral bouquets on her desk. "It looks like a second wedding," she remarked, and then got down to the business of participating in party caucus meetings and presenting legislation.[4] Later that same year Governor Robert P.

Robinson appointed Fannie Herrington to be his secretary of state. Miss Herrington was the first of her sex to serve in that capacity anywhere in the United States. It appeared that women were a rapidly rising force in state politics. Women's groups were among the best organized, least self-interested, and most persuasive lobbyists that legislators encountered. But what appeared to be the onset of a stream of wome legislators failed to materialize.Only one woman was elected to the legislature during the following decade.

Prohibition remains the most emblematic symbol of the "Jazz Age." Next to schools and taxes, that ill-fated reform was the most troubling and controversial issue to face the General Assembly in the 1920s. The Prohibition cause had strong defenders in Delaware, especially within certain religious groups, such as the Methodists, the largest denomination in the state. The most militant Prohibitionists belonged to the Anti-Saloon League, a group that kept a sharp eye on Prohibition enforcement and regularly lobbied the legislature.

Issues related to liquor came up at every session in the twenties. In 1923 advocates of a more relaxed approach to Prohibition presented a bill to permit doctors to prescribe remedies containing alcohol for medicinal purposes. The Anti-Saloon League saw that bill as the camel's nose of repeal sliding under the tent of rigorous enforcement. They dubbed it "the Bootleggers' Bill," and it went down to defeat.[5] In the 1925 session the "drys" took the offense with a proposal to increase the penalties on persons found with even a small amount of liquor in their possession. Here the "drys" encountered resistance. P.S. du Pont had led the unsuccessful fight for legalizing the use of medicinal alcohol. This time he and other anti-extremists won a victory when the so-called "hip flask" legislation failed to pass. The "hip flask bill" reappeared in 1929 and again went down to defeat as legislators slyly set it aside and allowed it to die a quiet death at the end of the session.

Other controversial bills of the 1920s included efforts to bring boxing matches and racetracks to Delaware. Aside from opposition on moral grounds, he main obstacle to the enactment of such legislation lay in the state constitution's prohibition of gambling. In 1929 proponents of horse racing thought they had found a clever way around the constitution. They proposed that Delaware create a state racing commission, and instead of charging racetracks a license fee, they figured to adopt a law to fine violators of the constitutional prohibition at the rate of $2000 a day. In that way the state could have its racetracks and the treasury could make money, all without violating the constitution.[6] It was a cunning scheme, but it failed to pass. Boxing also went down for the count. Both recreations seemed a bit too "racy" for Delaware's legislators at the time.

In 1925 the General Assembly marked its 100th regular session since the United States had declared its independence. To judge from their provision of $100 to celebrate the occasion the event was treated in a distinctly low-key fashion. It would be unpatriotic to leave discussion of legislative actions in the 1920s without noting the assembly's action in that same session to declare "Our Delaware" to be the state song "to inspire a love of our state," especially in school children.[7]

The song with its poetic images of each county has been doing just that ever since.

The 103rd General Assembly that gathered in Dover in January 1931 was the first assembly to meet following the stock-market collapse of 1929. Considering that an economic disaster had fallen upon the nation, the assembly went about most of its business much as usual. Republicans controlled both houses of the legislature, and a Republican, C. Douglass Buck, was governor. Governor Buck was able to report to the assembly that despite the effects of the Depression on tax receipts, the state's treasury held a surplus. That good news encouraged the Republican legislators to ignore their governor's advice and appoint a record number of legislative assistants.[8]

A last hurrah for the old State House shows the building, and its appendages built after the restoration of 1909, decorated for the inauguration of Governor C. Douglass Buck in January 1929. The legislature last met in the State House in November 1932. (Courtesy of the Delaware Public Archives)

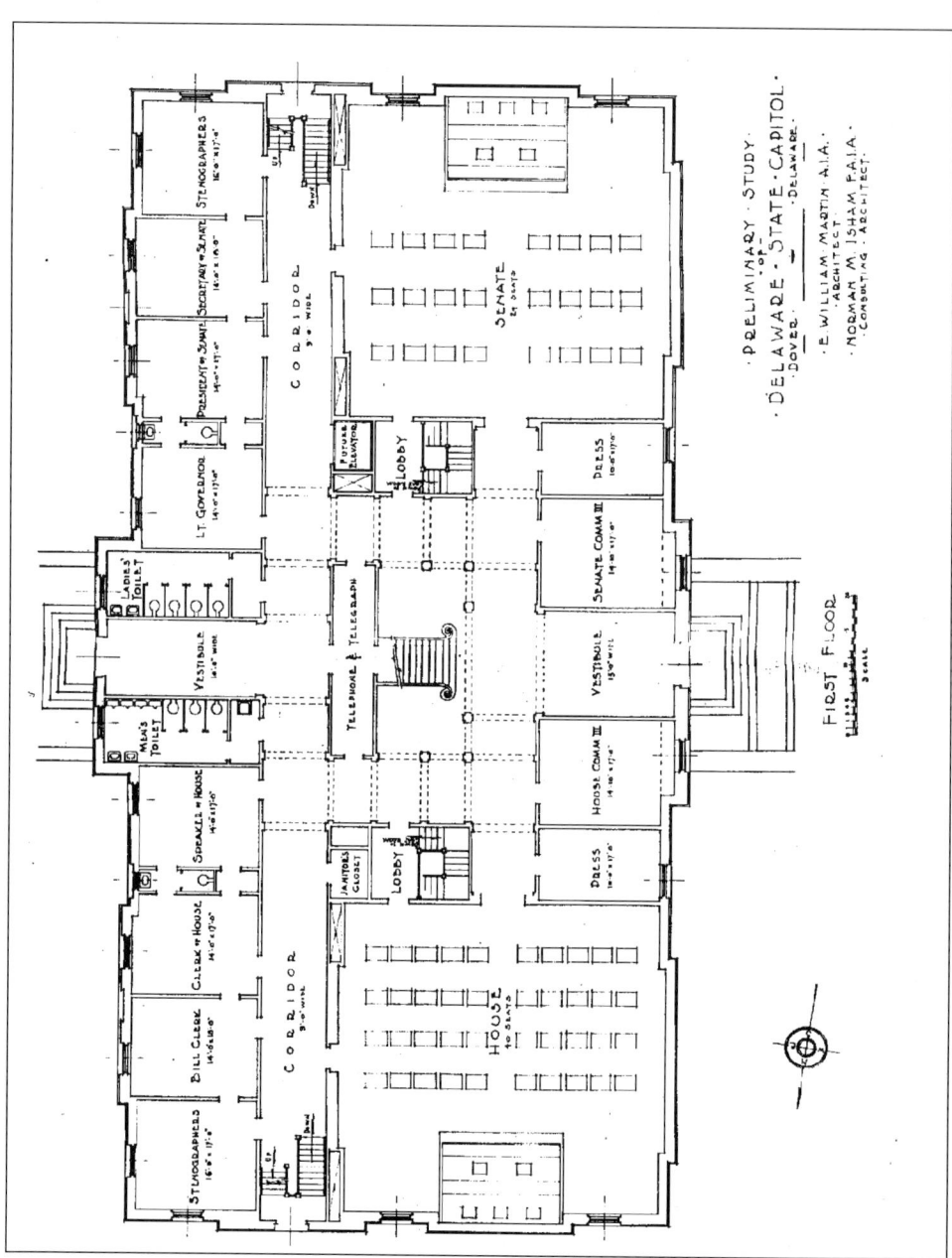

The preliminary plan for the first floor of Legislative Hall shows the dimensions and purposes for each room. (Courtesy of the Delaware Public Archives)

Sacrifice was not a high priority in the State House in another respect as well. The legislature authorized the creation of its new home. The assembly of 1929 had created a special commission to be appointed by Governor Buck to draw up plans for a new state government campus. Members of the commission included Judge W.W. Harrington and Mrs. Henry Ridgely of Dover, Henry L. Cannon of Bridgeville, and Hugh Rodney Sharp. Sharp was a brother-in-law of P.S. du Pont and the major force behind the creation of the University of Delaware's Green, with its Colonial Revival brick structures placed on either side of a swath of grass. Plans for the new capital complex conformed to a similar model.

Shortly into the 1931 session the commissioners presented to the legislature and the public an ambitious plan for a state-government campus. The centerpiece was to be a new Legislative Hall. The new hall would afford the legislators' greater space and dignity than they had in the State House. What's more, the new building could be designed in the colonial style to have moe "feel" of the eighteenth century than did the much-renovated, cramped but genuinely eighteenth-century structure that the General Assembly presently inhabited.

After consulting with architects at the nation's most famous colonial seats of government—Williamsburg, Virginia, and Annapolis, Maryland—the commissioners chose Norman Morrison Isham of Providence, Rhode Island, to direct the project. Isham had achieved national stature as an interpreter of colonial architecture. Most notably, Isham had designed the Rhode Island State House and had produced interior rooms in the Metropolitan Museum of Art in New York to be settings for the museum's American decorative arts collection. His in-state collaborator was architect E. William Martin of Wilmington.

The plan called for the state to purchase a large tract of land that extended from the old State House to the St. Jones River. The proposed Legislative Hall was to be placed at the head of a landscaped parkway facing the rear of the old State House from across a block-long field of grass. Additional colonial-style brick office buildings were to be built along the parkway as funding for them became available. The plan also called for the removal of the wings that had been added to the State House so as to restore the venerable building to its original 1790s appearance.[9]

The commissioners asked the assembly for $750,000 to complete the project. The legislature issued bonds to provide money to purchase the land, construct the proposed Legislative Hall, and undertake extensive landscaping. The commissioners produced a model of the plan to give the members of the assembly and the public a glimpse of what the new government campus would look like. The model was placed on display in the lobby of Wilmington's Hotel Du Pont, and a photograph of it appeared in the newspapers. In spite of, or possibly because of, the depressed times, the legislature rose to the occasion and voted the money to get the massive project underway. The landscaping and building provided jobs for many workers in Kent County during the worst days of the Depression.

The prolonged economic disaster prompted the assembly to take responsibility for Delaware's poorest and most vulnerable citizens. The legislature agreed to provide $1 million in each of the next two fiscal years for assistance to aged people living at home and voted to build a state welfare home to accommodate those who required institutional care. Alfred I. du Pont provided financial assistance to build the new facility just north of Smyrna, Delaware. With its completion the notorious county almshouses were closed forever.

Legislative Hall under construction in 1932. (Courtesy of the Delaware Public Archives)

It is ironic to note that in the midst of replacing those institutional relics of the dark side of colonial life, Delawareans were embarking on a veritable orgy of colonial remembrances. The design of the new state government buildings was but one manifestation of the pervasive activity that must have brought a sense of pride and security to a people buffeted by the Depression. It was in 1931 that the legislature created the Historical Markers Commission, which erected blue-and-gold colored signs at historically important spots throughout the state. The Zwannendael Museum, based on the design of the Town Hall in Hoorn, Holland,

and the statues of Caesar Rodney and John M. Clayton for Statutory Hall in the United States Capitol also received legislative support in that session.

The steely moralizing that had governed much government policy in the previous decade diminished in the Depression years. The notion that the state had to erect strong barriers to hold back the forces of immorality was being replaced by the attitude that activities such as boxing, horse racing, and even gambling should be permitted so long as they were carefully regulated. Probably the most important factor in changing the law to permit these activities was their potential as sources of state revenue. Whatever the motivation, the assembly adopted the boxing bill that had failed to pass in previous legislatures. The law created a State Athletic Commission to oversee boxing and wrestling matches.

In 1931 the assembly changed the way school districts were governed. The Republicans pushed through a bill to replace Wilmington's elected school board with a board to be appointed by the resident judge of the Superior Court. The new law so angered the Democrats that in retaliation they proposed a bill to extend the practice of judicially appointed boards to school districts throughout the state. To the Democrats apparent surprise, the Republicans accepted the idea.[10] The resulting legislation was un-democratic, but it took school boards out of politics and led to the selection of thoughtful, public-spirited board members who could operate independently of short-term public opinion.

Another hallmark of the 1931 session was the creation of a state board of budget directors to include the governor, state treasurer, and secretary of state. Governor Buck requested the measure to assist him in putting together a budget proposal to present to the assembly. The board increased the governor's control over state functions and ensured that future legislatures would receive a unified budget rather than an uncoordinated list of requests from the growing number of state institutions and agencies.[11] It marked the first step toward effective control over state spending.

The election of 1932 took place at the depths of the Depression. At the national level, Democrat Franklin D. Roosevelt defeated incumbent Herbert Hoover in a landslide that gave the Democrats control of Congress. In Delaware, however, the Republicans still retained some power. Although the GOP lost control of the Delaware House of Representatives, they maintained their majority in the Senate. The Republicans' gubernatorial candidate, C. Douglass Buck, also won re-election. Buck thus became the first governor in the state's history to hold a second term.

Immediately after the election, Governor Buck called the outgoing legislature into special session to consider his recommendation for relief. It would be the last time that a legislative session would meet in the old State House. The Depression had hit parts of the state in different ways. It reduced the value of farmland and depressed the prices that farmers received for their crops, but otherwise the Depression did not have so detrimental an effect on families engaged in agriculture as it did on those who were dependent on the industrial sector of the economy. Factory workers and office workers who lost their jobs had no way to maintain themselves. In Delaware, most of the industrially and commercially unemployed were located in or near the city of Wilmington. The governor's request thus had geographic implications.

This page and facing: two views of Legislative Hall photographed by Representative Frank R. Zebley in the 1930s. The interior view shows the Speaker's desk in the House of Representatives. (Courtesy of the Delaware Public Archives)

Governor Buck told the assembly: "I have summoned you to the Capitol to ask that you provide for the immediate needs of some 16,000 of our people who are looking to you to save them from starvation this winter."[12] Recognizing that the state could not provide enough direct relief to meet the emergency, he asked that the assembly provide work relief as well. The legislators responded with an act whereby Delaware took on $2 million in debt to distribute direct relief through an agency to be called the Emergency Relief Commission.[13] Having done their duty, members were invited to take their desks and chairs home with them since the next legislature would be meeting in its new home, with its new chairs and new desks.[14]

When the 104th General Assembly met in Legislative Hall on January 3, 1933, the splendor of their fresh, almost opulent, surroundings bore a striking contrast to the dark situation that confronted many of Delaware's people. In the Senate chamber the majority Republicans took a break from their internal squabble over which among them would be elected president pro tempore to hear Lieutenant Governor J. Henry Hazel pronounce his blessing on "this new and magnificent State Building. Here, for many generations," he predicted, "will be made the laws under which the people of the Commonwealth will live."[15] No one could disagree with that sentiment, and the Republicans resumed their battle for leadership while the Democrats happily seized their opportunity to control the outcome of the fight.

The messy clash in the Senate proved to be but a harbinger of the entire session. Finances, a rehash of the school-board issue, and Prohibition repeal kept the pot boiling well beyond the normal sixty-day limit. The session's most notable achievement may have been establishing a Racing Commission, a step that led to the construction of racetracks in Delaware and promised the state an additional source of income once the following legislative session agreed to modify the anti-gambling language in the state constitution.

The most time-consuming issue, however, was the repeal of Prohibition. With the death of the Eighteenth Amendment the legislature chose local option. Alcoholic drinks became legal in those parts of the state that voted to permit the sale of liquor. The legislature also created the Alcohol Beverage Control Commission to control the manufacture and sale of liquor in the state. Regardless of their personal opinions on the issue, legislators could look forward to another new source of revenue from the tax that they imposed on liquor sales. The new statutes respecting alcohol took up nearly 100 pages in the *Laws of Delaware* for 1933.[16]

Meanwhile, in Washington, Congress was busy enacting the Roosevelt administration's New Deal legislation. To bring Delaware into conformity with the National Industrial Recovery Act, Governor Buck recalled the General Assembly to Dover in October 1933. The legislators passed acts to enable cities and towns to undertake public works in cooperation with the new federal program, adopted a law to authorize the creation of housing authorities to participate in a federal program to build housing for the poor, and made more money from the state treasury available to provide relief in the coming winter.[17]

Tax policy dominated the assembly in its session in 1935. With the Republicans in charge of both houses there was a minimum of overt political infighting and nobody, except the Republican governor, to complain about the excessive number of attaches, or assistants, assigned to work in each house. Although the Depression had not abated, in 1935 the legislature voted to withdraw the state government from public assistance. In its place the legislators voted to allow New Castle County to impose additional taxes on its residents. The money raised was to be distributed among the county's needy through a matching program with the federal government to be administered by the Delaware Temporary Emergency Relief Commission.[18]

The state's corporate franchise tax presented the most interesting issue to come before the legislature in 1935 and again in 1937. Companies incorporated under Delaware law were required to pay an annual franchise tax based on the value of individual shares. That practice had worked well until the Depression, when some companies sought to lower their tax by reducing the par value of each share of their stock. As a result less money was flowing into Delaware's special fund to benefit the state's public schools.

At first the "low par" formula had little effect on state revenue because the state's tax was already so small that most companies were content to pay at the usual rate. But in the Depression decade some companies took advantage of the law to expand the number of their shares and thus reduce the value of individual shares. According to the calculations of State Tax Commissioner Pierre S. du Pont, by 1937 the "low par" formula was costing Delaware $1,250,000 a year in revenue.[19]

The franchise tax issue pitted one set of mainly Republican stalwarts, the members of the corporate bar, against the formidable business leader turned philanthropist, Pierre Samuel du Pont. What was a Republican legislator to do? One side raised the specter of corporations fleeing Delaware; the other side presented the equally unpalatable fact of declining revenue. P. S. himself admitted to the assembly, "I for one don't envy you gentlemen of the assembly who have to settle this question."[20] Not surprisingly, the dilemma so rattled the legislators that in 1935 they merely created a commission to undertake further study of the problem.

Governor Buck appointed P.S. du Pont to chair the commission. In 1937 du Pont presented his commission's report to the 106th General Assembly. The report called for a change in the franchise tax law that would, du Pont assured the legislators, restore the state's income without driving corporations out of Delaware. When the state's leading corporate lawyers, Democrat Hugh M. Morris and Republican Robert H. Richards, agreed to the change, legislators of both parties had little difficulty adopting a new formula for calculating the tax.[21]

In 1937 Delawareans inaugurated the state's first Democrat as governor since Ebe Tunnell had vacated the office in 1901. The new governor was Richard C. McMullen, a Wilmington leather manufacturer. He faced a split legislature in which his party held a majority in the House of Representatives while the Republicans continued to rule the Senate. Contrary to the New Deal's reputation for unconstrained government spending, Governor McMullen was an economy-minded fiscal conservative.

Members of the Joint Budget Committee, composed of the Senate's Finance Committee and the House Appropriations Committee, soon discovered that the governor's narrowly conceived view of economy could only be achieved at great cost to the state's responsibilities. Dr. M. A. Trumianz, the director of the State Hospital at Farnhurst, threatened to resign if his institution did not receive funds to overcome the institution's extremely overcrowded conditions. The director of the Ferris School for delinquent boys told the committee that at his facility Negro boys were being housed in a barracks "not fit for a hog to live in."[22]

The equality of the political parties in the assembly exacerbated tensions at a time when reduced state income clashed with expanding needs. In the Democrat-controlled House the chairman of the Appropriations Committee supported a relief bill, but Republicans, citing Governor McMullen's call for economy, voted it down in the Senate. Likewise, disagreement between the houses and between upstate and downstate members doomed a child-labor amendment. Unemployment compensation lost because the parties disagreed on the composition of the commission that would administer the program.[23] In short, a session that lasted sixty-eight days, eight days beyond the usual, produced little to warrant the $210,000 that the session cost tax payers.

In 1939 the GOP returned to power in both houses of the assembly and promptly appointed so many aides that Lieutenant Governor Edward W. Cooch, a Democrat, was forced to vacate his office on the second floor of Legislative Hall to give the Republican appointees more room.²⁴ The Republicans were feeling particularly cocky because shortly after the session began their senatorial candidate won a run-off election in Wilmington that assured them veto-proof majorities in both houses. It seemed a perfect situation for the majority party, but as is often the case in politics, things did not turn out as one might have expected.

The big battle of the session came over a bill to alter the composition of the State Highway Commission. When there had been a Republican in the governor's office, Republicans had been happy to give the governor power to choose the members of the commission. Now that a Democrat ruled, however, they voted to change the law to require bipartisan control and to prevent Republican employees from being replaced by Democrats. As expected, Governor McMullen vetoed the bill, calling it "purely partisan ripper" legislation.²⁵

The surprise came when a Sussex County Republican senator refused to vote to override the veto unless his designee was appointed to the commission. News stories of the discord that his action created jostled for readers' attention with Hitler's seizure of Czechoslovakia on the front page of the Wilmington press.²⁶ Governor McMullen broke with precedent to appear in person before the legislature to announce his veto of the "ripper" bill. He appealed to the senators' "better judgment as a group of honorable, high-minded men with the best interests of our state at heart."²⁷ The Republicans, however, were in no mood to compromise. The Democrats also hung tough by exploiting their threat to vote en mass against any measures, including the state budget, which required a three-fifths vote. Democrats now became strong supporters of civil-service reform. The Republicans claimed that they had no intention of firing all the Democrats who worked on the state's highways, but what Democrat would trust their word?

A session that had seemed to promise harmony had descended into petty squabbling over every issue. In the end the spoils system remained intact and the Democrats' refusal to vote for budget items cost numerous agencies, including fire companies and hospitals, the state aid that they usually received. The 107ᵗʰ General Assembly was one of the nastiest sessions on record. It revealed partisan politics at its worst. It is no surprise that Governor McMullen vetoed more bills that year than had any governor in the state's history. The session's two major accomplishments were creating a permanent budget commission to be chaired by the governor, and unifying the state treasury by eliminating the separate school and highway funds. For many decades thereafter there would be no separation of school and highway money from that in the general treasury.

In 1941 Delaware had a new governor, Walter W. Bacon, a Republican and a former mayor of Wilmington. With the Republicans also in charge of both houses, legislative leaders resolved to expedite the peoples' business without the embarrassing battles that had marred the preceding legislature.

While bombs rained down on London, Delaware's legislators debated the question of permitting communities to decide whether or not to allow theaters to show movies on Sunday. Most Republicans supported local option on the issue, so the Democrats balked as a tactical move to gain leverage over other more significant issues. In an effort to break the logjam, the Republicans in the Senate ordered Attorney General James R. Morford to enforce the colonial blue law in all its vigor. The resulting avalanche of arrests aimed at anyone engaging in "worldly employment" on the Sabbath was intended to demonstrate the anachronistic nature of a statute that had been adopted in 1740. On the Monday morning following the crackdown, several hundred gas-station operators, milk deliverymen, restaurant owners, and similarly employed people appeared en mass as defendants in state courtrooms.

The mass-arrest tactic struck at the dignity of some legislators, particularly those in the House, who responded with a resolution that members "will not be coerced or told by any fellow officer or department what it shall do." The dispute attracted national attention and prompted the editors of the *New York Times* to write that most states had similar unenforceable laws on their books. The editor asked: "How do we come to have laws which no one has the courage to enforce and no one has the courage to repeal?"[28]

The battle was between the two houses of the legislature, not between the attorney general and the legislature. The Senate had passed a bill sponsored by Senator Paul R. Rinard, a Wilmington Republican, calling for local option on the question of more than just movies on Sunday. The senators had included the possibility that communities could vote to permit horse races and other amusements on the Sabbath, as well. Since this legislation would alter town charters, concurrence in the House would require a two-thirds vote, an unlikely event.

A reporter described the discussions among legislators about the Sunday issue as being conducted "at a feverish pitch."[29] There were so many possible places to draw the line on what constituted acceptable behavior on the Sabbath. Some wanted to include sports, such as baseball and bowling; others were willing to even consider the possibility that communities might vote to permit dancing on Sundays. Some House members met privately with a group of ministers, including the president of the Anti-Saloon League, to find out what clergymen might think permissible. Those who attended the meeting returned prepared to permit the delivery of newspapers, milk, bread, and other essentials on Sundays, but definitely no dancing and no sports, except for playing tennis on private property.

The man who finally sliced the Gordian Knot was Representative Robert H. Richards, Jr., a lawyer and Republican from Wilmington. His bill side-stepped the two-thirds vote issue of the Rinard bill and permitted incorporated towns and cities to exercise local option on Sunday amusements. Despite the opposition of some members of the clergy, Richards's bill passed both houses and Governor Bacon signed it into law.[30]

Shortly thereafter Senator Rinard took a new job as the state's Adjutant General. Preparation for war fast overtook concerns about purely domestic matters during the latter half of 1941. In anticipation of the United States being drawn into the war, in 1941 the assembly created the State Council of Defense. Similar to the council of World War I, the S.C.D. was charged to oversee war production, defense, and transportation needs. In striking contrast to recent disagreements over the composition of commissions, there was unanimous support for the proposal to give the governor authority to select the council's members without regard for party affiliation.[31]

The General Assembly met twice in regular session and once very briefly in special session during the years in which the United States was engaged in World War II. The General Assembly convened in January 1943 in the midst of wartime austerity. War-related issues filled the assembly's agenda. To counter the state's loss of revenue from gasoline taxes, race tracks, and other usual sources, Governor Bacon requested that the legislature enact new taxes "for the duration" to maintain the state's solvency. The assembly voted to impose a special tax on cigarettes and added a 1 percent surcharge to the state income tax.[32] The legislature also voted to provide short-term aid to discharged servicemen. The Democrat minority quashed efforts to fund postwar highway construction projects, including the proposed bridge over the Delaware River, in retaliation for the Republicans' refusal to give the minority party some influence in the Highway Department. Similarly, the Democrats continued their longstanding opposition to the creation of a Family Court in New Castle County, which they feared the Republicans would control.

When the legislature met at its usual time in January 1945 the Battle of the Bulge was raging in Western Europe and American soldiers, sailors, and marines were engaged in desperate fighting against the armed forces of the Japanese Empire for control of far-off islands in the Pacific Ocean. Speaker of the House of Representatives Chester V. Townsend, Jr., of Dagsboro told his fellow representatives: "We are beginning our work in a distressing time. Sometimes we wonder if we are ever to have peace again. We have a great responsibility. Let us do our work in a businesslike manner."[33]

In 1944 the Republicans had triumphed in the contest for state offices. Walter Bacon had been re-elected governor, and his party continued its hold of the majority in both houses of the legislature. Once again, the big party battles were fought over a few issues that required either two-thirds or three-quarters votes, where a disciplined Democratic minority could affect the outcome. Quarreling and maneuvering on the Family Court issue and on money for highways and for the proposed bridge over the Delaware River consumed much of the legislators' time and dragged out the session.

Then, on April 12 came the unexpected news that President Franklin D. Roosevelt had died at Warm Springs, Georgia. The suggestion was proffered in the somber mood that followed to name the proposed bridge in his honor. The Republicans would have none of that, but within days the legislators enlarged that concept to make the bridge a memorial to all those in the service who had already lost, and were continuing to lose, their lives. Opposition melted, and the measure to bond the state for the bridge was passed unanimously.[34] The Democrats also gave up their resistance to postwar highway construction bonds, without which Delaware could lose federal matching funds.

Partisan contention then focused on the Family Court. Republicans planned to make the court as analogous as possible to the existing superior courts by providing for a judge to be appointed by the governor for a term of twelve years. Democrats insisted on a four-year term. In a rare show of compromise during the last frenzied hours of the session's final day, the contending parties reached accord on a six-year term.[35]

From the perspective of the legislature itself, perhaps the most important accomplishment of the 113th General Assembly of 1945 was its vote to create the Legislative Reference Bureau of Delaware. That body, to be composed of the governor, the Senate President Pro Tempore, and the Speaker of the House of Representatives, was to take responsibility for preparing and drafting legislation. The governor was empowered to appoint an attorney to act as the bureau's executive director.[36] Sponsors of the bill hoped that the bureau would expedite action in the General Assembly. Better time management was needed during the early weeks of each session when committees typically waited around for bills to come to them, only to receive them in an avalanche, often in skeleton form, when it was already too late to give proposed legislation more than a cursory reading. The effects of this new mode of operation would not be known until the spring of 1947.

The General Assembly that gathered in January 1947 promised to be the most "business-like" in many years. Republicans held both legislative chambers and the governorship. The Legislative Reference Bureau began meeting even before the fall elections of 1946 to put together the majority party's legislative package, including the state budget. When the assembly convened, the House speaker and Senate president pro tem moved quickly to assign fellow Republicans to legislative committees and to forward the budget and other legislative initiatives to them. The way seemed cleared for a smoothly efficient session.

Governor Walter Bacon made his program proposals public in his address to the legislature on its second day. Most significantly he urged the assembly to adopt a program of modest raises for the state's public school teachers, to enact restrictions on labor unions, and to require motorists to carry collision insurance. Regarding the state's finances, Governor Bacon sounded a cautionary note. In the immediate wake of the war, revenue remained down, and the modest surplus in the state treasury would be sufficient to see Delaware only through the biennium. By the time the next legislature met in 1949 it would be necessary to find additional sources of money to run the state.[37]

The governor's remarks did not sit well with teachers. In the postwar inflationary environment, they viewed the administration's projected raises of $200 as wholly inadequate when they were earning an average of between $2,000 and $3,000, which was less than many factory workers received. Governor Bacon responded that in 90 percent of Delaware's school districts the district did nothing to supplement the state's provision for teachers' salaries. Instead of asking more from the state, he suggested that districts tax themselves to provide higher pay to their teachers. Whatever its merits as a suggestion, the idea of locally administered taxes seemed unlikely to be forthcoming.

The teachers were not to be so easily subdued. They organized to fight back and enlisted PTA members in their support. The issue divided Republicans in the legislature and gave Democrats an opportunity to denounce the majority party. Democrats castigated their opponents for putting highways, the major source of patronage for the GOP, above education.

The Democrats then drew attention to the thoroughly undemocratic methods that the majority was employing to tame the legislature. They noted in particular the Republican leadership's refusal to appoint Democrats to legislative committees, to hold public hearings on important bills, or to make those bills available to the entire membership of the assembly prior to the floor vote. In short, the Democrats characterized the GOP's methods as a "steam roller pork barrel."[38]

The final showdown came on February 18 when the Senate took up the governor's controversial school bill. Before a hostile gallery filled with PTA members, a Republican senator invoked a parliamentary maneuver to cut off discussion of the bill on the floor and to table a proposed amendment that would have doubled teachers' raises. Amid a chorus of boos from the gallery, the senators proceeded to enact the bill on a straight party vote.[39] Still hoping to force reconsideration in the House, teachers from around the state drove to Dover and held a mass meeting in the Dover Field House before descending on Legislative Hall. At least one participant attached a sign to the rear of his car that read "TEACHERS Have Been BETRAYED By The Law Makers."[40]

The teachers' demonstration came at a particularly polarizing time in American labor relations. Mine workers were threatening to strike; the teachers of Buffalo, New York, were picketing before their schools; and Congress was about to adopt the union-weakening Taft-Hartley Labor Relations Act. In Dover the Republicans introduced their own version of Taft-Hartley called "An Act Regulating Labor Unions," but better known as HB 212. The bill was designed to weaken the hand of organized labor in the First State by denying unions some of their most effective bargaining tools such as closed shops, sit-down and slow-down strikes, and mass picketing. The Republicans' majority in both houses of the legislature ensured the passage of this highly controversial and divisive measure. Democrats shunned HB 212 as "un-American" interference with the rights of labor.

The assembly was also divided on issues of public welfare. In 1946 the federal government had approached Governor Bacon with a plan to cede Fort Du Pont to the state. The fort, located on the Delaware River just south of Delaware City, contained some sixty-five buildings in various states of repair. The governor had become increasingly concerned about overcrowding at the State Hospital at Farnhurst. He viewed the proposed gift as a godsend and promised the federal government's negotiators that if the fort were to be given to Delaware the state would use the facility to assist in its public-welfare responsibilities. At a ceremony on January 30, 1947, held before members of the General Assembly and other state officials, Governor Bacon officially accepted the deed to the property.[41]

Some legislators, particularly a few in the governor's own party, were inclined to look a gift horse in the mouth. Senator Harvey H. Lawson, a Millsboro Republican, called the acquisition "the biggest white elephant the state of Delaware ever had" and threatened to vote against the governor's proposal to spend over $1 million to refit the fort's buildings to be used as a hospital.[42]

Another skeptic was Vera G. Davis, a Dover Republican and the first woman to be elected to the state Senate. Senator Davis was no novice in politics or in dealing with public-health issues. Speaking from her perspective as a member of the State Board of Welfare and longtime activist in women's club work, she, too, labeled the fort a "white elephant." Her remark came in the course of a public sparing match with State Hospital head Dr. Tarumianz, who was eager to move alcoholics, crippled children, and epileptics into the fort's barracks.[43]

In the end Governor Bacon won. As part of the final all-night rush that marked the conclusion of every General Assembly, the weary legislators voted the $1,250,000 that the governor had requested to turn the fort into a hospital. Not long after the facility was renamed in his honor.

The General Assembly of 1947, begun with such high hopes for "business-like" efficiency, had turned out to be just as contentious as most of its predecessors. Not surprisingly it functioned best when dealing with matters on which Republicans could agree, such as support for state highways and the proposed bridge over the Delaware River, and restrictions on labor unions. There was a sense, however, that the Republicans might be in for a fall. Their policy of placing highways at the top of the state's budget agenda rankled not only with Democrats, but also with many teachers and PTA parents; and the Republicans support for HB 212 gave Democrats a big boost among labor-union members. The election year 1946 had been a good one for the GOP nationwide, but in Delaware the Republicans had dissipated much of their potential power with internal squabbling and divisive policies.

The election of 1948 stunned the Republicans both in Delaware and throughout the nation. Although Thomas E. Dewey, the Republican candidate for president, won in Delaware over the incumbent national victor, Harry S Truman, at the gubernatorial level Democrat Elbert N. Carvel of Laurel defeated the Republican candidate, Hyland George, by over 10,000 votes. Carvel attributed his victory to his campaign's emphasis on building schools and developing other state facilities, but the efforts of union leaders to get out the labor vote was also a factor.[44] After a decade of depression and a major war, the state and nation were engaged in a baby boom and were enjoying prosperity. As he prepared to meet the 115th General Assembly, Governor-elect Carvel knew that without tapping new sources of revenue the goals for which he had campaigned would be beyond reach. He also knew that Delaware needed those resources and could afford to pay for them.

It would not be unfair to characterize the legislative session of 1949 as the "session from Hell," not because it lacked accomplishment, but because in that year the legislature exceeded past extremes of party bickering. The session dragged on for eighty-six frustrating days. The root cause of the infighting was the absence of a workable majority. Although a Democrat was governor, the Republicans maintained control of both houses of the legislature, but only by one-vote margins. In the House the majority included a new representative for Wilmington's First District, William J. Winchester, the first African-American to serve in the General Assembly. The Republicans chose Harvey H. Lawson, formerly senator from Millsboro of "white elephant" fame, as their speaker. In recognition of his party's slender majority, Representative Lawson agreed to break precedent and to appoint two Democrats to every five-person House committee.

Vera G. Davis (1894-1974). In 1946 Mrs. Davis became the first woman to be elected to the State Senate and in 1949 she became its president pro tempore. Defeated for reelection to the Senate in an intra-party primary, she later won a seat in the House of Representatives, where she rose to be majority leader. (Courtesy of the Delaware Public Archives)

Things did not go so easily in the Senate with its nine Republicans and eight Democrats. Eight of the Republicans were split evenly between two candidates for president pro tempore. The ninth Republican, Vera Davis, also of "white elephant" fame, held aloof. The Democrats seized the opportunity to propose Senator Davis as president pro tempore. With her vote added to theirs, she won. The surprising coup caught the male Republicans off guard. They fumed when Senator Davis appointed Democrats to half of the Senate's attaché positions and, following the lead of Speaker Lawson, gave the Democrats two seats on Senate committees, all the while asserting that she had made no deal with the opposition.[45]

At the outset of the session, the strongly Republican *News Journal* papers, the state's only dailies, urged the assembly to take major steps to improve life in Delaware. The papers' list of necessary accomplishments included raising teachers' salaries, providing for road construction, creating an independent supreme court, and building a sewage disposal plant in Wilmington to clean up the heavily polluted Delaware River.[46] All were highly desirable actions, but each carried a price tag, and, as Governor Bacon had predicted two years before, the state treasury was no longer in surplus. The question of the moment was whether a deeply divided legislature, facing a governor of the opposite party, could summon the will to meet those important needs.

To increase the drama, there was the question of how long the session might last. In January no one paid much attention to the matter, but it was a factor because the previous two legislatures had voted to alter the state constitution respecting the formula by which members of the assembly were paid. In the past, members had received $600 for a sixty-day session. Under that plan if the legislature failed to complete its work in sixty days its members worked on at no pay. The effect had been to force legislators to stick to the limit, even if it meant conducting all-night sessions and fooling themselves as to the time by stopping the clock at midnight on the final night. But now the rules were changed. In future, assembly members could expect to receive a salary of $1000 regardless of how long the session might continue. The sixty-day limit had become history.

Add to that factor the politics surrounding the state's biggest employer, the State Highway Department. For twenty-two years Frank V. du Pont, T. Coleman's son, had ruled over the Highway Commission and had been the most powerful figure in the state Republican Party. When du Pont's term as commission chairman expired, Governor Carvel did not reappoint him. According to Carvel, "the Democrats were really up in arms about Frank du Pont. They hated his guts."[47] Even some Republicans thought him highhanded. In the 1947 legislature, Republican senators had become so irate at the commissioner's choice for chief of the state police that they adopted a resolution that removed the chief from office. The politics surrounding Frank du Pont's imperious reign and Carvel's refusal to reappoint him infected Legislative Hall.

The General Assembly of 1949 followed a trajectory unlike any before it. Everything moved at a glacial speed. The closing date for the admission of bills, which had always been in early March, did not come until a month later, by which time a record of 1,031 measures were before the legislature. A time-consuming debate over whether by law the appropriations bill had to be adopted by the session's fiftieth day kept the assembly from doing anything of substance for most of the month of April. Governor Carvel's call for increases in income, gasoline, liquor, and cigarette taxes provided an additional opportunity for infighting.

The result was a deadlock that took the legislature way beyond its usual sixty-day closing in early April, through the month of May and into June. Amazingly, things did eventually get done. Bipartisanship was forced on the Senate by the

Republicans' inability to overcome a united minority that could count on the support of President Pro Tempore Davis when she thought the state's welfare was at stake. In the House, progress on major bills sometimes hinged on deal making between Governor Carvel and Speaker Harvey H. Lawson. After weeks of bickering, Lawson agreed to accept the governor's budget in exchange for state funding to dredge the Indian River in his constituency.[48] The battle to revoke the previous assembly's labor legislation pitted the Democrats and Wilmington Republicans, who dared not vote against repeal, against the outnumbered Republicans representing rural districts. The session finally ended on June 3, with the legislators continuing their old habit of meeting all night to complete the people's business. In the final frenzy they passed the Wilmington sewage-plant bill and a school-construction bond bill.

Perhaps most important of all, after many years of failure, they voted for the constitutional amendment to create a separate and independent Supreme Court. When the legislature of 1951 also ratified that change, Delaware became the last state to adopt an independent supreme court. It is ironic that the creation of the Supreme Court, which earlier legislatures had shunned out of fear that the other party might get the opportunity to name the justices, was first ratified by an assembly so notable for its political volatility.

As the 115th General Assembly came to a close the *News Journal* editor could not resist calling the session "A Legislative Nightmare." In fairness, he added, "by the end of the session, if not before, most members were acting like Delawareans rather than like blind partisans. Which makes us all, we trust, one family again...."[49]

When the General Assembly next met in January 1951, the United States was at war in Korea and Republicans were cautioning voters about "creeping socialism" connected to Democrats' big-spending policies. Wartime anxieties and an effort to distance himself from negative images of his party were manifest in Governor Carvel's admonition to the legislators to resist unnecessary spending. Paradoxically, his plea came just as his administration announced that in 1950 the state's revenue from all sources had broken all previous records and had outdistanced the state's income in 1949 by a whopping 114 percent.[50]

At its outset, the 116th General Assembly appeared destined to be a repeat of its squabbling, politically divided predecessor. Although the Democrat-controlled Senate got off to a smooth start, in the Republican-controlled House, sparks flew over the choice of speaker. Harvey H. Lawson of Millsboro was eager once more to sit in the speaker's chair, but he faced opposition from F. Albert Jones of Claymont, who had the support of the majority of the GOP representatives. Just as the Democrats had taken advantage of a split in the ranks of the GOP majority in the Senate two years before, the House Democrats now rallied behind Lawson, who won the speaker's position with their support and that of Sussex County Republicans. Jones, who was the favorite of the Republicans of New Castle and Kent Counties, was rewarded with the position of majority leader.

Once the houses were organized the politically discordant assembly faced the usual number of difficult issues. State Attorney General H. Albert Young zealously presented the legislature with drafts of over thirty bills intended to reform Delaware's criminal code and anti-gambling statutes. Another thorny issue resulted from the state's promise made in 1945 to purchase the New Castle to Pennsville ferries when the Delaware Memorial Bridge made them redundant. Now the legislature would have to fulfill its commitment.

To the surprise and relief of most observers, and probably not a few legislators as well, the 116th General Assembly was among the most harmonious on record. The collaborations, compromises, and agreements that made it possible resulted from the decision to adopt a Draconian method designed to sort through and prioritize the hundreds of bills presented to the legislature. In the past those tasks were accomplished within the caucuses of the majority parties in each house. That method worked best, of course, when the same party controlled both houses. In 1951, however, not only did different parties control each house, but the House of Representatives was so internally divided that the speaker and majority leader led different factions within the majority party.

To avoid a stalemate, legislative and party leaders agreed to create a Legislative Conference Committee. Members of that committee included leaders from both houses as well as leaders from the state party organizations. Those backstage party managers, often called the assembly's third house, were, for a brief moment at least, placed directly in the public eye. The assembly agreed to cede to the Conference Committee the responsibilities usually exercised by the majority caucus. The novel mechanism made work go forward most expeditiously. The Conference Committee held hearings on major legislation, where proponents and opponents were allowed to voice their views, and then decided which bills it would recommend to the legislature. The members of the eight-member Conference Committee agreed among themselves to vote out only those bills that received at least six of their votes, so bills came to the full assembly with compelling recommendations.

The special committee, effective though it proved to be, struck some people both in and out of the General Assembly as undemocratic. But, as Jack Gibbons, a political reporter for the *News-Journal* papers noted: "The existence of the all-powerful caucus system in itself is scarcely democratic."[51] One of those who objected to the Conference Committee's power was Senator Ernest B. Benger, a Westover Hills Republican. Senator Benger could not democratize the Conference Committee, but he did succeed in removing the mystery behind the workings of the legislature's other most powerful committee: the Joint Budget Committee. Senator Benger presented a resolution to require that committee to provide a written report to members of the legislature explaining their budget recommendations. His idea was welcomed in the assembly, especially among those who felt powerless because they served on neither major committee. The "backbenchers" showed their appreciation for the Budget Committee's report by voting to accept their budget recommendation with only tiny alterations.[52]

The streamlined methods did help the legislature to accomplish a good deal. The assembly enacted many of Attorney General Young's crime and gambling bills into law. In addition, they bit the bullet by agreeing to purchase the Delaware River ferries, as their predecessors had promised to do, and they gave final approval to the constitutional amendment to create the independent Delaware Supreme Court. The assembly also voted to allow a zoning commission to undertake planning in rapidly suburbanizing New Castle County. Other accomplishments included providing money to stamp out tuberculosis and to undertake slum clearance in Wilmington. The legislators voted for a model adoption law and funded new structures at the University of Delaware. In fulsome praise of the accomplishments of the 116th General Assembly, the editor of the *Wilmington Morning News* wrote that the legislature had been "awake to the needs of the state, responsive to public opinion, conscientious and hard-working."[53]

Left in the dust, however, were several important initiatives, including the need for more formal structures to hold together the commissions, institutions, and offices of Delaware's burgeoning government. The state was now operating on a biennium budget of $52,678,194 with the same formal organizational structure that had been appropriate when the budget and all that it represented had been a tiny fraction of that size.

School district consolidation had also emerged as a partisan issue. Thirty years earlier the Republicans had led the way in consolidating Delaware's many school districts and in imposing a strong State Board of Education to control the state education system. At that time the Democrats had been the party of local, non-professional control of education. But in the wake of the New Deal, the parties had switched positions. In the 1940s and 1950s it was the Democrats who sought the consolidation of state agencies, especially those engaged in health and social services, and it was the Republicans who stood in the way.

In the summer of 1951 as the first motorists drove up the arched roadway of the Delaware Memorial Bridge, awestruck at the size and might of its massive towers and powerful steel cables, few could have imagined the other fundamental changes that lay in store for Delaware and Delawareans just over the horizon.

9
FEDERALISM IN ACTION, 1952-1972

In the early 1950s rural, conservative forces were in control of Delaware's General Assembly. During the two decades from 1952 to 1972 that control was to change dramatically. The origin of that profound change came from the United States Supreme Court. With the striking exceptions of the Revolutionary War and Civil War periods, Delaware and its legislature never experienced such a basic transformation. The doctrine of "states rights" was under assault. Although the General Assembly resisted the changes that were forced upon the state, the legislature ultimately adapted and became a better focused and more experienced lawmaking body.

Delaware's General Assembly took state sovereignty very seriously. The little state's legislators relished great powers that belonged to them alone. In no other state did a legislature possess the exclusive right to alter its state's constitution. Under the Delaware Constitution of 1897 amendments could be adopted only if they passed two consecutive legislatures with a two-thirds vote in each. No governor's signature was required and no popular vote could force the legislative hand. Delaware had no initiative, referendum, or recall legislation. For some, this remarkable legislative power was a comforting bulwark; for others, it was a troubling barricade designed to frustrate democracy.

During the third quarter of the twentieth century the federal government, most particularly the United States Supreme Court, intervened to change Delaware in ways that the state's citizens could hardly have imagined in 1952. In the landmark case *Brown* v. *Board of Education* in 1954 the Court undid the legal basis for the segregation of the races in American public schools. Eight years later in *Baker* v. *Carr* the Court required states to structure their legislative bodies according to the principle of "one man, one vote." Those judicial decisions had major impacts on the First State that transcended the implementation of desegregation and reapportionment. They heralded a new style of politics and government in Delaware. To fully comprehend the significance of the federal courts' mandates, consider what Delaware and its legislature were like in the early 1950s.

In 1952 Delaware operated a segregated school system. The state enforced an Innkeepers' Law adopted in 1875 that permitted restaurant and hotel owners to deny service to anyone whom they or their customers found offensive. Under this law black people were routinely denied service in establishments that catered to the white majority. In addition, real-estate agents and their white clients observed discriminatory practices that maintained the separation of the races in the housing market and restricted black citizens to the least desirable neighborhoods.

In 1952 a state judge sentenced a man to be whipped with a cat o' nine tails while shackled to a post. At that time Delaware alone among the United States retained the whipping post, a punishment that had been discarded by sister states and by most of the civilized world as a barbaric relic of the past. More than a century before, during the reform era of the 1820s and 1830s, when other states were abandoning the post, Delaware's leaders had urged the General Assembly to do likewise, but those admonitions had failed to convince a majority in the legislature.

Eventually Delaware stood alone in maintaining the whipping post. Adherents of the bloody punishment claimed that the threat of whipping kept criminals out of the state. Those governors and legislative leaders who opposed the punishment feared to raise the issue because to do so would draw national attention to a practice that had the support of a majority in the General Assembly. The legislature's one venture into dealing with the post in the twentieth century was in 1935 when the assembly outlawed the photographing of whippings. Their concern was to prevent the recurrence of the state's embarrassment when a Philadelphia newspaper had published a picture of a whipping at New Castle County's Greenbank prison. The message from the assembly was that whippings might appear barbaric but they prevented crime.

By mid-century the composition of the General Assembly was becoming increasingly unrepresentative of the state's population. The inequalities that rural interests had demanded in Delaware's Constitution of 1897 had grown increasingly egregious. According to the United States Census Bureau, the state's total population in 1950 was 318,085, of whom more than two thirds lived in New Castle County. The city of Wilmington alone accounted for 110,356 people. Yet Kent County with only 37,870 inhabitants and Sussex County with 61,336 each had ten representatives and five senators in the General Assembly, compared to Wilmington's five representatives and two senators. Leaving the city out of the equation, the rural portion of New Castle County alone accounted for more people than the populations of Kent and Sussex Counties combined. And yet rural New Castle County's representation in the legislature equaled that of each of its sister counties.

Never before had the clash of cultures represented by the urbanized industrial area north of the Chesapeake and Delaware Canal and the agrarian lands and small towns south of the canal been so powerful as in the middle of the twentieth century. New Castle County experienced exuberant postwar industrial expansion. Two automobile assembly plants opened there and Wilmington's chemical companies—Du Pont, Atlas, and Hercules—added many employees to their management and research staffs. The workers in those industries, white-

and blue-collar alike, sought homes in burgeoning suburban developments throughout northern New Castle County. Yet, how likely was it that the legislators who represented Kent and Sussex counties would vote in two successive legislatures to renounce their control over the assembly by distributing power more fairly to New Castle County?

An election ballot of 1952, the last election before Delaware adopted voting machines. (Courtesy of the Historical Society of Delaware)

Delaware's government had been designed for an agrarian age. People in rural areas were comfortable with a state government that relied on a myriad of commissions headed by citizen-commissioners appointed under laws that gave each county an equal number of seats. Residents of every rural town and village knew of a local person who was a commissioner of something or other. By contrast, New Castle County's urban and suburban residents were less likely to know a commissioner. A system that seemed home-grown to residents of a Sussex County town appeared disjointed, unresponsive, and unprofessional to New Castle County suburbanites.

Delaware's politics revolved around the counties and the concept of geographic rotation. The political parties were organized at the county level. Each party chose its candidates for statewide offices on the basis of county rotation and balance. Similarly, candidates for the General Assembly were selected from among the party faithful on the basis of rotation among the communities within each representative or senatorial district. The rotation of legislative candidates among the towns and villages within each district produced high turnover in Legislative Hall.

Despite seemingly ceaseless alterations to the laws governing registration and voting, election practices had really changed little since the days of John E. Addicks. In 1952 Delawareans still voted by marking large paper ballots. The system was rife with corruption. Both parties scrambled to distribute ballots among poor people, who were bribed with money and liquor to cast their vote for that party's slate.

While both parties indulged in bribing voters, the Republicans had deeper pockets and were acknowledged to be more effective at it than the Democrats. That advantage compensated the GOP for the Democrats stronger hold among New Castle County's industrial workers and southern Delaware's rural conservatives. Thus, despite the appeal of the Democratic Party to many Delawareans, the GOP remained the state's dominant political force. In the forty years beginning in 1916 and ending in 1956 Delaware voted for the Republican presidential candidate in every election except those held during the Depression and World War II, when Franklin D. Roosevelt carried the state.

In the early 1950s Delaware's General Assembly was low on experience and high on turnover. In 1956 Paul Dolan, then the state's major scholar in the study of Delaware government, published a book entitled *The Government and Administration of Delaware*. Professor Dolan described the legislators as short-term, part-time, parochial, and inexperienced. "It is extremely rare to find a member of the legislature who feels he is representing the people of the entire State. His primary and almost sole allegiance is to his constituency and to his county, particularly in the rural areas.... One member of a locality is considered no more gifted than the next to represent the interest of the community," he wrote. Because "members of the legislature are workaday citizens..., attendance at legislative sessions takes up too much time of a man's life." Farmers, who constituted a significant percentage of the body, usually stayed only one term because they found it difficult to attend to the state's business while managing their farms. Businessmen, bankers, and lawyers who won seats in the assembly were likewise inconvenienced and inclined to remain but a short time. One reason for their reluctance to stay on was the low pay of $1000 per session, which hardly compensated members for time lost from clients and customers.[1]

More insidious than the low pay were the frustrations that were endemic to legislative service. "No other group of folks in the state take more collective abuse than members of our General Assembly," wrote the editor of the *Delaware State News* in 1961.[2] Professor Dolan agreed. "There is a feeling among many legislators," Dolan reported, "that their efforts in Dover are wasted." Too often, deadlocks, stalemates, and snarls blocked important initiatives while only trivial, non-controversial bills, each designed to aid particular legislators' constituents, got passed. Legislators had no working space except for their desks on the floor of the house in which they served. They had no assistance beyond the largely untrained attaches appointed by the majority party as compensation for political services. Dolan concluded that "lack of working space and proper assistance have turned men from seeking reelection."[3]

The professor spoke of "men" because, as he noted, only four women had served in the assembly in the three and a half decades since women had gotten the vote. Most legislators were men in their fifties and sixties, but Dolan looked with some hope on the World War II veterans' generation that was beginning to infuse the institution with "more youthful blood."[4]

Paul Dolan cited the experience of one recent legislator to confirm his assertion that service in the Delaware General Assembly was rife with frustrations. His source was Ernest B. Benger, a senator from the wealthy Westover Hills area northwest of Wilmington. Benger was appalled by the disorganization and "undemocratic" practices that he found among his colleagues in Dover.[5] As a scientist employed by the Du Pont Company, he was used to the orderly, rational processes that governed decision-making in the chemical corporation.

Senator Benger published his observations of the assembly in a series of essays entitled "Your Legislature" that appeared in the *Wilmington Morning News* during the month of October 1951. The essays provide a window into the workings of an institution that was the antithesis of what modern corporations sought to be. He described his colleagues as parochial in their loyalties and shortsighted in their views. To the extent that members submitted to anyone's rule it was to the leadership of their party caucus. In the Senate the majority caucus led by the president pro tempore made all major decisions. Because senators had no offices, they were forced to meet colleagues and constituents in the crowded conditions of the Senate floor amid a sea of lobbyists. The railroads, oil companies, and teachers' organization, in particular, maintained lobbyists on the floor at all times during the sessions.

Although space was at a premium, money for attaches was not. There were about one hundred of those patronage employees, including five cloakroom attendants, nine sergeants at arms, and six messengers, who sat around waiting to be asked to pass papers from place to place. But there were few stenographers and only two lawyers available to assist members in gathering information or drafting legislation.[6]

Such disorder bordering on chaos gripped Benger and many of his colleagues with a feeling of purposelessness. "Visitors to Legislative Hall often comment on the confusion and lack of scheduling which they observe," he wrote. There were many frustrating delays. Members sat around not knowing why their leaders had disappeared or when they might return. The assumption was that the leadership was engaging in some high-level meeting, perhaps with the Speaker of the House and the governor, but nobody knew for sure. At such times, Senator Benger wrote, "the ordinary legislator wastes a prodigious amount of time standing around the chambers and corridors in casual conversation with his colleagues or visitors."[7]

Senator Benger wrote that 80 percent of the members of the House and 65 percent of the senators in the General Assembly of 1949 had no previous legislative experience. Yet little attention was paid to introducing the newcomers to the work of the bodies to which they had been elected. There was no manual of procedures and no pre-session orientation. Benger described his fellow lawmakers as "people who can spare the time, to whom $1000 a year is important" or people who have earned a reward from their party. Some, he said, liked "the game" of politics; he attributed more selfish motives to others. It was no wonder that members were easily persuaded to stick to their party's platform and leadership, even when their personal predilections might have been to vote otherwise.[8] Ordinary legislators were especially likely to take their cue from their party's leaders in voting on the budget, as few even attempted to master the state's complex finances.

The committee system was a sham. It was designed to give the appearance of communal input into legislation, but most often committees were but a mechanism for the leadership of the majority party to maintain control. No time was set aside for committee meetings on the legislative agenda, so committees seldom met "except on those rare occasions when they hold public hearings." Usually, Benger reported, the committee chair circulated the bills assigned to his committee among the members wherever he might encounter them to get their signatures. A majority of signatures in favor or "on its merits" would bring a bill to the full Senate, while a majority of signatures marked against a bill would kill it, all without holding a meeting of the committee.[9]

The most important committee was not a standing committee of either house, but rather the Conference Committee, aptly called the screening committee. This powerful group consisted of the leaders of the majority party from each house plus the state party leadership. During the final frantic days of a legislative session, when there were stacks of bills awaiting action and only a few hours in which to act, it was up to the Conference Committee to decide which legislation to push through and which to let die. In situations where different parties controlled the two houses, the process involved trades that were not so clear or simple.

Senator Benger intended to open the public's eyes to the serious flaws in the state's lawmaking body. The senator concluded his series of articles with a plea for greater citizen input into legislation. He pointed out that without hearing a wide range of public views, legislators were prone to vote the way their party leaders dictated, react to the persuasions of a few discontents, or accept the views of self-serving lobbyists.[10]

Several years later, in 1958, Arden E. Bing published the *Delaware Blue Book*, the first guide to the state's government. The book contained the names and short biographies of the members of the 119th General Assembly elected in 1956. The information strongly reinforced the impression of rural dominance in the legislature. By far the majority of legislators were Delaware-born, public-school educated Methodists who earned their livelihoods in farming. Several were veterans of World War II. Very few had earned college degrees, and union members were virtually nonexistent outside the delegations from Wilmington.[11]

The governor's voice was the greatest outside influence on legislators of his party, but his views only carried weight when his party controlled enough votes to pass his bills. In the years from 1949 through 1965 Delaware had two governors: Elbert Carvel, a Democrat from Laurel, and Caleb Boggs, a Kent County-born Republican who resided in New Castle County. Both men tried to strengthen the government of the First State, but their efforts were frequently blocked by the stubborn parochialism and narrow partisanship that infected the General Assembly.

In 1951 Elbert Carvel was in the middle of his first term as Delaware's chief executive. In that year he had helped persuade the legislature to create a separate state Supreme Court to be composed of full-time justices, a major accomplishment that previous General Assemblies had long resisted. Now Governor Carvel faced an equally difficult challenge: to prevail upon the Senate to elevate Vice Chancellor Collins J. Seitz to chancellor of the Court of Chancery.

Vice Chancellor Seitz had gained notoriety that transcended judicial circles in 1950 when he ruled to break the color barrier by admitting several black students to the University of Delaware. Carvel admired the vice chancellor's fairness and courage, but his reappointment was politically risky. Wilmington *News-Journal* columnist Bill Frank recalled attending a celebration in New Castle to mark the town's tercentenary. The members of the General Assembly were scheduled to participate in the ceremony, but they failed to appear on time. Frank later learned that the senators were delayed because they were engaged in tense negotiations with the governor over the Seitz confirmation. According to the newsman, the price the governor paid to secure a majority vote was the paving of some dirt roads in Sussex County.[12]

The Seitz appointment was destined to produce historic results. In 1952 the chancellor ruled in favor of several black plaintiffs who sought entry to all-white public schools in New Castle County, Delaware. The cases went to the federal courts on appeal and were among those incorporated in the United States Supreme Court's landmark decision in *Brown v. Board of Education of Topeka, Kansas, et al.* in May 1954.

On January 6, 1953, Elbert Carvel appeared before the newly elected,

Republican-controlled 117th General Assembly to give his final message. Delawareans were prosperous, he said, enjoying the highest per-capita income of any state, so there was reason to be optimistic about the state's ability to tackle its unmet needs. But all was not well. "A blight obscures the fair face of our beloved State. Our election laws encourage corruption in the way of vote buying and repeating by both of our major political parties."[13] He proposed that Delaware replace its paper ballots with less corruptible voting machines.

Incoming Governor Caleb Boggs, a Republican, agreed. Boggs made election reform a high priority for his administration. HB 2, "An Act to Provide for the Use of Voting Machines," was introduced in the House on January 23, 1953, the same day that Boggs gave his first speech to the legislature. Although in Delaware both parties bought votes, voting fraud had always favored the Republicans, so it took some political courage for the GOP majority to join their governor in voting to bring the less easily corrupted machines to the First State. It was also not too surprising that the Democrats won a majority of seats in the assembly in the next election of 1954.

Both Carvel and Boggs also supported another reform, the introduction of civil service. The chief executives recognized that Delaware's government had grown to a size and a complexity where politically appointed operatives could no longer be counted on to provide adequate public service. Neither governor could persuade the General Assembly to accept that view. A majority of the legislators of both parties refused to scrap a system that, however flawed, provided jobs for friends, neighbors, relatives, and, in some cases, themselves.

The State Highway Department was the biggest patronage prize. The department, which included the state police, mosquito control, and other functions, offered more state jobs and contracts than any other unit in Delaware's government. What's more, the Highway Department determined when and where roads would be constructed or improved. Its decisions could make a landowner richer or poorer.

The Highway Department had long been a Republican fiefdom. That changed quite dramatically in 1955 when the Democrats seized control of the General Assembly with the aid of the voting machines. Over Governor Boggs's strenuous objections, and even over the warnings of their own party leaders, the Democrats in the legislature voted to recast the Highway Commission into a Democrat-controlled organization. Taking a page from the Republican book, the Democrats enacted one of the most noteworthy pieces of "ripper" legislation in Delaware history. Instead of giving the governor the power to name the new commissioners, as was the custom, the "ripper" legislation included the names of the new commissioners in the bill.[14]

The Highway Commission Act could stand as a metaphor for the political deadlock that dominated executive-legislative relations during most of Caleb Boggs's eight-year administration. To the acute frustration of the Republican governor and GOP legislators, major bills were passed or defeated by the vote of the Democratic caucus without public debate or open hearings. In one session in the mid-1950s the Democrats overrode fifty-five of the governor's fifty-nine vetoes.[15]

The Republicans in the assembly retaliated against the Democrats' ripper legislation. They launched a barrage of accusations that the Highway Department's Democrat commissioners were engaging in corrupt practices, including conflicts of interest that involved some members of the legislature. The resulting probes yielded no indictments, but they kept the political pot boiling. More importantly, the bad publicity aroused public indignation and cynicism about state government in general, and the General Assembly in particular.

In the mid-1950s inflation was increasing the state's costs at a pace that exceeded its revenues. The short-term response to the problem was to borrow money. As the state's debt grew it became obvious to all that more fundamental changes were in order, but the two parties could not agree on how to solve the financial dilemma. While the debt continued to rise, the executive and legislative branches remained trapped in a stalemate. Governor Boggs's solution was to increase taxes and to create a department of finance to better manage the state's income and outgo. The Democratic majority in the General Assembly, however, was determined to cut taxes and to prevent significant changes in the inner workings of the state's finances and bureaucracy.

While the state's fiscal position deteriorated, each party battled to gain an advantage with the voters. The parties offered contrasting remedies and laid the blame for the problems at the feet of their opposition. Governor Boggs and the minority Republicans called for a reorganization of the government to render it more efficient. The Republicans called the Democrats' tax-cutting and service-cutting efforts "astounding evidence of financial irresponsibility."[16] The Democratic spokesman on financial matters was Senator Walter J. Hoey of Milford, who chaired the Joint Finance Committee. Senator Hoey displayed a machete behind his desk to signal his intent to slash the state budget. He refused to entertain the possibility of raising taxes because, he said, he had pledged as much to the voters. The two sides did agree, however, to create an annual budget to replace Delaware's historic biennial budgeting system, a relic of the Constitution of 1831.

On January 7, 1959, Governor Boggs told the legislators that "Delaware is at a crossroads." He described how the state's government might be reformed to be more effective yet less costly under a plan that he called "A New Day for Delaware." Noting the severity of the ongoing financial crisis, Governor Boggs told the assembly, "we are trying to meet the needs of a growing state with an antiquated governmental system." The state could not continue to operate with the methods that had served its citizens in the past, he said. Delaware was then the fourth-fastest growing state in the nation. Its population had risen more than 50 percent in the previous eleven years. Government had not caught up with that growth. By good fortune, the state had been saved from even more horrendous deficits thanks to a few timely tax windfalls from the estates of wealthy individuals.

The governor urged the legislature to authorize a referendum for a new constitution. In the meantime, he recommended the adoption of amendments to the present constitution to establish annual sessions of the General Assembly, to provide home rule for incorporated towns and cities, and, most important, to reapportion the legislative districts to better reflect present population patterns. He also called for legislation to reduce the number of school districts, to enact civil-service reform to help attract capable careerists, and to remove the State Police from the control of the politically-charged Highway Commission.[17]

On May 20, 1959, Governor Boggs again came before the legislature to present a more complete outline of what he hoped "New Day in Delaware" might accomplish. His goal was to replace the state's one-hundred-plus uncoordinated boards, agencies, and commissions with a few departments whose heads would report to the governor. Such a basic reform would be politically neutral, he declared, recalling that in 1950 a special bipartisan commission had offered a similar recommendation. Legislatures controlled by both parties had ignored that proposal. But the assembly should now think again, Boggs said, because within a year Boggs would be out of office and either party might command the executive branch when the proposed change was implemented.[18]

The 120th General Assembly to which Governor Boggs spoke was firmly under the control of the Democrats, who held a twenty-six to nine majority in the House and an eleven to six majority in the Senate. Sherman Tribbitt, a former banker and storeowner from Odessa in southern New Castle County, was Speaker of the House of Representatives. In the Senate two factions of the Democratic Party engaged in a very public power struggle for leadership. That split allowed the Republicans to dictate the outcome by casting their ballots for one of the Democratic contenders for president pro tempore.[19] The winner was Allen J. Cook of Kent County. Cook took a leave of absence from his job as a highway sign inspector for the State Highway Department to accept the position.

The Democrats showed no interest in releasing the "New Day" proposals from committee. In December 1959 the exasperated governor called the legislators back into special session to deal with what he called a "severe financial crisis." Boggs urged the legislators to put "reforms before taxes."[20] Speaker Tribbitt responded with a promise to hold open hearings to consider the governor's proposed sweeping reorganization of the executive branch as one big package rather than as a series of individual departmental bills. The Speaker also asked for a "detailed analysis of the tax dollar saving" to be realized through the reform.[21]

For a moment it appeared that something might be achieved from the "New Day" plan. The outcome proved otherwise. Despite Speaker Tribbitt's unified plan, Senate President Pro Tempore Cook decided to treat the reform in a piecemeal fashion. He sent its parts to various standing committees. Republican Senator Reynolds du Pont introduced a bill to form a joint ad hoc committee to treat the governor's proposal, but it predictably failed to pass. Commissioners and agency administrators were unified in their opposition. Citizens in southern Delaware in particular liked the myriad commissions ruling over politically appointed job holders, and lower Delaware had the votes to thwart the creation of a bureaucracy of civil servants who would report to the governor. Opponents rallied to smother the "New Day" proposal in each committee. Even the governor's most prized recommendation, the creation of a department of finance, went down to defeat.

The governor's "New Day" was not dead; it was just premature. Eventually every one of the major reforms that Governor Boggs championed in his "New Day for Delaware" plan would be enacted into law with the exception of the proposed new constitution.

Speakers of the House of Representatives of the 1960s through 1980s. Front row from left: Harold T. Bockman, George C. Hering III, Robert W. Riddagh, Kenneth W. Boulden, John P. Ferguson. Back row from left: Charles L. Hebner, Sr., Casimir J. Jonkiert, Orlando J. George, Jr., Sherman Tribbitt, John F. Kirk, Jr. (Courtesy of the Delaware Public Archives)

Crime and punishment issues also absorbed the legislature during the late 1950s and early 1960s. Both the 118th General Assembly and the 119th General

Assembly voted to abolish the death penalty on the strength of expert testimony that the penalty was an ineffective deterrent to crime. The abolition went into effect on April 2, 1958.

The legislature's action in discarding the noose was in contrast to the majority of legislators' continuing refusal to remove the whipping post from the state's arsenal of punishments. In 1959, without holding a hearing, the Senate adopted a bill to require mandatory whippings of anyone convicted of robbery. The vote was fifteen to two. Governor Boggs announced his intention to veto the mandatory whipping bill should it pass the House. He reasoned that the bill would remove judges' discretion, that whipping was no deterrent to crime, and that the practice was "incompatible with rehabilitation of criminals." The governor characterized whipping as "a barbaric, cruel, and inhuman method of punishment." Expanding its use would, he said, be "a long step backward for Delaware."[22]

The threatened veto put a stop to the mandatory whipping bill, but not to the sentiments from which it came. Senator Walton H. Simpson of the town of Camden in Kent County declared that the courts were too lenient on criminals and that it must fall to the legislature to "take a practical approach" to dealing with crime. Otherwise, he said, "people will have to keep their doors locked."[23] His point was a telling one. It demonstrated the contrasting expectations of security between those who lived in rural areas where strangers were rare and safety was expected, and those who inhabited the more fluid urban world where the necessity to lock doors was taken for granted.

In 1961 the expectation of personal safety was shattered in the Sussex County town of Laurel when a black hired man who was a former prison inmate murdered an elderly white couple. Shocked by the brutality of the crime, the legislators quickly restored the death penalty. The governor at that time was Elbert Carvel, who had been recently elected to a second non-consecutive term. Carvel was himself a citizen of Laurel so he had a vivid sense of the deep feelings that underlay public reaction to the crime. In spite of those factors, he believed that the General Assembly had taken a giant leap backwards by restoring the death penalty.

Governor Carvel issued a long, well-researched veto message. He produced charts to demonstrate that the death penalty did not reduce crime; and he admonished his fellow Delawareans to improve the state's woefully inadequate corrections and rehabilitation programs. His statement ended with a plea "that human life is God given and not for man to take away . . . who among us wishes to meet our Maker with the blood of our brother on our hands."[24] Several labor unions weighed in to support Governor Carvel's position, and the governor received a congratulatory telegram from Eleanor Roosevelt, but the legislators were listening to constituents' demands for the execution of murderers. The lawmakers ignored the governor's charts full of evidence and voted to override. Delaware's brief experiment with the abolition of the death penalty was at an end.

Governor Carvel also reached beyond the sentiments of many of his fellow

Sussex Countians to recognize the unfairness of the apportionment of seats in the General Assembly. In 1949 he proposed to recreate the General Assembly on the model of the federal Congress. In such a scheme New Castle County's larger population would give that county dominance in the House of Representatives, but each county would have an equal voice in the Senate. The issue didn't get very far, however, because no one could imagine that two successive legislatures would provide the two-third-vote majority needed to alter the state constitution. It seemed that no matter how large New Castle County's population became, the northern county's residents were doomed to remain the minority in Legislative Hall.

Then, in 1962 the United States Supreme Court shattered the conventional wisdom. In a case called *Baker* v. *Carr* that arose from the mal-distribution of legislative seats in Tennessee, the Court asserted federal control over state legislative apportionment. In the past, the United States Supreme Court had refused to adjudicate cases of that sort on the grounds that the apportionment of seats in state legislative bodies was a matter for state courts rather than the federal courts. Under Chief Justice Earl Warren, however, the Supreme Court took the view that such unfair representation infringed the Fourteenth Amendment's Equal Protection Clause.

The Supreme Court's decision in *Baker* v. *Carr* signaled to many states, including Delaware, that they, too, must reapportion their legislative seats. A group of New Castle County Republicans filed suit in federal court to ensure Delaware's compliance. In the meantime, Governor Carvel hoped to convince the legislature to enact reapportionment ahead of a federal decree. He appointed a broad-based committee, weighted toward his own party and section, to draw up a proposal. The committee proposed a plan modeled on the federal Constitution, exactly as Carvel had suggested earlier. With the committee's plan in hand, Governor Carvel called the General Assembly into special session in July 1962. The governor urged the assembly to adopt the plan by the two-thirds vote needed to satisfy the first half of Delaware's constitutional amendment process.

The governor's proposed amendment passed easily because it provided the minimum of change. Under the plan New Castle County would get ten more seats in the House, giving its representatives a clear majority of twenty-five of forty-five total seats in that body. In the Senate, however, Kent County and Sussex County would each receive two new senators to bring their numbers into equality with New Castle County's seven senators. In short, under the county equality principle, two-thirds of the senators would represent 31 percent of the state's people. Kent and Sussex would continue to rule in one house of the assembly.

The analogy of the proposed distribution plan to that of the United States Congress under the federal Constitution gave the plan's supporters hope that it would pass muster in the federal courts. Acting on that belief, the 122nd General Assembly promptly confirmed the vote of its predecessor on the amendment in January 1963. Thus, under threat of the federal judiciary, the legislature had done what no one had ever expected it to do: it had used the amendment process of the state constitution to alter the distribution of seats in the General Assembly.

Attention now shifted to the New Castle County Republicans' suit in federal court. The new distribution of legislative seats did not satisfy them, and they persisted in their suit in the Federal District Court. In April 1963 a three-judge panel headed by United States Circuit Court of Appeals Judge John Biggs, Jr., dismissed the state legislature's reapportionment plan as "irrational, arbitrary, and invidiously discriminating." Legislative leaders in Dover vowed to fight on against federal interference in the state's affairs. Their appeal eventually reached all the way to the United States Supreme Court in the case .[25]

When came before them, the Supreme Court was also considering a similar case from another state called *Reynolds* v. *Sims*. Both cases shared a key point: the legality of constituting a bicameral state legislature that based its upper house on a criterion other than population. In both cases Chief Justice Warren denied the validity of an analogy to the United States Senate. In the *Reynolds* case the Chief Justice declared: "Legislators are elected by voters, not farms or cities or economic interests." Therefore, he reasoned, "the Equal Protection Clause requires that the seats in both houses of a bicameral state legislature must be apportioned on a population basis." The principle that he invoked was called "one man, one vote."[26]

The Supreme Court announced its ruling in and *Reynolds* v. *Sims* on the same day. In both cases the Court denied arguments for a "federal analogy" as put forward by the State of Delaware's lawyers. The lawyers representing Delaware based their case on the claim that Delaware's three counties had been sovereign entities in colonial days when the little colony was called the Three Lower Counties on Delaware. Following that logic, Delaware's counties could claim equality in the state's upper house similar to that of the states in the United States Senate.

Chief Justice Warren dismissed Delaware's argument with the words: "Whatever the role of counties in Delaware during the colonial period, they never have had those aspects of sovereignty which the States possessed when our federal system of government was adopted. And it could hardly be contended that Delaware's counties retained any elements of sovereign power when the State was formed . . . there never was much and there is now no sovereignty in the Counties of Delaware . . . ."[27]

The history of government in Delaware fully bears out the Chief Justice's declaration. Counties were formed in the early colonial period to be conveniently sized geographical entities for the courts of justice and for the local administration of the law. From 1682, when William Penn called his first General Assembly, the counties have been wholly dependent on the legislature for their administrative form and powers. It is ironic that a legal brief presented on behalf of the Delaware General Assembly would have argued otherwise.

Chief Justice Warren gave the General Assembly the task of fulfilling the

Court's apportionment decree. He further suggested that Delaware's lawmakers could make their task less time-consuming and difficult if they would amend their state constitution to make apportionment a statutory matter. In that way, the legislature would not have to resort to the rigmarole attendant to the constitutional amendment process every time population moves necessitated redistributing legislative seats.

The federal courts had given the General Assembly the opportunity to remake Delaware's legislative districts in accord with the population of the state. The courts mandated quick action to satisfy the plaintiffs' plea for their constitutional right to fair representation. The Delaware legislature was required to enact the appropriate statute in time to put a constitutional apportionment plan in place for the 1964 election.

The political parties disagreed as to how apportionment should be accomplished. The Democrats had the majority, and they were determined to do it their way. Republicans were not welcome on the legislative committee charged to create the apportionment formula. The GOP's Senate minority leader, Reynolds du Pont, presented his party's objections to the one-sided process in a letter to Governor Carvel. Du Pont stressed the present unfair distribution of seats. In the most recent election, he said, more voters had elected the Republican minority than had chosen the Democrats' legislative majority. His plea for equal representation on the reapportion committee was ignored.

The plan that the Democrats passed into law in July 1964 was driven by political rather than sectional rivalries. Senator Curtis W. Steen of Dagsboro, the president pro tempore in the previous session, told his fellow senators that his party would "take care of the Democratic Party in the redistricting."[28] The Democrats' plan added one seat to the Senate for a total of eighteen but did not alter the number in House of Representatives, which continued to have thirty-five members. In obedience to the decree of the court, New Castle County was awarded most of the seats in both houses, but within the county, Democratic Wilmington received more than its fair share in comparison to the Republican-leaning suburbs.

The 123rd General Assembly elected in November 1964 more than fulfilled the Democrats' fondest expectations. In a year that saw Lyndon Johnson's landslide victory over Barry Goldwater for the presidency, Delaware's Democrats elected former judge Charles Terry to be the state's new governor and took thirty of the thirty-five seats in the House of Representatives and thirteen of the eighteen seats in the Senate. In his valedictory address to the newly elected assembly, Governor Carvel ignored his party's overwhelming majority to focus on how reapportionment had relocated power from the southern to the northern part of the state. He tactfully expressed the hope that "those located in the new center of power will use their authority in the same judicious manner demonstrated by those south of the canal during the past 178 years."[29]

The reapportionment issue refused to die as long as the original plaintiffs were willing to continue their suit. Angered by their party's exclusion from planning the reapportionment, the Republican plaintiffs appealed to the federal district court. On January 10, 1967, the court struck down the Democratic legislators' plan on the grounds that the district boundaries had been gerrymandered. The court did not invalidate the elections of the current members of the assembly, but it gave the legislators exactly one year, until January 10, 1968, to produce an acceptable plan to be implemented for the 1968 election.[30]

This time all sides recognized the need to achieve bipartisan consensus on a reapportionment plan. It was clear that the federal district court would not relent until it was satisfied that reapportionment had met the court's standard of fairness. But beyond the threat of further appeals to the court was the fact that the 124th General Assembly elected in 1966 was a very different animal from its predecessor. For one thing, the Republicans had captured the House of Representatives. For another, the even number of senators had resulted in that most-feared fiasco: an evenly balanced Senate of nine Republicans and nine Democrats.

The problem of deciding who would become president pro tempore in the Senate produced a memorable scene in which one side's crafty maneuvering outdid that of the other. The Republican strategy was to hold off the final vote until their party had a majority present on the floor. When they saw that they could not win on the first vote, several Republicans voted "not voting" so that the total number of votes would fall below the quorum of ten voting senators required by Senate rules.

The Republicans tactic failed. The Senate's presiding officer was Lieutenant Governor Sherman Tribbitt. Tribbitt was a veteran legislator who had served as speaker of the House of Representatives for three terms. Without hesitation, Tribbitt announced that the Democrats' candidate, Calvin McCullough, had received the majority of votes cast and was, therefore, elected president pro tempore. The astonished Republicans demanded that the lieutenant governor follow the Senate's quorum rule, to which Tribbitt replied that the Senate had not as yet established its rules for the session. Therefore, as presiding officer he had the power to decide the rules. With that pronouncement from the chair, Senator Margaret Manning, a New Castle County Republican, dramatically lifted her copy of the Senate Rulebook, walked to a nearby metal wastebasket and dropped it in with a resounding thump.[31]

The situation in the House of Representatives was quite different. There the Republicans held an overwhelming majority of twenty-three to twelve. Equally significant, twenty-one of the thirty-five members of the House were legislative freshmen, including nineteen of the GOP members. Some of them had never been to Dover before and had to ask directions to Legislative Hall.

The newcomers chose one of their own to be Speaker. He was George C. Hering III, a young attorney from Wilmington. Having no ties to past practices, Hering and his fellow newcomers brought a fresh perspective to the management of the lower house. The Speaker eliminated about one-half of the body's thirty standing committees and reduced the number of attaches while improving their quality. The freshmen also began the process of amending the state constitution to equalize the legislative processes of the odd and even numbered years. Their initiative removed the constitutional limitations of length of session and subject matter that had long circumscribed action in the second session of each two-year General Assembly. Thus did Delaware finally remove the last vestiges of the biennial legislative system that had been in place since 1831.[32]

Governor Elbert N. Carvel inspects one of the new voting machines in 1954. (Courtesy of the Delaware Public Archives)

Politicians of both parties recognized the necessity of reaching an accord on redistricting ahead of the federal court's deadline. To achieve consensus the assembly established a Legislative Council composed of five members from each party to construct a plan that would be acceptable to both. George C. Hering III, the Republican Speaker of the House, chaired the Council, while Democrat Calvin McCullough, the President Pro Tempore, served as its vice-chair.

As the deadline loomed on January 10, 1968, negotiations within the Council became intense. On the first of the year Governor Terry announced that he would not call the legislature into session until the two parties had reached an accommodation. The Council negotiated the remaining sticking points concerning district lines just in time. Two days before the deadline, the Council emerged from nineteen hours of intense negotiations to announce that they had reached an agreement on district lines for a nineteen-member Senate and a thirty-five-member House of Representatives.

The new legislative map was, not surprisingly, designed to preserve the seats of most incumbents. Following the population rather than the interests of one political party, the big winners were suburban areas of New Castle County. The big loser was Wilmington, which had received more than its fair share of seats under the Democrats' plan. Under the new plan, African American legislators found the representative districts in which blacks predominated reduced from three to one.

After vetting by the two political caucuses, the redistricting bill came before the legislature. It passed overwhelmingly, with only four negative votes—three of them cast by African American representatives from Wilmington. With the United States District Court's three-judge panel standing by should the state fail to act in time, Governor Terry signed the bill into law a mere fifty minutes ahead of the deadline.[33]

The notion that district boundaries were immune to alteration was dead. Less than four years later, in time for the election of the 127th General Assembly in 1972, the legislature enlarged both houses by two, thus creating a Senate of twenty-one and a House of Representatives of forty-one members. The General Assembly continues to maintain that size.

In addition to "one man, one vote," the push toward racial equality was a dominant theme at both national and state levels during the 1950s and 1960s. There were many African Americans in Delaware's rural communities, especially those located south of the Chesapeake and Delaware Canal, but black Delawareans were spread so evenly among the state's farms and small communities as to constitute a minority in every rural legislative district. During the 1950s, only Wilmington had a concentration of black people sufficient to elect one lone minority representative, until the short-lived redistricting plan of 1963 had briefly extended the number of majority black districts to three in the House of Representatives.

No African American had served in the Delaware Senate until Herman M. Holloway, Sr., a former city policeman and legislative attache, was elected in 1964. He was destined to remain in the Senate for over thirty years, setting a record for length of service that stood until the end of the twentieth century. Herman Holloway, Sr., arrived in Dover at an historic moment in the evolution of race relations. As the only black senator, he became the General Assembly's most visible advocate for racial equality.

A major piece of civil-rights legislation had come before the assembly in the session previous to Holloway's election. In response to mounting demands for civil-rights reforms, both in Delaware and throughout the nation, the General Assembly had taken the modest step of creating a Human Relations Commission. The commission had no direct power, but it provided a conduit for complaints and a launching pad for civil-rights legislation. In 1963 the commission introduced a public-accommodations bill into the legislature to replace the discriminatory Innkeepers Law of 1875. According to a reporter who was present in the Senate when the bill was announced, the commission's bill drew "snickers and some laughter" from senators hostile to integration.[34]

Throughout 1963, while civil-rights leaders led highly publicized national and local protests against segregation, the public-accommodations bill languished. Then, on November 22, 1963, President John F. Kennedy was shot in Dallas. Echoing a plea of President Lyndon B. Johnson before Congress, Governor Elbert Carvel called on the General Assembly to pass public accommodations as a tribute to Kennedy. Although snickers were no longer heard, the bill's sponsors still faced a daunting prospect.

Civil rights split both political parties. The bill passed the lower house, but its passage in the Senate was very much in doubt. There were nine Democrats and eight Republicans in the Senate. Five of the Republicans were willing to vote for it. Governor Carvel set out to win over the four Democratic votes necessary for a majority.

Many years later Elbert Carvel could recall in detail what happened next. His words give unusual insight into a governor's tactics in winning legislative votes. He described how he had spent several hours convincing Senator Calvin McCullough of New Castle to vote for the bill and thought he had finally secured his commitment. The governor also felt certain of Senator Curtis Steen's vote because Steen had many black voters in his Dagsboro district. As the roll call began it looked as if the nine votes would be there to pass the bill.

> Well, we sent the bill down for passage after we finally got Cal to agree and we had two votes from Wilmington to begin with. John Reilly (Democrat) was one of them. We had another Wilmington Democrat who voted for it. And we needed Cal McCullough and Curt Steen. All right, that would be nine votes, five for the Republicans, four for the Democrats. Well, I'm up in the balcony watching the vote and the vote comes up and Cal McCullough votes against it and Elisha Dukes (Secretary of State) is with me. I said, 'Elisha, go down and talk to Cal and find out what's wrong with him. He said he was going to vote for this bill.' So in the meantime I go down to the first floor, into the lobby of the legislature, and Elisha went in and talked to Cal. Elisha came out and said, "Cal says he had promised somebody that when it came up he was going to vote against it, but next time it comes up he'll vote for it." So I'm still there about to go upstairs and out comes Curt Steen. And remember, we had worked for hours on Cal to get him to agree to vote for this bill and Curt Steen who said he was going to vote for it . . . who was the last man to vote because he was the majority leader of the Senate . . . came barreling out of there. I said, 'Curt, where in the hell are you going?' He looked at me and he didn't expect to see me there, and he says, 'Governor, if I vote for that bill, they'll hang me when I get back to Dagsboro.' And I gave him a withering look and I said, 'Hang and be damned!' And I turned around and walked upstairs. Curt turned around and

went in and voted for it . . . . Curt Steen got the message immediately, 'If you don't vote for that bill you're done as far as I'm concerned.'[35]

The public-accommodations bill passed the Senate ten to seven with one vote to spare.

The most glaring remaining form of racial segregation was access to residential housing. Real-estate brokers maintained segregation throughout Delaware. In Wilmington black residents were forced to live in the least desirable sections of the city regardless of their aspirations or wealth. With the demolition of houses for urban renewal and the influx of newcomers from rural areas, the ghetto became ever more crowded.

In 1964 a coalition of religious leaders and civil-rights advocates took up the cause of open housing in Wilmington, but their efforts were thwarted by the realtors association's refusal to cooperate. Open-housing proponents then turned to the legislature. In 1965 the Human Relations Commission introduced a bill in the assembly to end housing discrimination. When that bill got nowhere, Senator Herman Holloway, Sr., put forward another bill authored by Delaware's leading African-American attorneys, Louis L. Redding and Leonard Williams. To Holloway's deep dismay, it, too, failed. Yet another attempt was made to introduce a compromise bill that contained a "Mrs. Murphy" clause that would permit resident property owners to discriminate. It had the backing of Governor Terry and the Wilmington Democratic machine, but it, too, failed to pass.[36]

Open housing provided the greatest legislative battle of the 1965 session. Both parties claimed to support the concept in principle, but neither could offer the votes to get the legislation adopted. The issue frightened legislators. Senator Allen J. Cook, a Kent County Democrat, suggested that open housing be submitted to a statewide voter referendum, but Delaware had no such precedent for letting the General Assembly off the hook. While the realtors lobbied to prevent any legislation, the NAACP held out for a strong bill with no "Mrs. Murphy" provision.

In 1966 Senator Holloway teamed up with Senator Louise Connor, a New Castle County suburbanite, to offer yet another bill to end racism in real estate. Like its predecessors, this version never emerged from committee. Desperate to secure some legislative step forward, Senator Holloway agreed to a compromise that would include the contentious "Mrs. Murphy" clause. His position did not sit well with NAACP leaders, who denounced the senator's "half a loaf" approach in a confrontational public meeting at a Wilmington church. Holloway was so angered that he retorted: "Here I am down in Dover among conservatives and bigots who use as an excuse, 'your own people don't want the bill.'"[37]

Recognizing the reality of the lone black senator's view, the NAACP relented on the resident-owner provision, but despite Senator Holloway's eloquent appeals, a Senate majority again defeated the open-housing bill with the "Mrs. Murphy" clause attached, while the emotionally drained Holloway wept.

Where the Delaware General Assembly failed, the United States Congress did not. In the wake of severe rioting that gripped Washington, D. C., following the assassination of the Reverend Martin Luther King, Jr., in the spring of 1968, Congress responded to the powerful persuasion of President Lyndon B. Johnson and adopted a national open-housing bill.

It is difficult to know what the reaction of the General Assembly might have been to open-housing legislation had the legislators received the equivalent in gubernatorial support. Unlike Elbert Carvel or President Johnson, Charles Terry was at best a lukewarm supporter of advances in civil rights. During the debates on the issue, he said that he would sign an open-housing bill if one came to his desk, but he did little to make that happen.

As the state's chief executive during the most contentious years of the civil-rights movement, Governor Terry focused his attention on efforts to prevent destructive, racially inspired riots that were then common in American cities. In August 1967 the governor called the assembly into special session to respond to a minor disturbance that had taken place in Wilmington. Although no one had been injured and there was little looting, the governor activated the State Police and used the incident to ask the assembly to adopt three anti-riot bills.

The legislators unhesitatingly passed the governor's anti-riot bills into law. One law gave the governor authority to declare a state of emergency and impose curfews; another outlawed the possession of Molotov cocktails and firebombs; and the third provided mandatory three-year jail terms for persons convicted of malicious destruction during a state of emergency.[38]

Governor Terry returned to the theme of threatened violence in his annual address to the General Assembly in February 1968. He proclaimed his readiness to meet threats with force. The governor was not unwilling to push for better housing and job opportunities for black Delawareans, but he displayed a visceral hostility to the confrontational tactics used by some minority petitioners. A group of welfare recipients from Wilmington came to Dover and joined students from Delaware State College to protest a reduction in welfare payments. At Legislative Hall the protesters met a phalanx of state policemen brought there by Governor Terry to remove them from the hall.

Many legislators took their cue from the governor. The House used the incident to defer consideration of the welfare bill on the grounds that they would not consider the measure in an atmosphere of "pressure, intimidation and fear caused by the demonstrating welfare recipients . . . ."[39]

A few days after the Legislative Hall confrontation, Martin Luther King, Jr., was killed in Memphis, and riots erupted in the black ghettoes of many American cities. At first it appeared that Wilmington might escape the destructive mayhem, but on the day of King's funeral rioting broke out on the city's near-west side. Fires were set, police cars were attacked, and fearful commuters rushed back to their suburbs. Fulfilling his earlier promise, Governor Terry used the authority that the legislature had given him to impose a state of emergency. Ignoring the pleas of Wilmington mayor John E. Babiarz to allow the city's police to handle the situation with minimal assistance from the National Guard, the governor sent the entire Delaware National Guard to Wilmington. Within a day the area of the riot returned to quiet, but Governor Terry ignored the mayor's pleas to remove the troops. National Guardsmen continued to patrol the city through the summer, fall, and winter until a new governor was inaugurated in January 1969.

State police evicted welfare demonstrators from Legislative Hall on March 28, 1968. (Courtesy of the Delaware Public Archives)

The 124th General Assembly's most memorable accomplishment was the passage of the Educational Advancement Act of 1968. The education bill was the work of a blue-ribbon committee chaired by Delaware Chief Justice Daniel Wolcott. The goal of the committee's proposal was to consolidate school districts throughout the state so that every district would be large enough to provide all the benefits of modern education from technical subjects through college-preparatory courses. The plan made alterations in every district in the state with the exception of the Wilmington district, because that district had already met the goals of consolidation. That exemption failed to raise suspicions of de facto segregationist intent at the time but it would become the center of a major lawsuit in the federal court a decade later. In 1968, opposition to the proposed law centered in southern Delaware, where many residents were reluctant to abandon their familiar local town-centered school districts.

The school-district plan had the support of leaders from both parties including Governor Terry and Representative Clarice Heckert, a Republican from the Wilmington suburbs who chaired the House Education Committee. She called the Educational Advancement Act "one of the most important bills for education to be considered by this House at any time."[40]

The Education Advancement bill passed the House in May 1968, a few weeks after the Wilmington riots. It also passed the Senate and was signed into law. In years to come, plaintiffs in the desegregation suit *Evans* v. *Buchanan* would cite the Education Advancement Act as proof of legislative intent to create a segregated school system in Wilmington and to prevent the integration of the suburban school districts, but no one saw that purpose in 1968.

By 1968 black students had become the majority in Wilmington's schools. In that spring, the most supercharged time of civil-rights protests in Delaware's history, African Americans did not protest the Educational Advancement Act. The black members of the assembly voted for the bill. After a century of being treated by Wilmington school administrators as an inferior, undesired minority, African Americans were poised to take control of the city's schools. With that prospect in mind, civil-rights leaders did not anticipate that the federal courts would view the outcome as segregationist in its effects.

The election held in November 1968 was the first to be conducted using the recently reapportioned district lines. Nationally it was a Republican year that saw Richard Nixon triumph over Hubert Humphrey for the presidency. In Delaware the Republican upsurge, coupled with the effects of the recent redistricting, produced Republican victories in both houses of the legislature. Equally significant was the narrow victory of a political newcomer, Republican Russell Peterson, over incumbent Governor Charles Terry.

Russell Peterson was not a native Delawarean, but he was representative of a significant group of Wilmington's suburban residents. He was a Midwesterner and a Ph.D. chemist who had come to Delaware to work for the Du Pont Company. Many Du Ponters were active in their communities and school PTAs, but Peterson took civic responsibilities several steps further than most. As he rose through the ranks into the top echelon of the chemical company, Peterson also displayed an unusual willingness to engage in the search for solutions to some of the community's most controversial and intractable problems. He led a citizen-based effort to shift the state's correctional policies away from punitive punishments toward rehabilitation; and he championed racial integration and environmental protection. His work on behalf of corrections reform introduced Peterson to state government and to the leaders of the Republican Party, who suggested that he run for governor against Terry.

The Terry-Peterson contest took place against the backdrop of the National Guard's continuing presence in Wilmington. The new governor's first official act was to remove the last remnants of the Guard patrols from the city's streets. This was but the first of a series of gubernatorial initiatives that would change Delaware and its government during the next few years.

In the late 1960s Delaware's legislature was being transformed into a careerist lawmaking body filled with members who sought and won reelection to multiple terms. Reapportion increased the legislative seats in the state's urban north where institutional and corporate employees were freer than self-employed people such as farmers to accept the commitments of legislative service without losing income. Another factor in members' decisions to seek reelection was the increase in the financial rewards of legislative service. In the past, legislators' pay had been insufficient to compete with the demands of tending to one's farm or business. Then, incrementally, the legislators raised their pay, first from $1,000 to $3,000 and then in 1968, to $6,000. The legislators also voted themselves into the state's pension plan.

By the 1960s it was the rare legislator who did not run for and win the same legislative seat for up to five and six times. Indeed, the parties' jostling over district lines during the reapportionment negotiations of the 1960s was not only to create boundaries that would assist one party or the other, but also to secure the reelection of particular incumbent members.

The days when the General Assembly had been nearly an all-male club were also coming to a close. In the 1950s members gathered in the basement office of Speaker James R. Quigley, a brash New Castle Democrat who was Speaker of the 118th General Assembly. Lobbyist-supplied liquor flowed in those informal sessions in the Speaker's office, which was dubbed the "snake pit."[41] It was hardly a tea party atmosphere. Quigley served only one term as Speaker, but he continued to represent his New Castle district until 1966, by which time the locker-room world of the "snake pit" and the rowdy behavior that went on in its precincts had entered into legislative legend.

In the 1960s an increasing number of women entered the legislature and affected its tone. Most among the new wave of female legislators were married to husbands who were their families' main breadwinners, thus freeing up the women legislators to give most of their time and attention to their legislative responsibilities.

Typically, women legislators got involved in politics through their volunteer work for community-based organizations.[42]

In the late 1960s Legislative Hall itself underwent a major overhaul. For years members had complained about the building's limitations. There were few meeting rooms, and only officers had individual offices. Lobbyists were everywhere. Legislators met constituents and lobbyists at their desks in the legislative chambers or, if the houses were in session, they transacted business in the front lobby, connecting hallways, or the men's room.

The first effort to build an addition to the building in 1961 came to nothing. The matter came up again in 1966, and this time the legislature adopted a joint resolution to proceed with the project. Governor Terry appointed a committee to recommend a building plan. The committee consisted of twelve members, including seven members of the assembly and Lieutenant Governor Sherman Tribbitt.

The committee members had no difficulty in justifying the need for an addition. In their report they noted that "a visit to Legislative Hall on any day that the General Assembly is in session reveals the sorry spectacle of crowded corridors, where representatives of the news media, lobbyists—both professional and amateur—and interested citizens share the frustrations of looking for, and seldom finding, a particular legislator if he is not in his 'office' on the floor."[43]

Happily, money was available from the state's tax windfall from the Du Pont-General Motors divestiture to pay for the addition. George Fletcher Bennett, a Dover-based architect noted for his mastery of the Delaware colonial-revival style, was hired to provide new offices and meeting rooms. In keeping with the eighteenth century's penchant for symmetry, Bennett extended the building equally on both sides so that the façade was wider, but it maintained its colonial-revival appearance. The extensions were completed in 1970 in time for occupancy by the 125th General Assembly. At last each legislator had a quiet spot to call his or her own in an office, most often shared with a colleague, where he or she could meet with constituents, do correspondence, read reports, or just put one's feet up and relax in a private setting.

The Delaware General Assembly was becoming a body of long-serving members who viewed their service as a major component in their careers. Members developed strong constituent ties that served them well at election time. All strove to build reputations as supporters of programs that were popular with the people of their districts. Some became experts in particular areas of state government.

Reapportionment ensured that the legislators reflected the make-up of the state's people and industries. Some members' present or former employment gave them strong ties to particular business interests—the chemical industry, farming, or labor unions—but the most interesting new development was the election of men and women who had worked, or were working, for state government or for state-supported institutions, especially public-school teachers and state policemen.

In the 1960s the momentum of growth in the responsibilities of state government that had been accelerating since World War II reached a critical point.

In the twenty years from 1940 to 1960 the State of Delaware's annual budget had increased from about $15,000,000 to over $145,000,000. Even veteran legislators had difficulty comprehending or controlling the expenditure of those funds as they were divided among over one hundred agencies. To give the legislators a better handle on the state's budget, the General Assembly created the office of Controller General in 1969. That officer continues to provide the professional expertise that underlies the financial and budgeting work of the Joint Finance Committee and the Joint Bond Bill Committee.

The state now operated on annual, rather than biennial, budgets. The governor presented his budget to the legislature in a speech that came several weeks after his state of the state address. The Joint Finance Committee then held hearings and discussions to massage the budget figures before they recommended passage of the budget bill at the end of the legislative session in June. The number of agencies and institutions that received state aid had grown to a point that precluded the legislature's visits to state institutions that had once been a part of the legislative experience.

In 1958 Governor Boggs had offered his ill-fated "New Day for Delaware" proposal to tame the myriad, ungovernable agencies. A few years later some members of the General Assembly were forced to agree. In 1964 Senator Allen Cook, one of the Democratic Party's leaders on Joint Finance, took the floor to remark that state agencies were thwarting the intentions of the legislature by reallocating money that had been designated for one area into another. "They have seen fit to ignore us," said the frustrated senator.[44]

In the days when the number of the state's facilities had been small, the legislature's power to provide or withhold money gave its members the opportunity to engage directly in institutional policy making and to influence the appointment, retention, and removal of employees. By the 1960s the legislators had relinquished much of their earlier hands-on administration of state agencies. In part, that development resulted from the growing professionalism among state employees, who now included physicians, accountants, criminologists, and the like. Most legislators now recognized that the management of the agencies should lie with the governor.

A good example of the changed perception of the legislative role came in 1966 when the General Assembly appointed a joint committee to investigate the operation of the Delaware Home and Hospital for the Chronically Ill at Smyrna. Shortly thereafter, Governor Terry appointed his own committee to make a similar enquiry. On learning of the governor's action, the assembly dissolved its investigative committee on the grounds that the management of the hospital was an executive function.[45] That same year, after years of procrastination, the assembly voted to create a merit system for state employees. Patronage appointments for rank-and-file state employees were dealt a blow.

In 1968, the Republicans won control of the executive and legislative branches of the state. The opportunity that Governor Boggs had sought for a strengthened executive in his "New Day for Delaware" had finally come. Senator Dean C. Steele, a gruff Republican from the north Wilmington suburbs, set the stage in January 1969 in his report on the findings of the previous session's ad hoc Joint Committee to Investigate Nonessential State Expenditures. In the guise of discussing wasteful spending practices, Senator Steele denounced numerous state agencies for harboring lazy, incompetent employees and for being out of the control of elected officials. In conclusion, Senator Steele remarked, "Delaware has been sauntering through her resources and through the mazes of her politics with easy nonchalance."[46]

Liberal and conservative Republicans of the 1960s disagreed on many things, but they were united in their demand for a more efficient and accountable state government. The old model was one of a myriad of state agencies overseen by politically-based citizen commissioners. That model would soon be replaced by a cabinet system that fixed responsibility on the governor and on his or her department heads. The new system would copy the organization of the federal government, and it was based on Governor Peterson's corporate experience.

During the six weeks between the election and his inauguration, Governor-elect Peterson met with Senate President Pro Tempore Reynolds du Pont and House Speaker George Hering III to plan the introduction of his government reorganization proposal. The governor explained his intention to ask the assembly for authority to appoint a blue-ribbon task force to plan the reorganization.[47] Speaker Hering and President Pro Tempore du Pont agreed to co-chair an ad hoc joint committee to see the task force recommendations through the General Assembly.

The governor and legislative leaders took lessons from the failed "New Day for Delaware" proposal. That plan had been subjected to open hearings before a legislative committee, where the many commissioners and agency administrators who feared for their power and jobs ganged up to denounce it. This time, the process would be different, there would be not one, but a series of bills. Each activity, such as highways or health and social services would be treated separately. There would, of course, be opponents to each portion, but not so many at one time.[48]

The strategy worked because the governor had a friendly legislature. The assembly voted in April 1969 to establish the task force and in that same legislation affirmed: "It is declared to be the public policy of this state that the commission form of government shall be abolished and a cabinet form of government shall be adopted."[49] The first of the proposed cabinet rank departments to come before the legislature for confirmation was Health and Social Services, which combined the units that had been most hostile to combination in the past. Once that hurdle was cleared, the others became progressively easier; and the entire process of turning over 100 semi-independent boards, agencies, institutions, and commissions into ten cabinet departments was completed in 1970.

That major reorganization could not have been accomplished but for the political unity that held sway following the election of 1968; and that election would not have turned out as it had without the court-ordered reapportionment that preceded it. Governor Peterson did what he could to mitigate the inevitable hostile reaction of many, especially among rural Delawareans. He created citizen advisory boards to assist the new departments. Those boards allowed former commissioners to retain ties to the units they had once controlled. He also transferred many higher-level administrators from the old to the new system. Perhaps most important, his plan left untouched the largest and most pervasive bureaucracy in the state, the Board of Education, which was to remain unaffected by the cabinet system for nearly thirty years.[50]

The introduction of the cabinet system marked another notch downward in the General Assembly's direct involvement in the management of state institutions. A good example of that reality came in 1973 when Representative Daniel E. Weiss accompanied *News-Journal* columnist Bill Frank on a visit to the Biggs Building at the Delaware State Hospital. The representative and journalist were shocked by what they saw and smelled there, especially urine-soaked floors that produced an "outrageous odor." They reported to the legislature that the stinking facility was overcrowded, understaffed, and disintegrating.[51]

Based on that report, the legislators specifically authorized improvements to the Biggs Building. A year later Representative Weiss followed up to see what had been accomplished. He was disappointed to discover that only a few changes had been made. Even more frustrating was the response of the Secretary of Health and Social Services. The secretary was not pleased. In a letter to the Speaker of the House of Representatives the secretary complained that members of the legislature should consult with him through proper channels before sounding off and making specific demands. The secretary declared that he had to contend with many problems more pressing than the smell-filled, overcrowded Biggs Building.[52] One wonders what other horrors went unreported to the legislature or the public. The main point was that direct legislative involvement in the affairs of the state's cabinet departments was perceived as meddling.

While the cabinet system got a good deal of publicity, the expulsion of the whipping post from the state's arsenal of criminal punishments was introduced more quietly. After such a long history of failed efforts to remove the lash, some had feared that Delaware would never abandon the infamous "Red Hannah." The feat was accomplished through an updated criminal code that simply did not include the whipping post. The leaders of that reform were two legislative lawyers from the Wilmington area, Senator Michael N. Castle and Representative W. Laird Stabler. The 125th General Assembly enacted the new code without the necessity of debating that most highly divisive issue because it was not there to be debated. Governor Peterson signed the new code into law on July 6, 1972.

Updating the corporation law also fell into the category of the General Assembly's un-debated actions. The state's corporate lawyers constantly monitored the law, and in 1967 and again in 1973 the Delaware Bar Association offered recommendations to the assembly to keep Delaware competitive with other states seeking to lure corporate business their way. From the legislature's point of view the most important goal was to maintain the tax base represented by the corporations that chose Delaware as their home base.

In 1967 the legislature passed a new corporation law based on the recommendations of a commission appointed by the secretary of state. According to an article that later appeared in *The Connecticut Bar Journal,* one of the commissioners denigrated the legislators as "just a bunch of farmers" who were presumably incapable of comprehending the law's intent.[53] If that remark was in fact made, it was incorrect in its presumption that the legislators were unable to understand what they were enacting, or that their ranks were filled with farmers. It would, however, be fair to say that few members of the legislature waded through the details of such lengthy and legalistic legislation. They relied instead on explanations from lawyers, both in and out of the legislature, whom they had learned to trust.

It is an understatement to note that the social churning and relative economic health of 1960s and early 1970s provided the impetus for the creation of new government institutions. Delaware's new institutions ran the gamut from a new college to a new prison. In April 1966 Governor Charles Terry introduced his plan for a two-year post-secondary technical college. Shortly after, the legislature took the first of several steps that produced the Delaware Technical and Community College. The college was to operate from campuses in all three counties and to run programs in cooperation with the University of Delaware. A few years later, in Governor Peterson's administration, Delaware constructed its first modern statewide prison, located at Smyrna, as part of a concerted effort to reform Delaware's approach to crime and criminals.

Of all the initiatives of the Peterson years, the one that remains most closely identified with the governor himself is the Coastal Zone Act of 1971. Thirty years later, the Coastal Zone Act remains Delaware's greatest and most comprehensive legislative achievement toward maintaining a livable environment.

Laws respecting the environment reach back to the General Assembly's earliest days when killing wolves and ditching marshland were high priorities. From the first, legislation concerning the environment focused on the Delaware Bay and River. In the nineteenth century the legislature adopted numerous laws to protect the lower bay's oyster beds and maintained a watch boat to guard against outsiders raiding the beds. In the twentieth century, as industrial enterprises became common along the Delaware River from New Castle northward to Trenton, the fishing industry that had once provided food and employment for the river's watermen slowly died away.

The Delaware Bay and River offer significant advantages to a number of industries, particularly those that require facilities for large seaborne carriers. The needs of the oil industry fit that profile particularly well. In 1957 the Tidewater Oil Company opened a refinery at Delaware City. Four years later the Shell Oil Company purchased wetlands at the mouth of the Smyrna River, company planned to build a refinery adjacent to a major Atlantic flyway bird sanctuary. By 1970, unknown to Delawareans, the Nixon administration was promoting the development of super-tanker ports, including an artificial island to be built in the Delaware Bay, and a consortium of oil companies was planning to construct refineries there.[54]

Governor Russell W. Peterson addressing a joint session of the General Assembly, June 29, 1971. (Courtesy of the News Journal Company)

Governor Peterson adamantly opposed the construction of additional refineries along Delaware's shoreline. In 1970 he imposed a moratorium on the development of the coast to delay construction and established a task force to develop a plan that would allow Delaware to deny the oil companies and other potential heavy industries the use of Delaware's remaining natural coastline.

On January 13, 1971, the governor addressed the newly elected 126th General Assembly. In the speech he briefly noted his belief that Delaware should welcome clean, high-employment industries but should reject heavy industries that pollute and offer few jobs. Governor Peterson's low-key presentation belied the careful preparation for the battle that he knw was about to come. The same month, the governor assigned Fletcher Campbell, Jr., an experienced counsel, to draft a bill designed to protect the coast from heavy industry that would stand up to legal challenge.

There were major opponents against restraining further industrial development of the bay and river. The Delaware State Chamber of Commerce and the AFL-CIO, organizations that often clashed, both strongly opposed restrictions. To counteract these powerful forces, the governor convinced the United Automobile Workers and numerous civic groups to endorse the bill. He also worked closely with the Republican leadership in the legislature to ensure the major party's support. Senate leader Reynolds du Pont favored the bill, as did sportsmen and nature-lovers from around the state. In the House the Republican caucus was emerging from an intra-party fight that had toppled George Herring III from the Speaker's chair in favor of William L. Frederick, the candidate of a group of iconoclasts who styled themselves "the parking lot gang."[55]

Despite their internal differences, most House Republicans favored protecting the coastal zone. Andrew Knox, a freshman member of the lower house, agreed to introduce HB 300, the Coastal Zone bill, because it was too much of a "hot potato" for older hands.[56] Knox, like the governor, was a Ph.D. chemist who had honed his management skills at the Du Pont Company. His role promoted the idea that the environmentally sensitive legislation was scientifically sound and that it was not anti-business as its detractors were claiming.

The real battle was fought at the grass-rots level. The legislators held a series of well-attended hearings throughout Delaware. In Sussex County, where HB 300 was especially controversial because of conflicting economic interests, former Governor Elbert Carvel announced his support for the legislation, but few other prominent political figures in Sussex followed his lead.

The Shell Oil Company planned to begin construction of its refinery in 1973. In an effort to derail the legislation, the company invited a group of thirteen legislators on a free first-class trip to see the company's clean, modern refineries in New Orleans and Seattle. The trip had its intended effect. All but four of the thirteen returned to Delaware convinced that refineries need not be polluters, said their spokesman, J. Donald Isaacs, a Republican senator from Townsend.[57]

HB 300 came before the House of Representatives for a vote on June 21, 1971. Legislative Hall was packed with lobbyists and reporters for the showdown. Democrats Sherman Tribbitt and Clifford Hearn, Jr., led a last-minute effort to weaken the bill with an amendment drafted by oil company lawyers that would have created a commission to decide on applications for industrial development within the coastal zone on a case-by-case basis. At 9:30 p.m. the roll call began on the amendment that supporters feared would gut the bill. Governor Peterson looked down anxiously from the balcony as the members announced their votes. The amendment lost, but only by one vote: twenty to nineteen. Several of the amendment's backers then followed Sherman Tribbitt's lead and voted for the original bill.

The vote in the Senate the next day was also a cliffhanger. There were thirteen Republican senators to only six Democrats, but three of the Republicans, including their spokesman, J. Donald Isaacs, were opposed. The defection of only one more Republican would kill the bill. Governor Peterson captured the urgency of the moment in his memoir.

> Republican leaders in the Senate, Reynolds du Pont and Frank Grier, along with Lieutenant Governor Gene Bookhammer and I, worked to hold our ten votes. Lobbyists cornered senators every time they left the sanctuary of the senate chamber. By dinner it appeared we held only a bare majority of the votes.
>
> After dinner an aide rushed into my office to say that two Republican senators had been turned around by lobbyists during dinner. That meant the opposition now had eleven votes to our eight. I asked those two senators to meet with me and the senate leadership in my office. We impressed on them the need to maintain party unity, to respect the will of the people, to remember who elected them to office and who could send them packing, to consider the well-being of future Delawareans.
>
> After about an hour, the two agreed to support the bill.
>
> When the Senate went back into session, I was watching again from the balcony. Shortly before 11 p.m., the final vote came. It was sixteen to three. The margin in our favor seemed overwhelming, but this is an illusion. As in the final house vote, many of the senators, when they saw which way the vote would go, joined the winning side in what had become a motherhood issue. But motherhood or not, the reality was that our bill had eked by, in both chambers, with only one vote to spare.[58]

Senator Isaacs had tried to win a majority for four amendments designed to provide some latitude for heavy industrial development along the coastline, but all failed. Senator Calvin McCullough called the governor a "dictator" for his hardball maneuvering, but it did not matter.[59] The governor had scored a major victory for the fledgling environmental movement that captured the attention of the nation. "It was a grand occasion," he said.[60]

A Rip Van Winkle who had gone to sleep in Delaware in 1952 and awakened in 1972 would have been astonished by the changes in his state. Suburbs had eaten up most of the farmland of northern New Castle County. Shopping malls had replaced the retail stores of Wilmington's Market Street. Legal segregation was gone in the state's public schools, restaurants, theaters, and housing market. An interstate highway, the Delaware River Bridge, and the Lewes-Cape May Ferry connected the state to the entire Atlantic seaboard.

Many of the remarkable changes of those years occurred in the organization of state government. An independent Supreme Court now capped Delaware's judiciary. The whipping post had disappeared from the inner yard at the New Castle County Work House; and the workhouse itself had been replaced by a new state correctional facility at Smyrna. The state's more than 100 commissions had disappeared; and the governor was now truly a chief executive with the power and the responsibility to administer state agencies through his appointed cabinet secretaries. Voters now used machines rather than easily corruptible paper ballots to choose their leaders and representatives. Since 1967, state offices and the General Assembly's Joint Finance Committee had begun using computers to handle the budget process.

Not the least of the changes affected the General Assembly itself. The assembly had been reapportioned to reflect the location of population. The members of the assembly were reasonably compensated, and many were being re-elected multiple times. There were more women members. In 1971 the women members included Henrietta Johnson, the first African American woman elected to the House of Representatives. The legislature, the people's house, had become more reflective of the people themselves.

Underlying the changes that marked those two decades was the United States Supreme Court. Given its border state history and conservative social structure, Delaware would not have integrated its schools, public accommodations, or housing market had it not been for the United States Supreme Court, together with the actions of presidents and the Congress. The Supreme Court forced Delaware to redistribute the seats in its General Assembly according to the principle of "one man, one vote." The General Assembly's new orientation shifted power from the rural to the suburban part of the state and opened Delawareans to new ways of thinking about their state's organization, resources, and future.

10

THE CITIZEN LEGISLATORS, 1973-2004

Three bronze plaques dominate the landing on the central staircase in Legislative Hall. The plaques bear the names of those who have served twenty years or more in the General Assembly. Three names honor eighteenth-century assemblymen. There are no names from the nineteenth century, and only two from the twentieth century before World War II. In the mid twentieth century the number of long-serving legislators began to climb. By 1973 the number of names had grown to a total of seventeen. It was about then that the real take-off began. By 2003 the list of names had expanded to forty-four.

The plaques reveal an important truth about recent legislative life. The late twentieth century witnessed the rise of long incumbencies in the General Assembly not seen in the assembly's three-hundred-year history. Those modern-day long-term lawmakers and their colleagues have faced and overcome major challenges that made the late twentieth century one of the most significant eras in the history of the Delaware General Assembly.

The past thirty years present a movement towards a more professional, structured, and business-like approach to governance in both the executive and legislative branches of Delaware's government. The political antagonism that once crippled the ability of governors and legislators to work together across party lines has diminished. Citizen legislators of both major parties have come to the fore to tackle issues ranging from health care to saving parkland to improving public education. Although party affiliation no longer dictates votes as much as it once did, battles continue between supporters of business and labor, between the heavily developed upstate and the developing downstate, and between social liberals and social conservatives. But, on the most serious issues concerning the state's economic and fiscal health, legislators from all sides have learned to work in harness, if not in total harmony.

The financial crisis of the 1970s was a watershed in the history of the General Assembly. The American economy was in recession, and the economic troubles hit Delaware at a most inopportune time. In 1972 Governor Russell Peterson lost his bid for re-election to former Speaker of the House Sherman Tribbitt, in part because the Peterson administration had failed to predict a decline in the state's income and to budget accordingly. As governor from January 1973 to January 1977, Sherman Tribbitt faced the brunt of the recession with similar inability to foretell the state's income or to control its costs.

The election of 1972 that had brought Democrat Sherman Tribbitt to the governor's office was also historically significant for the General Assembly. As part of the redistricting of the state following the 1970 census of the United States, the assembly had added two seats to each chamber, raising the number of seats in the Senate from nineteen to twenty-one and in the House from thirty-nine to forty-one. The voting process changed also. The election of 1972 was the first in Delaware to do away with the "Big Lever" that had encouraged voters to vote a straight party ticket with one flick of the hand. Starting in 1972 voters had to go down the list of candidates for each office and pull a series of little levers to make their selection for each office. The practice encouraged ticket-splitting and assisted the re-election of incumbents over less- established opponents.

The election of 1972 seemed to promise a political stalemate in Dover because there would be a Democrat governor and a Republican-controlled General Assembly. But Sherman Tribbitt was not an old hand in Legislative Hall for nothing. In the two months between the election and the opening of the 127th General Assembly the governor-elect maneuvered behind the scenes to bring the Senate, formerly the province of Republican leader Reynolds du Pont, into the Democratic fold. His co-conspirators were two Republican Senators: J. Donald Isaacs, whose Middletown farm lay close to Tribbitt's home in Odessa; and Anthony J. Cicione, a butcher from the Wilmington working-class suburb of Elsmere. Reportedly, even though he ran in a majority Democrat district, Isaacs had received little Republican support in his last campaign. Cicione was likewise disenchanted with the Republicans. The pairs' defections made good political sense.

In January 1973 the General Assembly convened amid the usual flutter of first-day swearing-in ceremonies conducted before the proud families and friends of the new legislators. Hardly had the ceremony ended in the Senate when Lieutenant Governor Bookhammer yielded the floor to Senator Allen J. Cook. In short order the rumored defections became plain. There followed a flurry of motions, tablings, and tablings of tablings that befuddled all but the most seasoned and clued-in members. In each roll call the first to vote was the only senator whose name began with the letter "A," Thurman G. Adams, Jr., a newly elected Democrat from Bridgeville. In the confusion, Adams looked vainly around him for assistance to determine how a good Democrat should cast his vote.[1]

Senator Adams must have voted correctly, because at the end of the day J. Donald Isaacs and Anthony Cicione had bolted from the Republicans to the Democrats, giving the governor's party a majority. Isaacs had gotten the grateful Democrats' votes to make him president pro tempore. The maneuver removed veteran Senator Calvin McCullough of New Castle from leadership of the Senate Democrats, but McCullough may have enjoyed seeing the embittered reactions from the other side of the aisle, even as he experienced power slipping from his own grasp.

Reynolds du Pont and the other Republicans were furious and only a bit assuaged by Isaacs's promise to let stand most of his former leader's committee assignments. The editorials in the du Pont family-owned Wilmington News Journal papers were scathing in their indignation at the turnabout. The *Morning News* denounced Senator Isaacs as "a right-wing blowhard whose concept of legislative initiative is to attack anything progressive."[2]

Reynolds du Pont was the last Republican president pro tempore in the twentieth century. In 1974 he declined to run again for the Senate, relinquishing his safe Republican seat to House veteran Andrew Knox. Senator du Pont had been the source of election funds for Republican candidates in both houses of the General Assembly. He had led his party in the legislature since the late 1950s and had served as president pro tempore during the four years that Russell Peterson was governor.

The politically divided assembly that gathered in January 1973 had few tools with which to govern. Just two years before, a major national study had ranked the Delaware General Assembly a sorry forty-eighth among American legislative bodies. The ranking was based on criteria such as functionality, accountability, independence, and knowledge of issues.[3] The authors of the study admitted that many state legislatures functioned poorly. But even in comparison to other dysfunctional state legislatures, they placed Delaware's among the worst. The First State's legislature, they said, lacked trained staff to research issues and to prepare bills. Furthermore, they admonished the Delaware lawmakers for their cavalier approach to the potentialities of legislative committees. Respecting committees, Delaware was ranked dead last, with the comment that "for all practical purposes, committees can hardly be said to exist."[4]

It didn't require expert knowledge to observe flaws in the General Assembly. A combination of antiquated rules, spiteful partisanship, and parliamentary trickery substituted for structure, careful preparation, and open discussion in determining the outcome of legislation. Unwritten skeleton bills were a thing of the past, but the procedure of tabling the roll call was still practiced. By that maneuver either a proponent or an opponent could postpone a vote with the intent to recall a bill at a moment when his or her side could muster a majority of members present and voting. End-of-term logjams, never to be completely avoided no matter how well managed a legislative body might be, had reached inhuman proportions in the final days of each session in Dover. A succession of all-night sessions that left members so weary they could not concentrate were the norm in late June. Former Senator Roger Martin recalls the twenty-two-hour meeting on June 30, 1974, as his most hellish experience in Legislative Hall.[5]

The General Assembly was a reactive body. Its members had virtually no professional staff to help them research issues and prepare legislation. The attaches were patronage appointees, go-fers, and ornaments. United States Congressman Michael N. Castle recalls staying up all night to draft his own bills when he was a member of the legislature in the 1960s.[6] Fortunately for him, he was a trained lawyer capable of undertaking work that would confound most legislators. More typically, members of the assembly took their bills from lobbyists or from administrators in the executive branch of government. On the important issues of the state's budget and capital spending, legislators had even less guidance than the inadequately informed governor.

The recession that afflicted the world economy in the early 1970s had frightened many people in Delaware into a reexamination of the Coastal Zone Act of 1971. Some thought the act sent an anti-business signal that would ultimately doom the state's economy. There were fears that its enforcement would especially undermine the nation's ability to overcome the energy crisis. Eugene Bookhammer, the Republican lieutenant governor and a former legislator from Lewes, led a movement to establish a mega-docking facility at Big Stone Beach in the Delaware Bay. There huge ships could unload coal and crude oil, which would be transferred to smaller vessels to be shipped to refineries and factories up river. As a legislator, Governor Tribbitt had sought to weaken the coastal zone law, but now he used his influence to maintain the coastal zone against proposed encroachments. The legislation held.

Readers may be surprised that Delaware had a governor and a lieutenant governor of opposing parties. Under Delaware's Constitution of 1897 candidates for the state's two top executive offices run separately rather than as a team. As a result, there have been occasions when an officer of the executive branch whose party affiliation is different from the governor's has held the potential tie-breaking vote in the Senate.

In the 1960s a committee of legislators undertook to draft a new constitution that would bring the state constitution into greater conformity with that of the federal government and of most other states. Reformers sought to have the governor and lieutenant governor run on one ticket and to reduce the much-amended 1897 document's excessive verbiage. However improved it might have been, the proposed constitutional revision was ill-starred. During the Peterson administration it passed both houses in the requisite two separate legislative sessions only to be killed by the secretary of state's failure to place a timely advertisement in the press.

The revised constitution came back to the legislature again in 1974, only to be trounced in an even more bizarre fashion. On the last day of the legislative session, June 30, 1974, the constitution came before the House of Representatives. The revision had already passed in the Senate with the two-thirds vote required for a constitutional amendment. The last day is notorious for vote trading as members scramble to get their pet bills adopted in the rush of the final hours. In her perceptive eyewitness study of modern-day Delaware politics, *Only in Delaware*, political reporter Celia Cohen recalled the constitution's demise. "There were a number of representatives angling for votes for their pet bills," she writes, "but none was more cagey than John Matushefske, the mischief-making Wilmington Manor Democrat . . . ."[7]

"Matty" was an extreme example of an old-time "pol," who, Cohen says, "combined a cherubic disposition with buccaneering wiles in a creative approach to politics." According to Cohen, Matushefske once explained, "If I take the money and do the favor the same day, it's a bribe. If I do the favor the next day, it's a campaign contribution." [8] On this occasion Matushefske wanted to help some friends in the road-construction trade more than he wanted a new state constitution. He traded his intention to vote for the constitution with some downstate legislators who opposed it in order to get their votes for an asphalt contractor he wanted to help. His defection left the constitution bill with but one vote to spare. At that point, Representative John G. S. Billingsley, a Newark Republican, became so disgusted by the lack of gravity in the House regarding the new constitution that he refused to vote for it. Thus, the revision of the state's fundamental law lost by one vote.

In the recriminations that followed, Representative Matushefske laid the blame at Billingsley's door. Celia Cohen quoted the Wilmington Manor representative as saying, "Billingsley is a phony, [he] went around telling Common Cause and the League of Women Voters he was for it, and then he killed it." Matushefske ascribed the real reason for Billingsley's sour reaction to the failure of the Newark representative's own pet legislation to pass. As for the asphalt bill, Governor Tribbitt vetoed it, so it died together with the constitution.[9]

The state's citizenry could be forgiven for thinking that their legislature was doing little to improve anything in Delaware. A measure to raise the number of justices on the state Supreme Court was lost because the Republicans in the House didn't want a Democrat governor and Democrat Senate to name two new justices when the Senate had recently refused to confirm a superior court justice that the Republicans favored. There were also party battles over teachers' pay and over the bond bill.

The legislators did yield to public pressure to adopt a disclosure bill whereby candidates for the assembly would have to reveal the sources of their funds. No one was surprised to discover that the two largest benefactors for candidates in legislative races in the fall of 1974 were Reynolds du Pont for the Republicans and the United Auto Workers for the Democrats. The interesting aspect of this information was the smallness of the gifts from the biggest donors: $7,265 from du Pont and $6,200 from the U.A.W., which demonstrated just how little it cost to run for a seat in the General Assembly.[10]

The election in November 1974 took place at the height of public disgust over the Watergate scandals of Richard M. Nixon's Republican administration. Delaware voters were also angry that the previous legislature had failed to resolve important issues. The election brought new blood to the legislature, especially in the House of Representatives. Thirteen seats changed hands in the House that gave the Democrats a clear majority. Among the newcomers to the House were two future Speakers: Democrat Orlando J. George, Jr., and Republican Charles L. Hebner, Sr. In addition, a future governor, Ruth Ann Minner, formerly a legislative secretary, was elected to the House to represent the Milford area. The Senate also went Democratic. Thomas B. Sharp, a future president pro tempore, was elected that year, as was Nancy Cook, a former attache and the widow of long-time Senator Allen J. Cook, who was chosen to replace her late husband in a special election.

A reunion of the "Class of '74," photographed on March 23, 1989. Front row from left: Orlando J. George, Jr., Gerard A. Cain, and Robert L. Maxwell. Back row from left: Charles L. Hebner, Sr., Al O. Plant, C. Leslie Ridings, Nancy W. Cook, Robert L. Byrd, Gwynne P. Smith, Thomas B. Sharp, and Ruth Ann Minner. Photograph by Gary Emeigh. (Courtesy of the News Journal Company)

At a critical moment in the state's history the members of the "Watergate class of '74" brought a spirit of purpose and optimism to the possibilities of government. Robert L. Maxwell, a social-studies teacher and a new member of the House of Representatives, recalls his excitement at being elected. Despite, or perhaps because of the crisis mode in Delaware's finances, he and his classmates brought "a feeling of invincibility" to their new responsibilities.[11] Orlando (Lonnie) George remembers how he and his fellow classmates believed that they "were on a mission" to build an environment where the operative idea would become "good government is good politics."[12] At their first Democratic caucus in the House the newcomers refused to go along with the old timers' call for revenge against the Republicans. In the face of serious problems, the practice of partisanship for its own sake was finally under challenge.

In 1975 the overriding issue before the legislature was how to pay the state's bills. Inflation was sapping everyone's income and driving up the cost of borrowing money. Because of the stalled economy traditional sources of funds were in decline. Casting about for new income, Governor Tribbitt and his fellow Democrats fixed their gaze on the Getty Refinery at Delaware City. A special tax on Getty seemed worth a try. News of the tax reached the ears of the reclusive J. Paul Getty at his English estate. The billionaire oil entrepreneur called Tribbitt on the telephone and threatened to pull up stakes in the First State should the tax stand. The Democrats were in too cavalier a mood to be frightened by the billionaire refinery owner; but they proved more amenable to the pleas of the refinery's union workers whose jobs were threatened.

Once again the irrepressible John Matushefske stood at the center of a major drama in Legislative Hall. Night fell as the House prepared to vote on a compromise bill the Democrats had devised to reduce their proposed tax on Getty. Members decided to break for dinner. As was common, a swarm of people buttonholed the hungry representatives as they left the chamber. When the representatives returned, John Matushefske informed Speaker Casimir S. Jonkiert that he could not vote for the tax. He then explained that a Getty worker to whom he owed a big favor had approached him during the dinner break. It seems that the worker's wife had once served on the jury that had acquitted Matushefske of malfeasance.[13]

Without Matty's vote, the Getty tax lost. The legislature's only remaining recourse was to raise income taxes to their all-time high of 19.8 percent for those in the highest bracket. The cumulative effect of the coastal-zone restrictions, the attempted tax on Getty, and the high tax on the state's most prosperous earners increased the impression that Delaware had become "anti-business."

To add to the state's financial woes, the Farmers Bank of Delaware faced bankruptcy. The General Assembly had chartered the bank in 1807 to be the state's official repository. For nearly 170 years the state had deposited the money it earned from taxes and fees in the Farmers Bank. To protect that trust and to earn additional income for the state, the original legislation had provided for Delaware to own a 20 percent interest in the bank. The directors' seats that came with the state's investment had always been among the General Assembly's most significant plums. In the bank's early days the legislature had appointed leading citizens with financial experience to occupy those seats. But with the passage of time and the rise of other state banking institutions that transcended the Farmers Bank in deposits and prestige, the legislature took a more relaxed approach and appointed men, often legislators or former legislators, who knew little of banking and viewed their appointments not so much as positions of oversight but as opportunities to secure loans on favorable terms for themselves and for their friends.

The impending failure of the state's bank came as a shock. The bank was poorly managed. In light of the economic downturn, its officers had indulged in excessively optimistic policies. By 1975 the bank was in deep trouble and was about to go down, taking the state's deposits with it. In a closed-door meeting, an officer of a major New York investment firm told a stunned governor and legislators that Delaware, too, faced bankruptcy.[14] If ever there was a wake-up call to state leaders this was it, but it would take several years for the executive and legislative branches to forge a strong financial structure for the state. In the meantime, mostly behind the scenes, Sherman Tribbitt fought and won the battle to keep the Farmers Bank afloat and the state's deposits safe.

Governor Tribbitt's Herculean efforts may have saved the state, but they could not save him. In 1976 he lost his re-election bid to Pierre S. du Pont IV, a great nephew of his namesake, the philanthropist whose money had built Delaware's first modern schools. Pete du Pont won the governorship on his promise to provide new, assertive "Leadership for a Change" to raise the battered state out of its troubles.

Based on past experience there was little prospect that a Republican governor could work with a Democratic legislature. One needed only to recall the failure of Governor Caleb Boggs's well-conceived "New Day for Delaware" in the 1950s. In addition, the new governor had slight respect for the General Assembly. Du Pont recalled that during his own service there some years before he had found the atmosphere in Legislative Hall to be informal and dysfunctional. It had been a place where members carried their hand-written bills around in their back pockets and where petty personal deal-making trumped procedural policy.[15] Now du Pont faced a legislature in which the Democrats were in firm control of both houses. The potential was present for the executive and legislative branches to become mired in a hopeless political clash as Delaware's credit careened to the bottom, its government ceased functioning, and its citizens lost faith in politics and politicians.

On the evening of du Pont's inaugural ball in January 1977 two House Democrats, both with university degrees in economics, asked the new governor to take a stroll with them behind a curtain. The men were Orlando George, a mathematics instructor who chaired the House Appropriations Committee, and Gerard Cain, a bank officer who served on the House Revenue and Finance Committee. They told du Pont that they recognized the seriousness of the state's financial troubles and promised that, while they were likely to disagree with the Republican governor on many issues, they would do what they could to cooperate on matters affecting the budget.[16] The walk behind the curtain was the first glimmer that there might be a way out of the financial and political morass.

There was hope for agreement on finance issues on the Senate side as well. The new president pro tempore was Richard S. Cordrey, the partner in an agricultural business in Millsboro. Senator Cordrey understood the need for careful money management. His father, who had owned farms and a milling business in Sussex County, died while Richard and his brother were in their teens, leaving them to carry on. Young Cordrey had learned the hard necessity of cost saving in order to meet the weekly payroll. He brought that same perspective to the state's finances.

Two Republican governors, J. Caleb Boggs (left) and Pierre S. du Pont IV, receiving U.S. Vice President George H.W. Bush on a visit to Delaware (Courtesy of the Historical Society of Delaware)

The newly elected 129th General Assembly opened with the outgoing governor's sobering final budget message and the new governor's impolitic admission that Delaware was "bankrupt." Leaders of both parties knew that the state could not continue to borrow its way out of its financial troubles. Delaware had to tap new revenue sources and its leaders had to control spending. Regarding the latter, a key issue that divided the parties was the automatic cost of living adjustment (COLA) that had been built into state employees' salaries as a hedge against inflation. The governor demanded its repeal. The Democrats in the legislature found that a hard proposition to swallow because they had strong ties to union workers, including the teachers' union, the Delaware State Education Association (DSEA). The governor told them that if the Democrats insisted on keeping COLA they would have to take the blame for raising the new tax dollars to pay for it.

The confrontation over the COLA issue set the tone for Governor du Pont's relationship with the Democratic assembly. The battle demonstrated that neither side would give way unless it got something in return. The governor brought the Republican members of the legislature on board to vote against the COLA and asked the reluctant Democrats to supply the extra votes needed to pass the bill. The Democrats agreed to provide enough votes, but only on condition that du Pont would not raise the salaries of his cabinet members and close aides.[17]

The Budget Bill for fiscal 1978 provided the next test of wills. It proved to be the most significant battle in modern Delaware political history and is recognized today as a major defining moment in the evolution of the General Assembly into a more responsible body.

There was too much partisan hostility for anyone to have predicted a positive outcome. The Democrats believed that the governor's lean budget projections were wrong. They expected the state to take in more money than the governor anticipated and, therefore, demanded a higher level of spending. Some Democrat legislators were openly resentful of the governor's family name and upper-class background. Some were indignant that du Pont sent emissaries to meet with them to discuss the budget rather than coming to bargain with them in person. Republican legislators were not happy either. They refused to go along with any tax increases, even when their party's governor supported moderate increases as part of a negotiated compromise with the majority Democrats. Democrats sneered that du Pont could not command his own partisans, much less the entire assembly.

The last day of June dawned with no compromise in sight. As usual on the final day of the session, the assembly struggled to pass last-minute bills amid the sea of lobbyists and special-interest advocates who mobbed Legislative Hall. The midnight deadline to begin fiscal 1978 came and went with no budget. It was apparent that political compromise was still not in sight. The Democrats decided to vote their version of the budget and dare the governor to veto it.

The Democrats were not simply being optimistic about the state's income projections for 1978. Their faith was based on numbers supplied by Orlando George, the chairman of the Joint Finance Committee. Representative George brought unusual strengths to his position that gave credence to his calculations. He had the confidence of his Democratic colleagues because he had a professional's understanding of the probable effects of economic change on Delaware's income. The governor's budget people predicted that the Democrats' projected budget of $454,000,000 would outstrip Delaware's income by $9,000,000. Not so, said George, who argued that the state's tax income would rise to pay the bills.

On July 2 weary legislators ended months of debate and voted along straight party lines for the Joint Finance Committee's version of the budget bill. As anticipated, Governor du Pont vetoed the bill during the Fourth of July recess, two days later the Democrats held together to override the veto.

The override vote could have been the final nail in the coffin of executive-legislative cooperation for the remainder of Governor du Pont's term in office. Instead it was the jolt needed to restore life to a near-bankrupt state government. To the Democrats' relief and the governor's amazement, the Joint Finance Chairman's prediction concerning the state's revenue for 1978 proved true. The legislature gained pride and confidence in their new-found professionalism. Pete du Pont was impressed.

It was Governor du Pont who made the first overtures at reconciliation.

Setting aside what had appeared to be an aloof disdain for the state's senators and representatives, he now invited the legislators to his home, "Patterns," a modern villa overlooking the Brandywine River across from the powder yards that his ancestors had established. He took them on picnics and to see big-league sports. He got to know the members of the legislature personally; and they got to know him. Little by little mutual respect and trust grew between the patrician governor and the more plebian representatives of the people at large.

The reconciliation could hardly have come at a more opportune time. In 1978 Alexander F. Giacco, the president of the Hercules Powder Company, then Wilmington's second-largest private employer, announced that his company was seriously contemplating leaving the state because of what he termed Delaware's anti-business climate. With the outspoken and energetic Giacco at its helm Hercules would not go quietly. Giacco got together with Du Pont Company President Irving Shapiro and leaders of other major businesses to lobby all levels of government for change.[18]

Speaking on behalf of business leaders, the president of Hercules said that he was "tired of deficits, tax increases, and no growth" in the First State.[19] He was particularly hostile to the 19.8 percent state income tax that he and other wealthy people viewed as a serious disincentive to attracting new high-paying, nonpolluting industries to locate in Delaware. Delawareans heard a barrage of accusations that the state was "anti-business," just as they heard after the passage of the Coastal Zone Act in 1971. There were real problems. The First State's economy was sluggish; there was a dangerously large state debt; and the high tax rate that so disturbed corporate executives was threatening to bring even greater economic pain.

Thanks to the spirit of cooperation on fiscal affairs that leaders in the General Assembly were forging with the du Pont administration, remedies could be implemented to counter the state's economic difficulties. Financial prudence became the state's primary strategic tool. In the Senate, President Pro Tempore Richard S. Cordrey proposed an amendment to Delaware's constitution to require the state to put 2 percent of its annual budgeted funds into a reserve account, popularly dubbed the "rainy day fund." In addition, Governor du Pont worked with Democrats in the legislature to adopt another amendment to require a three-fifths vote to raise taxes. Both amendments passed easily.

Orlando George and Gerard Cain, the young Democrats who had spoken to the governor behind the curtain at the inauguration, had now risen to leadership in the House of Representatives. They took seriously Al Giacco's complaints about the state's high tax rate and promised to cut the top income tax from 19.8 to 13.5 percent over two years. With that promise, together with a tax-cushioned deal whereby Hercules got a new office building in Wilmington with the aid of public money, Giacco assured Governor du Pont that the chemical company would remain in the state.

Delaware emerged from its late 1970s fiscal malaise with a strong fiscal structure. The rainy day fund and the three-fifths rule on tax increases have provided effective insurance for the state government's financial health ever since. The rainy day fund has become so sacrosanct that no governor or Joint Finance Committee has dared to suggest that the accumulating money be used for any purpose but to stand in reserve.

    Members of the legislature of both parties are proud of their roles in rescuing the state from near bankruptcy. Democrats and Republicans alike praise Governor du Pont for his leadership in partnership with the General Assembly. It was a joint effort in which many members could take credit. Robert F. Gilligan, currently the House minority leader, ranks his own role in helping to pass the financial safeguards as his proudest achievement in thirty years of service in the legislature.[20] Fellow Democrat Richard S. Cordrey, who served as president pro tempore of the Senate for eight terms, is likewise convinced that his proposal for the rainy day fund represented his most significant service to the state. Delawareans in and out of government were tired of the upward trend in taxes, Cordrey said, and expected the state to be run like a business.[21]

New members of the House of Representatives being sworn in at the opening of the 128th General Assembly in 1979. Photograph by Kevin Fleming. *(Courtesy of the News Journal Company)*

In the election of 1978 the Democrats retained their hold on the Senate, but in the House, where eighteen seats changed hands, the Republicans picked up five additional representatives. The GOP now held twenty seats to the Democrats' twenty-one. In September 1979, Democratic Representative Daniel A. Kelly, a schoolteacher from the Newport area, died, leaving the two parties tied for control of the House.

Both parties worked with utmost vigor to capture the seat made vacant by Kelly's death. A Republican win would give the GOP control of one house in the assembly and much more bargaining power with the Senate Democrats. Governor du Pont personally went door to door with the Republican candidate, Donald J. Van Sciver. Voters of the 16th district were heavily Democratic, but there was a big turnout for this particularly significant special election. A majority of the voters responded to their governor's pleas to elect Van Sciver.[22] Except for the years 1983 and 1984, the Republican Party has maintained its majority in the House of Representatives into the twenty-first century.

As the 1980s began, leaders of both parties in the General Assembly had learned to approach issues of fundamental importance to the First State's economy in a spirit of cooperation. That sense of a common purpose that joined Republicans and Democrats and the executive and legislative branches of government proved crucial to enacting the state's next major economic bill: the introduction of credit-card banking.

Like many other states in the post-industrial Northeast, Delaware hoped to lure well-paying, white-collar, non-polluting companies to make their home in the First State. Banks fit the profile: not retail banks of the sort that Delawareans knew, where customers have checking accounts and take out loans and mortgages, but a new type of service that was just then arising from the nation's major commercial banks — the issue of credit cards to millions of customers scattered throughout the nation and the world.

The key to profitability in credit-card banking lies in volume and the freedom to demand very high interest, often in excess of 18 percent, on loans that may extend over a lengthy period of time. Most states, including Delaware, had usury statutes that precluded such high rates of interest. South Dakota was the first state to repeal its usury law in hopes of attracting large New York banks to relocate their credit-card operations to their state. But not many bankers chose to move to the Great Plains. Delaware, with its easy access to major east coast cities, offered a far more alluring location.

Two premier New York banks, the Chase Manhattan and the Morgan Guaranty Trust, entered into a quiet courtship with the First State. After much negotiation, the bankers promised the governor that they would move their credit-card divisions to Delaware and provide jobs for Delawareans, but only if the state met their conditions, which included repealing its usury law and offering them a favorable tax rate. The banks also demanded that the state demonstrate its commitment by acting fast. If the necessary legislation failed to pass both houses between the outset of the 131st General Assembly in January 1981 and the assembly's recess in February for six weeks of budget hearings, the deal would be off.

Delaware's principal negotiators in the very quiet early stages of the credit-card deal were a bipartisan group that included Democrats William McLaughlin, the mayor of Wilmington, and O. Francis Biondi, one of Wilmington's leading lawyers. Biondi made a dramatic helicopter trip to Sussex County to inform President Pro Tempore Cordrey and Senator Thurman G. Adams, Jr., of the bankers' proposal.[23] Those legislative leaders' support would prove crucial in convincing their Democratic colleagues in the Senate to vote for the bill.

When the new legislature assembled in January 1981, Representative John M. Burris, the Republican majority leader, introduced the banking bill into the House. The governor's office had provided a skillfully crafted name for the legislation, calling it the Financial Center Development Act. John Burris was a compelling advocate for the legislation. He was a businessman from Milford, the son of the founder of Burris Foods, one of Southern Delaware's most important companies. Burris was determined to move the bill through the House as quickly as possible. "I took the position, the faster we'd do this, the more pressure we'd put on the Senate."[24]

The bill passed the House, but not without opposition. A few members of both parties complained that there should have been an open hearing to explore the bill's potential effects on consumer debt. Representative William A. Oberle, Jr., a Republican representing a blue-collar district, led the opposition. Two other members of the House joined him in refusing to vote for the bill on the grounds that there had been no opportunity to discuss its ramifications on consumer credit.

The credit-card bill then went to the Senate. Celia Cohen, who reported the scene in the upper house for the News Journal Papers, described the intense atmosphere there as the bill's supporters battled to hold onto the votes of uncommitted Senators. Cohen writes:

> By now, national consumer groups were alerted . . . Ralph Nader . . . issued a warning of dire consequences . . . . A local consumer lawyer raised objections. A cascade of amendments was prepared—with the very real threat that if any one of them passed, the bill would have to be returned to the House, creating a dangerous game of Ping-Pong and likely as not, missing the deadline for adoption.[25]

The Senators discussed and debated the proposed legislation, together with a slew of potential restrictive amendments for many hours. Finally came the roll call that would make or break Delaware's opportunity to become the nation's most desirable credit-card bank haven. As Governor du Pont and members of his staff sat on the floor of a Senate anteroom and listened nervously to hear the votes over a loudspeaker, the senators voted down amendment after amendment.[26] One amendment was rejected by a single vote. Then finally came the vote on the Financial Center Development Act in its original form. It passed fourteen to seven.

No one, even among the bill's most eager supporters, could have imagined how the Financial Center Development Act would transform Delaware's economy. MBNA Bank, now Delaware's largest private employer, was a small, unknown bank in Maryland. Neither it nor Bank One, which became the second most prominent credit-card operation in Delaware, was part of the original compact. Nor did anyone predict that the state's chemical giants of that time—DuPont, Hercules, and Atlas—would be subject to mergers, sell-offs, and employee downsizing that have greatly reduced the chemical industry's profile in Delaware.

In the same years that saw the legislative and executive branches working together to overcome financial catastrophe, Delaware's government was also reacting to a series of powerfully transformational federal court decisions respecting the desegregation of New Castle County's public schools.

It took Delaware's school districts a decade to implement the United States Supreme Court's *Brown* v. *Board* decision of 1954. Integration was introduced in the Wilmington public schools immediately following the Court's decision, but it did not become the norm in other parts of the state until the mid-1960s. Then, in 1968, the legislature adopted the Educational Advancement Act. Designed to consolidate small school districts throughout the state, the act froze the boundaries of the Wilmington district, the state's largest. During that same period the racial balance in the Wilmington public schools underwent dramatic change as white city dwellers moved to suburbs and rural black families moved to the city. By 1970 the Wilmington schools had become overwhelmingly black, while white children populated newly built suburban schools.

Responding to their new population, the Wilmington schools de-emphasized college preparatory courses in favor of programs aimed at lower-income students. Racial tensions and disorder became endemic in city high schools. Those phenomena led some middle-class white students in the city to seek transfers to suburban schools. Their efforts were rebuffed. The suburban districts cited the state's Educational Advancement Act of 1968 to deny cross-district transfers from the city on the grounds that the law had specifically declared the Wilmington district to be complete and self-contained.

The students' parents did not give up. They found allies among city officials and the American Civil Liberties Union. The lawyers for the plaintiffs recognized the futility of fighting the Educational Advancement Act in the state's courts. Instead, they launched their challenge in federal court under the umbrella of the federal courts' burgeoning opinions concerning school-district desegregation in urban areas throughout the United States. The Delaware case re-opened a prior federal integration case in the state called *Evans* v. *Buchanan*.[27]

By 1974, when *Evans* v. *Buchanan* went before a three-judge panel at the federal courthouse in Wilmington, the major issues raised by the case far transcended the question of city-suburban transfers. In light of recent federal-court decisions in the states of Michigan and North Carolina, the judges were asked to consider whether state and local government policies had contributed to the creation of the racially divided pattern of housing and school attendance that characterized northern Delaware. Lawyers for the plaintiffs convinced a majority of the judges that the Educational Advancement Act of 1968 had done just that. Although the legislature's action had been intended to consolidate rural districts rather than to isolate the Wilmington school district, the court held that the effect of the act had been to re-segregate the schools of New Castle County.

The case then entered the remedy phase under District Court Judge Murray M. Schwartz. Given the findings of the three-judge panel, Judge Schwartz could settle for nothing short of a plan that would co-mingle students from the city with those in the suburban districts. By then citizen groups had formed to exert their influence to prevent changing district lines and attendance patterns. The largest and most powerful group was the Positive Action Committee (PAC). PAC used every method short of violence to prevent the use of "forced busing" to desegregate the districts.

The legislature, too, got involved. Judge Schwartz urged the General Assembly to take responsibility for fashioning an acceptable remedy. The problem was that the General Assembly reflected the views of its members' constituents, who were overwhelmingly opposed to the federal courts' mandated changes in school-enrollment patterns. The legislators refused to take the responsibility that the judge thrust onto them. The assembly did, however, take one important step. They established a special joint committee to keep them informed on the case and to prepare their colleagues to take legislative action at the appropriate time.[28]

It was a difficult time to be a legislator from New Castle County. Members of the assembly faced angry, frustrated constituents at meeting after meeting. Robert Maxwell, who chaired the General Assembly's special committee, can recall being in schools where parents held up photos of their children and yelled that this would be the last time their children would be seen in that school if desegregation were to be implemented. Every legislator took pains to keep abreast of constituents' sentiments and to behave accordingly. In 1976 voters elected several new representatives on the basis of endorsements from the PAC. At least one legislator lost his seat because his opponent portrayed him as weak on that all-consuming issue.

Since the assembly had refused to enact the necessary legislation, Judge Schwartz had no recourse but to impose his own solution. As feared, his remedy was indeed draconian. The judge required the dissolution of school districts in Wilmington and its suburbs into a single district. Students were to attend schools in the city in the middle grades and to attend schools in the suburbs in the primary grades and high school. Teachers' pay would be adjusted to the highest level among the districts, which was in Wilmington. "Forced busing" would be required to implement the decree and the state and unified district were to be responsible for the associated costs.

The legislators were in the worst possible position. Having refused Judge Schwartz's invitation to craft a solution acceptable to the court, most members were now appalled by the judge's solution. But they were not out of the game yet. Wise heads warned that for the present, their best course was to be prudent. As Professor Jeffrey A. Raffel, who participated in Delaware's desegregation experience, observed, the legislature was "concerned with the legal propriety of its actions."[29] After all, it had been the seemingly innocent Educational Advancement Act of 1968 that had landed New Castle County's school districts in trouble with the federal courts.

By a stroke of good fortune, the legislature's special committee hired one of America's most outstanding legal scholars to advise them on how best to protect the interests of the state. Their advisor was Philip B. Kurland of the University of Chicago Law School. Professor Kurland warned the legislators to take no action that might re-enforce the federal court's perception that Delaware was attempting to thwart school integration. According to Representative Robert Maxwell, Kurland's advice was the essential element that restrained the General Assembly from exacerbating their conflict with the federal court.

Another important factor was the presence of the much-respected Herman Holloway, Sr., the Senate's only black member. As on many other occasions, Holloway demonstrated his statesmanship as a mediator who could defuse racial tensions among his colleagues.[30] Holloway no doubt reminded his colleagues that many black citizens of Wilmington disliked busing as much as white suburbanites did. Not only were small black children to be bused far from home, but the new unitary district deprived blacks of their newly won control of the Wilmington School Board.

Philip Kurland's legal advice and Herman Holloway's efforts at conciliation could not entirely stop legislators from inventing ways to assert their will over the federal court's decree. The assembly considered an amendment to the state constitution to prohibit changing school-district boundaries, but then recognized that the federal court could trump that move. In frustration they tried to subpoena Judge Schwartz to appear before them, but that move, too, proved more bluster than substance.

On March 15, 1976, Philip B. Kurland appeared before the General Assembly to answer legislators' questions. He emphasized their impotence to affect the court's decision. He deflated various schemes that were floating around Legislative Hall, such as the notion that they could bring busing to a halt by refusing to pay the bus drivers to transport children across the old district lines. He left the lawmakers with one clear concept that carried a reproach when he said, "The time for phased desegregation, which was immediately after the Supreme Court decree of 1954, is no longer acceptable . . . . The time for desegregation is now."[31]

The legislators may have been chastened, but they continued to seek some compromise in a last-ditch effort to prevent the implementation of Judge Schwartz's busing plan. The assembly passed a "Freedom of Choice" law under which parents could request reassignment of their children to another district. But when the plan was put to the test in the fall of 1976, the voluntary reassignments failed to desegregate the schools. The assembly also enacted a bill to create special-interest "magnet" schools, but it too seemed unlikely to bring about enough racial mixing to assuage the court.

In December 1977 Governor du Pont called the General Assembly into special session to consider a multi-district plan. The plan was designed to meet the court's demand for full desegregation, but within the context of four districts rather than the single district that the judge had put forward. The proposal offered opponents of busing but small consolation, and the legislature rejected it.[32] Three years later, in 1981, the assembly revisited the idea and adopted the four districts.

In his account of desegregation, Jeffrey Raffel credits a number of educational and community leaders with the peaceful imposition of desegregation by "forced busing" in the fall of 1978. As busing loomed, school and public officials formed the Breakfast Group to work through the desegregation process, to defuse tensions, and to create a desegregation plan compatible with Judge Schwartz's decree. By contrast, Raffel wrote, "the legislature, almost unanimously, exploited the passions around the issue and avoided the substance."[33]

It would have been unrealistic to expect the legislature to assume a positive role in the process similar to that of the school administrators of the Breakfast Group. The General Assembly is an elected body that acts as a mediator between the electorate and their government. The legislature represents "the people," and in this context "the people" were angry, alarmed, and frustrated at their inability to stop the action of a federal court. The wonder is that the legislators behaved with as much restraint as they did considering that they could have chosen the path of active obstruction.

Throughout the desegregation process the legislature acted as a vent for public emotions. It collected those angry resentments and frustrations. Most of its members shared them. But much though the lawmakers strove to dilute the court's decree, the legislators never tried to prevent the implementation of the District Court's remedy, nor did they incite angry citizens to commit violent and unlawful acts. They neither cooperated with those who worked to smooth the way for the single-district plan nor did they put up illegal barriers of resistance. Their unsuccessful efforts to adopt compromise measures only proved the futility of resistance to the federal court's decree.

The state's near financial collapse and the desegregation upheavals of the 1970s brought a more serious spirit to Legislative Hall. In the governor's office, Pierre S. du Pont IV introduced a business-like, professional approach to the management of the executive departments that his successors have emulated.

The culture of the General Assembly also underwent significant change. Little by little old-school, narrowly-focused, self-interested, wheeler-dealers were defeated or retired. The newcomers were less parochial, more professional, and better focused on solving problems. Voters demanded candidates for the General Assembly whom they could count on to be capable, hardworking, and intent upon addressing issues of significance to the electorate. Partisan tensions abated; business flowed more smoothly; and the most egregious forms of institutionalized games-playing were eliminated. The days when members carried around bills in their pockets written on the backs of envelopes were gone; and the boozy "snake pit" in the basement was relegated to Legislative Hall legend.

The Senate of 1987-88. Front row from left: Ruth Ann Minner, William C. Torbert, Harris B. McDowell III, Thomas B. Sharp, Richard S. Cordrey, Myrna Bair, Robert T. Connor, James P. Neal. Second row from left: Nancy W. Cook, James T. Vaughn, Roger A. Martin, Margo Ewing Bane, Robert I. Marshall, Third row from left: Jacob W. Zimmerman, Herman M. Holloway, Sr., William S. Slatcher, Robert Berndt. Fourth row from left: Thurman Adams, Jr., David B. McBride, Robert T. Still, Andrew G. Knox. (Courtesy of the Delaware Public Archives)

Although cooperation across party lines became more common on issues crucial to the state, political parties remained at the center of the assembly's organization. The basic decision-making group in the General Assembly, as in other American legislatures, remains the party caucus. The majority caucus in each house chooses the leadership that will control the composition of committees and the disposition of legislation. Newcomers whose previous experience has been in civic associations, charities, and good-government groups often find it difficult to adjust to a system that accords so little power to members of the minority party, even as it bestows great power on the majority of members within the majority caucus.

Party affiliation is the most significant factor in the formal internal structure of the legislature, but it is only one among a number of factors that determine the assembly's voting blocs. Upstate and downstate continue to be important divisions. Geographic divisions are pronounced on social issues, where southern Delawareans hold to more traditional views, and on land-use issues, where overdeveloped northerners generally want more limits than do southerners. Business versus labor is also a significant divider, but not always along party lines. There are "labor" Republicans who represent blue-collar districts in New Castle County and "business" Democrats who represent areas where small business is strong and organized labor is weak or non-existent.

In addition to organizational and ideological divisions, the arcane procedures that old-timers employ to outflank the uninitiated can be intimidating to legislative newcomers. The sure-footed and determined soon learn ways to function with some degree of effectiveness within this maze-like power structure, where the big prize is seeing your legislation adopted with your name attached to it, but where you may count yourself lucky to settle for getting your bill through with the sponsorship of someone who is more powerfully placed in the majority leadership.

The United States Constitution created a model for the separation of powers between the executive and legislative branches of government to be tempered by checks and balances in their respective powers. It is a model that the state constitutions have emulated. It encourages a healthy antagonism between the governor and the legislature, but it is to be a tension of powers that must be checked by realism in pursuit of the public good. In the course of Pete du Pont's administration, the governor and legislature rediscovered how to make their relationship work, and the pattern that emerged to characterize dealings between the executive and legislative branches during du Pont's administration has been continued through subsequent administrations.

Legislators appreciate a governor who takes them seriously. They insist on being consulted. They want the governor to recognize the rhythm of legislative sessions, to deal with their leaders, and to come to them personally to negotiate important matters. Governors who fail to do those things can expect opposition.

In 1985 the voters showed their support for the du Pont administration by electing Michael Castle, Pete du Pont's lieutenant governor, to be the governor's successor. Castle maintained the atmosphere of healthy legislative-executive relations that his predecessor had set. As a former state senator Governor Castle was well acquainted with the denizens of Legislative Hall. When he sensed that the assembly was testing his resolve by adopting a bond bill larger than he thought prudent, Castle vetoed it. The legislators got the message and negotiated.

In 1992, with the election of Thomas R. Carper, the Democrats broke the Republicans' sixteen-year hold on the executive branch. Carper, a former state treasurer, had most recently been Delaware's lone United States Representative. He, too, became a two-term governor. Unlike his three immediate predecessors, Carper had never been a member of the General Assembly, and some members grumbled at his Washington, D.C., style of governing that seemed remote in the context of Delaware's intimate politics. The governor sought to rectify that perception by inviting legislative leaders of both parties to weekly lunch meetings to discuss issues and impending legislation.

The Castle and Carper administrations enjoyed sixteen years of economic prosperity. The healthy economy, together with the financial reforms of the previous decade, allowed the state to build and to expand services while enjoying a good bond rating on Wall Street. The legislature responded to good times with discretion, but also with opportunities for members to realize their various hopes to improve life in the First State.

New financial mechanisms were put in place during the period of recovery from near bankruptcy to keep the state on track. The executive branch reformed the state Tax Office and created the Delaware Economic and Financial Advisory Council (DEFAC) to advise the governor on the state's projected income. The legislature acquired its own full-time professional financial advisors in the office of the Controller General. When the professional money people talk, the elected officials in both branches of government listen.

Next to education and social services, transportation is the state's most important and most costly responsibility. Potholes and bottlenecks get voters' attention. The state took a major step forward toward securing a funding base for its roads and highways when it created the Transportation Trust Fund during the Castle administration to be a stand-alone fund separate from the state's general fund. The fund has permitted the Transportation Department, known as DelDOT, to plan several years in advance in the knowledge that the money will be available to complete projects.

Even more significant from the perspective of legislators, was the creation of a new funding category called "street money," which assigns a fixed amount, now $300,000, to each member of the General Assembly for the member to designate for road repairs in his or her district. The "street money" policy protects DelDOT from undue pressure from the rich and powerful in deciding whose potholes should receive premier attention. It also ensures that repair funds will go where the population lives and works.

"Street money" has tied legislators more closely to neighborhood groups and civic associations in their districts. Lawmakers rely on those groups to help them prioritize their street-improvement spending accounts. The only grumbling with the system comes from senators, whose allocations equal those of representatives, even though their districts are twice as large. In Wilmington, where the city is responsible for street repairs, a lawmaker got into trouble for using street money for projects that had nothing to do with transportation. More savvy Wilmington legislators use the funds for roadway enhancements such as lampposts, trees, and sidewalks.[34]

Three major enduring influences from the 1980s have produced a less partisan, more collaborative culture in the General Assembly. First and most important in forging the necessity for cooperation has been the seemingly permanent division of the two houses between a Democratic Senate and a Republican House of Representatives. Second has been the emergence of what Celia Cohen aptly named "the Age of Incumbency," which has been characterized by a large proportion of legislators serving multiple terms and developing long-term working relationships with one another.[35] Third has been an increase in the number of women legislators, a phenomenon that has increased the core of issue-oriented citizen-lawmakers in Legislative Hall.

Incumbency and redistricting are closely tied. Redistricting is the most partisan action that the General Assembly undertakes. After every census, each house is responsible for redistricting itself. This practice has operated to protect the majority party's continued control of that chamber and to protect incumbents' seats. Incumbents also have a big advantage in raising funds and in name recognition, particularly among voters who have received constituent services from the incumbent. Some people familiar with the legislature argue that term limits would bring new faces and ideas into the assembly. Others argue that long incumbencies are beneficial because they permit members of the assembly to develop professional relationships with their fellow lawmakers. Long-time legislators know how to work with others to get things done in Legislative Hall. In many cases, those working partnerships, based on mutual trust, guide legislative action.

The majority party elects the leadership and controls the legislative agendas, but the long-time control of each house by a different party has made cooperation necessary to get things done. Accommodation politics takes various forms. Ability has replaced pure patronage in selecting legislative staff. There is agreement that partisanship should not inhibit process. A good example of this concept in action is the method used to designate the chairperson of the Joint Finance Committee. The chair of this most important joint standing committee is either the chair of the Senate Finance Committee or the chair of the House Appropriations Committee. In the past, the two chairs and their respective chamber leadership had haggled over which one was to assume the premier position. When the houses were held by opposite parties, the battle could be especially prolonged. Finally, Senator Robert J. Berndt, a Du Pont Company chemist, made the sensible suggestion that the Joint Finance Chairmanship should rotate between the House and Senate committee chairs. The Berndt plan eliminated politics from the equation and has saved a lot of time and energy for more important matters.[36]

Long incumbencies have had a marked effect on the operations of the Joint Finance and Bond Bill committees. Those committees have seen little change of leadership in two decades. Senator Nancy W. Cook, a Democrat from Kenton in Kent County, has been chair or vice-chair of Joint Finance for most of the time since the early 1980s. She shares that leadership with Representative Joseph G. DiPinto, a Republican from Wilmington. Another Republican, Roger P. Roy of Hockessin, has had an equally long run as the ranking Representative on the Bond Bill Committee, where his counterparts have been Senator Robert L. Venables, Sr., and Senator Patricia Blevins. These individuals have accumulated incomparable knowledge of the state budget and have mastered the art of negotiating with one another and with their committee colleagues on the intricacies of where the state should spend its money.

The changing nature of Delaware's population and economy has also affected membership in the General Assembly. The largest employment category for those elected to the General Assembly in 2000 was state-financed positions, mostly in schools and colleges. Those employed in various capacities in the private economy came second, but a strong third went to people listed as retired or as full-time legislators. While each of those groups contained fifteen or more individuals, the assembly included only five farmers and four lawyers. About two-thirds of the members held college degrees, including twenty who had earned advanced degrees. Several other legislators had earned college credits or had completed post-high-school training programs.

Women have become more visible as members and leaders in Delaware's General Assembly. In 1971 women constituted 9 percent of the state's lawmakers. Twenty years later, in 2001, women made up 26 percent of the members of the assembly. Ruth Ann Minner, who formerly served in every rank in Legislative Hall from secretary to representative, senator, and lieutenant governor, had risen to be Delaware's chief executive officer.

The presence of more women has influenced the legislature's culture and concerns. Typically, women legislators are no-nonsense folk intent on furthering particular legislative agendas. They are not inclined to remain after hours at receptions and dinners that keep them from their families. Newly elected women often seek out more experienced colleagues of their own sex to be their mentors. Women legislators sometimes meet together across party lines, a phenomenon that makes their male colleagues anxious to know what they may be discussing.

Women demand to be accepted as equals. When Liane Sorenson, a New Castle County Republican, was first elected to the House of Representatives in 1992 she objected to the inclusion of "Mrs." on the sign on her office door because the men did not have "Mr." preceding their names. Male colleagues were bemused and asked her "don't you like your husband?" She assured them that it was her equality as a legislator, not her family life, that was the issue, and the sign was changed.[37]

Nancy Cook, a former legislative staffer who was elected to replace her deceased husband, already knew the players and the plays before she acquired the title "senator." It has been her intense concentration on the details of the budget, her excellent memory, and her determination to maintain control of the budgetary process that has made her a formidable and powerful legislator.

Women legislators often come to the legislature after years of working as volunteers or professionals in educational or social service organizations. Ada Leigh Soles of Newark was known for her support of public libraries. Liane Sorenson first came to Dover as president of an umbrella group called the Agenda for Women to testify for measures such as family medical leave and improved foster care. Once elected to the legislature, she teamed up with Democratic Senator Patricia Blevins to sponsor a law to require privacy in medical testing.[38] Senator Blevins, who succeeded Herman Holloway, Sr., as chairperson of the Senate Committee on Health and Social Services, led an effort to reform Delaware's domestic violence laws.[39] Myrna Bair, a Ph.D. chemist and pro-business Republican from northern New Castle County, learned that some children were being mishandled in the state's children's services agencies because the agencies did not communicate with one another. In 1983, she pushed through legislation to create the cabinet-level Department of Children, Youth, and Their Families to unite the state agencies that deal with children.[40]

Another suburban wife and mother legislator, Republican Jane Maroney, became a nationally known advocate for issues relating to children and health. In 1983, as a freshman legislator in the minority party, the leadership ignored her. She turned to the National Council of State Legislatures to find issues, discovered that Delaware's child-support enforcement was shockingly inadequate, and, when the Republicans returned to the majority, became chair of the House Committee on Health and Social Services, where she turned that once moribund committee into a positive force for change. "You had to earn respect. Once you have trust, all sorts of doors open to you," she says.[41] Among her many successes were laws to address Delaware's high rates of infant mortality and cancer.

Senator Margaret Rose Henry of Wilmington is the first black woman to be elected to the Senate. She sponsored the Neighborhood Assistance Act to encourage investment in low-income areas and has been the leading voice for legislation against hate crimes and for the rehabilitation of youthful offenders.[42] As the Senate's only black member, Senator Henry occupies a unique position. Black Delawareans from all parts of the state turn to her for help. The only other African Americans currently serving in the General Assembly are Representatives Dennis P. Williams and Hazel Plant, both also of Wilmington.

Senator Henry is the only member currently serving in the legislature who has changed her party affiliation while in office. She was elected in 1994 with the support of the Republican Party to replace Herman Holloway, Sr., when the legendary senator died in office. After her election she became increasingly uncomfortable with the National Republican Party's move to the political Right. She bolted to the Democrats just when the Republicans were on the verge of accomplishing their long-awaited goal of capturing control of the Senate.

The most powerful woman in Delaware's political history is Governor Ruth Ann Minner. The governor first entered state government as an attache and clerk in the House of Representatives and then as receptionist in the office of Governor Sherman Tribbitt. She attributes her decision to run for a seat in the House of Representatives in 1974 to her experience with a law that adversely affected women. Suddenly widowed at age thirty-two, she needed a car in order to work to support herself and her children. She applied to her bank for an auto loan, only to be told that without the signature of a male it could not be granted. Several years later when she became a member of the assembly, she convinced banks to eliminate such sexist policies.

Unlike suburban citizen-legislator women, Ruth Ann Minner represented the rural, coastal area north of Milford. Her constituents were truckers, farmers, and fishermen. She sponsored legislation to assist farmers and bay community residents and helped to bring land and water conservation issues to the fore in the General Assembly. As a senator she was the prime sponsor of the Delaware Land and Water Conservation Act.

During her years in the House of Representatives from 1975-1982 Ruth Ann Minner chaired the long dormant Rules Committee and made a lasting contribution to the evolution of the General Assembly. It was a period when the House was poised between the two parties. In that precarious situation there was bipartisan support for her committee's efforts to restructure power and procedures to make the rules operate more fairly for all members regardless of party.[43]

Among the most important changes to the House Rules was the elimination of the practice of tabling roll calls. The old procedure was a crafty, deceptive tactic used to postpone a vote until a moment when, after hurried consultations and deal-making, one's supporters happened to outnumber opponents on the chamber floor. Thanks to Representative Minner's efforts, the House of Representatives disallowed the practice of tabling roll calls and did away with other unfair, manipulative vestiges from the past. In the Senate, however, where Harris Mc Dowell championed similar reforms, there was less support for change. The small, club-like Senate maintained its traditional culture.[44]

The spirit of reform has reduced, but hardly eliminated, opportunities to mislead one's colleagues. Even with the inclusion of a synopsis at the beginning of each bill, members must read the fine print to know the full effect of the legislation they are called upon to enact. Changing the rules cannot eliminate instances of personal greed, excessive chumminess with private interests, and similar conflicts of interest, but the new rules have made it more difficult to hide such actions from view.

In the 1980s four members of the General Assembly had to resign their offices because of malfeasance. In 1981 following an FBI wiretap, Senator William M. Murphy, Jr., of Dover went to federal prison for accepting money to assist a mobile-home dealer to secure legislation favorable to that industry. Two years later, Representative Richard J. Myers was caught stealing money from his civic association. Then Representative Herman Holloway, Jr., son of the venerable African American senator, was found guilty of tax evasion. Lastly, John H. Arnold, the Republican whip in the Senate, resigned his seat when it was discovered that he had voted to move his district line to accord with the location of his new home without disclosing his personal interest in the measure.[45]

The House of Representatives and the Senate each has its own characteristic procedures and group interactions. As the larger body, the House of Representatives has created a more formal structure, while the smaller Senate has clung to its traditional ways. A combination of factors, which include not only the different sizes of the two bodies but also the personalities of the leaders in each chamber, accounts for their divergent development.

The forty-one members of the House all stand for election every two years, so re-election can never be far from representatives' minds. Each continually needs to earn and re-earn the support of a majority among her or his constituents. Considerations of that sort help to explain why the House has embraced reformed rules designed to expedite business and to give each member a fair chance to have his or her bills considered.

The House depends on its committees to sort through proposed legislation. There are twenty-three standing committees in the House, each with a membership of from six to fourteen members. Most members serve on a half dozen, or more, committees. Because more bills are filed in the House, its committee structure could easily become overburdened. To solve the problem of how to find time for the representatives to attend to all of their committee assignments, the House has clustered its committees by similarity of function. Each member is appointed to serve on one cluster of committees, and meetings within the cluster are arranged so as not to overlap. In that way, representatives can find time in their crowded schedules to meet regularly during sessions to accomplish their committee work.

Among the most important rules in the House is a requirement that every bill that is introduced by a member of either the majority or minority party be sent to the appropriate committee. The majority caucus, meeting behind closed doors, can decide to oppose a bill, but the majority cannot stop a bill from being presented before a committee. The committee has but twelve working days in which to vote to bring the bill before the full House or to dismiss it. The majority party enjoys a majority of seats on each committee, so if the majority has decided in caucus to oppose a bill and if its committee members stand together, they can prevent a bill from coming out of committee. The committee chairperson cannot duck an issue by refusing to allow his or her fellow committee members their vote, as can happen in the Senate. Because House committees must meet regularly they often hold public hearings on proposed legislation, where interested parties can present evidence and opinions before the committee. House hearings take place in one or another of the large meeting rooms in Legislative Hall.

Just as in colonial days, the Speaker appoints committees and conducts meetings on the House floor. He (there has yet to be a she) determines the order in which members will be called upon to speak. That power allows him to control action on the floor. The Speaker works in harmony with the Majority Leader, who sits immediately in front of the Speaker's platform. Together, they ensure that issues are brought up at a time and in a fashion favorable to the majority's legislative agenda. It is the Majority Leader's responsibility to determine which bills on the House agenda are brought forward for debate by the House as a whole and to conduct meetings of the party caucus. Senators note that under House rules the Speaker can refuse to permit a bill to be introduced regardless of the determination of the sponsoring committee, but no Speaker in recent memory has made use of that prerogative.

The present Speaker is Representative Terry Spence, whose district is located in central New Castle County. Representative Spence has been Speaker for sixteen years, making him the longest serving Speaker in the history of Delaware's House of Representatives. He is regarded by all as an unusually affable man dedicated to maintaining harmony rather than to exercising potentially contentious power. Spence believes that it is the Speaker's job to allow "every elected official to be part of what's happening in Dover."[46] Thus, in the House there are no structural barriers to prevent members of either party from moving their bills forward, at least until the appropriate committee takes its vote.

Since the mid 1990s, Representative Wayne A. Smith, an investment banker with strong interests in American history and political science, has been the House Majority Leader. Spence and Smith make a good team. Whereas Spence is laid back and hates to say "no" to requests, the more intensely intellectual Smith gives primacy to accomplishing the legislative goals espoused by his party. Beyond their differences in temperament, Spence and Smith share compatible political views and are committed to providing an atmosphere of fair play.

The Senate, with only twenty-one members, operates under its own procedures. The Senate's committee system is less developed than that of the House. There are twenty-five standing committees in the Senate, more than one per member, but most seldom meet. The majority caucus decides the fate of many bills. Hearings often take place within the less public confines of the president pro tempore's office. Aside from the all-important committees that deal with finances, Senate committees operate as much or as little as their chairpersons decide.

Senate committee chairs have the power to prevent their committees from voting on a bill. In 2001, Senator Robert L. Venables, Sr., a Democrat from Laurel, did just that to squash a controversial bill to extend equal rights to gays. Senator Venables's action may have prevented the adoption of the bill, but it also relieved his fellow senators of the necessity to cast their votes on a divisive "hot button" issue.

To refute the arguments of those who decry such maneuvers as dictatorial, Senate leaders proudly point out that their body is so small that it operates as a committee of the whole. As in the House, non-members who have special knowledge or concern about a particular piece of legislation are permitted to address the Senate. Moreover, unlike the House Speaker, the President Pro Tempore cannot prevent a bill from coming to the floor. But, a determined President Pro Tempore can kill a bill by sending it to a hostile committee, knowing that the bill will never be reported to the floor.

Two men dominated the Senate leadership as president pro tempore for nearly three decades from 1977 until 2002. The first was Richard S. Cordrey, the Millsboro Democrat and sponsor of the "rainy day fund." Cordrey, who embodied the conservative Democratic traditions of eastern Sussex County, relied on his own courteous personality to create and maintain a workable majority. His was a "quiet leadership that you almost took for granted."[47] He worked with the Republicans, especially on issues affecting the state economy; but under his leadership the Senate's inherited rules that gave him great power remained intact.

Senator Cordrey's successor as president pro tempore was Thomas B. Sharp, a building construction foreman who represented a working-class, pro-labor district located in New Castle County between Wilmington and Newark. Senator Sharp managed the Senate as he had managed his construction sites, with a keen ability to bring many disparate elements into cohesion quickly and with a minimum of fuss. He possessed good political instincts and the fortitude to defend his views and his caucus in contentious situations. Senator Sharp was comfortable with the exercise of power and friends and adversaries alike always knew where he stood on controversial issues. He could be very intimidating, a strong friend or an unforgiving enemy. He dominated the Senate, and others crossed him at their peril.

President Pro Tempore Sharp hated to waste time and hated to get home late. He discontinued the practice of extending the legislative day into the evening hours. In the past the Senate had often broken for dinner, especially during the final weeks in June. Some senators drank too much and either slept or rambled on to no effect when the session resumed in the evening.

Not everyone shared Sharp's urge for early adjournments. Nancy Cook had a penchant for keeping the Joint Finance Committee in session until the wee hours of the morning. Some thought she used her night-owl powers to outlast others and get her way. Sharp warned her to change her ways. She did not, and he removed her from the chairmanship.[48]

Senator Sharp used his power to achieve another change: he insisted that the Joint Finance and Bond Bill committees give their colleagues the final form of their proposed portions of the state budget at least two days before the end of session. His demand was met. For the first time in more than a century, members had time see the budget before the frantic final night on June 30.

Senator Sharp did not, however, alter the Senate's long-standing custom that restricts members of the minority party to sponsoring only one bill per session. In theory any senator can present a bill for consideration on the floor of the Senate. In practice, under Senator Sharp the one-bill custom held sway. Senate Republicans with important legislation had to learn the skill of "coalition-building" with Democratic colleagues amenable to presenting their bills.[49] As president pro tempore, Senator Sharp reduced the size of Senate committees. His purpose was to allow each member to concentrate on only a few committee assignments. The effect was to reduce the number of minority party members on each committee from two to one.

Despite partisan chafing, the Senate remained a collegial place. In Sharp's time, as in Cordrey's before, at the end of each day's session all members as well as lobbyists and other guests were invited to an open house in the president pro tempore's office to intermingle and have a drink, alcoholic or otherwise.

Senator Sharp retired from the Senate in 2002. His successor as president pro tempore is Thurman Adams, Jr., the owner of an agribusiness company in Bridgeville. The man who spent his first day in the Senate back in 1973 vainly seeking to figure out what was happening during the Isaacs' take-over, is now a knowledgeable, respected old-hand. Although Senator Adams is comfortable with the Senate and its rather antique ways, he exercises his powers more gently than did his predecessor. Senator Nancy Cook is back as chair of Joint Finance; and members of both parties anticipate that other relaxations of the previous president pro tempore's policies may follow.

In all of his many actions as a senator, Thurman Adams, Jr., counts as his most important legislation the bill that created Emergency 911 in Delaware. E 911 allows police and ambulance services to track the location of calls from distressed people. The law is an example of the assembly's intention to inaugurate life-saving changes in Delaware.

Since they took control of the Senate in 1973, the Democrats' majority caucus has seldom broken ranks with their leadership. They did so, however, on one memorable occasion in 1989. The impetus was a last-minute addition to the budget bill to provide a significant increase in legislators' pensions. Some senators of both parties thought it outrageous. If adopted the measure would have paid long-term legislators more to retire than to remain in office. The provision had been inserted into the budget bill's epilogue, the portion of the bill that provides the details on how money will be spent. Trusting to their leaders and members of the Joint Finance Committee, few members bothered to read the epilogue, except, perhaps, to check on provisions in which they had a special interest. On that occasion, however, Senator Robert T. Connor, the minority whip and an administrator in the Colonial School District, discovered the pension addition. Having alerted his fellow Republicans, he wrote a less generous substitute bill and prepared to do battle.

Ordinarily, the Democrats would have had no trouble passing the budget bill over united Republican opposition. But this was no ordinary bill. Some Democrats were unwilling to associate themselves with a maneuver that appeared both selfish and secretive. Three Democrats simply failed to show up for the vote, thus ensuring a tie. The chastened Democrat leaders had no choice but to accept Senator Connor's substitute language into the budget bill. It was a rare, and much relished, victory for the minority Republicans.[50]

Legislators have been careful to limit their own raises to amounts consistent with the salary increases awarded to other elected officers. In the years since Robert F. Gilligan, currently the longest serving member of the assembly, was first elected to the House in 1973, legislative salaries have risen from $6,000 to $35,000. Leaders also receive additional income to compensate for their greater responsibilities, and all members receive an additional $6,600 for expenses.[51]

Another significant change can be seen in the professionalizing of the legislative staff. In 1969 the assembly took its first step in that direction when it created the Office of Controller General to provide professional quality information about the state's budget to the Joint Finance and Bond Bill committees. Armed with those data, the legislative committees were no longer beholden to the executive branch for accurate estimates of future income and outgo. Similarly, the legislature created the Legislative Council with professional staff to assist the lawmakers in research and preparation of bills. Employees of those offices have sometimes been chosen with political considerations in mind, but their offices are expected to function in a nonpartisan manner.

In 1982 another staffing milestone came with the introduction of the Legislative Fellows Program. The Fellows are specially trained students from the University of Delaware who provide assistance to the assembly. The University and the General Assembly share the program's expenses. It took a few years to build a productive relationship between the students and the legislators. The Fellows were first assigned to assist in the House of Representatives, where they worked with the party caucuses under the supervision of seasoned legislative staff. Fellows later became engaged with the Senate, as well. Incredibly, these college students serve as the only staff for House committees and have become indispensable for the functioning of Delaware's modern General Assembly.

While larger states assign professional staff to each legislator, Delaware has found this less expensive, university-based alternative to be effective in educating students and legislators alike. The program's founder and chief administrator, Jerome Lewis of the University of Delaware, says, "ours is a unique Delaware experience."[52] Both President Pro Tempore Thurman Adams, Jr., and Speaker Terry Spence second Lewis's enthusiasm. The Speaker calls the Fellows the "golden keys" that make the assembly function.[53]

Each of the four legislative caucuses also maintains its own permanent professional staff. Those workers are indispensable for keeping the General Assembly moving. They track legislation, keep on top of mounds of paper work, answer phones, and make appointments. They are especially important in assisting members to resolve constituents' myriad problems.

In addition to its improved staff support, the legislators of the 1970s and 1980s took more responsibility for doing their own research than had their predecessors. Members looked to national associations such as the National Council of State Governments (NCSG) and the National Conference of State Legislatures (NCSL) to provide assistance. Those organizations hold national and regional meetings where legislators can gain insights into issues and learn how other states are handling common problems. The participants discuss legislative initiatives from around the nation, including the pitfalls that have beset some states and the successes that others brag about.

National legislative organizations retain permanent staff to provide research assistance to individual legislators and to legislative committees. That help is especially important to a state like Delaware, where members of the permanent legislative staff are capable but few. In numerous instances Delaware's legislators have drawn upon those resources to shape their bills and inform their reports. This pattern is particularly true in regard to particularly complex matters of policy that affect every state, such as education, environmental control, and social services. For example, Governor Ruth Ann Minner credits her research at NCSG for the success of the environmental proposals she championed as a legislator.[54]

Alan V. Sokolow, the Director of the Eastern Office of the Council of State Governments, interacts with many legislatures in states both large and small. He is impressed by Delaware's effective use of his organization's services. Where in larger states legislators typically depend on in-house staff to research and draft bills, Delaware's legislators are more likely to make their own inquiries at the NCSG. As a result, the First state's lawmakers learn their subject first hand and can discuss it effectively. A well-informed legislator can often preempt challenges from less-well-prepared colleagues. Sokolow also notes that Delaware's legislators are encouraged to attend regional and national legislative conferences that the media in some states unfairly dismiss as "junkets." [55]

The life of a legislator has become more complex and demanding, but its essence remains simple. As one former member of the General Assembly put it, "When a legislator wakes up and looks in the mirror, the first thing that person says is 'what can I do today to keep my seat?'" [56] Pleasing one's constituents comes ahead of pleasing one's party or leadership.

Just as "practice, practice, practice" is the road to Carnegie Hall, most legislators begin their careers in public service or politics before they run for a seat in the General Assembly. For some the motivation to run may come from a commitment to social-reform causes. For others, the urge to run may be motivated by employment in a state-supported job, such as teaching or the state police. Another likely route to Legislative Hall lies through involvement in civic associations, service clubs, Little League, Boy Scouts or similar organizations that give the potential candidate a base of support as a well-known community leader. Yet others decide to run because they find politics intriguing and come to the attention of party leaders for their work on behalf of other party candidates. A few are born into or marry into politically active families.

The easiest way to get elected to the legislature is to be asked to run by your party in a district where the incumbent is retiring and the fledgling candidate's party holds a majority. Lacking that full set of advantages, it behooves the candidate to prepare carefully, run hard, and emphasize his or her zeal for a popular issue where the opponent can be made to appear to be weak. In the 1970s in suburban New Castle County a strong anti-busing stand was particularly effective. Hostility to the development of the last unused land in an area has also been a winner in that part of the state. Once elected, however, the issues may change. It will then be service to constituents, support for the current set of popular measures, and maintaining a profile of personal responsibility and availability that will keep voters pulling the incumbent's lever.

It costs money to reach the voters. Representative Robert F. Gilligan recalls that he spent $3,000 to get elected to his first term in 1972. By the year 2000 his campaign cost nearly $40,000.[57] The change is due to several factors. Delaware's population has escalated, but seats in the General Assembly have not, which means that each legislative district contains more people. In addition, voters have come to expect to receive an eye-catching, multi-colored brochure, complete with smiling family photo that describes the candidate's qualifications and goals. Voters also notice the flimsy but professionally printed cardboard signs that appear at every crossroad in the weeks before the election.

It costs a lot of money to create and distribute the brochures and signs. In the past candidates, their families, friends, and volunteer party workers put the brochures in mailboxes throughout the district by hand in what is known as a "lit drop." Today most brochures are printed and mailed from out of state. The rising cost of campaigning has aroused the public's fear that candidates can be "bought and paid for" by private interests. To combat that perception, the legislature adopted a disclosure law that created the Public Integrity Commission to monitor the sources of candidates' campaign contributions. But with or without disclosure, the idea that one can acquire an adequate campaign chest by including a discrete announcement of one's candidacy in Christmas cards, as Jane Maroney did successfully in 1978, now seems quaint. Today's candidates rely on contributions from lobbyists, like-minded supporters, and co-workers to raise the sums needed for a chance at victory.

For incumbents and newcomers alike, there is no substitute for shoe leather in campaigning for a seat in the General Assembly. Roger Martin, a high-school German teacher who served in the Senate from 1973 through 1993, described the process vividly in his autobiographical *Memoirs of the Senate.* In the summer before the election he began the grueling task of going door to door to the 8,000 to 10,000 households in his suburban Newark district. He recalls that "walking the streets in the July heat was almost unbearable."[58] The real push to reach voters begins after Labor Day. From then until the election, candidates knock on as many doors as possible every weekday in the late afternoon when someone is likely to be at home, and all day on weekends.

The door-to-door method is more difficult in the rural districts of southern Delaware, where candidates can walk the towns but must drive from farm to farm. Attending "meet the candidates" evenings, visits to community events, and appearances at church suppers, union halls, and other similar organizational events can play a significant role in all parts of the state, but particularly so in rural communities. In New Castle County candidates have found that there is no substitute for knocking on doors.

A newcomer may have to demonstrate special talents to win over skeptics. As a professor of nursing, Democrat Bethany Hall-Long had to prove to her would-be constituents in the rural Middletown area that she knew about issues beyond health care. She relied on her experiences growing up in a farming community in southern Delaware to demonstrate her understanding of farmers' problems and to show that she could excel in trapshooting.[59]

Bethany Hall-Long won a seat in the House of Representatives on her second try in 2002. As one of six new members she attended orientation day in December. She was pleasantly surprised to receive warm welcomes from Speaker Spence and Majority Leader Smith, as well as from Robert F. Gilligan, the minority leader. A lawyer from the Legislative Council and the chief clerk of the House conducted the orientation. The new members received copies of the rules, got identification cards and office keys, and learned about House procedures and policies.[60]

One of the presenters was veteran Representative Roger Roy, who can recall a very different beginning to his legislative career in 1977. There was no orientation program in those days. Representative Roy had never visited Dover before the first day of the session and had to ask directions to Legislative Hall.[61] His was not a unique experience in those days.

For a freshman, Legislative Hall was not so welcoming a place in the 1970s. The additions put onto both ends of the building had provided office space for every legislator, but only those in leadership positions had private offices. Regular members shared small offices with two or three other legislators. What members gained in familiarity with their office mates they lost in lack of privacy to conduct business.

By the late 1980s there were plans to construct two large wings onto the east facade of the building. The Architects Studio, Inc., of Wilmington carried out the work. Completed early in 1994, those matching additions provided handsome meeting rooms and made it possible for the first time in the history of the Delaware General Assembly for every member to have her or his own private office.

Delaware has a citizen legislature that reflects the variety among its people. Learning to work with people from diverse backgrounds and with different interests is, therefore, essential to becoming a successful legislator. In the General Assembly there are old and young, black and white, people with high-school diplomas as well as those with Ph.D.s, a few rich, and many members who would call themselves "middle class." There are legislators with labor union backgrounds, teachers, members accustomed to working in big companies or government bureaucracies, self-employed people, and homemakers. Some have lived in the same town all their lives; others came to Delaware as adults. It would be hard to find another organization in the state that represents such diversity of backgrounds and life experiences. The General Assembly is, after all, intended to be representative of all citizens of the First State.

It takes a lot of stamina to be a legislator. As Representative Stephanie Ulbrich aptly puts it, "the true mark of a legislator is how many things you can juggle at the same time."[62] Sessions meet annually from January to June. For members of the House, the two-year election cycle that fills every spare moment in the summer and fall recurs with disconcerting frequency. From January through June, the only respite for those who are not members of the Joint Finance Committee or the Bond Bill Committee comes in February, when the assembly breaks for budget hearings. Budget makers forego any respite.

The assembly meets in the afternoons on Tuesday, Wednesday, and Thursday. On a typical meeting day a member may eat an early breakfast at a restaurant with a constituent, go to work at his or her regular job for the rest of the morning, then grab a sandwich and beverage to consume in the car while attempting to arrive in Legislative Hall in time for the gavel to fall at 2:00 p.m. It is no wonder that lawyers are reluctant to run for election because they will lose so many billable hours, or that corporations, such as DuPont, have so tightened their policies on worker-legislators that few now seek office. The Du Ponters now serving in the assembly are retirees. It's no easier for blue-collar workers. Thomas B. Sharp recalls the difficulty of changing from mud-drenched boots and workman's attire into a business suit while making the dash to be in his Senate seat.[63]

When the session adjourns sometime in the late afternoon or early evening, the day is far from over. There may be a caucus meeting and then there will be receptions to attend. Among Dover's many hotels and restaurants there are only three large reception rooms. Members of the General Assembly know them all well. Groups rent those facilities to entertain lawmakers. Most try to attend, if only for a short time. The sponsoring organizations' purpose is to make contact with legislators and to explain their legislative concerns.

Members of the General Assembly may have purposes of their own for attending receptions. Such events provide opportunities to talk to members from the other chamber and from across the aisle in one's own. Equally important may be the chance to consume some shrimp cocktail, cheese and crackers, and a beverage to stand in place of dinner as the legislator dashes back to his or her district to attend one or more civic association meetings scheduled for that evening. The next morning the whole process starts again.

By January 1993, when Thomas R. Carper was inaugurated governor, the Delaware General Assembly had assumed its modern form. As is usual when the legislature first interacts with a new governor, there was a period of mutual testing of power. In 1993 the perennial issue of legislative pensions provided a testing ground. A law adopted in 1984 had created the Delaware Compensation Commission to set officials' salaries and benefits. The commission's decisions were to be final, subject only to the General Assembly's intervention. In 1993 the commission proposed a generous hike in officials' pensions that would include members of the General Assembly.

Just as in 1989, the issue of their own pensions divided members of the General Assembly. The Senate's Democratic leadership tried to avoid a vote and thus allow the increase to stand, but the new governor felt the heat of public disapproval. After initially going along with his fellow Democrats, he then changed his mind and called the assembly into special session to confront the issue during the budget recess. His fellow Democrats in Legislative Hall were not happy, and a few never forgave him.[64]

Executive-legislative relations were never comfortable in the Carper administration. Democrats and Republicans alike criticized the governor and his associates' inability to sense the rhythms of legislative life. But by the end of the 1993 session, the growing consensus was that the legislature could work with Governor Carper. Senator Robert I. Marshall, a Wilmington Democrat, told a *News Journal* reporter, "Carper will listen to reasonable suggestions. He's willing to dig in, but he's enough of a politician to compromise."[65]

The renewal of a proposal to put slot machines into Delaware's ailing racetracks illustrated the distance between the two branches. Governor Castle had vetoed a slots bill in 1989. Carper was inclined to do the same. In 1994, however, he chose to allow the General Assembly to take the lead as sponsors of the gambling bill, but he refused either to sign it or veto it. The bill's supporters claimed that slots would revive the tracks. More significantly, they argued that taxing the revenue from the gambling machines would preclude the need to raise money by increasing other taxes. In fact, the enhancement to the state's revenue stream set the stage for decreases in the state income tax during the prosperous 1990s to a maximum of 5.9 percent.

As farmland throughout the state continued to give way to the construction of housing developments, office complexes, strip malls, and big box stores, land conservation took on a new urgency in the 1990s. Where many members of the assembly had once accepted the dictates of free-market forces on land use and had believed that there was no downside to the jobs and income that development brings, by the 1990s many acknowledged the need for state intervention.

Senate President Pro Tempore Thomas B. Sharp was a significant convert to the cause. He challenged the expansion plans of the MBNA Bank. He also used his clout in Legislative Hall to secure a valuable piece of undeveloped suburban property in his district known as the Hugh M. Morris Tract. The tract belonged to the University of Delaware, which was planning to sell it to developers. Using his power on the Bond Bill Committee to good effect, he convinced the University to sell the land to the state at a reduced rate. The tract is now a state park.[66]

Legislative Hall is a beehive of activity, especially at the end of session, as shown here on June 30, 1998. Photograph by Gary Emeigh. (Courtesy of the News Journal Company)

Senator Ruth Ann Minner's Delaware Land and Water Conservation Act created the Delaware Open Space Council. The council was to preserve farmland and to assist the development of greenways through the state. Those programs received a boost in 1995 when the legislature voted to make them the major recipients of the state's multi-million dollar settlement from a corporate securities lawsuit with New York State. In keeping with its policy to maintain fiscal prudence, the state used none of the money for operating expenses or as the down payment for long-term debts. Instead, the legislature created an instrument called the Twenty-first Century Fund to channel the windfall into projects designed to enhance Delaware's infrastructure and to preserve its citizens' quality of life.[67] Farmland preservation and greenways fit that profile.

At the beginning of the new millennium the biggest "quality of life" issue in Delaware was the pollution of land, air, and water. While everyone can agree that pollution is a bad thing, it is not so easy to decide what to do about it. The legislature and governor are called upon to make hard choices. The refinery at Delaware City, once owned by Getty but now owned by a consortium of oil companies under the name Motiva, presents the state with a major environmental conundrum. The facility is designed to refine "dirty" oil, which has a high sulfur content. Only with costly, sustained effort can the refinery and the factories nearby that use its products be made free of pollution. In July 2001 a worker died at the facility due to improper maintenance, putting the issue of Motiva's impact on the environment back into the headlines. Legislators face the dilemma of where to draw the line between retaining the refinery and its workforce and providing enough legal enforcement to protect all Delawareans from polluted air, water, and land.

Delaware has an unusually high cancer rate. In 2002 the assembly took aim at the state's number-one health problem and adopted a law that makes restaurants and bars in the First State smoke free. The owners of slots casinos and bar rooms were furious that their establishments had been included in the ban. In 2003 they and their smoking patrons besieged Legislative Hall with petitions to exempt bars and casinos from the law.

The smoking ban was one of those "hot button" issues that politicians love to duck. The contest pitted two concepts of freedom: the freedom to smoke and the freedom from smoke. Governor Minner stood firm behind the ban. Partly from similar resolve and partly to put the onus of maintaining the ban on the governor, the House Republicans voted to maintain the law. In early April it was the Senate's turn to vote. Lobbying on behalf of both sides was intense. Bar owners complained bitterly of their loss of income; and casino promoters warned that patrons from out of state might take their business elsewhere. On the opposite side were health officials, cancer victims, and, most persuasively, barroom workers who feared for their own health if the smoking ban were lifted. By a vote of fourteen to seven in the Senate the advocates of clean air prevailed. Nearly all of those who voted to relax the ban were from southern Delaware.

In the 1990s and beyond, the overriding concern for Delaware's lawmakers remains public education. As Representative Joseph G. DiPinto has succinctly stated, rectifying the problems of education "would try Job."[68] The legislature and school officials view one another warily. The school bureaucracy wants the legislature to provide the money they request but seeks to avoid the legislature's interference in how the schools are run. Speaker Terry Spence learned as much in the early 1990s when he sponsored a bill that would require school administrators to report serious discipline problems to the police. Spence's bill passed, but the issue drew a hostile response from education bureaucrats who feared bad publicity.[69]

Most education-related issues of recent years can be divided into two interrelated components that can be loosely labeled under the headings of "busing" and "accountability." All three branches of the state government, as well as the federal government and the business community, have used their various powers to intervene into Delaware's educational system. In 1991 the state superintendent of schools launched a multi-year project called "New Directions" that was intended to improve how instruction was delivered and measured in the state's public schools.

While the executive branch was pursuing "New Directions," the General Assembly became involved once more in the issue of busing. In the years that followed implementation of the federal court's inter-district decree in 1978 the enrollment of white students in the busing area had fallen by half. New private schools sprang up throughout Wilmington's suburbs, attracting several thousand students, mostly whites. By 1993 Delaware led the nation in the percentage of its students enrolled in private schools.[70]

Both whites and blacks were discontented with busing. Some whites thought that too many black students came to school with low educational expectations and engaged in disruptive behavior. Some blacks thought that the teachers and school officials subjected them to derogatory stereotyping. A group of black Delawareans formed the Coalition to Save Our Children to protest what they perceived as white teachers' racially inspired disciplinary actions and the failure of the integrated schools to address the educational needs of black students. Many parents of both races criticized long bus rides as a waste of time and complained that it was difficult to participate in their child's school if it was far away.

In 1993 the Delaware State Board of Education asked the Federal District Court for Delaware to recognize the successful integration of New Castle County's schools and to end the court's control over school-district lines and pupil assignments. The Coalition to Save Our Children also weighed into the action. The coalition demanded that a reversal of the busing order must be accompanied by a set of specific actions designed to support minority students and their parents against what the group perceived as a hostile educational system.

In an effort to demonstrate to the court that Delaware had complied with the court's requirements, the state board worked with the coalition to craft a consent decree. Under the court's mandate, the consent order was to become the basis for the restoration of state and local control over the four Wilmington area school districts. The Coalition to Save Our Children demanded that the consent order require the General Assembly to fund additional counselors, trouble-shooters, and affirmative-action initiatives. In November 1993 the parties agreed to a Consent Order that met those requirements.[71]

The Consent Order was contentious. Much as members of the legislature yearned to end busing, the majority was loath to accept the Consent Order's terms. Senator John C. Still, a former teacher, spoke for many of his colleagues when he told the court that the order implicitly undermined the disciplinary actions necessary to maintain order in the schools.[72] On the other side, the Consent Order received the editorial blessing of the Wilmington *News Journal* and the support of Governor Carper. But the legislature turned it down. *News Journal* editor Norman Lockman placed the blame on "mischief-making politicians." That was a broad category, for it included Joseph R. Petrilli, the House majority leader, William A. Oberle, chairman of the House Desegregation Committee, Wayne Smith, a future majority leader, Thomas Sharp, the Senate president pro tempore, and several other prominent New Castle County legislators.[73]

The end to this fruitless battle came in an unexpected way. A new federal judge was assigned to oversee the case. Judge Sue L. Robinson rejected the Consent Order formula and declared that Delaware had fulfilled the federal court's requirements to desegregate. She thus opened the path for the Delaware General Assembly, the State Board of Education, and local school boards to resume control of the schools in the four districts contiguous to Wilmington.

The legislature lost no time in introducing new educational initiatives. In 1995 Representative Stephanie A. Ulbrich and Senator David P. Sokola sponsored legislation to introduce publicly funded, privately managed charter schools into Delaware. A separate bill provided parents with the option of school choice, which meant that parents could send their children to any public school. The business community strongly endorsed the charter movement because charter schools were to emphasize basic subjects. As finally passed by the legislature, however, the stated purpose of charter schools to "improve student learning" through "innovative or proven schools environments and methods," embraced both the tried-and-true as well as the experimental.[74]

The Choice program was less innovative, but equally unheard of during the years of the federal court's control. Under Choice, parents could enroll their children in public schools other than the ones to which they were assigned so long as the parents provided the transportation to a bus stop in the receiving district. Sponsors hoped that Choice would introduce a healthy breath of competition into an educational system grown complacent.

Passage of the two bills required negotiation between the two chambers. There was opposition to the Choice bill from Kent and Sussex County senators who worried that the program might disrupt the accepted town-rural relationships that the school districts reinforced. The House Republicans, whose strength was in New Castle County, responded by holding the Charter bill hostage. It was a maneuver that the Wilmington *News Journal* described as a "game of chicken."[75] Some observers, including the state PTA president, counseled a go-slow approach to study the proposals, but Governor Carper and the House Republicans were

President William J. Clinton posed with Governor Thomas R. Carper and Assembly leaders in Legislative Hall on May 8, 1998. Front row from left: House Speaker Terry R. Spence, President Clinton, Senate President Pro Tempore Thomas B. Sharp, Governor Carper. Back row from left: Robert J. Voshell, Robert F. Gilligan, Harris B. McDowell III, Myrna L. Bair, Charles W. Welch, Wayne A. Smith. (Courtesy of Jo Ann M. Hedrick, Chief Clerk of the House of Representatives)

intent upon passing both bills, and they zoomed through the assembly on the 1995 session's final day.[76]

Delaware's public-school innovations attracted national attention at the highest level and even brought a sitting president of the United States of America to Legislative Hall on May 8, 1998. It was the first time that a President of the United States had addressed a joint session of the Delaware General Assembly. The President was William Jefferson Clinton, and his subject was education.

President Clinton spoke in the Senate Chamber to an audience that included most members of the General Assembly, Governor Carper and his cabinet, and the state judiciary. The President showered compliments on the First State. In a modernized extension of Thomas Jefferson's famous comparison of Delaware to a diamond, Clinton called the state a "silicon chip" that packed much power into a small size. Small is good, he said. "I love your Capitol Building. I like the feel of your Legislature. I like the size of your Legislature." As in his native Arkansas, he felt that in Delaware "people learn to treat each other as people. They learn to listen to people on opposite sides of the aisle."[77]

The President chose Delaware's Legislative Hall to be his backdrop for a campaign to increase federal aid to education. He praised the state's willingness to embrace innovative educational policies; and he advocated federal aid to hire teachers, refurbish buildings, and establish national learning standards. Most legislators liked what they heard, but not all. Representative Wayne Smith, a conservative Republican, did not like the idea of federal intervention. He was "not convinced that his [Clinton's] educational plan is in the best interests of Delaware's public school children." Nor was the editorial writer at the *News Journal* persuaded that Delaware had as yet earned the President Clinton's glowing praise. "If Delaware is any example," the reporter wrote, "the solutions will be neither quick nor easy."[78]

In 1998 the legislature was again embroiled in the highly controversial issue of educational accountability. Whose job was it to produce educated graduates—teachers, administrators, parents, students? The General Assembly was about as democratic a venue as there could be to discuss those difficult issues, but that fact only served to exacerbate the difficulty in resolving them. The legislature was composed of past and present teachers as well as parents. On this complex subject being the "voice of the people" was impossible because the "people" did not speak with one voice. After much debate, the legislature adopted an accountability statute that put the state ahead of the federal government's "No Child Left Behind" legislation of 2002.

In 2000 House Majority Leader Wayne Smith sponsored a bill to take the state beyond Choice and Charter to re-institute neighborhood schools in New Castle County. The bill permitted students to attend the school nearest their homes. It appeared to meet the District Court's standard and it offered parents and students the end to the busing that they claimed to be seeking. The Neighborhood Schools Act was not as thoroughgoing as its sponsor had intended. Some districts were reluctant to dismantle the intricate educational programs and funding policies that they had developed during the twenty years of court-decreed desegregation. Furthermore, 2000 was an election year and Governor Carper was running for a seat in the United States Senate. Concerned that the governor might veto his bill, Smith permitted the governor to add qualifiers that weakened the bill and has allowed some districts to continue their busing patterns.[79]

Governor Ruth Ann Minner presenting her budget address to a joint session of the General Assembly, January 30, 2003. Photograph by Gary Emeigh. (Courtesy of the News Journal Company)

The problems inherent in finding workable paths forward in public education are illustrative of the perpetual dilemmas of lawmaking in a democratic culture. The legislature represents and reflects the variety of points of view to be found in a democracy. Thoughtful legislators approach new proposals with questions like "what makes sense?" "is it right?" and "is it what my constituents want?" They try to foresee the effects of the law of unintended consequences. Shades of gray dominate over black or white, good or bad, or even Delaware's colonial blue and buff.

The millennial year of 2000 brought forth another United States Census and its corollary, the redistricting of the General Assembly. The greatest increases in Delaware's population were in Sussex County and the greatest relative losses were in the city of Wilmington. In the assembly the shift translated into a southward movement of seats. The redistricting process was particularly politically sensitive in the Senate, where the altered boundaries put several Republican incumbents into unfamiliar districts. In 2002 in the new oddly drawn Sixth District, which encompasses the extreme northwest of northern New Castle County, veteran Senator Liane Sorenson defeated a Democratic challenger, former Representative Richard A. DiLiberto, Jr., on turf that was partly new to both. Theirs was the most expensive legislative election in Delaware history to date. Between them, Sorenson and DiLiberto spent upwards of $100,000. Meanwhile, in the House, where Republicans controlled redistricting, a similar case of gerrymandering occurred at the opposite end of the state. There, Democrat Representative John R. Schroeder's Lewes district was recast into a new configuration that cost him his seat to Republican Joseph W. Booth.

Several disturbing aspects have emerged in the selection of members of the General Assembly. The legislature's redistricting in response to the United States Census of 2000 was rigged by each house to favor the interests of one party or the other, or of particular incumbents. That politically charged process threatens to undermine a sense of fairness in elections that Delaware has struggled mightily to achieve.

From the electorate's perspective the most disturbing aspect of the election of 2002 was not gerrymandering per se but the proliferation of unopposed candidates that are the result of engineering districts to serve the interests of one party or one candidate. In a Senate of twenty-one, nine seats were filled unopposed; in the House of Representatives, eighteen of forty-one candidates faced no opposition. Left unchecked, this trend can strangle democracy.

Another issue is that of representation of minority groups. Historically, every legislator of African American descent has been elected from Wilmington. It will be a major step forward in Delaware when African American candidates are also elected from districts where they do not hold an advantage in numbers. Also underrepresented are Latinos. There is a growing population of Guatemalans in Sussex County and people of Puerto Rican descent in Wilmington, but no one of Latin origin has yet been elected to the General Assembly.

At the conclusion of the first three hundred years of Delaware's independent General Assembly one senses once again that change is on the horizon. The era that began with the late 1970s is at an end. For a quarter of a century, Delaware's government has worked in accord with the reconciliation that Governor Pete du Pont and the Democrat-led legislature forged over spending and saving. That consensus has produced fiscal health and economic growth in the First State. Today, the future of major established revenue streams are under threat. Economic events on a national and international scale have reduced the state's income from the franchise tax on corporations. Nearby states, especially Maryland, may decide to permit slot machines and thus deprive Delaware of another lucrative way into the pockets of out-of-state residents.

General assemblies of the future will be challenged to deal with these financial problems, together with their ongoing efforts to improve public education and to provide a healthy environment. As one era ends and another begins Delawareans will yet again turn to their citizen legislators for vision, resolve, and the careful listening that will be needed if the First State is to have a bright future. In that quest, history can provide no answers, only examples of past successes and failures. It is not enough to erect monuments to the past; we must study its lessons and learn from them. Delaware has developed an ever more inclusive democracy that is embodied in the people who represent their fellow citizens in the General Assembly. That evolution has brought Delaware closer to William Penn's quest for a legislature noted for its members "sobriety, wisdom, and integrity" than we have seen for a long time. But as history tells us, maintaining democracy will require constant vigilance to keep a General Assembly that is truly representative of the people and effective in resolving their problems and improving their lives.

This photograph by Kevin Fleming appeared in the News Journal on January 4, 1980. The accompanying text read: "The walls are freshly painted, desks and chairs are in order, and state custodian Walter Buckworth puts finishing touches on the floor of the Senate Chamber in preparation for Tuesday's opening of the General Assembly session." (Courtesy of the News Journal Company)

NOTES

Chapter 1

1. Jean R. Soderland, ed., *William Penn and the Founding of Pennsylvania, 1680-1684, A Documentary History* (Philadelphia: University of Pennsylvania Press, 1983), 189.
2. *Votes and Proceedings of the House of Representatives of the Province of Pennsylvania*, in *Pennsylvania Archives*, 8th ser., 8 vols. (Harrisburg: Pennsylvania State Library, 1931-1935), Appendix, 1:331-33.
3. Richard S. Dunn and Mary M. Dunn, eds., *The Papers of William Penn*, 5 vols. (Philadelphia: University of Pennsylvania Press, 1987), footnote, 2:313.
4. *Votes and Proceedings*, 1:1-4.
5. Robert Proud, *History of Pennsylvania in North America* (Philadelphia: Poulson, 1797), 206-7.
6. Ibid., 207.
7. *Votes and Proceedings*, 1:17.
8. Dunn and Dunn, *Papers of William Penn*, 2:621-24.
9. Ibid., 2:543.
10. Gary B. Nash, *Quakers and Politics in Pennsylvania, 1681-1726* (Boston: Northeastern University Press, 1968), 122.
11. *Votes and Proceedings*, I:95-109.
12. *Votes and Proceedings*, Appendix, 1:341-50.
13. *Votes and Proceedings*, 1:277.
14. Nash, *Quakers and Politics*, 131.
15. Ibid.
16. Dunn and Dunn, *Papers of William Penn*, 3:295-99.
17. Ibid., 3:328.
18. *Votes and Proceedings*, 1:352-53.
19. Barbara E. Benson, "Courthouses in New Castle County," *Delaware Lawyer*, 20 (2002-3):22.
20. *Votes and Proceedings*, 1:258.
21. *Minutes of the Provincial Council of Pennsylvania*, 10 vol. (n.p.: published by the state, 1851-1852), 2:49-50.
22. Proud, *History of Pennsylvania*, 442.
23. *Votes and Proceedings*, 1:311.
24. Dunn and Dunn, *Papers of William Penn*, 4:104-9
25. Proud, *History of Pennsylvania*, 450.
26. *Votes and Proceedings*, 1:356-84, passim.
27. Lawrence A. Gipson, "An Anomalous American Colony," *Pennsylvania History*, 27 (1960):149.
28. John A. Munroe, *Colonial Delaware: A History* (Millwood, New York: KTO Press, 1978), 129.
29. Ibid., 223.
30. *Laws of the Government of New Castle, Kent and Sussex Upon Delaware* (Philadelphia: B. Franklin and D. Hall, 1752), 120-22.
31. Ibid., 124.
32. Ibid., 125-26.
33. *Minutes of the House of Assembly . . . 1739*, reprinted in *Early Government Records of Delaware* (Wilmington, Delaware: Public Archives Commission, 1929), 37.
34. Ibid., 15.

35. The first printing of the *Laws* bears the date 1741 because England and her colonies had not yet adopted the Gregorian calendar.
36. *Minutes of the House of Assembly . . . 1741*, reprinted in *Early Government Records of Delaware* (Wilmington, Delaware: Public Archives Commission, 1929), 41.
37. *Minutes of the House of Assembly . . . 1740*, reprinted in *Early Government Records of Delaware* (Wilmington, Delaware: Public Archives Commission, 1929), 13.
38. Letter dated October 23, 1762, in *Votes and Proceedings of the House of Representatives . . . 1762,* reprint ed. (Wilmington, Delaware: Public Archives Commission, 1930), 10.

Chapter 2
1. William H. Williams, *Slavery and Freedom in Delaware, 1639-1865*, paperback ed. (Wilmington, Delaware: SR Books, 1999), 16.
2. Claudia L. Bushman, Harold B. Hancock, and Elizabeth Moyne Homsey, eds., *Proceedings of the Assembly of the Lower Counties on Delaware, 1770-1776, of the Constitutional Convention of 1776, and of the House of Assembly of the Delaware State, 1776-1778* (Newark, Delaware: University of Delaware Press, 1986), 562.
3. *Minutes of the House of Assembly . . . 1773*, reprinted in *Early Government Records of Delaware* (Wilmington, Delaware: Public Commission, 1931), 113.
4. *Minutes of the House of Representatives . . . in the Years 1765-1770,* reprinted in *Early Government Records of Delaware* (n.p.: Public Archives Commission of Delaware, 1931), 10.
5. William T. Read, *Life and Correspondence of George Read* (Philadelphia: J. B. Lippincott & Co., 1870), 29-30.
6. *Minutes of the House of Representatives . . .* , 59-61.
7. Ibid., 121.
8. Ibid., 158.
9. Ibid., 166-70.
10. *Proceedings of the Assembly of the Lower Counties . . .* , 145-46.
11. *Letters to and from Caesar Rodney, 1756-1784*, ed. George H. Ryden (Philadelphia: University of Pennsylvania Press, 1933), 79-80.
12. *Proceedings of the Assembly of the Lower Counties . . .* , 212.
13. Gordon S. Wood, *The Creation of the American Republic, 1776-1787* (Chapel Hill: University of North Carolina Press, 1969). See Chap. 4, "The Restructuring of Power," 127-61.
14. J. Thomas Scharf, *History of Delaware, 1609-1888*, 2 vols. (Philadelphia: L. J. Richards, 1888), 1:236.
15. *Proceedings of the Assembly of the Lower Counties . . .* , 213.
16. Ibid., 256.
17. Ibid., 267.
18. Ibid., 328-29.
19. Ibid., 319.
20. Read, *Life and Correspondence*, 285-86.
21. Ryden, *Letters*, 241.
22. *Minutes of the Council of the Delaware State from 1776 to 1792* (Dover, Delaware: James Kirk and Son, 1886), 141-47.
23. *Proceedings of the Assembly of the Lower Counties . . .* , 343-44.
24. Read, *Life and Correspondence*, 298.
25. Ibid., 300-1.
26. Ibid., 304
27. Ryden, *Letters,* 260-67.

28 Ibid., 305-6.
29 *Timoleon's Biographical History of Dionysius, Tyrant of Delaware*, ed. John Munroe (Newark, Delaware: University of Delaware Press, 1958).

Chapter 3
1 *Laws of Delaware*, vol. 2, chap. 121, pp. 818-19.
2 Ibid., chap. 140, p. 866.
3 Ibid., chap. 45, pp. 668-69.
4 Ibid., chap. 145, p. 884.
5 Ibid., pp. 884-87.
6 William T. Read, *Life and Correspondence of George Read* (Philadelphia: J. B. Lippincott & Co., 1870), 389, 405.
7 Ibid., 403.
8 Claudia L. Bushman, Harold B. Hancock, and Elizabeth Moyne Homsey, eds., *Proceedings of the House of Assembly of the Delaware State, 1781-1792 and of the Constitutional Convention of 1792* (Newark, Delaware: University of Delaware Press, 1988), 467.
9 Ibid., 477.
10 *Laws of Delaware*, vol. 2, chap. 222, p. 1002.
11 *Proceedings of the House of Assembly*, 485.
12 Ibid., 657-58, 692.
13 Ibid., 538.
14 See *Proceedings of the House of Assembly*, 692, for Broom's expenditure report for his extra work as leader of the committee.
15 Ibid., 599-611.
16 Ibid., 757-58.
17 Richard L. Mumford, "Constitutional Development in the State of Delaware, 1776-1897" (Ph.D. diss., University of Delaware, 1968), 2 vols., 1:111-46, passim.
18 Ibid., 2:844-45, 856.
19 *Minutes of the Council of the Delaware State from 1776 to 1792* (Dover, Delaware: James Kirk and Son, 1886), 1267-68.
20 *Laws of Delaware*, vol. 2, chap. 105, p. 1296; *Laws of Delaware*, vol. 2, chap. 133, p. 1352.
21 *Journal of the Senate*, 1806.
22 John A. Munroe, *Federalist Delaware, 1775-1815*, paperback reprint (Newark, Delaware: University of Delaware, 1987), 213.
23 Bruce A. Bendler, "The Emergence of Rural Federalism: Political Culture in Delaware, 1760-1812" (Ph.D. diss., University of Delaware, 2000), 1.
24 *Journal of the House of Representatives*, 1801, pp. 12-13.
25 Ibid., 1810, p. 25.
26 *Laws of Delaware*, vol. 3, chap. 182, p. 393.
27 *Journal of the House of Representatives*, 1796, p. 72.
28 *Laws of Delaware*, vol. 4, chap. 190, p. 409.
29 *Journal of the House of Representatives*, 1812, pp. 4-6.
30 *Journal of the House of Representatives*, 1819, p. 14; 1826, p. 51; 1827, pp. 37-40; 1830, pp. 53-54; and 1833, pp. 149-51.

Chapter 4
1 *Journal of the House of Representatives*, 1857, pp. 3-4.
2 Ibid., 1817, p. 181.
3 Ibid., 1824, pp. 10-11.
4 *Laws of Delaware*, vol. 7, chap. 99, pp. 184-97.

[5] *Journal of the House of Representatives*, 1839, p. 110.
[6] Ibid., 1841, p. 301.
[7] *Laws of Delaware*, vol. 8, chap. 257, p. 283.
[8] Ibid., vol. 9, chap. 480, p. 532.
[9] *Journal of the House of Representatives*, 1818, p. 38.
[10] *Journal of the Senate*, 1823, p. 73.
[11] *Journal of the House of Representatives*, 1824, pp. 11-12.
[12] Ibid., 1835, pp. 11-13.
[13] Ibid., 1839, pp. 8, 99, 220.
[14] Ibid., 1841, p.10.
[15] *Laws of Delaware*, vol. 10, chap. 396, p. 397.
[16] Ibid., vol. 8, chap. 320, p. 356; vol. 11, chap. 114, p.118.
[17] Ibid., vol. 10, chap. 186, pp. 178, and chap. 200, p. 195.
[18] *Journal of the House of Representatives*, 1843, p. 299.
[19] John A. Munroe, *History of Delaware*, 2d ed. (Newark, Delaware: University of Delaware Press, 1987), 125.
[20] *Journal of the House of Representatives*, 1841, pp. 434-35.
[21] *Laws of Delaware*, vol. 8, chap. 22, p. 49.
[22] Ibid., vol. 8, chap. 343, p. 383.
[23] Ibid., vol. 9, chap. 216, p. 263.
[24] Ibid., vol. 10, chap. 569, pp. 562-64.
[25] Ibid., vol. 10, chap. 358, pp. 342-50.
[26] Ibid., vol. 10, chap. 692, pp. 698-99.
[27] Ralph D. Gray, *The National Waterway: A History of the Chesapeake and Delaware Canal, 1769-1965* (Urbana, Illinois: University of Illinois Press, 1967), 92-98.
[28] Ibid., 114.
[29] *Laws of Delaware*, vol. 10, chap. 45, p. 42.
[30] *Journal of the House of Representatives*, 1852, pp. 161-68; *Laws of Delaware*, vol. 10, chap. 622, pp. 698-99; vol. 11, chap. 87, pp. 81, 652-55.
[31] *Journal of the House of Representatives*, 1857, pp. 282-85.
[32] *Laws of Delaware*, vol. 8, chap. 20, p. 45; vol. 9, chap. 429, p. 466.
[33] Richard L. Mumford, "Constitutional Development in the State of Delaware, 1776-1897" (Ph.D. diss., University of Delaware, 1968), 153-200.
[34] *Journal of the House of Representatives*, 1829, p. 52.
[35] Ibid., 1835, pp.126-27.
[36] *Laws of Delaware*, vol. 8, chap. 353, p. 395.
[37] Ibid., vol. 11, chap. 323, p. 340.
[38] Mumford, "Constitutional Development," 212-82, passim.
[39] Patience Essah, *A House Divided: Slavery and Emancipation in Delaware, 1638-1865* (Charlottesville: University Press of Virginia, 1996), 3.
[40] *Journal of the House of Representatives*, 1818, pp. 61-62.
[41] Ibid., 1819, p. 178.
[42] Ibid., 1829, pp. 195-196.
[43] *Laws of Delaware*, vol. 8, chap. 176, pp. 208-10.
[44] Ibid.
[45] *Journal of the House of Representatives*, 1837, p. 10.
[46] William H. Williams, *Slavery and Freedom in Delaware, 1639-1865*, paperback ed. (Wilmington, Delaware: SR Books, 1999), 189.
[47] *Laws of Delaware*, vol. 10, chap. 334, p.319; chap. 411, pp. 412-14; chap. 591, p. 591.
[48] *Journal of the House of Representatives*, 1843, p. 307.
[49] Ibid., 1839, p. 153.

[50] Ibid., 1833, pp. 101-2.
[51] Ibid., p. 86.
[52] Ibid., 1849, p.163.
[53] Ibid., 1855, p. 47.
[54] *Laws of Delaware*, vol. 11, chap. 664, p. 759.
[55] *Journal of the House of Representatives*, 1853, p. 386.
[56] Ibid, 1859, pp. 9-22.
[57] Ibid.
[58] Ibid., 1859, p. 89.

Chapter 5

[1] This issue is discussed in the Republican newspaper, *Delaware State Journal and Statesman*, Jan. 28, 31, 1862.
[2] Harold B. Hancock, *Delaware During the Civil War: A Political History* (Wilmington, Delaware: Historical Society of Delaware, 1961), 48.
[3] *Journal of the Senate*, 1861, p. 155.
[4] Ibid., 163.
[5] Hancock, *Delaware During the Civil War*, 106-10; *Delaware Gazette*, Feb. 14, 1862.
[6] *Journal of the House of Representatives*, 1863, pp. 9-24.
[7] *The Delawarean*, Jan. 24, 1863.
[8] *Journal of the House of Representatives*, 1863, pp. 89-106.
[9] *Laws of Delaware*, vol. 12, chap. 341, p. 387.
[10] Ibid., vol. 12, chap. 326, pp. 361-62.
[11] Ibid., chap. 305, pp. 330-34.
[12] Ibid., chap. 316, pp. 348-49.
[13] Ibid., chap. 336, pp. 381-84.
[14] Ibid., 383.
[15] *Delaware State Journal & Statesman*, Jan. 15, 1863.
[16] *Laws of Delaware*, vol. 12, chap. 462, pp. 481-87.
[17] *Journal of the House of Representatives*, 1864, pp. 212-13.
[18] Ibid., pp.199, 215.
[19] Ibid., 1865, p.11.
[20] Both editorials were quoted in the *Delaware State Journal & Statesman*, Feb. 17, 1865.
[21] Ibid.
[22] *Journal of the House of Representatives*, 1867, pp. 224, 226.
[23] *Laws of Delaware*, vol. 13, chap. 81, p. 87.
[24] Ibid., vol. 14, chap. 613, pp. 687-89.
[25] See Amy Hiller, "The Disfranchisement of Delaware Negroes in the Late Nineteenth Century," *Delaware History*, 13 (1968-69):124-53; Harold Livesay, "Delaware Negroes, 1865-1915," *Delaware History*, 13 (1968-69):87-123.
[26] *Laws of Delaware*, vol. 15, pt. 1, chap. 50, pp. 84-85.
[27] J. Thomas Scharf, *History of Delaware*, 2 vols. (Philadelphia: L. J. Richards, 1888), 1:386-87.
[28] *Laws of Delaware*, vol. 15, pt. 1, chap. 50, pp.85-87.
[29] Ibid., chap. 194, p. 322.
[30] Ibid., vol. 13, chap. 390, pp. 358-89.
[31] *Journal of the House of Representatives*, 1875, p. 15.
[32] Ibid., 1871, pp. 17-19.
[33] *Laws of Delaware*, vol. 12, chap. 572, p. 663; vol. 14, chap. 80, p. 95; vol. 14, chap. 550, pp. 638-40; vol. 15, chap. 165, pp. 289-90.
[34] Ibid., vol. 17, pt. 2, chap. 670, pp. 956-57.

Chapter 6
[1] *Laws of Delaware*, vol. 17, pt. 2., chap. 649, pp. 945-46; chap. 679, pp. 961-62.
[2] *Journal of the House of Representatives*, 1889, pp. 15-16.
[3] Ibid., 18.
[4] *Journal of the Senate*, 1891, Appendix, p. 1660.
[5] *Journal of the House of Representatives*, 1895, p. 14.
[6] The Addicks challenge is well covered in John A. Munroe, *History of Delaware*, 2d ed. (Newark, Delaware: University of Delaware Press, 1987), 176-78, and in Henry M. Canby, "J. Edward Addicks, A History of His Political Activities in Delaware, 1889-1906" (B.A. thesis: Princeton University, 1932), copy in the collections of the Historical Society of Delaware.
[7] Munroe, *History of Delaware*, 166.
[8] *Debates and Proceedings of the Constitutional Convention of the State of Delaware*, 5 vols. (Milford, Delaware: Milford Chronicle Publishing Co., 1958), 2:1153-54, 1215-46; Constitution of Delaware (1897), Art. X, Sec.1.
[9] Robert G. Caldwell, *The New Castle County Workhouse*, 13th ser. of *Delaware Notes* (Newark, Delaware: University of Delaware, 1940), 234-36.
[10] *Debates and Proceedings*, 3:2011.
[11] Ibid., 1:236 and 3:2053.
[12] Ibid., 3:2049.
[13] Ibid., 3:2098-100, 2135.
[14] Ibid., 3:2136.
[15] Ibid., 1:336-39.
[16] Ibid., 2:1042-1152.
[17] Ibid., 1:425.
[18] Ibid., 2:1001.
[19] Ibid., 2:1002-41.
[20] *Laws of Delaware*, 1898, vol. 21, pt. 1, chap 4, pp. 7-8; chap. 65, p. 166; chap. 147, p. 284.
[21] Ibid., 1899, vol. 21, pt. 2, chap. 273, pp. 445-503.
[22] *Journal of the House of Representatives*, 1901, pp. 23-28.
[23] Ibid., 29.
[24] Ibid., 1308-92.
[25] Canby, "J. Edward Addicks," 75.
[26] Ibid., 76; *Wilmington Every Evening*, Jan. 15- Mar. 17, 1903.

Chapter 7
[1] *Laws of Delaware*, vol. 22, pt. 2, chap. 380, pp. 729-37.
[2] Ibid., vol. 23, pt. 1, chap. 124, pp. 213-18.
[3] *Wilmington Sunday Star*, Feb. 19, 26, 1911.
[4] *Laws of Delaware*, vol. 26, chap. 189, pp. 374-96.
[5] Richard B. Carter, *Clearing New Ground: The Life of John G. Townsend, Jr.* (Wilmington, Delaware: Delaware Heritage Press, 2001), 165.
[6] Ibid., 173-74.
[7] *Journal of the Senate*, 1915, p. 65.
[8] *Journal of the House of Representatives*, 1907, p. 138.
[9] Ibid., 1913, p. 25.
[10] Carter, *Clearing New Ground*, 217.
[11] *Journal of the Senate*, 1915, pp. 72-74.
[12] Joseph J. Wall, *Alfred I. du Pont, The Man and His Family* (New York: Oxford University Press, 1990), 369.

[13] *Wilmington Sunday Star*, Jan. 21, 1917.
[14] *Laws of Delaware*, vol. 29, chap. 227, pp. 734-38.
[15] Ibid., vol. 24, pt. 1, chap. 121, pp. 213-18.
[16] *Journal of the Senate*, 1918, p. 14.
[17] Robert J. Taggart, *Private Philanthropy and Public Education: Pierre S. du Pont and the Delaware Schools* (Newark, Delaware: University of Delaware Press, 1988), 48.
[18] Ibid., 53.
[19] *Wilmington Every Evening*, Mar. 21, 1919.
[20] *Wilmington Evening Journal*, Mar. 7, 1919.
[21] *Wilmington Morning News*, Mar. 22, 1919.
[22] *Wilmington Every Evening*, Mar. 22, 1919.
[23] *Wilmington Morning News*, Mar. 27, 1919.
[24] Ibid.
[25] *Laws of Delaware*, vol. 30, pt. 2, chap. 157, pp. 352-433.
[26] *Journal of the Senate*, 1920, p. 18.
[27] Carol E. Hoffecker, "Delaware's Woman Suffrage Campaign," *Delaware History*, 20 (1983):164.
[28] *Laws of Delaware*, vol. 32, chap. 3, p. 6.
[29] Taggart, *Private Philanthropy*, 81-84.
[30] Ibid., 84-85.
[31] *Journal of the Senate*, 1920, pp. 19-20.
[32] Ibid., 123-124.
[33] Ibid., 236.
[34] *Wilmington Sunday Star*, Mar. 6, 1921.
[35] Ibid., Mar. 13, 1921; *Wilmington Evening Journal*, Mar. 15, 1921.
[36] *Laws of Delaware*, vol. 32, chap. 9, pp. 20-45.
[37] *Wilmington Evening Journal*, Mar. 26, 1921.
[38] Taggart, *Private Philanthropy*, 152.
[39] *Journal of the Senate*, 1921, p. 55.

Chapter 8

[1] *Wilmington Evening Journal*, Mar. 15, 1929.
[2] Ibid., Feb. 28, 1925.
[3] Robert J. Taggart, *Private Philanthropy and Public Education: Pierre S. du Pont and the Delaware Schools* (Newark, Delaware: University of Delaware Press, 1988), 154.
[4] *Wilmington Evening Journal*, Jan. 6, 1925.
[5] Ibid., Feb. 19, 1923.
[6] Ibid., Feb. 21, 1929.
[7] By composer George B. Hynson (*Laws of Delaware*, vol. 34, chap. 253, pp. 564-65).
[8] *Wilmington Evening Journal*, Jan. 3, 8, 1931.
[9] Ibid., Jan. 10, 1931.
[10] Ibid., Mar. 10, 25, 1931.
[11] *Laws of Delaware*, vol. 37, chap. 81, p. 309.
[12] *Journal of the Senate*, 1932, p. 22.
[13] *Laws of Delaware*, vol. 38, pt. 1, chap. 1, p. 3.
[14] *Journal of the Senate*, 1932, p. 46.
[15] *Wilmington Morning News*, Jan. 4, 1933.
[16] *Laws of Delaware*, vol. 38, pt. 2, chaps. 11-19, pp. 53-151.
[17] Ibid., vol. 39, chap. 1, pp. 16, 21.
[18] Ibid., vol. 40, chap. 115, pp. 396-405; *Wilmington Journal-Every Evening*, Feb. 28, 1935.

[19] *Wilmington Journal-Every Evening*, Feb. 2, 1937.
[20] Ibid., Mar. 25, 1935.
[21] Ibid., Feb. 2, Apr. 2, 1937.
[22] Ibid., Feb. 26, 1937.
[23] Ibid., Apr. 17, 20, 21, 1937.
[24] Ibid., Jan. 6, 1939.
[25] Ibid., Feb. 24, 1939.
[26] Ibid., Mar. 14, 1939.
[27] Ibid., Mar. 24, 1939.
[28] Ibid., Mar. 4, 1941.
[29] Ibid., Mar. 7, 1941.
[30] *Laws of Delaware*, vol. 43, chap. 285, pp. 1016-17.
[31] Ibid., 1173.
[32] Ibid., vol. 44, chap. 7, pp. 14-20, and chap. 9, pp. 22-31.
[33] *Wilmington Journal-Every Evening*, Jan. 3, 1945.
[34] Ibid., Apr. 16, 17, 1945.
[35] Ibid., Apr. 18, 1945.
[36] *Laws of Delaware*, vol. 45, chap. 296, pp. 1077-80.
[37] *Wilmington Journal-Every Evening*, Jan. 8, 1947.
[38] Ibid., Feb. 4, 1947.
[39] Ibid., Feb. 19, 1947.
[40] Ibid., Feb. 26, 1947.
[41] Ibid., Jan. 30, 1947.
[42] Ibid., Mar. 14, 1947.
[43] Mary Sam Ward, ed., *Delaware Women Remembered* (Wilmington, Delaware: Modern Press, 1977), 79; *Wilmington Journal-Every Evening*, Apr. 1, 1947.
[44] Roger A. Martin, *Elbert N. Carvel*, Oral History Series No. 1 (Wilmington, Delaware: Delaware Heritage Commission, 1997), 85-87.
[45] *Wilmington Journal-Every Evening*, Jan. 4-10, 1949.
[46] Ibid., Jan. 12, 1949.
[47] Martin, *Carvel*, 49.
[48] *Wilmington Journal-Every Evening*, May 12, 1949.
[49] Ibid., Jun. 4, 6, 1949.
[50] Ibid., Jan. 9, 19, 1951.
[51] *Wilmington Morning News*, May 28, 1951.
[52] Ibid.
[53] Ibid.

Chapter 9
[1] Paul Dolan, *The Government and Administration of Delaware* (New York: Thomas Y. Crowell Co., 1956), 46.
[2] *Delaware State News*, Dec. 14, 1961.
[3] Dolan, *Government*, 47.
[4] Ibid., 48.
[5] *Wilmington Morning News*, May 28, 1951.
[6] Ibid., Oct. 3, 1951.
[7] Ibid., Oct. 9, 1951.
[8] Ibid., Oct. 10, 11, 1951.
[9] Ibid., Oct. 4, 1951.
[10] Ibid., Oct. 13, 1951.
[11] Arden Ellsworth Bing, *Delaware Blue Book, 1957-1958* (Milford, Delaware: Milford

Chronicle Publishing Co., 1958).
[12] Bill Frank, *Bill Frank's Delaware*, ed. Joseph J. Hanson (Wilmington, Delaware: Middle Atlantic Press, 1987), 285-87.
[13] *Journal of the House of Representatives*, 1953, p. 25.
[14] *Wilmington Morning News*, Jun. 9, 1955.
[15] Roger A. Martin, *A History of Delaware Through Its Governors, 1776-1984* (Wilmington, Delaware: McClafferty Printing, 1984), 480-81.
[16] *Journal of the Senate*, 1958, p. 677.
[17] Ibid., 1959, pp.14-26.
[18] Ibid., pp.177-80.
[19] *Delaware State News*, Jan. 7, 1959.
[20] *Journal of the Senate*, 1959-1960, p. 384.
[21] Ibid., 396-97.
[22] Ibid., 84, 161-62.
[23] Ibid., 188-89.
[24] Ibid., 1961, 461-67.
[25] *Roman v. Sincock*, 377, U.S. 695 (1964).
[26] Bernard Schwartz, *A History of the Supreme Court*, paperback ed. (New York: Oxford University Press, 1995), 278
[27] *Roman v. Sincock*, 9.
[28] *Journal of the House of Representatives*, 1967, p. 118.
[29] *Journal of the Senate*, 1965, p. 14.
[30] *Wilmington Morning News*, Jan. 11, 1967.
[31] Interview with Margaret Manning, Feb. 6, 2003 (notes of this and all subsequent interviews in the possession of the author).
[32] Interview with George C. Hering III, Feb. 25, 2003.
[33] *Wilmington Morning News*, Jan. 3, 5, 6, 8, 9, 10, 11, 1968.
[34] Ibid., Dec.18, 1963.
[35] Roger A. Martin, *Elbert N. Carvel*, Oral History Series No. 1 (Wilmington, Delaware: Delaware Heritage Commission, 1997), 67.
[36] Carol E. Hoffecker, *Corporate Capital, Wilmington in the Twentieth Century* (Philadelphia: Temple University Press, 1983), 195.
[37] *Wilmington Morning News*, May 1, 1967.
[38] *Journal of the House of Representatives*, 1967, pp. 307-8, 311-13.
[39] Ibid., 1968, p. 516.
[40] Ibid., 476; *Wilmington Morning News*, May 8, 1968.
[41] Celia Cohen, *Only in Delaware: Politics and Politicians in the First State* (Newark, Delaware: Grapevine Publishing, 2002), 90.
[42] Manning interview.
[43] Legislative Hall Exhibit Folder, Delaware Public Archives, Dover, Del.
[44] *Journal of the Senate*, 1963-1964, p. 424.
[45] Ibid., 1966, p.526.
[46] Ibid., 1969, pp. 19-26.
[47] The Task Force chairman was E. Norman Veasey, who was later appointed Chief Justice of Delaware.
[48] Interview with Russell Peterson, Jan. 28, 2003.
[49] *Journal of the Senate*, 1969, p. 452.
[50] Cohen, *Only In Delaware*, 170.
[51] *Journal of the House of Representatives*, 1973, pp. 79-92.
[52] Ibid., 1974, pp. 838-39.
[53] James Phelan and Robert C. Pozen, *The Company State*, paperback ed. (New York:

Grossman Publishers, 1973), 317.
[54] Russell W. Peterson, *Rebel with a Conscience* (Newark, Delaware: University of Delaware Press, 1999), 125-27.
[55] Cohen, *Only in Delaware*, 165-72.
[56] Interview with Andrew G. Knox, Jan. 30, 2003.
[57] *Wilmington Evening Journal*, Jun. 16, 1971.
[58] Peterson, *Rebel With a Conscience*, 148.
[59] *Wilmington Evening Journal*, Jun. 23, 1971.
[60] Peterson, *Rebel with a Conscience*, 148.

Chapter 10
[1] Interview with Thurman G. Adams, Jr., Apr. 3, 2003 (notes for this and all subsequent interviews in the possession of the author).
[2] *Wilmington Morning News*, Jan. 12, 1973.
[3] John Burns, *The Sometime Governments, A Critical Study of the Fifty American Legislatures* (New York: Bantam Books, 1971), 49.
[4] Ibid., 107.
[5] Former Senator Roger A. Martin describes the agony of all-night sessions in his book *Memoirs of Twenty-two Years in the Delaware State Senate* (n.p: 1995), 28-29.
[6] Interview with Michael N. Castle, Apr. 21, 2003.
[7] Celia Cohen, *Only in Delaware: Politics and Politicians in the First State* (Newark, Delaware: Grapevine Publishing, 2002), 219.
[8] Ibid.
[9] Ibid., 221.
[10] *Wilmington Morning News*, Jan. 20, 1975.
[11] Interview with Robert L. Maxwell, Apr. 22, 2003.
[12] Interview with Orlando J. George, Jr., Apr. 4, 2003.
[13] Cohen, *Only in Delaware*, 235.
[14] Interview with Thomas B. Sharp, Apr. 23, 2003.
[15] Interview with Pierre S. du Pont IV, Mar. 31, 2003.
[16] Ibid.
[17] Ibid.; interview with Nancy W. Cook, Apr. 3, 2003.
[18] Al Giacco, *Maverick Management Strategies for Success* (Newark, Delaware: University of Delaware Press, 2003), 214-20.
[19] Ibid., 215.
[20] Interview with Robert F. Gilligan, Apr. 24, 2003.
[21] Interview with Richard S. Cordrey, Apr. 15, 2003.
[22] Cohen, *Only in Delaware*, 267-68.
[23] Ibid., 273-74.
[24] Ibid., 279.
[25] Ibid., 280.
[26] Du Pont interview.
[27] Carol E. Hoffecker, *Corporate Capital: Wilmington in the Twentieth Century* (Philadelphia: Temple University Press, 1983), 245-47.
[28] Jeffrey A. Raffel, *The Politics of School Desegregation: The Metropolitan Remedy in Delaware* (Philadelphia: Temple University Press, 1980), 5.
[29] Ibid., 90.
[30] Maxwell interview.
[31] Raffel, *Politics of School Desegregation*, 91-93.
[32] Ibid., 97-98.
[33] Ibid., 100.

34 Interview with Joseph Di Pinto, Apr. 11, 2003.
35 Cohen, *Only in Delaware*, 313.
36 Cook interview.
37 Interview with Liane M. Sorenson, Mar. 21, 2003.
38 Ibid.
39 Interview with Patricia M. Blevins, Apr. 9, 2003.
40 Interview with Myrna L. Bair, Apr. 10, 2003.
41 Interview with Jane P. Maroney, Apr. 17, 2003.
42 Interview with Margaret Rose Henry, Apr. 21, 2003.
43 Interview with Ruth Ann Minner, May 12, 2003.
44 Ibid.
45 Cohen, *Only in Delaware*, 315-18.
46 Interview with Terry R. Spence, Apr. 17, 2003.
47 Blevins interview.
48 Sharp interview.
49 Interview with Steven H. Amick, Apr. 7, 2003.
50 Bair interview.
51 Gilligan interview.
52 Interview with Jerome Lewis and Lisa Moreland, Apr. 14, 2003.
53 Spence interview.
54 Minner interview.
55 Interview with Alan V. Sokolow, May 27 2003.
56 Maxwell interview.
57 Gilligan interview.
58 Martin, *Memoirs of the Senate*, 6.
59 Interview with Bethany Hall-Long, Apr. 28, 2003.
60 Ibid.
61 Interview with Roger Roy, Apr. 15, 2003.
62 Interview with Stephanie Ulbrich, Apr. 18, 2003.
63 Sharp interview.
64 Cohen, *Only in Delaware*, 378-79.
65 *Wilmington News Journal*, Jul. 4, 1993.
66 Sharp interview.
67 *Delaware Code Annotated*, vol. 4 (2001), pp. 429-30.
68 DiPinto interview.
69 Spence interview.
70 William W. Boyer, *Governing Delaware: Policy Problems in the First State* (Newark, Delaware: University of Delaware Press, 2000), 201; Raymond R. Wolters, "The Consent Order as Sweetheart Deal: The Case of School Desegregation in New Castle County, Delaware," *Temple Political & Civil Rights Law Review*, 4(1995): 282.
71 Wolters, "The Consent Order," 283-87.
72 Ibid., 287.
73 Ibid., 291.
74 *Laws of Delaware*, vol. 70, chap. 179, p. 445.
75 *Wilmington News Journal*, Jun. 23, 1995.
76 Ibid., Jun. 29, 1995.
77 Ibid., May 9, 1998.
78 Ibid.
79 Interview with Wayne A. Smith, Jun. 20, 2003.

Index

A

Abolition 3, 52, 60, 68, 80, 90, 91, 93
Act of Union 10, 12, 17, 18
Adams, Thurman G., Jr. 230, 242, 247, 257, 258
Addicks, John Edward O'Sullivan 3, 120, 123, 125, 138, 139, 150, 198
Alcohol Beverage Control Commission 182
Alison, Francis 29, 33
Allee, J. Frank, Jr. 155, 159, 165
American Anti-Slavery Society 92
American Civil Liberties Union 243
Arnold, John H. 254
Atlas Powder Company 154, 196, 243
Attaches 170, 182, 199, 210, 231

B

Babiarz, John E. 215
Bachman, Frank P. 157, 158, 160, 167
Bacon, Walter W. 184–189, 191
Bair, Myrna 247, 252
Baker v. Carr 207
Bank One 243
Banking 141, 235, 241, 242
Banks 65, 241
Bassett, Richard 42, 45, 53, 55, 57, 65, 67
Battell, Elizabeth 56
Bayard, James A. 65, 80, 87, 89, 100
Bayard, Thomas F. 100, 111, 150
Bedford, Gunning, Jr. 55
Benger, Ernest B. 193, 199, 200
Bennett, Caleb P. 81, 94
Bennett, George Fletcher 219
Berndt, Robert J. 247, 250, 251
Betts, Edward 101
Biggs, Benjamin T. 123–125
Biggs, John, Jr. 208
Billingsley, John G.S. 233

Bing, Arden E. 201
Biondi, O. Francis 242
Blackwell, Captain John 12, 14
Blevins, Patricia 251, 252
Boggs, J. Caleb 201, 202, 236, 237
Bookhammer, Gene (Eugene) 226, 230, 232
Booth, Joseph W. 271
Braddock, General Edward 28
Bradford, Edward G. 126, 131, 134
Broom, Jacob 55, 57
Brown v. Board of Education of Topeka, Kansas, et al. 195, 201, 243
Buck, C. Douglass 171, 175, 177, 179, 180, 182, 183
Burris, John M. 242
Burton, William 96, 101, 105

C

Cain, Gerard A. 234, 236, 239
Calvert Family 11, 39
Campbell, Fletcher, Jr. 225
Cannon, Henry L. 177
Cannon, William 103, 105, 109
Carper, Thomas R. 249, 262, 263, 267–270
Carvel, Elbert N.
  189, 191, 192, 201, 202, 206, 207, 209, 211, 213, 215, 225, 282, 283
Castle, Michael N. 231, 249, 263
Catt, Carrie Chapman 134, 162
Causey, Peter F. 96
Charter of Privileges 18, 19
Chesapeake and Delaware Canal 73, 83, 86, 196, 212
Child Labor Commission 150
Cicione, Anthony J. 230
Clark, David S. 134
Clark, John 76
Clayton, John M. 74, 80, 84, 86, 95, 125, 150, 179
Clayton, Joshua 62
Clinton, William Jefferson 268, 269
Coalition to Save Our Children 266, 267
Coastal Zone Act 223, 232, 239
Cohen, Celia 232, 233, 242, 250
Collins, John 76
Collins, Thomas 55, 56
Comegys, Cornelius P. 81
Compensated Emancipation Plan 102, 103
Connor, Louise 214

Connor, Robert T. 247, 257, 258
Continental Congress 2, 38, 40, 49
Cooch, Edward W. 183
Cooch, J. Wilkins 126, 134
Cook, Allen J. 204, 214, 220, 230, 234
Cook, Nancy W. 234, 247, 251, 252, 256, 257
Cordrey, Richard S. 236, 239, 240, 242, 247, 256, 257
Corporation law (see Incorporation Law)
Council of Defense 157, 158, 185
Court of Chancery 39, 201

D

Davis, Colonel Samuel Boyer 70
Davis, Vera G. 189, 190, 192
Delaware Association for the Educational Advancement and Moral Improvement of the Colored People 113
Delaware Bar Association 173, 222
Delaware College 113–115, 150, 151, 160
Delaware Compensation Commission 263
Delaware Economic and Financial Advisory Council 249
Delaware Memorial Bridge 193, 194
Delaware Railroad 84–87, 101, 117, 118
Delaware School Auxiliary Association 164, 168, 171
Delaware State Board of Education 161, 167, 168, 194, 222, 266, 267
Delaware State College 165, 167, 215
Delaware State Education Association 237
Delaware Supreme Court 68, 147, 194, 201, 233
Delaware Technical and Community College 223
Delaware Temporary Emergency Relief Commission 182
Denney, William D. 148, 165, 168
Department of Children, Youth, and Their Families 252
Department of Health and Human Services 221
Department of Transportation (DelDOT) 249
Dickinson, John 30, 32, 33, 35, 49, 50, 55, 59, 62
DiLiberto, Richard A., Jr. 271
Dingee, Daniel 46
DiPinto, Joseph G. 251, 266
Dolan, Paul 198, 199
DSAA 172
Du Pont, Alfred I. 142, 155, 158, 159, 161, 163–165, 168, 172, 178
Du Pont, Colonel Henry Algernon 126, 131, 142, 155, 172
Du Pont Company 141, 142, 154, 155, 225
Du Pont, Frank V. 191
Du Pont, P.S. (Pierre S.) (Pierre Samuel) 3, 142, 165, 166, 172, 174, 177, 183

Du Pont, Pierre S. IV (Pete) 236–238, 246, 248, 249, 271
Du Pont, Reynolds 204, 209, 221, 225, 226, 230, 231, 233
Du Pont, Thomas Coleman 3, 139, 142–149, 154, 155, 158, 159, 163, 168, 169, 173, 191
Dukes, Elisha 213

E

Educational Advancement Act 216, 217, 243–245
Emancipation (*See* abolition)
Emancipation Proclamation 103, 106
Emergency Relief Commission 180
Environment 27, 83, 147, 223, 265
Evans, John 19–21
Evans v. Buchanan 243

F

Family Court 186, 187
Farmers Bank 68, 235, 236
Financial Center Development Act 242, 243
Fisher, George P. 102
Flexner, Abraham 157, 158, 160
Frame of Government 8–11, 14, 15, 18
Frank, Bill (William P.) 201, 222
Franklin, Benjamin 25, 26
Frederick, William L. 225
Freeman, John 56, 57
French and Indian War 27, 30, 32
French, John 21

G

Gambling 52, 83, 100, 174, 179, 182, 193, 194, 263
George, Orlando, J., Jr. (Lonnie) 205, 233, 234, 236, 238, 239
Getty, J. Paul 235
Giacco, Alexander F. 239
Gilligan, Robert F. 240, 258, 260, 261, 268
Gookin, Charles 21
Gray, George 126, 136, 148
Grier, Frank 226

H

Hall, Willard 76, 77, 79, 89
Hall-Long, Bethany 261
Hamilton, Robert 63

Hanby, Florence M. 173
Harrington, W.W. 177
Hart, Walter E. 163
Haslet, Colonel John 47
Haslet, Joseph 70
Hastings, Daniel O. 145
Hazel, J. Henry 181
Hazzard, David 92, 94
Hearn, Clifford J. 225
Hebner, Charles L. 205, 233, 234
Heckert, Clarice 217
Henry, Margaret Rose 252
Hercules Powder Company 239
Hering, George C. III 205, 210, 211, 221
Herrington, Fannie 174
Higgins, Anthony 111, 125
Highways 27, 67, 100, 139, 143, 184, 186, 188, 189, 221
Hilles, Florence Bayard 162, 164
Hoey, Walter J. 203
Holloway, Harry V. 171
Holloway, Herman M., Jr. 254
Holloway, Herman, Sr. 212, 214, 245, 247, 252
Hope Farm 173
Houston, Margaret 134
Human Relations Commission 212, 214

I

Income tax 152, 154, 156, 167, 172, 186, 235, 239, 263
Income tax law 155
Incorporation law 88, 120, 129, 133, 136, 173, 222, 223
Insane 67, 68, 75, 80, 82, 96, 123
Isaacs, J. Donald 225, 226, 230, 231, 257
Isham, Norman Morrison 177

J

Jackson, Andrew 72, 80
Jail 9, 67, 68, 75, 129
James Duke of York (King James II) 7, 14, 17
Jason, W.C. 165
Johnson, Everett 157
Johnson, Henrietta 227
Johnson, Lyndon B. 209, 213, 215
Jones, F. Albert 192

Jonkiert, Casimir S. 205, 235
Junction & Breakwater Railroad 85, 100, 101

K

Kelly, Daniel A. 241
Kent County Courthouse 60, 61
Kidd, Captain William 15
King Charles II 7
King George III 34, 35, 39
King, Martin Luther, Jr. 215
King William III and Queen Mary II 14
Knox, Andrew 225, 231
Kollock, Jacob 33
Kurland, Philip B. 245

L

Land and Water Conservation Act 253, 265
Lawson, Harvey H. 189, 190, 192
Layton, Dr. Caleb 155
Layton, Landreth 164
Legislative Council 211, 258, 261
Legislative Fellows Program 258
Legislative Hall 4, 176-178, 180, 198, 200, 207, 215, 216, 219, 225, 231, 235, 236, 238, 246, 247, 249, 250, 251, 255, 259, 261, 263–265, 269
Legislative Reference Bureau 187
Lewis, Jerome 258
Lincoln, Abraham 101, 109, 115
Liquor 24, 31, 52, 79, 82, 151, 158, 174, 182, 191, 198, 218
Lockman, Norman 267
Lord Baltimore 7, 8, 10, 11, 19, 20, 22
Lotteries 37, 82, 83, 100, 101

M

Manlove, Boaz 46
Manning, Margaret 210
Maroney, Jane 252, 260
Marshall, Robert I. 247
Martin, E. William 177
Martin, Roger A. 231, 247, 260
Marvil, Joshua H. 130
Matushefske, John 232, 233, 235
Maxwell, Robert L. 234, 244, 245
MBNA Bank 243, 263

McCullough, Calvin 210, 211, 213, 226, 230
McDowell, Harris B. III 247, 268
McKean, Thomas 2, 32–36, 38, 40, 42, 46, 48–50, 65
McKinly, Dr. John 45–49
McLaughlin, William 242
McMullen, Richard C. 183, 184
McNabb, John E. 161, 163
Mentally ill 3, 67, 82, 96
Mifflin, Warner 60
Militia 27, 28, 31, 32, 40, 48, 49, 67, 69, 70, 71, 105
Miller, Charles I. 167
Miller, Charles R. 150
Minner, Ruth Ann 233, 234, 247, 251, 253, 259, 265, 270
Mitchell, Nathaniel 68
Morford, James R. 185
Morris, Hugh M. 183, 263
Mother's Pension Commission 156
Motiva 265
Munroe, John A. 64
Murphy, William M., Jr. 254
Myers, Richard J. 254

N

Nader, Ralph 242
National Council of State Governments 259
National Council of State Legislatures 252
National Guard 149, 215, 218
New Castle and Frenchtown Railroad 84, 86, 87
New Castle County Workhouse 130, 138
Nixon, Richard M. 217, 224, 233

O

Oberle, William A., Jr. 242, 267
Open housing 214

P

Penitentiary 67, 81, 96, 123
Penn, John 22
Penn, Richard 22
Penn, Thomas 22
Penn, William 1, 6, 8–19, 22
Pennewill, Simeon S. 151
Pennsylvania Railroad 84, 118
Peterson, Russell 217, 221–226, 229, 231, 232

Petrilli, Joseph R. 267
Plant, Hazel 252
Polk, Charles 92
Poll tax 88, 89, 111, 113, 123, 125, 134, 135
Ponder, James 112
Poorhouse 67
Positive Action Committee 244
Prison 81, 196, 223
Prohibition 158, 163, 174, 181, 182
Public accommodations 114, 213, 227
Public Integrity Commission 260
PW & B Railroad 84, 86, 95, 114

Q

Queen Anne 19–21
Quigley, James R. 218

R

Racing Commission 174, 181
Raffel, Jeffrey A. 245, 246
Railroads 3, 73, 75, 86–88, 100, 114, 122, 129, 136, 143, 153, 199
Randall, John, Jr. 86
Raskob, John J. 157
Read, George 2, 32–38, 40, 42, 45, 48–50, 53, 55, 57, 150
Redding, Louis L. 214
Reilly, John 213
Reynolds, Robert 125
Reynolds v. Sims 208
Richards, Charles F. 126
Richards, Robert H. 145, 183
Richards, Robert H., Jr. 185
Ridgely, Dr. Charles 38, 42, 45, 46
Ridgely, Mrs. Henry (Mabel) 177
Ridgely, Nicholas 59, 60
Rinard, Paul R. 185
Ripper bills 170
Roads 3, 22, 32, 66, 75, 119, 123, 143, 149, 168, 169, 173, 201, 202, 249
Robertson, James W. 161
Robinson, Robert P. 172, 174
Robinson, Sue L. 267
Robinson, Thomas 38, 46
Rodeney, William 32
Rodney, Caesar 2, 31–33, 35, 36, 38, 41, 42, 48–50
Rodney, Caesar A. 64, 65, 79

Roman v. *Sincock* 208
Roosevelt, Franklin Delano 169, 179, 186, 198
Ross, William H. 95
Roy, Roger P. 251, 261

S

Saulsbury, Eli 95, 100
Saulsbury, Gove 100, 106, 109
Saulsbury, Willard 106, 112
Saulsbury, William 126, 133
School Code 128, 159–161, 163, 164, 167, 171, 172
Schools 62, 68, 76–79, 96, 109, 113, 123, 128, 135, 141, 142, 145, 158, 159, 163, 164, 167, 169–171, 173, 174, 177, 184, 191, 202, 243, 266, 272
Schroeder, John R. 271
Schwartz, Murray M. 244–246
Seitz, Collins J. 201
Service Citizens of Delaware 157, 160
Shapiro, Irving 239
Sharp, Hugh Rodney 177
Sharp, Thomas B. 234, 247, 256, 257, 262, 263, 267, 268
Shippen, Joseph 20
Simpson, Walton H. 206
Skeleton bill 170, 231
Slavery 3, 12, 30, 35, 44, 52, 53, 60, 68, 69, 73, 80, 89, 96, 99–103, 105–111, 113–115, 118, 127, 129
Smith, Wayne A. 255, 261, 267–270
Sokola, David P. 267
Sokolow, Alan V. 259
Soles, Ada Leigh 252
Sorenson, Liane 251, 252, 271
Spence, Terry R. 255, 258, 261, 266, 268
Spruance, William C. 126, 131, 134
Stabler, W. Laird 222
Stamp Act 32–35
Stamp Act Congress 33
State Athletic Commission 179
State Board of Welfare 189
State Council of Defense 157, 158, 185
State Highway Commission 143, 184
State Highway Department 149, 168, 171, 173, 191, 202, 204
State Hospital 170, 173, 183, 188, 189, 222
State Hospital for the Insane 124, 138
State House 60, 61, 63, 88, 89, 94, 102, 105, 110, 112, 118, 119, 124, 126, 135–137, 171, 175, 177, 179

State Police 191, 202, 204, 215, 216, 259
Steele, Dean C. 220
Steen, Curtis W. 209, 213
Still, John C. 267

T

Temperance 80, 82
Terry, Charles L., Jr. 209, 211, 212, 214–220, 223
Thomas, Charles 76, 81
Thomas, George 24, 25
Thompson, Mary Wilson 162–164
Torbert, William 64
Townsend, Chester V., Jr. 186
Townsend, John G., Jr. 147, 149, 152, 153, 155–158, 160–165, 168
Townshend Duties 35–37
Transportation Trust Fund 249
Tribbitt, Sherman 204, 205, 210, 219, 225, 229, 230, 236, 253
Trumianz, Dr. M.A. 183
Tunnell, Ebe W. 126, 135, 136, 183
Turnpikes 65–67

U

Ulbrich, Stephanie 262
United Auto Workers 233
United States Constitution 4, 56–59,
    92–94, 105, 110, 115, 127, 150, 154, 158, 162, 164, 248
United States Supreme Court 4, 133, 195, 201, 207, 208, 227, 243
University of Delaware 170, 177, 194, 201, 223, 258, 263

V

Van Sciver, Donald J. 241
Vandyke, Nicholas 53
Venables, Robert L., Sr. 251, 255
Vernon, Mabel 162
Vines, John 10
Vining, John 36

W

War of 1812 51, 70, 73, 83
Warren, Earl 207
Washington, George 40, 42, 46–49, 57, 61, 64, 65, 72, 94, 136
Weiss, Daniel E. 222
Welfare 80, 128, 156, 158, 173, 178, 188, 215, 222

Welfare home 173
Whipping post 61, 81, 82, 151, 196, 206, 222, 223, 227
White, John 12–14
Williams, Dennis P. 252
Williams, Leonard 214
Wilson, Woodrow 141, 156, 158, 163
Winchester, William J. 190
Wolcott, Daniel 217
Wolcott, Josiah O. 155
Woman's Suffrage 134, 162–164
Women's College of Delaware 150
Workhouse 67, 81, 123, 129, 227

142nd GENER

SENATE MEMBERS ABOVE

Front Row:	Anthony J. DeLuca, Thurman Adams, Jr., John C. Carney, Jr., Harris B. McDowell, III, Liane Sorenson, John C. Still III
Second Row:	Nancy W. Cook, Margaret Rose Henry, Patricia M. Blevins, Robert L. Venables, Catherine L. Cloutier
Third Row:	Karen E. Peterson, Robert I. Marshall, Steven H. Amick, George H. Bunting, Dorinda A. Connor
Fourth Row:	David P. Sokola, James T. Vaughn, Charles L. Copeland, F. Gary Simpson
Not in Photo:	David B. McBride, Colin J.R. Bonini

HOUSE MEMBERS RIGHT

Front Row:	Representatives Clifford G. Lee, Wayne A. Smith, Speaker Terry R. Spence, John F. VanSant, Robert F. Gilligan
Second Row:	Representatives John J. Viola, Hazel D. Plant, William I. Houghton
Third Row:	Representatives Richard C. Cathcart, Melanie L. George, Pamela S. Maier, Nancy W. Wagner, Tina Fallon
Fourth Row:	Representatives Pamela J. Thornburg, David H. Ennis, Roger Roy, Bruce C. Ennis, Helene M. Keeley
Fifth Row:	Representatives Vincent A. Lofink, Gregory F. Lavelle, Donna D. Stone, Joseph E. Muro, Bruce C. Reynolds
Sixth Row:	Representatives V. George Carey, Deborah D. Hudson, Peter C. Schwartzkopf, Gerald A. Buckworth, Bethany Hall-Long, Gerald W. Hocker
Seventh Row:	Representatives Joseph W. Booth, Stephanie A. Ulbrich, Robert J. Valihura, Jr.
Back Row:	Representatives J. Benjamin Ewing, John C. Atkins, William A. Oberle, Jr., Timothy U. Boulden
Not in Photo:	Representatives G. Wallace Caulk, Joseph P. DiPinto, Michael P. Mulrooney, George Robert Quillen, Dennis P. Williams